AI Impacts on Market Analysis and Investment Strategy

Soly Mathew Biju
https://orcid.org/0000-0003-1323-7480
University of Wollongong in Dubai, UAE

Sangeeta Trott
ITM Skills University, India

IGI Global
Scientific Publishing
Publishing Tomorrow's Research Today

VP of Publishing Ethics & Research Integrity Melissa Wagner
Director of Acquisitions Mikaela Felty
Director of Book Development Jocelynn Hessler
Production Manager Mike Brehm
Cover Design Jose Rosado

Published in the United States of America by
IGI Global Scientific Publishing
701 East Chocolate Avenue
Hershey, PA, 17033, USA
Tel: 717-533-8845 | Fax: 717-533-7115
Website: https://www.igi-global.com E-mail: cust@igi-global.com

Library of Congress Cataloging-in-Publication Data

Names: Biju, Soly, 1976- editor | Trott, Sangeeta editor
Title: AI impacts on market analysis and investment strategy / [edited by] Soly Mathew Biju, Sangeeta Trott.
Description: Hershey, PA : IGI Global Scientific Publishing, [2027] | Includes bibliographical references and index. | Summary: "This book provides a comprehensive, practice-oriented understanding of how AI transforms market analysis and investment strategy. It integrates algorithmic trading, sentiment analysis, and risk modeling strands into a unified, interdisciplinary framework"-- Provided by publisher.
Identifiers: LCCN 2026014689 (print) | LCCN 2026014690 (ebook) | ISBN 9798337396453 hardcover | ISBN 9798337396460 paperback | ISBN 9798337396477 ebook
Subjects: LCSH: Artificial intelligence--Financial applications | Investment analysis
Classification: LCC HG4515.5 .A3845 2026 (print) | LCC HG4515.5 (ebook) | DDC 332.028563--dc23/eng/20260508
LC record available at https://lccn.loc.gov/2026014689
LC ebook record available at https://lccn.loc.gov/2026014690

British Cataloguing in Publication Data
A Cataloguing in Publication record for this book is available from the British Library.

Table of Contents

Preface xi

Chapter 1
AI-Driven Financial Decision-Making: Evidence From Centralized and Decentralized Financial Markets 1
Shradha Attri, Central University of Himachal Pradesh, India
Sanjeev Gupta, Central University of Himachal Pradesh, India
Sachin Singh, Central University of Himachal Pradesh, India

Chapter 2
Artificial Intelligence in Market Analysis and Investment Decision-Making: A Behavioural Finance Perspective 29
Pratibha Gupta, Symbiosis Centre for Management Studies, Symbiosis International (Deemed to be) University, Pune, India
Pawan Pant, Chandigarh University, Mohali, India
Azmee Zaheer, Chandigarh University, Mohali, India
Kaushal Kishore Mishra, Chandigarh University, Unnao, India

Chapter 3
From AI-Based Market Forecasting to Investment Strategy: Cross-Firm Machine Learning Signal Evaluation in the Technology Sector 57
Fares A. Dael, İzmir Bakırçay University, Turkey

Chapter 4
AI-Driven Trading and Portfolio Optimization Platform With Risk and Forecasting Integration 95
Neha Garg, Delhi Technical Campus, India
Sharad Gupta, Delhi Technical Campus, India
Yashdeep Saxena, Delhi Technical Campus, India

Chapter 5
Artificial Intelligence and the Future of Investment Strategy: Data-Driven Markets, Behavioural Indicators, and Adaptive Portfolio Management 127
Rizwan Khan, Haji Taufeeq Ali Mahavidyalaya, India
Mohammad Taqi, Bahrain Polytechnic, Bahrain

Chapter 6
AI-Enabled Green Finance and Triple Helix Governance for Renewable Energy Investment Integrity 163
José G. Vargas-Hernández, Business School, Universidad LaSalle Bajìo, Mexico
Selene Castañeda-Burciaga, Universidad Politécnica de Zacatecas, Mexico
Omar A. Guirette, Broward International University, USA & Universidad Politécnica de Zacatecas, Mexico

Chapter 7
Applicability of Artificial Intelligence in the Financial Domain 203
Ameya Anil Patil, Dr. Vishwanath Karad MIT World Peace University, India

Chapter 8
Machine Learning Techniques for Market Forecasting 223
Yogita Yashveer Raghav, K.R. Mangalam University, Gurugram, India
Aman Jatain, DPG Institute of Technology and Management, India
Prashanth Kumar Katta, King Faisal University, Al Ahsa, Saudi Arabia
Abhishek Bhardwaj, Government Polytechnic, Indri, India

Chapter 9
AI Applications in Behavioral Finance: Integrating Machine Learning With Investor Psychology 251
Khalil Omar, University of Petra, Jordan
Hussam Fakhouri, Al-Balqa Applied University, Jordan
Faten Hamad, Sultan Qaboos University, Oman & University of Jordan, Jordan

Chapter 10
Deep Sentiment, Deeper Insights: LSTM and GRU Models for Reliance Stock Price Forecasting... 281
Tarun Sai Raavi, KL University, India
P. S. SubhaPradha, Aurora University, India
Radhika Ramanchi, GITAM University, India

Compilation of References 313

About the Contributors 345

Index 353

Detailed Table of Contents

Preface xi

Chapter 1
AI-Driven Financial Decision-Making: Evidence From Centralized and Decentralized Financial Markets 1
Shradha Attri, Central University of Himachal Pradesh, India
Sanjeev Gupta, Central University of Himachal Pradesh, India
Sachin Singh, Central University of Himachal Pradesh, India

The global financial ecosystem is undergoing a profound transformation with the integration of advanced digital technologies, particularly Artificial Intelligence (AI). Financial markets that once relied heavily on human intuition and traditional analytical methods are increasingly adopting AI-driven tools to enhance investment decision-making, risk assessment, and portfolio management. The rise of AI has significantly reshaped how investors interact with financial information, enabling more data-driven, efficient, and predictive investment strategies. At the same time, the financial system itself has evolved into two major structures: centralized finance (CeFi) and decentralized finance (DeFi). Technologies such as machine learning, natural language processing, and predictive analytics allow financial institutions to analyze large volumes of financial data and generate investment insights with high accuracy. The convergence of AI with these two financial systems is creating new opportunities and challenges for investors

Chapter 2
Artificial Intelligence in Market Analysis and Investment Decision-Making: A Behavioural Finance Perspective 29
Pratibha Gupta, Symbiosis Centre for Management Studies, Symbiosis International (Deemed to be) University, Pune, India
Pawan Pant, Chandigarh University, Mohali, India
Azmee Zaheer, Chandigarh University, Mohali, India
Kaushal Kishore Mishra, Chandigarh University, Unnao, India

The relationship between Artificial Intelligence (AI) and Behavioural Finance has been examined through three (3) case studies that showcase AI technology in the current investment environment. These three (3) case studies on AI-driven platforms demonstrate how the use of algorithms, Natural Language Processing (NLP) and predictive analytics provides a mechanism to enhance the accuracy of analysis, allowing investors/investment professionals to make more informed investment decisions and a better understanding of how investors behave. The use of analytics in each case study enables analysis of investor sentiment, recognition of irrational trading behaviour, and the generation of data-driven recommendations for both retail and institutional investors. The use of these platforms has the potential to help eliminate cognitive biases from the decision-making process, including overconfidence, loss aversion, and herd behaviour; thus, improving the quality of decisions made by investors.

Chapter 3
From AI-Based Market Forecasting to Investment Strategy: Cross-Firm Machine Learning Signal Evaluation in the Technology Sector 57
Fares A. Dael, İzmir Bakırçay University, Turkey

This chapter examines the role of artificial intelligence in transforming market analysis and investment strategy through machine learning-based stock direction forecasting. It proposes a standardized and reproducible evaluation framework that integrates predictive modeling, cross-firm robustness assessment, and risk-adjusted economic evaluation within a unified methodology. Using five large-cap technology firms as an empirical illustration, the chapter demonstrates how machine learning-generated market signals can support investment decisions and be evaluated using predictive accuracy, cumulative returns, Sharpe ratio, and maximum drawdown. The findings indicate that ensemble learning methods, particularly XGBoost, provide more robust predictive signals and superior risk-adjusted performance across multiple firms. The chapter emphasizes methodological rigor, economic validation, and cross-firm consistency, providing a practical framework for AI-driven financial forecasting and investment decision support.

Chapter 4
AI-Driven Trading and Portfolio Optimization Platform With Risk and Forecasting Integration 95
Neha Garg, Delhi Technical Campus, India
Sharad Gupta, Delhi Technical Campus, India
Yashdeep Saxena, Delhi Technical Campus, India

Artificial Intelligence (AI) and machine learning technologies have significantly transformed financial markets and replaced intuition based strategies by data-driven intelligent systems. AI-driven trading and portfolio optimization platforms, which integrate advanced analytics, predictive modeling, and automated decision-making to enhance investment performance. The chapter explores the design and application of AI enabled trading platforms in modern financial markets. These platforms support technologies such as machine learning algorithms, deep learning models, natural language processing, and big data analytics to analyze market trends, detect trading opportunities, and construct optimized investment portfolios. By combining real-time and historical data, AI generate predictive insights for informed investment decisions and risk management strategies. The chapter discusses the evolution of algorithmic trading and AI's growing role in financial market analysis. It examines key components including data acquisition modules, predictive analytics engines, automated trading systems, and portfolio optimization models. Challenges such as model interpretability, regulatory compliance, data privacy, and algorithmic bias are also addressed. A conceptual framework is proposed for effective deployment of these technologies.

Chapter 5
Artificial Intelligence and the Future of Investment Strategy: Data-Driven Markets, Behavioural Indicators, and Adaptive Portfolio Management 127
Rizwan Khan, Haji Taufeeq Ali Mahavidyalaya, India
Mohammad Taqi, Bahrain Polytechnic, Bahrain

Artificial intelligence (AI) is fundamentally transforming investment strategies by enabling data-driven decision-making, behavioural insights, and adaptive portfolio management. This chapter examines the evolving role of AI in financial markets by integrating theoretical perspectives, including market efficiency and behavioural finance, with emerging empirical evidence. It explores the growing importance of big data, algorithmic trading, and AI-driven sentiment analysis in shaping market dynamics. The study further analyzes adaptive portfolio strategies, highlighting the role of machine learning and robo-advisory platforms in enhancing efficiency and personalization. In addition, it addresses key regulatory, ethical, and governance challenges, including algorithmic transparency, data privacy, and systemic risk. Through case-based insights, the chapter identifies both opportunities and limitations of AI adoption. It concludes by emphasizing the need for responsible innovation, human AI collaboration, and robust policy frameworks to ensure sustainable and inclusive financial markets.

Chapter 6
AI-Enabled Green Finance and Triple Helix Governance for Renewable Energy Investment Integrity 163
José G. Vargas-Hernández, Business School, Universidad LaSalle Bajìo, Mexico
Selene Castañeda-Burciaga, Universidad Politécnica de Zacatecas, Mexico
Omar A. Guirette, Broward International University, USA & Universidad Politécnica de Zacatecas, Mexico

This chapter reframes sustainable economic models and green finance for renewable energy through an AI-enabled green finance lens aligned with the Triple Helix (University, Government, Industry) framework. The synthesis identifies four cross-cutting AI-enabled mechanisms that can reduce these frictions: (1) AI driven risk and scenario analytics (2) NLP based disclosure intelligence (3) AI supported MRV (including alternative data) and (4) integrity analytics to detect inconsistencies and support anti greenwashing controls. The chapter also integrates ethical, legal, and societal implications (ELSI), emphasizing explainability, accountability, fairness, data governance, and energy justice as conditions for legitimate scaling. Implications are derived for green bonds, blended finance, and carbon-pricing ecosystems, proposing a practical agenda for trustworthy AI adoption in sustainable finance.

Chapter 7
Applicability of Artificial Intelligence in the Financial Domain 203
Ameya Anil Patil, Dr. Vishwanath Karad MIT World Peace University, India

Technology, especially AI is becoming ubiquitous in various functional areas.This chapter delves into the integration of AI technologies with a focus on neural networks within the financial domain. Neural networks excel in processing amounts of data identifying nonlinear patterns and adapting to changing market conditions. The article explores two applications of AI in finance; stock prediction and bankruptcy prediction including fraud detection in statements. These areas rely on analytics, where AI algorithms analyze data to forecast market trends stock prices and economic indicators. The potential for networks to revolutionize prediction capabilities in these domains is highlighted through a review of research and methodologies. AI is also increasingly used in bankruptcy prediction, associated with the probability of financial failure of a corporation. Financial data, such as those included in popular bankruptcy prediction and fraud detection models such as Altman's Z-score, Beneish's M-score are fed as inputs to the neural networks.

Chapter 8
Machine Learning Techniques for Market Forecasting 223
Yogita Yashveer Raghav, K.R. Mangalam University, Gurugram, India
Aman Jatain, DPG Institute of Technology and Management, India
Prashanth Kumar Katta, King Faisal University, Al Ahsa, Saudi Arabia
Abhishek Bhardwaj, Government Polytechnic, Indri, India

Market forecasting plays an important role in economic planning, investment, and business decision-making. Traditional forecasting methods often struggle with the increasing complexity of modern markets driven by globalization, digitalization, and large volumes of data. Machine learning techniques provide data-driven approaches that can capture nonlinear patterns and adapt to dynamic market conditions. This chapter discusses key ML methods for market prediction, including data preprocessing, supervised and unsupervised learning, deep learning models, and evaluation metrics.

It also highlights applications, challenges, and emerging trends for developing reliable and responsible forecasting systems.

Chapter 9
AI Applications in Behavioral Finance: Integrating Machine Learning With Investor Psychology 251
Khalil Omar, University of Petra, Jordan
Hussam Fakhouri, Al-Balqa Applied University, Jordan
Faten Hamad, Sultan Qaboos University, Oman & University of Jordan, Jordan

Behavioral finance questions the rational-investor assumption, with empirical evidence of systematic cognitive biases which contribute to market outcomes. In this chapter, machine learning is combined with the behavioral theory of finance in terms of three empirical studies based on publicly available Kaggle datasets, FinBERT to predict sentiment, XGBoost and LightGBM to predict tabular data, an LSTM to predict sequence learning, and SHAP to interpret the results. Findings are inconsistent to the extent that the daily-index herding hypothesis is rejected; a momentum signature dominates over overreaction-reversal; a small loss-aversion drift ratio of 1.267 comes out that is lower than the prospect-theoretic canonical value of 2.25. The chapter maintains that explanation-driven validation is what makes a difference between scale-dependent attenuation and true refutation, showing that the scale-dependent attenuation is not due to the complexity of the algorithm used to compute it but rather to the fact that certain behavioral biases are the ones that can be detected.

Chapter 10
Deep Sentiment, Deeper Insights: LSTM and GRU Models for Reliance Stock Price Forecasting 281
Tarun Sai Raavi, KL University, India
P. S. SubhaPradha, Aurora University, India
Radhika Ramanchi, GITAM University, India

In this research, the impact of financial news sentiment on enhancing stock price forecasting is analyzed by incorporating sentiment features with market historical data and applying deep learning models. With a representative example of Reliance Industries Limited, LSTM and GRU are implemented to analyze nonlinear temporal pattern in stock prices. A lexicon-based and a domain-specific method have been applied to measure sentiment from financial news. The findings show that sentiment-augmented models consistently outperform price only models on a variety of performance measures such as forecasting accuracy and directionality prediction. The models are evaluated on their performance, and GRU outperforms the other models, especially in cases of fluctuations in the stock market data, suggesting its ability to deal with noisy financial information. The results of this study validate the theory of behavioral finance and point to the need to include qualitative data into quantitative forecasting models to be useful in financial decision making.

Compilation of References 313

About the Contributors 345

Index 353

Preface

The rapid advancement of Artificial Intelligence (AI) is fundamentally reshaping the way financial markets are analyzed, interpreted, and navigated. As financial ecosystems become increasingly data-intensive, interconnected, and dynamic, traditional approaches to market analysis and investment decision-making are being complemented—and, in some areas, transformed—by machine learning, natural language processing, predictive analytics, automation, and deep learning. Against this backdrop, *AI Impacts on Market Analysis and Investment Strategy* brings together contemporary perspectives on how intelligent technologies are influencing financial decision-making, investment strategy, risk management, market forecasting, and the broader evolution of financial systems.

The growing availability of structured and unstructured financial data has created new opportunities for investors and financial institutions to identify patterns, evaluate risks, forecast market movements, and develop adaptive investment strategies. At the same time, the increasing use of AI introduces important questions concerning transparency, explainability, data privacy, algorithmic bias, regulatory compliance, market stability, and the appropriate balance between human judgment and automated decision-making. This book therefore approaches AI in finance not merely as a technological development, but as a multidimensional transformation with economic, behavioural, organizational, ethical, and societal implications.

The chapters in this volume reflect the breadth of current research and practice at the intersection of AI, market analysis, and investment strategy. They examine both established and emerging applications, ranging from AI-supported financial decision-making and robotic process automation to behavioural analysis, sentiment modelling, portfolio optimization, market forecasting, and sustainable finance. Several contributions employ empirical modelling and machine learning techniques to demonstrate how AI can generate actionable insights, while others provide conceptual frameworks for understanding the strategic, governance, and ethical dimensions of AI adoption.

Particular attention is given to the relationship between quantitative financial analysis and human behaviour. Behavioural finance has demonstrated that investors do not always act according to the assumptions of purely rational decision-making. Cognitive biases, investor sentiment, herding, overconfidence, loss aversion, and other behavioural factors can influence market outcomes. AI and machine learning provide new mechanisms for identifying and interpreting these patterns, potentially allowing investment professionals to incorporate behavioural indicators into more sophisticated decision-making frameworks.

The volume also recognizes that the future of AI-driven finance depends not only on predictive accuracy but also on the quality, robustness, interpretability, and responsible application of analytical systems. A model that produces strong predictions but lacks transparency or fails under changing market conditions may have limited practical value. Accordingly, the chapters consider issues such as cross-firm robustness, risk-adjusted performance, explainability, regulatory requirements, data governance, and responsible innovation. The discussion extends beyond conventional investment markets to include decentralized finance, green finance, renewable energy investment, and emerging models of technology-enabled financial governance.

OVERVIEW OF THE CHAPTERS

1. The opening chapter examines the transformation of financial decision-making through AI across centralized and decentralized financial markets. It considers how machine learning, natural language processing, and predictive analytics can support investment decisions, risk assessment, and portfolio management while highlighting the opportunities and challenges associated with the convergence of AI and evolving financial architectures.
2. The second chapter approaches AI and investment decision-making from a behavioural finance perspective. Through case-based analysis, it explores how algorithms, natural language processing, predictive analytics, and sentiment analysis can help identify investor behaviour and potentially mitigate cognitive biases such as overconfidence, loss aversion, and herd behaviour.
3. The third chapter focuses on machine learning-based market forecasting and the evaluation of investment signals across technology-sector firms. It emphasizes methodological consistency, predictive performance, cross-firm robustness, and risk-adjusted economic evaluation, illustrating how ensemble learning approaches can contribute to more reliable investment decision support.
4. The fourth chapter examines the architecture and application of AI-enabled trading and portfolio optimization platforms. It discusses data acquisition, predictive analytics, automated trading, portfolio construction, and risk forecasting

while also addressing practical challenges involving regulation, privacy, and algorithmic bias.

5. The fifth chapter considers the future of AI-driven investment strategy through the combined lenses of data-driven markets, behavioural indicators, and adaptive portfolio management. It explores big data, algorithmic trading, sentiment analysis, machine learning, and robo-advisory systems while emphasizing the importance of human-AI collaboration, governance, transparency, and responsible innovation.
6. The sixth chapter extends the discussion of AI into green finance and renewable energy investment. It examines how AI-enabled risk analysis, disclosure intelligence, monitoring and verification, and integrity analytics can strengthen sustainable finance. It also highlights the importance of accountability, explainability, fairness, data governance, and energy justice within technology-enabled sustainable investment ecosystems.
7. The seventh chapter provides an overview of AI applications within the financial domain, with particular emphasis on neural networks. It explores the use of AI for stock prediction, bankruptcy prediction, and financial statement fraud detection, demonstrating how advanced analytical techniques can identify complex and nonlinear relationships in financial data.
8. The eighth chapter presents machine learning techniques for market forecasting. It discusses data preparation, supervised and unsupervised learning, deep learning, evaluation approaches, practical applications, and emerging trends, while considering the challenges involved in developing reliable forecasting systems for increasingly complex and dynamic markets.
9. The ninth chapter investigates the integration of machine learning with behavioural finance. It applies contemporary analytical techniques to examine phenomena such as herding, momentum, overreaction, and loss aversion, while emphasizing the importance of interpretability and explanation-driven validation when using complex machine learning models to study investor behaviour.
10. The concluding chapter examines the integration of financial news sentiment with historical market data for stock price forecasting. Through deep learning approaches, it demonstrates how qualitative information can complement quantitative market variables and explores the effectiveness of recurrent neural network architectures in dealing with nonlinear and volatile financial time series.

Taken together, the contributions in this volume demonstrate that AI is becoming an increasingly important component of modern financial analysis and investment strategy. Yet, the value of AI should not be measured solely by computational sophistication or predictive performance. Its long-term contribution will depend on the ability of financial institutions and investors to combine technological capabilities with sound financial reasoning, domain expertise, ethical principles, and effective governance.

The future financial landscape is likely to be characterized by greater interaction between human expertise and intelligent systems. AI can process vast quantities of information, identify complex relationships, detect behavioural and market signals, and support increasingly personalized and adaptive investment strategies. Human decision-makers, however, remain essential for interpreting context, exercising judgment, establishing objectives, managing uncertainty, and addressing ethical and societal considerations that cannot be reduced to numerical optimization.

This book is intended to contribute to that evolving conversation. By bringing together empirical evidence, analytical methodologies, conceptual perspectives, and practical applications, it seeks to provide researchers, academics, financial professionals, investors, policymakers, and students with a comprehensive understanding of the opportunities and challenges created by AI in market analysis and investment strategy. Ultimately, the volume emphasizes that the future of intelligent finance will depend not simply on creating more powerful algorithms, but on developing financial systems in which innovation, resilience, transparency, and responsible human oversight advance together.

Soly Mathew Biju
University of Wollongong in Dubai, UAE

Sangeeta Trott
ITM Skills University, India

Chapter 1
AI-Driven Financial Decision-Making:
Evidence From Centralized and Decentralized Financial Markets

Shradha Attri
http://orcid.org/0000-0002-5649-1318
Central University of Himachal Pradesh, India

Sanjeev Gupta
http://orcid.org/0000-0002-9032-9437
Central University of Himachal Pradesh, India

Sachin Singh
http://orcid.org/0009-0009-5522-2093
Central University of Himachal Pradesh, India

ABSTRACT

The global financial ecosystem is undergoing a profound transformation with the integration of advanced digital technologies, particularly Artificial Intelligence (AI). Financial markets that once relied heavily on human intuition and traditional analytical methods are increasingly adopting AI-driven tools to enhance investment decision-making, risk assessment, and portfolio management. The rise of AI has significantly reshaped how investors interact with financial information, enabling more data-driven, efficient, and predictive investment strategies. At the same time, the financial system itself has evolved into two major structures: centralized finance (CeFi) and decentralized finance (DeFi). Technologies such as machine learning, natural language processing, and predictive analytics allow financial institutions

DOI: 10.4018/979-8-3373-9645-3.ch001

to analyze large volumes of financial data and generate investment insights with high accuracy. The convergence of AI with these two financial systems is creating new opportunities and challenges for investors

1. INTRODUCTION

The integration of advanced digital technologies with Artificial Intelligence (AI) has emerged as a focal point of a multidimensional transformation in the global financial ecosystem. Traditionally, the financial markets operate on human judgment, experience, a conventional analytical framework, and fundamental analysis. Investment decisions were primarily influenced by historical trend analysis, fundamental analysis, expert/broker opinions, and friend/family opinions and advice (Attri et al., 2025b). Even though these approaches to making investment decisions have worked well in the past, in the present dynamic financial ecosystem, the real-time complexity is not delivering strong results. In the present global scenario, with an increasingly interconnected, volatile global economy and vast, complex data, the modified digital technologies can safeguard investors.

The exponential growth of data, often referred to as "Big Data," has fundamentally altered the informational landscape of financial markets. The macroeconomic indicators, real-time price movements, new reports, social media sentiment, and fear of missing out (FoMo) make investment decisions difficult with the traditional approaches (Attri et al., 2025a). Thus, the complexity of information makes it nearly impossible for a retail investor alone to efficiently process and extract meaningful insights. This is where AI has emerged as a transformative enabler, bridging the gap between data availability and actionable decision-making.

With the help of AI-driven tools and techniques, particularly machine learning (ML) and deep learning (DL) algorithms, have a significant capacity of financial systems to analyse large datasets with speed and precision (Singh et al., 2025). Unlike traditional techniques, these technology-driven methods are capable of identifying hidden patterns, detecting anomalies, and generating predictive insights. (Singh et al., 2025) concluded that a deep neural network (DNN) yields better results than traditional techniques of price forecasting. ML models can analyse historical market data alongside real-time inputs to forecast asset price movements, while natural language processing techniques can evaluate news sentiment and its potential impact on financial markets. As a results, AI empowers investors to make more informed, evidence-based decisions rather than relying solely on intuition or limited analytical frameworks.

Moreover, the integration of AI has revolutionized investment decision-making processes by introducing automation and efficiency (Huynh et al., 2020). Algorithmic trading systems, powered by AI, can execute trades within milliseconds based on predefined criteria and evolving market conditions (Ben Hamadou et al., 2025). These systems not only enhance trading speed but also reduce human biases, such as overconfidence, herding behaviour, and emotional decision-making, which have historically influenced market outcomes. Similarly, AI-driven Robo-advisors provide personalized investment recommendations by analysing risk profiles, market trends, and financial goals, thereby democratizing access to sophisticated financial advisory services (Bai, 2024; Bhatia et al., 2022).

Risk assessment and management, critical components of financial decision-making, have also been significantly improved by AI techniques (Singh et al., 2026b). Traditional risk management approaches often rely on static models and historical data, which may not adequately capture the dynamic nature of financial markets. In contrast, AI-based risk models continuously learn and adapt to changing market conditions, enabling more accurate identification of potential risks and uncertainties. Financial institutions increasingly use AI to detect fraudulent transactions, assess creditworthiness, and monitor market volatility, thereby enhancing the resilience and stability of financial systems. Another important dimension of AI-driven transformation is the shift towards predictive and proactive investment strategies. Unlike traditional reactive approaches, where decisions are made based on past events, AI enables forward-looking analysis by leveraging predictive modelling techniques. Investors can anticipate market trends, identify emerging opportunities, and respond to potential risks in a timely manner. This predictive capability is particularly valuable in highly volatile markets, such as cryptocurrency, where rapid price fluctuations and market sentiment are crucial (Attri et al., 2025a; Buthelezi, 2024; Tripathy et al., 2025).

Furthermore, AI has redefined how investors interact with financial information. The use of intelligent dashboards, real time analytics platforms, and automated reporting systems allows investors to access and interpret complex data in a more intuitive and user-friendly manner. This not only improves decision-making efficiency but also enhances transparency and accessibility within financial markets. Retail investors, who previously had limited access to advanced analytical tools, can now leverage AI-powered platforms to compete more effectively with institutional investors. However, while the adoption of AI offers numerous advantages, it also introduces new challenges and considerations. The increasing reliance on algorithmic decision-making raises concerns related to transparency, accountability, and ethical implications. AI models, often described as "black box, may produce outcomes that are difficult to interpret, potentially leading to issues of trust among investors. Additionally, the widespread use of AI-driven trading systems can contribute to market volatility, especially during periods of high uncertainty or systemic shocks.

Despite these challenges, the role of AI in financial markets continues to expand, driven by ongoing technological advancements and increasing demand for data-driven insights. The convergence of AI with other emerging technologies, such as blockchain and cloud computing, is expected to further accelerate this transformation, creating more integrated and intelligent financial ecosystems.

2. BACKGROUND OF FINANCIAL MARKET TRANSFORMATION

Existing studies have predominantly examined AI adoption in centralized financial institutions, whereas comparatively limited attention has been devoted to AI-enabled decision-making in decentralized finance. Moreover, few studies have compared these two ecosystems within a unified conceptual framework. This chapter attempts to bridge this gap by synthesizing evidence across both financial environments. The transformation of financial markets is the result of a long-term evolutionary process shaped by economic development, technological innovation, regulatory changes, and shifting investor behaviour. Financial markets, which initially functioned as simple platforms for the exchanges of capital, have progressively evolved into complex, technology-driven ecosystems that facilitate global financial integration and sophisticated investment activities. Understanding this transformation is essential to contextualizing the growing role of AI in modern financial decision-making. Financial markets were characterized by physical trading environments where transactions were conducted face-to-face. Early stock exchanges operated through open outcry systems, and information dissemination was slow and uneven. Market participants relied heavily on personal networks, broker advice, and limited publicly available data. This environment often led to information asymmetry, where certain investors had access to better or faster information than others, resulting in inefficiencies in price discovery and investment decisions. The first major wave of transformation occurred with the digitization of financial markets in the late 20th century. The introduction of computers and electronic trading systems revolutionized how financial transactions were executed. Trading shifted from physical floors to digital platforms, enabling faster execution, improved accuracy, and reduced transaction costs. This transition marked the emergence of electronic financial markets, where investors could participate remotely and access real-time market information. The digitization process also facilitated the development of online trading platforms, significantly increasing retail investor participation. Alongside digitization, the forces of globalization played a critical role in transforming financial markets. Capital flows became increasingly international, linking domestic markets with global financial systems. Investors gained the ability to diversify portfolios across borders, while multinational corporations accessed funding from international capital markets. This interconnectedness enhanced market efficiency but also introduced new risks, such financial contagion and systemic instability, as witnessed during global financial crises. Another significant driver of transformation has been financial innovation. The development of complex financial instruments, such as derivatives, exchange-traded funds (ETFs), and structured products, expanded investment opportunities and risk management strategies. While these innovations improved market efficiency and liquidity, they also increased the complexity of financial systems, making them more difficult to regulate and understand. This growing complexity created the need for advanced analytical tools, paving the way for the integration of AI and data-driven technologies.

The early 21st century witnesses the rise of algorithmic and high frequency trading, which further accelerated market transformation. These technologies enable automated trading based on predefined rules and real-time data analysis, significantly increasing market speed and efficiency. However, they also raised concerns about market volatility, flash crashes, and the dominance of institutional investors with access to advanced technological infrastructure. More recently, the emergence of financial technology (FinTech) has reshaped the financial landscape by introducing innovative solutions that enhance accessibility, efficiency, and user experience. FinTech applications, including mobile banking, digital payments, peer-to-peer lending, and Robo-advisory services, have democratized access to financial services. This shift has empowered retail investors and reduced reliance on traditional financial intermediaries (Singh et al., 2026a).

A major milestone in the transformation of financial markets has been the development of blockchain technology and DeFi. Blockchain introduced the concept of distributed ledgers, enabling secure, transparent, and tamper-proof recording of transactions without the need for centralized authorities. This innovation gave rise to cryptocurrencies and decentralized financial platforms, which challenge the traditional centralized financial system by offering peer-to-peer financial services and greater user autonomy. Concurrently, the exponential growth in data generation and computational power has created an environment in which advanced technologies like AI can thrive. Financial markets now generate vast amounts of real-time data from multiple sources, including trading activities, economic indicators, and digital interactions. AI systems leverage this data to provide predictive insights, automate decision-making processes, and enhance risk management practices.

The transformation of financial markets has also been influenced by regulatory evolution. Governments and regulatory bodies have continuously adapted to technological advancements and market innovations to ensure stability, transparency, and investor protection. While centralized financial markets operate within well-defined regulatory frameworks, decentralized markets often exist in a relatively ambiguous regulatory environment, creating both opportunities and challenges. In essence, the background of financial market transformation reflects a shift from manual, localized, and intermediary-driven systems to digital, globalized, and technology-driven ecosystems. This transformation has not only improved efficiency and accessibility but has also increased complexity and dynamism of financial markets.

3. CENTRALIZED VS. DECENTRALIZED FINANCIAL SYSTEM

The modern financial ecosystem can broadly be divided into two major structures: Centralized Financial System (CeFi) and Decentralized Financial System (DeFi). Both systems aim to facilitate financial transactions, investment activities, lending, borrowing and wealth creation; however, they differ significantly in terms of governance, operational mechanisms, transparency, regulation, and technological foundations.

3.1. Centralized Financial System (CeFi)

CeFi refers to a traditional financial structure where financial activities are managed and supervised by central authorities such as banks, stock exchanges, governments, and regulatory institutions. In this system, intermediaries play a crucial role in facilitating transactions, ensuring trust, maintaining records, and enforcing financial regulations. Examples of CeFi: commercial banks, stock exchanges, mutual funds, insurance companies, brokerage firms, and central banks.

3.2. Decentralized Financial Systems (DeFi)

DeFi refers to a blockchain-based financial ecosystem where financial services are provided without traditional intermediaries. Transactions occur directly between participants using peer-to-peer networks, smart contracts, and decentralized applications (dApps). DeFi emerged primarily through blockchain platforms like Bitcoin and Ethereum, which introduced the possibility of conducting secure financial transactions without centralized control. Examples of DeFi: Cryptocurrencies, decentralized exchanges (DEXs), Peer-to-Peer lending platforms, smart-contract-based insurance and decentralized autonomous organizations (DAOs).

3.3. Comparison of CeFi and DeFi

Table 1. CeFi vs DeFi

Basis of Comparison	CeFi	DeFi
Control	Controlled by institutions and regulatory bodies.	Controlled by blockchain protocols and smart contracts.
Intermediaries	Requires intermediaries such as banks, brokers, and payment processors.	No intermediaries; peer-to-peer transactions
Trust mechanism	Trust is placed in financial institutions.	Trust is placed in technology and blockchain networks.
Regulation	Highly regulated and governed by legal frameworks.	Limited or evolving regulatory oversight.
Transparency	Moderate transparency; internal processes may not be fully visible.	High transparency; transactions are recorded on public ledgers.
Accessibility	Requires KYC, documentation, and compliance procedures	Open access with an internet connection and a digital wallet
Transaction speed	Comparatively slower due to institutional verification	Faster due to automated smart contracts
Transaction cost	Higher fees because of intermediary charges.	Lower fees due to the removal of intermediaries.
Security	Protected by institutional safeguards and legal systems.	Depends on blockchain security and smart contract reliability.
Volatility	Relatively stable and less volatile.	Highly volatile, especially in cryptocurrency markets.
Investor protection	Strong legal protection and dispute resolution mechanisms.	Limited legal recourse and investor protection.

4. ROLE OF AI IN CEFI AND DEFI

AI has emerged as a transformative force in modern financial systems, significantly influencing how financial decisions are made, risks are managed, and investment opportunities are identified. Both CeFi and DeFi increasingly rely on AI-driven technologies to improve efficiency, accuracy, and transparency in financial operations. Although the application of AI differs across these two systems due to their structural and operational differences, its role in enhancing financial decision-making remains critical in both environments.

CeFi manage vast amounts of financial data and requires advanced analytical tools for decision-making. AI plays a crucial role in optimizing operations and improving strategic financial management. *(a) Algorithmic and high-frequency trading:* AI-powered algorithms analyse real-time market data, identify trading opportunities, and execute transactions within milliseconds (Devi et al., 2025; Wilhelmina Afua Addy et al., 2024). These systems improve trading efficiency, reduce manual errors, and enhance profitability by responding instantly to market fluctuations. *(b) Portfolio management and Robo-advisory*: AI helps financial institutions offer personalized investment advice through Robo-advisors (Wah, 2025). These platforms access investor preferences, financial goals, and risk tolerance to create optimized portfolios and provide automated recommendations. A prominent example is Betterment, one of the world's leading robo-advisory platforms. Betterment uses AI-driven algorithms to recommend customized portfolios based on an investor's financial objectives, risk profile, and time horizon. The platform automatically rebalances portfolios, supports goal-based investing, and offers tax-loss harvesting to improve after-tax returns, enabling investors to manage their investments efficiently with minimal human intervention. *(c) Credit Scoring and Risk Assessment:* Banks and lending institutions use machine learning models to evaluate borrower profiles, credit histories, and repayment behaviour. This improves the accuracy of credit scoring and reduces default risks. *(d) Fraud Detection and Cybersecurity:* AI systems detect suspicious transactions, unusual account activities, and potential fraud patterns in real time. This strengthens financial security and protects both institutions and customers. Fraud detection is one of the most mature applications of AI in the banking industry. JPMorgan Chase uses machine learning algorithms to monitor millions of financial transactions in real time. These systems analyse transaction characteristics such as payment amounts, locations, device information, spending patterns, account histories, and transaction frequencies to identify unusual or suspicious activities. Unlike traditional rule-based fraud detection systems, AI models continuously learn from new transaction data and adapt to emerging fraud patterns. When a transaction deviates significantly from a customer's normal behavior, the AI system generates an alert for further investigation or automatically blocks the transaction until verification is completed. This real-time monitoring improves fraud detection accuracy while reducing false positives, thereby protecting both customers and the institution from financial losses. *(e) Customer Service and Financial Inclusion:* Chatbots and AI-based customer support systems enhance the customer experience by providing instant assistance, financial guidance, and greater service accessibility, particularly in digital banking environments. *(f) Market Forecasting:* AI models use predictive analytics to forecast stock prices, interest rate changes, and economic trends, helping investors make informed decisions based on data rather than intuition (Hossain, 2025).

DeFi operates on blockchain technology without traditional intermediaries. Due to high volatility, complexity, and limited regulatory oversight, DeFi requires intelligent systems that can process large-scale decentralized data and improve investment safety. *(a) Cryptocurrency Price Prediction:* AI models analyze historical price trends, blockchain transactions, and market sentiment to forecast cryptocurrency prices(Attri et al., 2025c). This helps investors manage risks in highly volatile markets (Bhowmik et al., 2025; Islam et al., 2025). *(b) Blockchain Analytics*: AI assists in analyzing on-chain data such as wallet activity, token movement, liquidity flows, and transaction volumes (Garg, 2022). These insights help investors identify profitable opportunities and detect unusual market behaviour. *(c) Smart Contract Auditing:* AI systems are used to identify vulnerabilities and coding errors in smart contracts. This reduces the risk of hacks, fraud, and financial losses in DeFi platforms. *(d) Sentiment Analysis:* Natural Language Processing (NLP) tools analyze news reports, social media discussions, Reddit communities, and investor forums to understand market sentiment and predict short-term price movements. *(e) Fraud and Scam Detection:* AI helps detect rug pulls, phishing attempts, Ponzi schemes, and suspicious token launches by identifying abnormal transaction patterns and security risks. *(f) Yield Optimization:* AI-driven DeFi platforms assist users in selecting the most profitable staking, lending, or liquidity farming opportunities by analyzing returns, risks, and protocol reliability.

5. HUMAN DECISION-MAKING VS AI DECISION-MAKING

Decision-making is a fundamental process in every field, particularly in finance, where accurate and timely decisions significantly influence investment outcomes and risk management. Traditionally, decision-making has been primarily human-driven, relying on experience, intuition, judgment, and emotional understanding. However, with the rapid advancement of technology, AI has emerged as a powerful tool that supports and, in some cases, replaces human decision-making processes. While both human and AI decision-making aim to achieve optimal outcomes, they differ significantly in terms of speed, accuracy, emotional influence, adaptability, and accountability.

Human decision-making is based largely on personal experience, expertise, intuition, and cognitive reasoning. Individuals often use their knowledge, past experiences, and emotional understanding to interpret situations and make judgments. In financial markets, for example, investors may rely on their perception of market trends, expert opinions, and instinct when making investment decisions. Human decision-making is particularly valuable in situations that require creativity, ethical judgment, strategic thinking, and the ability to handle uncertainty. Humans can adapt quickly to unfamiliar circumstances and make decisions even when complete information is not available. However, human decisions are often influenced by emotions such as fear, greed, overconfidence, panic, and herding behavior. These emotional and psychological biases can lead to irrational decisions, especially in highly volatile financial markets (Singh et al., 2026b). Additionally, human beings have limited capacity to process large volumes of complex data quickly. As financial systems generate massive amounts of real-time information, relying solely on human analysis becomes increasingly difficult and inefficient.

In contrast, AI decision-making is based on algorithms, machine learning models, and data-driven analysis. AI systems are designed to process vast amounts of structured and unstructured data rapidly and identify patterns that may not be visible to human analysts. In finance, AI can analyze market prices, economic indicators, social media sentiment, and historical trends to generate predictive insights and support investment decisions. AI-driven systems such as algorithmic trading platforms, robo-advisors, and fraud detection tools can make decisions in real time with high speed and consistency. One of the major advantages of AI decision-making is its objectivity. Unlike humans, AI is not directly influenced by emotions or personal judgment, which reduces the risk of impulsive or biased decisions. AI can continuously monitor market conditions and execute transactions based on predefined logic, making it highly effective for repetitive, high-frequency, and data-intensive tasks. It also improves risk assessment by using predictive analytics and statistical modelling to identify potential threats and opportunities.

Despite these advantages, AI decision-making has its own limitations. AI lacks human intuition, creativity, moral reasoning, and contextual understanding. It depends heavily on the quality of the data used for training and may produce biased outcomes if the input data itself is biased. Many advanced AI models also operate as "black boxes," meaning their decision-making processes are difficult to interpret or explain. This creates concerns regarding transparency, trust, and accountability, particularly in high-stakes financial decisions. When an AI system makes an incorrect decision, determining responsibility can be challenging. Another key difference lies in adaptability. Humans can respond effectively to unexpected situations, ambiguous environments, and new problems without prior training. AI systems, however, usually require retraining, reprogramming, or updated data to perform effectively in changing environments. While AI excels in speed and efficiency, humans remain superior in strategic decision-making that requires ethics, empathy, and innovation.

In practical terms, the most effective approach is not choosing between human or AI decision-making, but combining both. AI can serve as a powerful support system that enhances human judgment by providing data-driven insights, while humans provide oversight, ethical reasoning, and strategic direction. In financial markets, for instance, portfolio managers may use AI-generated forecasts to support investment decisions while still applying their professional judgment and market understanding. Human decision-making and AI decision-making each possess unique strengths and limitations. Human decisions are flexible, intuitive, and ethically grounded, while AI decisions are fast, consistent, and data-driven. The future of financial decision-making lies in the integration of both approaches, where AI enhances efficiency and precision, and human intelligence ensures accountability, trust, and strategic balance. This synergy is essential for building smarter, more reliable, and more sustainable financial systems.

Table 2. Human vs AI Decision-making

Basis of Comparison	Human Decision-Making	AI Decision-Making
Meaning	Decisions made based on human judgment, experience, intuition, and emotions	Decisions made based on algorithms, data analysis, and machine learning models
Speed	Slower, especially when handling large volumes of data	Faster due to real-time processing and automation
Data Processing Capacity	Limited ability to process large and complex datasets	Can process vast amounts of structured and unstructured data quickly
Emotional Influence	Highly influenced by emotions such as fear, greed, overconfidence, and bias	Mostly objective and less influenced by emotions
Consistency	May vary depending on mood, experience, and circumstances	Highly consistent as decisions follow programmed logic
Learning Ability	Learns from experience, observation, and judgment	Learns from historical data and continuous model training
Creativity and Intuition	Strong ability in intuition, creativity, and abstract thinking	Limited creativity; depends on programmed patterns and data
Bias	Subject to personal, cognitive, and behavioural biases	May inherit bias from poor-quality or biased training data
Transparency	Reasoning can often be explained verbally	Some AI models operate as "black boxes" and are difficult to interpret
Risk Assessment	May rely on perception and subjective judgment	Uses predictive analytics and statistical models for objective risk evaluation
Adaptability	Can adapt quickly in uncertain and unfamiliar situations	Requires retraining or updated algorithms for new conditions
Cost	Higher due to salaries, expertise, and manual effort	Lower in the long term after system development and implementation
Accountability	Humans can be held directly responsible for decisions	Accountability may be unclear when decisions are fully automated
Examples in Finance	Portfolio manager choosing investments based on market experience	Robo-advisors, algorithmic trading systems, fraud detection models
Best Use	Strategic decisions requiring ethics, judgment, and creativity	Repetitive, data-driven, and high-speed decision processes

6. THEORETICAL FRAMEWORK FOR DECISION-MAKING

Decision-making is a complex process influenced by cognitive, psychological, social, and technological factors. In the context of financial markets, investment decisions are not made solely on the basis of rational calculations; they are also shaped by investor behaviour, perceptions, trust, risk tolerance, and the availability of technological support such as AI. To understand how AI influences decision-making in CeFi and DeFi, it is important to establish a strong theoretical framework that explains investor behaviour and technology adoption.

While AI has significantly enhanced the speed and accuracy of investment analysis, its effectiveness depends heavily on the quality of training data, model design, and market conditions. AI models trained on historical datasets may struggle to adapt to unprecedented events, such as financial crises or geopolitical shocks, limiting their predictive accuracy. Moreover, excessive reliance on automated systems may reduce human oversight, potentially increasing systemic risks in financial markets.

This study draws upon multiple theories to explain AI-driven financial decision-making, particularly focusing on Behavioural Finance Theory, the Theory of Planned Behavior (TPB), the Technology Acceptance Model (TAM), and the Unified Theory of Acceptance and Use of Technology (UTAUT). These theories collectively provide a comprehensive understanding of how investors perceive, adopt, and utilize AI tools in making financial decisions.

A. Behavioural Finance Theory

Behavioral Finance Theory explains how psychological factors and emotional biases influence investor decision-making. Unlike traditional finance, which assumes that investors are fully rational and always seek to maximize utility, behavioral finance recognizes that individuals often make irrational decisions due to cognitive biases and emotional reactions.

Common biases include:

- Overconfidence bias
- Herding behavior
- Loss aversion
- Fear of missing out (FOMO)
- Anchoring bias
- Confirmation bias

In both CeFi and DeFi markets, investors may make impulsive decisions based on fear, greed, or social influence rather than objective analysis. AI helps reduce these biases by providing data-driven recommendations and predictive insights. For example, algorithmic trading systems and robo-advisors can support rational investment decisions by minimizing emotional interference. Thus, Behavioural Finance Theory helps explain why AI is valuable in improving decision quality and reducing behavioural distortions in financial decision-making.

B. Theory of Planned Behavior (TPB)

The Theory of Planned Behavior, developed by (Ajzen, 1991), explains how an individual's behavior is influenced by intention, which is shaped by three major factors:

a) Attitude

The degree to which an investor has a favourable or unfavourable evaluation of using AI for investment decisions.

b) Subjective Norms

The influence of family, peers, financial experts, and social networks on the investor's decision to adopt AI-based financial tools.

c) Perceived Behavioural Control

The extent to which investors believe they have the knowledge, skills, and resources to use AI technologies effectively.

According to TPB, if investors have a positive attitude toward AI, receive social support for its adoption, and feel confident in using it, they are more likely to develop investment intention, which leads to actual investment decisions. This theory is highly relevant in understanding AI adoption in financial markets, particularly among retail investors.

C. Technology Acceptance Model (TAM)

Davis (1989) Technology Acceptance Model explains how users come to accept and use new technologies. It was developed by Fred Davis and is based on two key constructs:

a) Perceived Usefulness

The extent to which an investor believes that AI improves investment performance and decision quality.

b) Perceived Ease of Use

The extent to which investors believe that using AI-based financial tools is simple, understandable, and convenient.

If investors perceive AI tools such as robo-advisors, trading bots, or predictive analytics platforms as useful and easy to use, they are more likely to adopt them for financial decision-making. TAM is especially useful in explaining the acceptance of AI in both centralized and decentralized financial systems.

D. Unified Theory of Acceptance and Use of Technology (UTAUT)

Venkatesh et al. (2003) Unified Theory of Acceptance and Use of Technology expand TAM by incorporating additional factors that influence technology adoption. It includes:

a) Performance Expectancy

Belief that AI will improve investment outcomes

b) Effort Expectancy

Ease associated with using AI technologies

c) Social Influence

Pressure from social networks and professional communities

d) Facilitating Conditions

Availability of infrastructure, internet access, financial literacy, and technical support

UTAUT provides a broader understanding of why investors adopt AI tools in CeFi and DeFi environments and how institutional and technological support systems influence this adoption.

E. Proposed Integrated Framework

Based on these theories, the chapter proposes an integrated framework for AI-driven financial decision-making:

Figure 1. AI adoption and Investment Decision process

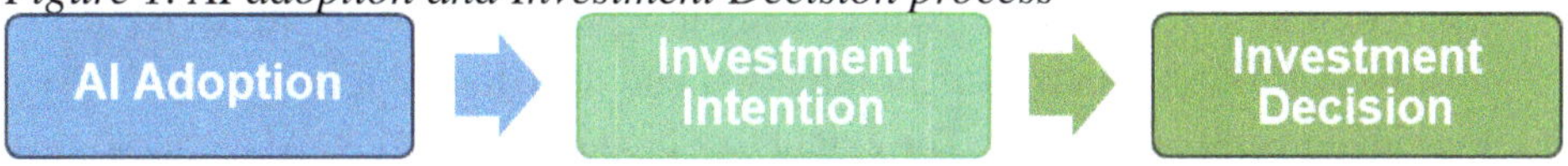

In this framework:

- AI adoption is explained by TAM and UTAUT
- Investment intention is explained by TPB
- Behavioural distortions are explained by Behavioural Finance Theory

This relationship can be further influenced by moderating variables such as:

a) **Trust in AI systems:** The degree to which investors believe that AI-based financial tools are reliable, accurate, secure, and capable of providing beneficial investment recommendations (Koroma et al., 2022). If investors trust AI technologies such as Robo-advisors, algorithmic trading systems, and predictive analytics platforms, they are more likely to use them for financial decision-making. Higher trust increases adoption and strengthens investment intention.

b) **Perceived Risk:** An investor's subjective assessment of the uncertainty and potential financial loss associated with using AI-driven investment tools or participating in financial markets, especially in decentralized finance (DeFi). Investors may fear system errors, cyber fraud, market volatility, or poor investment outcomes (Lee, 2009; Rahardja et al., 2023). Higher perceived risk often reduces confidence and negatively affects investment decisions.

c) **Financial Literacy:** The knowledge and understanding of financial concepts such as investment, risk diversification, portfolio management, interest rates, and market behaviour. It helps investors evaluate financial opportunities more effectively and understand how AI tools support investment decisions. Investors with higher financial literacy are generally better at using AI technologies and making rational financial decisions.

d) **Herding Behaviour:** The tendency of investors to follow the actions and decisions of others rather than relying on their own analysis. In financial markets, investors often buy or sell assets simply because others are doing so, especially during periods of uncertainty (Gupta & Shrivastava, 2022). AI can help reduce herding behaviour by providing objective, data-driven insights, but social influence may still affect investor decisions.

e) **Financial Self-Efficacy:** An investor's confidence in their own ability to manage financial matters, evaluate investment options, and make sound financial decisions. Investors with strong financial self-efficacy feel more capable of using AI-based financial tools and taking independent investment decisions. It positively influences investment intention and decision quality.

f) **Perceived Innovativeness:** The extent to which investors view AI technologies as modern, advanced, and beneficial innovations in financial markets. If investors perceive AI tools as useful innovations that improve investment efficiency and outcomes, they are more likely to adopt them. This variable reflects openness toward new financial technologies and digital transformation.

g) **Regulatory Awareness:** The investor's understanding of financial rules, legal protections, compliance requirements, and government policies related to AI-based finance, cryptocurrencies, and investment platforms. Investors who are more aware of regulations feel safer and more confident while making investment decisions. In decentralized finance, regulatory awareness becomes especially important due to legal uncertainty and market risks.

This integrated approach provides a strong conceptual foundation for understanding how AI influences investor decisions across centralized and decentralized financial markets. The theoretical framework of decision-making provides the academic foundation for understanding the relationship between AI and investment behaviour. Behavioural Finance Theory explains the psychological limitations of human decision-making, while TPB, TAM, and UTAUT explain how investors adopt AI technologies and translate that adoption into financial decisions. Together, these theories demonstrate that AI-driven financial decision-making is not only a technological process but also a behavioral and psychological phenomenon.

7. EMERGING TRENDS IN AI-DRIVEN FINANCIAL DECISION-MAKING

The rapid advancement of AI is fundamentally transforming financial markets and investment decision-making processes. Emerging technologies such as Explainable Artificial Intelligence (XAI), Generative AI, Large Language Models (LLMs), AI governance frameworks, and Responsible AI are reshaping how financial institutions, investors, and regulators interact with intelligent systems. Simultaneously, the convergence of AI with blockchain technology, decentralized finance (DeFi), and digital identity solutions is creating new opportunities while introducing complex ethical, regulatory, and cybersecurity challenges.

7.1. Explainable Artificial Intelligence (XAI) in Financial Decision Support

As AI models become increasingly sophisticated, many financial institutions rely on complex machine learning and deep learning algorithms to support investment decisions, credit assessments, fraud detection, and portfolio management. However, these models often operate as **"black-box" systems**, producing highly accurate predictions without providing clear explanations of how decisions are generated. This lack of transparency can reduce investor confidence and create challenges for financial institutions attempting to comply with regulatory requirements.

XAI has emerged as an important solution to this challenge. XAI refers to AI systems designed to provide transparent, interpretable, and understandable explanations for their predictions and recommendations (Černevičienė & Kabašinskas, 2024). Rather than simply generating an investment recommendation, XAI enables investors and financial professionals to understand which variables, market indicators, or economic factors contributed to the decision. In financial decision-making, XAI improves transparency in credit scoring, loan approvals, portfolio optimization, investment advisory services, and fraud detection (Rane et al., 2023). Investors are more likely to trust AI-generated recommendations when they understand the rationale behind them. Moreover, regulators increasingly encourage the adoption of explainable AI to ensure fairness, accountability, and compliance with financial regulations. Consequently, XAI is expected to become a key component of trustworthy AI-driven financial systems.

7.2. Generative AI and Large Language Models in Investment Analysis

The emergence of Generative AI and Large Language Models (LLMs) has significantly expanded the role of AI in financial markets. Unlike traditional machine learning models that primarily analyze numerical data, Generative AI can generate text, summarize complex financial reports, interpret economic news, and assist investors in analyzing large volumes of unstructured information. Large Language Models, such as ChatGPT, can support financial professionals by summarizing annual reports, earnings announcements, central bank communications, regulatory updates, and macroeconomic news (Krause, 2023). These models also assist investors in understanding technical financial concepts, comparing investment alternatives, and interpreting market sentiment. Generative AI further supports investment analysis through automated report generation, financial research assistance, scenario analysis, and market intelligence. Financial analysts can use AI to identify emerging trends, summarize research findings, and improve decision-making efficiency. Despite these advantages, Generative AI also presents challenges. AI-generated content may occasionally contain inaccurate information, outdated knowledge, or fabricated references if not carefully verified. Therefore, human oversight remains essential to validate AI-generated insights before making investment decisions.

7.3. AI Governance and Regulatory Compliance

The increasing use of AI in financial markets has highlighted the need for effective governance mechanisms that ensure AI systems operate responsibly, transparently, and in compliance with regulatory standards. AI governance refers to the policies, procedures, and institutional frameworks that guide the ethical development, deployment, and monitoring of AI systems (Eisenberg et al., 2025). The Unified Control Framework: Establishing a Common Foundation for Enterprise AI Governance, Risk Management and Regulatory Compliance. Financial institutions must ensure that AI models comply with legal requirements related to consumer protection, anti-money laundering (AML), know-your-customer (KYC) regulations, data privacy, cybersecurity, and financial reporting standards. Regulatory authorities worldwide are increasingly developing AI-specific governance frameworks to address issues such as accountability, explainability, model validation, and risk management. Strong AI governance promotes investor confidence, reduces operational risks, and ensures that AI technologies support sustainable financial innovation while maintaining market integrity.

7.4. Responsible AI and Ethical Decision-Making

As AI assumes a greater role in financial decision-making, ethical considerations have become increasingly important. Responsible AI emphasizes that intelligent systems should be designed and implemented in ways that are fair, transparent, accountable, secure, and beneficial to society. In financial services, responsible AI requires institutions to ensure that automated decisions do not discriminate against individuals based on demographic or socioeconomic characteristics. Financial institutions must also establish mechanisms for human oversight, allowing experts to review AI-generated decisions when necessary. Ethical AI is particularly important in investment advisory services, lending decisions, insurance underwriting, and wealth management, where algorithmic decisions can significantly affect individuals' financial well-being. Responsible AI therefore promotes trust between financial institutions and their customers while reducing reputational and regulatory risks.

7.5. AI Fairness, Transparency, and Algorithmic Bias

Although AI is often considered objective, AI systems are only as reliable as the data used to train them. Historical financial data may contain biases that unintentionally influence AI predictions, leading to unfair investment recommendations or discriminatory lending decisions. Algorithmic bias may arise from incomplete datasets, unbalanced training samples, or inappropriate model design. Such biases can affect credit scoring, fraud detection, customer segmentation, and investment recommendations. To address these challenges, financial institutions increasingly adopt fairness-aware machine learning techniques, regular model audits, bias detection tools, and explainable AI methods (Panarese et al., 2026). Transparency in AI decision-making enables regulators, investors, and customers to better understand how AI systems operate and ensures greater accountability.

7.6. Cybersecurity Risks in AI-Driven Financial Systems

As financial institutions increasingly depend on AI, cybersecurity has become a critical concern. AI systems process large volumes of sensitive financial information, making them attractive targets for cybercriminals (Thapaliya, 2024). Potential threats include data breaches, adversarial attacks on AI models, identity theft, phishing attacks, ransomware, and manipulation of AI algorithms. In decentralized finance, vulnerabilities within smart contracts and blockchain protocols may expose investors to additional risks. To address these threats, financial institutions employ AI-powered cybersecurity solutions capable of continuously monitoring network activity, detecting anomalies, and responding to suspicious behaviour in real time. Nevertheless, cybersecurity remains an ongoing challenge requiring continuous investment in advanced security technologies and regulatory compliance.

7.7. Human–AI Collaboration Rather Than AI Replacement

One of the most significant emerging trends is the recognition that AI should complement rather than replace human expertise. Although AI excels at processing large datasets, recognizing complex patterns, and generating predictive insights, it cannot fully replicate human judgment, ethical reasoning, creativity, or contextual understanding. In financial markets, AI functions most effectively as a decision-support system that enhances human intelligence rather than replacing financial professionals. Portfolio managers, investment analysts, and financial advisors continue to play an essential role in interpreting AI-generated recommendations, evaluating qualitative factors, considering regulatory implications, and making final strategic decisions (Fügener et al., 2026). The concept of Human-in-the-Loop (HITL) has therefore gained increasing importance, whereby AI performs analytical tasks while human experts provide supervision, validation, and ethical oversight. This collaborative approach combines the computational power of AI with human experience, resulting in more balanced, transparent, and trustworthy financial decision-making.

The emerging trends discussed above demonstrate that AI-driven financial decision-making is evolving from simple automation toward intelligent, transparent, and collaborative financial ecosystems. Innovations such as Explainable AI, Generative AI, Responsible AI, and advanced governance frameworks are improving the reliability and accountability of AI applications, while developments in cybersecurity and human–AI collaboration are addressing critical operational and ethical challenges. As centralized and decentralized financial systems continue to converge, these emerging trends will shape the future of intelligent finance by promoting innovation, trust, regulatory compliance, and sustainable financial decision-making.

8. IMPLICATIONS

The study provides several important implications for investors, financial institutions, policymakers, and researchers. As AI continues to transform both CeFi and DeFi, understanding its practical and theoretical implications becomes essential for ensuring efficient, transparent, and sustainable financial systems.

AI-driven tools such as robo-advisors, algorithmic trading systems, predictive analytics, and sentiment analysis platforms enable investors to make more informed, faster, and data-driven decisions. In centralized financial markets, investors can use AI for portfolio optimization, risk diversification, and credit evaluation, while in decentralized markets, AI assists in cryptocurrency forecasting, blockchain analytics, and fraud detection.

For banks, stock exchanges, insurance firms, brokerage houses, and other financial institutions, this chapter emphasizes the strategic importance of integrating AI into core financial operations. AI enhances efficiency in risk management, fraud detection, customer service, compliance monitoring, and investment advisory services. Institutions that effectively adopt AI can improve operational performance, reduce costs, and gain a competitive advantage in rapidly changing financial markets. As AI-driven decision-making becomes more prominent, there is a growing need for regulatory frameworks that address issues such as algorithmic transparency, accountability, data privacy, cybersecurity, and ethical AI governance. In decentralized finance, where regulatory uncertainty remains high, policymakers must develop balanced regulations that encourage innovation while protecting investors from fraud, market manipulation, and systemic risks. The study supports the need for adaptive policy mechanisms that can govern both traditional financial institutions and emerging blockchain-based financial platforms. This study contributes to the academic literature by bridging the gap between AI applications in centralized and decentralized financial systems. It provides a comparative understanding of how AI influences investment decision-making across both environments and opens avenues for future empirical and theoretical research. Researchers can further explore topics such as investor trust in AI systems, behavioral responses to AI-assisted decisions, ethical dimensions of financial automation, and the integration of AI with blockchain and FinTech innovations.

9. CONCLUSION

While previous studies have examined Artificial Intelligence in traditional financial markets or decentralized finance independently, this chapter provides an integrated perspective by comparing AI applications across centralized and decentralized financial systems. It combines insights from behavioral finance and technology adoption theories to explain how AI influences investment decision-making in different market environments. Furthermore, the chapter proposes a conceptual framework that can serve as a foundation for future empirical research on AI-driven financial behavior. The financial landscape has undergone a remarkable transformation over the past few decades, driven by technological innovation, globalization, financial liberalization, and the emergence of digital ecosystems. Traditional financial markets, once dominated by physical trading floors, institutional intermediaries, and manual decision-making processes, have evolved into highly interconnected, technology-driven systems that operate in real time across global boundaries. This transformation has fundamentally reshaped how financial activities are conducted, how investment decisions are made, and how risk is managed. At the center of this transformation lies the distinction between Centralized Finance (CeFi) and Decentralized Finance (DeFi). Centralized financial systems continue to provide stability, regulatory protection, and institutional trust through established entities such as banks, stock exchanges, brokerage firms, and financial regulators. These systems offer structured governance, investor safeguards, and relatively lower market volatility, making them suitable for long-term financial planning and institutional participation. In contrast, decentralized financial systems have emerged as a disruptive force powered by blockchain technology, cryptocurrencies such as Bitcoin and Ethereum, smart contracts, and peer-to-peer financial services. DeFi offers transparency, autonomy, global accessibility, and reduced dependence on intermediaries. However, it also introduces challenges such as regulatory uncertainty, technological vulnerabilities, and extreme market volatility. Both CeFi and DeFi represent distinct approaches to financial market operations, yet both are increasingly converging toward a hybrid financial model that combines institutional reliability with technological innovation. Within this evolving financial ecosystem, Artificial Intelligence (AI) has emerged as one of the most influential and transformative technologies. AI has shifted financial decision-making from intuition-based judgments to data-driven, predictive, and automated systems. Through machine learning, deep learning, natural language processing, and predictive analytics, AI enables investors and institutions to process vast amounts of structured and unstructured data with greater speed and accuracy than ever before.

In centralized financial systems, AI supports algorithmic trading, portfolio optimization, credit scoring, fraud detection, robo-advisory services, and customer relationship management. It enhances institutional efficiency, reduces operational risks, and improves the precision of investment decisions. In decentralized finance, AI plays a critical role in cryptocurrency price prediction, blockchain analytics, smart contract auditing, fraud detection, and yield optimization. It helps investors navigate highly volatile and less regulated environments by providing intelligent insights and risk management mechanisms. The role of AI in decision-making extends beyond operational efficiency. It improves predictive capabilities, reduces emotional and cognitive biases, strengthens risk management practices, and enables proactive strategic planning. By transforming financial information into actionable insights, AI allows both institutional and retail investors to make more rational, timely, and informed decisions. This is particularly valuable in modern financial markets where complexity, speed, and uncertainty require intelligent decision support systems. However, the adoption of AI also brings significant challenges. Issues related to algorithmic transparency, ethical concerns, data privacy, cybersecurity, and regulatory compliance remain critical. The "black-box" nature of many AI models raises questions of accountability and trust, while the lack of clear regulations in decentralized markets further complicates implementation. Therefore, responsible AI governance, transparent regulatory frameworks, and ethical standards are essential to ensure sustainable and inclusive financial innovation. Ultimately, the integration of AI into both centralized and decentralized financial systems represents not just a technological advancement, but a structural shift in the future of global finance. The synergy between AI, CeFi, and DeFi is redefining investment behaviour, market efficiency, and financial accessibility. As these systems continue to evolve, the future of finance will likely be shaped by intelligent hybrid models that combine the strengths of traditional financial institutions with the openness and innovation of decentralized technologies. In conclusion, AI-driven financial decision-making is no longer a future possibility—it is a present reality that is reshaping the foundations of financial markets. Understanding this transformation is essential for investors, financial institutions, researchers, and policymakers seeking to navigate the next era of intelligent and inclusive financial systems. Thus, this chapter contributes to the literature by offering an integrated comparison of AI-driven decision-making across centralized and decentralized financial systems, proposing a theoretically grounded framework, and identifying emerging research directions that may guide future empirical investigations.

REFERENCES

Ajzen, I. (1991). The Theory of Planned Behavior. *Health Communication*, *50*(11), 187–211. DOI: 10.1080/10410236.2018.1493416

Attri, S., Gupta, S., & Singh, S. (2025a). Empirical Analysis of Cryptocurrency Investors' Perception: Insights into Investment Behaviour and Market Dynamics. In *Concept, Theories, and Management of Cryptocurrencies* (pp. 251–274). IGI Global. DOI: 10.4018/979-8-3693-5986-0.ch009

Attri, S., Gupta, S., & Singh, S. (2025b). Risk Forecasting Using Artificial Intelligence and Machine Learning: Evidence From Stock and Cryptocurrency Markets. In *Artificial Intelligence for Financial Risk Management and Analysis* (pp. 187–196). DOI: 10.4018/979-8-3373-1200-2.ch009

Attri, S., Gupta, S., & Singh, S. (2025c). Examining cryptocurrency versatility: Is it a currency or an investment asset? *Journal of Economic and Administrative Sciences*. DOI: 10.1108/JEAS-01-2025-0037

Bai, Z. (2024). Examining the association between robo-advisory and perceived financial satisfaction. *Review of Behavioral Finance*, *16*(4), 668–681. DOI: 10.1108/RBF-10-2023-0268

Ben Hamadou, F., Mezghani, T., Zouari, R., & Boujelbène-Abbes, M. (2025). Forecasting Bitcoin returns using machine learning algorithms: Impact of investor sentiment. *EuroMed Journal of Business*, *20*(1), 179–200. DOI: 10.1108/EMJB-03-2023-0086

Bhatia, A., Chandani, A., Divekar, R., Mehta, M., & Vijay, N. (2022). Digital innovation in wealth management landscape: The moderating role of robo advisors in behavioural biases and investment decision-making. *International Journal of Innovation Science*, *14*(3–4), 693–712. DOI: 10.1108/IJIS-10-2020-0245

Bhowmik, P. K., Chowdhury, F. R., Sumsuzzaman, M., Ray, R. K., Khan, M. M., Gomes, C. A. H., Al Helal, M. A., Siam, M. A., & Gomes, C. A. (2025). AI-Driven Sentiment Analysis for Bitcoin Market Trends: A Predictive Approach to Crypto Volatility. *Journal of Ecohumanism*, *4*(4), 266–288. DOI: 10.62754/joe.v4i4.6729

Buthelezi, E. M. (2024). Navigating Global Uncertainty: Examining the Effect of Geopolitical Risks on Cryptocurrency Prices and Volatility in a Markov-Switching Vector Autoregressive Model. *International Economic Journal*, *38*(4), 564–590. DOI: 10.1080/10168737.2024.2393589

Černevičienė, J., & Kabašinskas, A. (2024). Explainable artificial intelligence (XAI) in finance: A systematic literature review. *Artificial Intelligence Review*, *57*(8), 216. DOI: 10.1007/s10462-024-10854-8

Davis, F. D. (1989). A Technology Acceptance Model for Empirically Testing New End-User Information systems: Theory and Results. *Science*.

Devi, P., Kishore, R., Giri, S., Srivastava, S. P., Vishnoi, A., Sharma, P., & Balyan, A. (2025). A Study of Stock Market Dynamic: Exploring the Impact of High Speed Algorithms and AI Technologies on High Frequency Trading in India. *Proceedings - International Conference on Next Generation Communication and Information Processing, INCIP 2025*, 298–303. DOI: 10.1109/INCIP64058.2025.11019692

Eisenberg, I. W., Gamboa, L., & Sherman, E. (2025). *The Unified Control Framework: Establishing a Common Foundation for Enterprise AI Governance, Risk Management and Regulatory Compliance*. 1–31. https://arxiv.org/abs/2503.05937

Fügener, A., Walzner, D. D., & Gupta, A. (2026). Roles of Artificial Intelligence in Collaboration with Humans: Automation, Augmentation, and the Future of Work. *Management Science*, *72*(1), 538–557. DOI: 10.1287/mnsc.2024.05684

Garg, A. (2022). Unified Framework of Blockchain and AI for Business Intelligence in Modern Banking. *International Journal of Emerging Research in Engineering and Technology*, *3*(4), 32–42. DOI: 10.63282/3050-922X.IJERET-V3I4P105

Gupta, S., & Shrivastava, M. (2022). Herding and loss aversion in stock markets: Mediating role of fear of missing out (FOMO) in retail investors. *International Journal of Emerging Markets*, *17*(7), 1720–1737. DOI: 10.1108/IJOEM-08-2020-0933

Hossain, M. A. (2025). Artificial Intelligence-Driven Financial Analytics Models for Predicting Market Risk and Investment Decisions in U.S. Enterprises. *ASRC Procedia: Global Perspectives in Science and Scholarship*, *01*(01), 1066–1095. DOI: 10.63125/9csehp36

Huynh, T. L. D., Hille, E., & Nasir, M. A. (2020). Diversification in the age of the 4th industrial revolution: The role of artificial intelligence, green bonds and cryptocurrencies. *Technological Forecasting and Social Change*, *159*, 120188. Advance online publication. DOI: 10.1016/j.techfore.2020.120188

Islam, M. S., Bashir, M., Rahman, S., Al Montaser, M. A., Bortty, J. C., Nishan, A., & Haque, M. R. (2025). Machine Learning-Based Cryptocurrency Prediction: Enhancing Market Forecasting with Advanced Predictive Models. *Journal of Ecohumanism*, *4*(2), 2498–2519. DOI: 10.62754/joe.v4i2.6663

Koroma, J., Rongting, Z., Muhideen, S., Akintunde, T. Y., Amosun, T. S., Dauda, S. J., & Sawaneh, I. A. (2022). Assessing citizens' behavior towards blockchain cryptocurrency adoption in the Mano River Union States: Mediation, moderation role of trust and ethical issues. *Technology in Society*, *68*, 101885. DOI: 10.1016/j.techsoc.2022.101885

Krause, D. S. (2023). Large Language Models and Generative AI in Finance: An Analysis of ChatGPT, Bard, and Bing AI. *Bard, and Bing AI*, 1–31. https://ssrn.com/abstract=4511540

Lee, M. C. (2009). Factors influencing the adoption of internet banking: An integration of TAM and TPB with perceived risk and perceived benefit. *Electronic Commerce Research and Applications*, *8*(3), 130–141. DOI: 10.1016/j.elerap.2008.11.006

Panarese, P., Grasso, M. M., & Solinas, C. (2026). Algorithmic bias, fairness, and inclusivity: A multilevel framework for justice-oriented AI. *AI & Society*, *41*(4), 2803–2825. DOI: 10.1007/s00146-025-02451-2

Rahardja, U., Chen, S., Lin, Y., Tsai, T., Aini, Q., Khan, A., Oganda, F. P., Dewi, E. R., Cho, Y., & Hsu, C. (2023). Evaluating the Mediating Mechanism of Perceived Trust and Risk toward Cryptocurrency: An Empirical Research. *SAGE Open*, *13*(4), 1–17. DOI: 10.1177/21582440231217854

Rane, N., Choudhary, S., & Rane, J. (2023). Explainable Artificial Intelligence (XAI) Approaches for Transparency and Accountability in Financial Decision-Making. SSRN *Electronic Journal*. DOI: 10.2139/ssrn.4640316

Singh, S., Singh, M., & Attri, S. (2025). Mapping stock market dynamics: A tripartite neural network approach using modified grid search for stock market prediction. *Expert Systems with Applications*, *278*(February), 127243. DOI: 10.1016/j.eswa.2025.127243

Singh, S., Singh, M., & Attri, S. (2026a). Dynamic volatility linkages among crude oil, exchange rate, interest rate, gold and equity markets: An empirical Asian perspective. *Managerial Finance*, *52*(1), 160–182. DOI: 10.1108/MF-01-2025-0016

Singh, S., Singh, M., & Attri, S. (2026b). Unraveling two decades of volatility in financial markets: Insights and emerging themes. *Global Knowledge, Memory and Communication*, •••, 1–20. DOI: 10.1108/GKMC-01-2025-0038

Thapaliya, S. (2024). Examining the Influence of AI-Driven Cybersecurity in Financial Sector Management. *The Batuk*, *10*(2), 129–144. DOI: 10.3126/batuk.v10i2.68147

Tripathy, N., Mishra, D., Hota, S., Mishra, S., Das, G. C., Dalai, S. S., & Nayak, S. K. (2025). Bitcoin volatility forecasting: A comparative analysis of conventional econometric models with deep learning models. *International Journal of Electrical and Computer Engineering*, *15*(1), 614–623. DOI: 10.11591/ijece.v15i1.pp614-623

Venkatesh, V., Morris, M. G., Davis, G. B., & Davis, F. D. (2003). User acceptance of information technology: toward a unified view. *Management Information Systems Quarterly*, *27*(3), 425–478. DOI: 10.2307/30036540

Wah, J. N. K. (2025). AI-Powered Wealth Management: Transforming Financial Literacy, Personalized Investments, and Risk Assessment Through Robo-Advisors and Predictive Analytics for the Future of Finance. *Chinese Science Bulletin, 70*(02), 4401–4420. 02.1706/Csb.28.02.2025.01

Chapter 2
Artificial Intelligence in Market Analysis and Investment Decision-Making: A Behavioural Finance Perspective

Pratibha Gupta
http://orcid.org/0009-0007-5121-7604
Symbiosis Centre for Management Studies, Symbiosis International (Deemed to be) University, Pune, India

Pawan Pant
http://orcid.org/0000-0003-1774-5650
Chandigarh University, Mohali, India

Azmee Zaheer
http://orcid.org/0000-0002-6281-2608
Chandigarh University, Mohali, India

Kaushal Kishore Mishra
http://orcid.org/0000-0001-6466-0575
Chandigarh University, Unnao, India

ABSTRACT

The relationship between Artificial Intelligence (AI) and Behavioural Finance has been examined through three (3) case studies that showcase AI technology in the current investment environment. These three (3) case studies on AI-driven platforms demonstrate how the use of algorithms, Natural Language Processing (NLP) and

DOI: 10.4018/979-8-3373-9645-3.ch002

predictive analytics provides a mechanism to enhance the accuracy of analysis, allowing investors/investment professionals to make more informed investment decisions and a better understanding of how investors behave. The use of analytics in each case study enables analysis of investor sentiment, recognition of irrational trading behaviour, and the generation of data-driven recommendations for both retail and institutional investors. The use of these platforms has the potential to help eliminate cognitive biases from the decision-making process, including overconfidence, loss aversion, and herd behaviour; thus, improving the quality of decisions made by investors.

1. INTRODUCTION

1.1 Background and Motivation

At the intersection of Artificial Intelligence and Behavioural Finance lies one of the most revolutionary paradigms in Financial Markets today. Traditionally, Finance has been taught on the basis of the Efficient Market Hypothesis (EMH) as well as Rational Expectations, which assumes that an investor will rationally assess all information available to them and form consistent preferences, (Fama, 1970); however, through decades of empirical evidence within the field of Behavioral Finance (Kahneman & Tversky, 1979), we have discovered that human decision making is not logical and has many systematic deviations from logic due to cognitive bias, emotional bias and heuristics. Some of the Behavioural Anomalies documented include loss aversion, overconfidence, confirmation bias, herding, and mental accounting. Because of these Anomalies, we see many instances in which investors do not achieve optimal returns on their investments, and we also see market inefficiencies and increased volatility.

At the same time, the Financial Services industry has gone through an enormous technological evolution. The exponential Growth in Computational Power, the availability of Big Data, and Advanced Machine Learning Algorithms (e.g., Neural Networks) have led to the Development of artificial intelligence systems capable of processing massive amounts of information at a rate never seen in the history of the Financial Markets. By 2026, the Artificial Intelligence in Finance Market is projected to surpass $17 billion, achieving a compound annual growth rate (CAGR) of 25.9% and showing widespread use among both institutional and retail users (corporate report submission, Qubit Capital, 2025). As such, the use of artificial intelligence systems is clearly growing among traditional financial services businesses such as investment banks, asset management, hedge funds, and a number of new fintech companies, and is being deployed for a wide spectrum of applications from algorithmic trading and risk assessment to portfolio optimisation and personalised financial services.

The combination of insights from Behavioural Finance and the capabilities offered by Artificial Intelligence presents a unique opportunity to address many of the challenges in Investment Management. Artificial Intelligence systems, in theory, have no emotional biases and can analyse multidimensional datasets to identify and mitigate irrational behavioural patterns (as per Kahneman & Tversky, 1979) that continue to undermine investor performance. For example, Natural Language Processing (NLP) algorithms can measure sentiment from millions of news articles, social media postings and financial filings to determine market psychology, Machine Learning models can identify patterns within trading behaviours that are indicative of cognitive biases, and Reinforcement Learning agents can optimise Portfolio Allocation Strategies while taking into consideration the Non-rational Behaviours of investors.

1.2 The Behavioural Finance Framework

The discussion surrounding behavioural finance arises from the field of economics within the last 40 years or so; this topic places non-typical, systematic patterns of irrationality in financial decision making at the forefront of research (Thaler, 2015), and extends to the work that has been done by several main researchers in this area. The explorers of behavioural finance have categorised the behavioural characteristics of investors that can lead to irrational behaviour along a number of different dimensions:

1. **Heuristics and Biases**; Investors often utilise "mental shortcuts" (heuristics) to assist in the process of making decisions related to their investments, and these types of shortcuts can lead to systematic errors in the decision-making process.
2. **Prospect Theory and Loss Aversion**; Kahneman and Tversky (1992) articulated Prospect Theory as an alternative to the "expected utility" theory under which decision-makers make their assessments of potential investments. Specifically, they found that investors evaluate potential outcomes relative to a "reference point" rather than their absolute values. Investors who face potential losses typically exhibit loss aversion, as they tend to experience losses approximately twice the magnitude of an equivalent gain; this asymmetry leads to "risk-seeking" behaviours in the domain of possible losses and "risk-averse" behaviours in the domain of possible gains.
3. **Overconfidence and Illusion of Control**: Investors tend to overestimate their level of knowledge, expertise, and the accuracy of their forecasts. Consequently, these behaviours lead to excessive trading, under-diversification of their invest-

ments, and inadequate risk hedging. The Illusion of Control leads investors to believe they can control or predict the outcomes of inherently uncertain events.

4. **Herding and the Social Influence of Other Investors**; When one or more members of the financial markets are investing based upon the actions of other investors, they can create herding behaviour that can cause the actual value of securities to deviate significantly from the fundamental value of the securities. The phenomenon of herding behaviour creates "bubbles" and "crashes," as well as momentum, in financial markets.
5. **Mental Accounting and Framing Effects**: Investors typically keep their money within different mental accounts and base their investment decision-making process around the way something is framed versus the way that something actually is in real life. This behaviour will typically lead to inconsistent risk-taking preferences and optimal asset allocation decision-making.

1.3 The Promise of AI in Addressing Behavioural Biases

Behavioural bias detection and mitigation are achieved through multiple routes using artificial intelligence. One way is through machine learning algorithms that use past trading patterns to identify real-time occurrences of behaviour driven by bias. For instance, a high frequency of trades in a volatile market could indicate overconfidence, while reluctance to accept losses or sell a position could indicate loss aversion (Mezzi, 2025). By continuously monitoring investor performance using established behavioural finance models, AI can deliver timely interventions, including cognitive nudges, alerts, and automatic portfolio rebalancing, to mitigate irrational behaviours.

Financial sentiment can be estimated using natural language processing techniques on large volumes of textual data from news media outlets, financial reports, analyst recommendations, and social media. Sentiment analysis algorithms can identify timeframes associated with excessive optimism or pessimism, suggesting herding or bubble behaviour.

Deep reinforcement learning (DRL) has recently emerged as one of the more promising techniques for applying behavioural finance principles to algorithmic trading strategies. Recent investigations have shown that a DRL model utilising behavioural biases such as loss aversion and overconfidence outperforms traditional rational models and even human participants (Nature Scientific Reports, 2026). These "behaviourally aware" AI systems understand that optimal trading strategies in real-world markets should account for the behavioural dynamics of other market participants, since no two markets operate in the same way.

2. LITERATURE REVIEW

2.1 Foundations of Behavioural Finance

Research in behavioural finance has exploded, offering powerful evidence of systematic deviations from rationality in financial decision-making. The development of Prospect Theory by Kahneman and Tversky showed that people make decisions based on their reference point and the potential losses from their choices. This runs counter to the theory of Expected Utility (Kahneman & Tversky, 1979). Many of the anomalies in the stock market, such as the disposition effect, where investors sell winning shares too quickly and hold losing shares too long, and the Equity Premium Puzzle, can be explained by Prospect Theory.

Since Kahneman and Tversky's work, an increasing number of behavioural biases affecting decision-making have been identified. Barber and Odean showed that overconfident investors trade excessively and incur losses of approximately 6.5% more than they would if they had not traded at all (Barber & Odean, 2000). Shiller's study of irrational exuberance discussed how the psychology of investors and social interactions lead to bubbles and crashes in asset prices (Shiller, 2000). De Bondt and Thaler showed that investor psychology leads to overreaction or underreaction in stock prices rather than a change in the company's fundamentals. (De Bondt & Thaler, 1985).

2.2 AI Technologies in Financial Services

There are many machine learning techniques used in finance today, including supervised, unsupervised, and reinforcement learning. Supervised learning algorithms such as random forests, gradient boosting machines, and neural networks are employed for tasks including predicting the likelihood of a borrower defaulting on a loan, forecasting stock market returns, and classifying financial markets into different regimes, according to Gu and Xiu (2020). Both clustering and dimensionality reduction, which are part of unsupervised machine learning, can also assist in identifying financial market segments, detecting trade anomalies, and identifying the latent factors that drive returns on investments in financial assets.

Natural language processing (NLP) has also been leveraged for use in financial analysis. NLP systems use transformer architectures and large language models (LLMs) to process unstructured text in documents, such as market reports, newspapers, and social media posts. Applications of NLP include analysing sentiment in financial news and social media, applying algorithms to automate the preparation of certain financial documents, transcribing and analysing earnings calls, and providing conversational-style financial advice via chatbots (Amundi Research Centre,

2025). Studies have demonstrated that sentiment indicators derived from NLP have statistically significant predictive power for stock market returns and volumes, as well as for volatility in financial markets.

Finally, deep reinforcement learning is widely regarded as the most advanced application of AI in financial services. Agents of Deep Reinforcement Learning (DRL) can learn optimal trading strategies and portfolio allocation policies through trial and error, maximising risk-adjusted returns over the long term (Nature Scientific Reports, 2026).

2.3 AI and Behavioural Finance

Many studies have illustrated the ability of machine learning-based methods to detect behavioural biases from trading data. Researchers have developed machine learning algorithms to classify traders'/investors' susceptibility to specific biases, thereby enabling customised interventions (Journal of Investment Economics Research, 2024). By analysing investment patterns such as holding duration, the timing of realisation, and responses to market changes, AI systems can identify loss-averse investors and offer Standard Operating Procedure (SOP) coaching to overcome these biases.

The growing body of literature examines "behaviourally informed" AI models constructed using behavioural inputs. In doing so, these AI models view market participants as behaving in a (non-rational) manner, rather than as being rational actors (Surmount AI, 2025).

Researchers have suggested that by outsourcing all decision-making functions to algorithms, robot-advisors and automated trading systems may diminish investors' financial literacy and create instances of "learned helplessness" (Frontiers in Behavioural Economics, 2024). Researchers have also suggested that by training AI systems on historical data and using those datasets to run the algorithm, AI systems may perpetuate, magnify, and amplify behavioural biases that existed within the historical datasets used for development (AInvest, 2025).

As recent studies have begun to examine the psychological and social effects of AI investment strategy management practices, researchers are investigating investor confidence in algorithm-based recommendations, the transparency and explainability of algorithmic behaviour, and the potential for AI systems to contribute to increasing wealth disparity. To fully understand the multifaceted implications of increasing AI use in investing, interdisciplinary collaboration will be necessary to integrate Computer Science, Economics, Psychology, and Sociology.

2.4 Literature Gaps

Despite growing integration of AI and behavioural finance, key research gaps remain. Limited longitudinal field studies exist, with most research relying on back-testing or laboratory methods. Existing literature largely focuses on equities, overlooking fixed income, commodities, cryptocurrencies, and alternative assets. Additionally, studies often isolate single biases, whereas investors typically exhibit multiple interacting biases. Regulatory and ethical frameworks for AI-driven investment management, including accountability, transparency, and consumer protection, remain underexplored. This paper addresses these gaps through real-world case studies, multi-bias analysis, and regulatory insights.

3. RESEARCH OBJECTIVES

The purpose of the research paper is to investigate AI's contribution to market analysis and investment decision-making, in the context of behavioural finance, based on selected case studies. The paper has the following specific objectives:

1. To examine case-based evidence as to how artificial intelligence techniques—such as machine learning, natural language processing, and predictive analytics—can identify and mitigate cognitive biases (e.g., overconfidence, loss aversion, and herd behaviour) in investment decision-making.
2. To analyse case-based evidence of AI-driven platforms in both institutional and retail investment contexts, focusing on their effectiveness in improving decision quality through sentiment analysis and detection of irrational trading patterns.

4. METHODOLOGY

4.1 Research Design

Qualitative case study methodology was used in this study. Case study research is well-suited to examining complex contemporary phenomena in their natural environments, particularly when the boundaries between the phenomenon and its context are not clearly delineated (Yin, 2018). The integration of AI and behavioural finance in investment management is a complex, contemporary phenomenon comprising multiple aspects, including technological, psychological, economic, and organisational dimensions.

This research employed a multiple-case study design with three cases, all involving the application of AI to investment decision-making. The cases selected are: (1) BlackRock's Aladdin platform as related to large-scale institutional asset management, (2) Minotaur Capital's Taurient AI system as representative of boutique hedge fund use, and (3) the robo-advisory industry model as relevant to retail investor use. The range of cases will enable cross-case comparisons and provide insight into the varying contexts of AI-behavioural finance integration. An extensive review of industry-related materials, such as white papers, case studies, and technical documentation issued by financial institutions, fintech companies, and technology providers, was conducted to extract and compile practical information on AI-behavioural finance integration and quantitative performance metrics for use in this research.

5. CASE STUDIES

5.1 Case Study 1: BlackRock's Aladdin Platform

5.1.1 Background and Context

BlackRock was founded in 1988 and, by 2026, will be the world's largest asset management company, with approximately $10 trillion in assets under management. The main driver of BlackRock's success has been Aladdin (Asset, Liability, Debt, and Derivative Investment Network), an EMLO integrated system used to manage all investment assets globally, currently approximately $21 trillion, for BlackRock and many other types of institutional clients (pension funds, insurance companies, sovereign wealth funds, etc.) across the world (Redress Compliance, 2025).

Aladdin was created in the 1990's primarily as a risk management tool following the catastrophic losses in mortgage-backed securities; then it evolved over 30 years to become an integrated investment management platform that encompasses all aspects of managing a portfolio, including portfolio management, trading, operations, risk analytics, and increasingly, artificial intelligence. The platform performs millions of transactions per day, utilises massive datasets such as market prices, economic indicators, corporate fundamentals, and alternative datasets, and provides investment professionals with integrated tools that support decision-making.

BlackRock has recently increased Aladdin's AI capabilities, most notably by introducing Aladdin Copilot; an AI-powered assistant designed to help investment managers across the Aladdin platform; using generative AI through large language models and machine learning, providing investment managers with an AI-based, scalable solution to rapidly analyse data; generate insights; and identify potential investment opportunities; as well as facilitate the process of making informed investment decisions (BlackRock., 2025).

5.1.2 Behavioural Challenges Addressed through Aladdin

The AI integrated into the Aladdin platform has been designed to directly address the many well-documented behavioural biases that impact all aspects of institutional investment management. Institutional portfolio managers are also regularly exposed to large amounts of information (i.e. thousands of securities, several data points for each security, constantly changing news, and complex inter-asset dependencies) which creates conditions for PF managers to develop confirmation bias where they focus mostly on information that agrees with what they already believe and tend to ignore any information that contradicts or disputes those beliefs leading to bad decisions about where to allocate their capital. Experienced portfolio managers form strong pattern-based beliefs by analysing their past experience in the marketplace; however, these beliefs may not be grounded in reliable relationships and, in some cases, lead to poor investment decisions. Excessive reliance on specific historical periods to form pattern-based beliefs leads a manager to overconfidently take on excessive risk and under-diversify their portfolio. Managers also suffer from recency bias/anchoring effects, which add to inefficiencies in their decision-making, as the price at which they first purchase a security, or the immediately preceding price, influences their investment decisions rather than the security's current relative value from a fundamental perspective. Lastly, even large multi-faceted institutional investors (i.e., hedge funds, mutual funds) exhibit herding tendencies, particularly during times of extreme stress, with career-related incentive structures favouring group (i.e., consensus) thinking versus individual (i.e., contrarian) philosophies, regardless of whether there is independent and/or fundamental support for differing from the group (i.e. market) position.

5.1.3 AI Technologies and Implementation

Aladdin employs several AI technologies to help portfolio managers address behavioural challenges and improve decision-making. It uses machine learning for predictive analytics of asset returns, volatility, correlations, and macroeconomic variables, drawing on supervised learning methods such as neural networks, ensemble techniques, and time-series models. These systems analyse both structured data, including prices, volume, and fundamentals, and unstructured data, such as news, social media, and satellite imagery, enabling predictions with less human bias. The ability of models to be continuously updated with larger datasets enables them to adapt to the ever-changing nature of the marketplace. Aladdin incorporates natural language processing to analyse substantial amounts of text, including but not limited to earnings call transcripts, analyst reports, news items and regulatory filings, so that it can extract material information, identify changes in sentiment, track emerging themes, as well as identify inconsistencies between narrative and numerical data and limit biases due to confirmation. Furthermore, Aladdin's Copilot product leverages generative AI and large language models to synthesise insights, respond to sophisticated portfolio inquiries, and rapidly surface relevant themes and investment opportunities. Aladdin's risk analytics and stress-testing capabilities simulate thousands of scenarios and tail events, helping limit both overconfidence and complacency. Finally, behavioural nudges assist managers in making critical decisions by helping them distinguish between rational rebalancing and loss aversion, while offering contrarian perspectives on crowded trades.

5.1.4 Performance results and evidence

BlackRock's use of Artificial Intelligence in its Aladdin success has provided benefits in operational and risk management functions; however, comparative data on portfolio-level returns are not publicly available because the associated holdings remain private. BlackRock asserts that its AI tools have enabled more efficient thematic research by using LLM-based analytics to create streamlined workflows that deliver timely results from complex investigations and enable rapid scaling of research efforts (BlackRock, 2025). In addition, the Aladdin platform's AI capabilities enable enhanced stress testing and scenario analysis by identifying hidden concentrations, correlations, and potential downside risks within portfolios, which may ultimately increase portfolio resilience during periods of market volatility.

Adoption of Aladdin has continued to grow, with more than 200 institutions using the platform to manage approximately $21 trillion in assets. The use of AI-driven decision support may also help mitigate bias by facilitating the implementation of more fundamental, contrarian investment positions and reducing herd behaviour through enhanced diversification across risk factors (BlackRock, 2025). At the same time, BlackRock's emphasis on privacy controls and guardrails within Aladdin Copilot reflects its overall commitment to transparency and the responsible application of AI in support of investment decision-making (BlackRock, 2025).

5.1.5 Challenges and Limitations

While Aladdin has been successful, the case study highlights important challenges.

Concerns about Black Box Models and Explainability: Aladdin's AI models are so complex that their transparency and explainability are in question. Both clients and portfolio managers need to understand why the system has made specific recommendations, especially regarding regulatory compliance and fiduciary duty obligations. Although BlackRock has invested heavily in explainable AI methodologies, tensions remain between model complexity and interpretability.

Risk of Algorithmic Bias: AI models built on historical data risk perpetuating existing biases in the market. For instance, if historical data have shown a systematic underpricing of companies with female CEOs or ethnic-minority management, then an AI model would learn to impose a penalty on such companies and to exaggerate, rather than correct, market inefficiencies. Although BlackRock attempts to address issues such as bias by implementing bias detection and fair testing processes, these should remain areas of focus for the firm.

Risk of Overreliance and Deskilling: As AI systems become more capable, there is a risk of overreliance on algorithmic decision-making at the expense of critical thinking, insight, and knowledge. This deskilling could be particularly damaging during unusual events when historic relationships fail, and the ability to use one's best judgment is needed.

Systemic Risk/Homogeneity: If multiple large asset managers employ the same AI system, the correlated signals their models receive will enhance trade synchronisation, which could ultimately increase volatility in their respective markets. Examples of algorithmic trading used to magnify market shocks include flash crashes in equity and currency markets. Regulatory authorities have also expressed concerns that the widespread adoption of AI in asset management poses a potential risk to systemic stability.

Garbage-in, Garbage-out Data Quality: An AI model's performance is only as good as the data upon which it has been trained. If there is an error, bias, or manipulation in the training data, the model's results will be affected. Furthermore, as the use of alternative data acquisition methods (e.g., social media, satellite imagery, and web scraping) increases, the data quality issues they pose must be monitored and validated on an ongoing basis.

5.2 Case Study 2: Minotaur Capital's Taurient AI System

5.2.1 Background and Context

Minotaur Capital, a unique Australian asset manager, operates in a completely different operational context from BlackRock's institutional level. Minotaur, which began in the 2010s, is primarily focused on finding unique, high-conviction investment opportunities by analysing global equities and using contrarian strategies that may not be on the minds of larger market players. Minotaur manages several hundred million dollars across multiple strategies and competes against much larger, better-financed funds.

The company was facing issues finding alpha-generating opportunities due to the vast amount of information available to them and a very competitive environment, and therefore built an internal Artificial Intelligence-based research platform called Taurient. Taurient combines the latest technologies, such as natural language processing, machine learning, and knowledge graphs, to analyse an extraordinarily large database of financial information to develop "investment insights" for Minotaur (Smart Dev, 2025). In addition to using the new Taurient research platform, the company reviews more than 35,000 articles, reports, and forms every week from myriad sources, including all forms of financial media, industry publications, regulatory filings, and research reports.

Taurient is a useful illustration of how a smaller asset manager can use AI to become a more effective competitor by leveraging analytical capabilities previously available only to the largest institutions. Furthermore, this case study demonstrates the potential of AI to democratise investment management by addressing the unique behavioural finance-related issues facing boutique funds.

5.2.2 Issues Addressed in Behavioural Finance

Implementing AI will enable Minotaur Capital to address the following behavioural biases commonly exist for smaller asset managers: Availability Bias and The Limited Coverage of Available Information: Human analysts working at smaller asset managers can only monitor a limited number of potential investment opportunities; therefore, they will always have Availability Bias—overemphasising those opportunities that have been easily found or come to their minds since they are limited in their coverage of companies that can be found or thought of in the first place. Many smaller asset managers concentrate their investments in the larger, more established, and therefore more publicly proven large-cap stocks with extensive information, while also missing opportunities for significant value in the less widely known and followed smaller- and mid-cap stocks. Confirmation Bias in Assessing Thematic Research - When analysts pursue investment themes or theses, they naturally look for evidence to support these views, thereby including any contrary evidence and creating a bias that leads to overrating poor investments, resulting in risk being identified only when losses occur.

Anchoring to Historical Examples - As analysts evaluate how best to approach new investment opportunities, they often look to historical examples. While using the past as a guide can help, relying solely on past examples may cause you to miss opportunities created by new events or changes in overall market conditions.

Limited Scope and Siloed Analysis - Because analysts tend to operate in "silos" (i.e., covering specific industries/regions), there is not ample opportunity for cross-pollination; therefore, connections across regions of the global economy may result in missed investment opportunities.

Time constraints and quality of analysis - Managers at boutique firms, because of high levels of pressure, are often managing multiple responsibilities, including research, portfolio management, client relations, and administrative tasks; therefore, decisions may end up being made quicker and with less rigour than if an analyst had sufficient time to appropriately conduct thorough research.

5.2.3 AI Implementation and Supporting Technologies:

Taurient utilizes multiple AI technologies that work together to provide its customers with superior investment research utilizing natural language processing (NLP) (i.e., advanced NLP algorithms) to read hundreds of thousands of documents each day and extract relevant information (i.e., important companies, executives, products, events, etc.) based on the relationships between various facts, sentiment, etc. during the daily search process.

Constructing A Knowledge Graph - By constructing knowledge graphs, Taurient will dynamically connect companies to one another, to various industries, technologies, market trends, regulatory changes, and global economic factors. Using these types of information visualisation (e.g., graphs), the investment management system can discover unexpected relationships and implications in investments. The system may, for example, find that a new regulatory change in one country impacts multiple companies in other areas, or that new battery technologies will have implications across many industries due to both the development of electric vehicles and their role in grid storage.

The system implements machine learning algorithms to detect anomalies, inconsistencies, and emerging trends in the knowledge graph. The algorithms flag unusual combinations of events and track major shifts in "sentiment" regarding individual stocks, as well as discrepancies between market expectations and underlying developments.

In contrast to relying solely on quantitative 'screening' criteria to identify new stocks, the Taurient system develops coherent sets of investment "themes" supported by data from numerous sources/types of information. It develops investment hypotheses and provides the analyst with supporting evidence that can subsequently be evaluated, modified, and potentially used to make investment decisions.

Modules exist within the Taurient system to identify analyst biases in research ("cognitive bias"). One such example is when the analyst repeatedly searches for evidence to support an investment-related conclusion, with no regard for contrary empirical evidence, and thus would be said to exhibit "confirmation bias." Conversely, if the analyst continually focuses on a relatively small number of well-known companies in their research, the system will recommend expanding their information sources to avoid judgement errors/reduce their subjectivity when making investment-related conclusions.

5.2 Performance Results and Evidence

The use of the Taurient research system in conjunction with traditional fundamental analysis has yielded superior results for Minotaur Capital:

Superior Returns: The Minotaur Global Opportunities Fund has achieved a 23.5% return through mid-2025 (as of writing), compared to 17.4% for the MSCI ACWI index, its performance benchmark (SmartDev., 2025). The Alpha of 6.1 is a significant value creation for the boutique fund relative to much larger institutions.

Research efficiency was drastically improved: The fund has reduced its research cycle time by 60%, enabling its analysts to review more investments and place trades with greater confidence and better timing. The fund's ability to identify and analyse potential investments within days rather than weeks has contributed significantly to its overall performance.

Diversity of ideas: The analysis of the fund's portfolio indicates that investment ideas generated using Taurient exhibit greater diversity across sectors, geographic areas, and market capitalisations than the fund's previously held investments. This indicates a reduction in available bias and an increase in the number of opportunities available. The fund has been able to recognise value in certain small-cap stocks and emerging economies that analysts would not otherwise have analysed.

Risk management: The fund has managed risk while seeking outsized returns. The volatility and maximum drawdown measures indicate that the fund did not achieve its outperformance by taking on greater risk than the benchmarks used to measure performance. The Sharpe ratio of the investment portfolio using AI technology was significantly higher than that of the benchmark portfolios.

Scalability and capacity: Taurient has enabled Minotaur to scale the fund's research and resources without proportionate increases in the number of analysts. The firm has increased the universe of companies it will consider for investment by more than threefold, from approximately 500 to over 3,000. This has been especially valuable to boutique firms that have fewer resources. Section 4.2.5 discusses three primary limitations and obstacles associated with Taurient's Minotaur case study.

I. **Data Source Dependency** - Taurient's ability to generate high-quality investment recommendations is contingent upon the diversity and comprehensiveness of data sources available to it; limitations in the overall coverage of the data may result in the omission of investment opportunities or incomplete representations of investment options. There may also be instances where a particular recommendation is an inaccurate portrayal of the investment opportunity because the underlying comprehensive inclusion of all available investment research data for that opportunity is lacking.

II. **False Positive Issues** - As in evaluating any other type of investment opportunity, AI generated investment ideas will inevitably contain some degree of "false positive" investment opportunities, expecting AI generated investment ideas to present investment opportunities exist that appear to have all the characteristics of being good investments; however, human investment analysts must critically evaluate and filter through AI generated investment opportunities before presenting any of these as viable investment options; without oversight from qualified human investment analysts that possess significant financial expertise, misidentifying an investment opportunity by solely relying on AI produced recommendations can adversely affect the investment performance of any entity using these recommendations.

III. **Market Adoption** - The effectiveness (alpha-generating potential) of any AI approach used to generate investment ideas has the tendency to diminish as other users adopt AI as users or customers of AI; alpha-generating potential is typically only temporary in nature as the market approaches pricing efficiency over time. Consequently, Taurient's Minotaur must continue to advance its AI capabilities to remain competitively advantageous.

IV. **AI Training and Behavioral Bias** - The ML models that power Taurient's minotar are trained on historical data that are representative of historical market participants' behavior; consequently, should the characteristics that describe particular market behaviors change in a manner that are inconsistent with previous historical observations (i.e., should value strategies be supplanted by growth strategies or should certain business sectors undergo disruptive structural changes), then the ML model outputs suggest misleading suggestions.

V. **Regulatory and Compliance** - The use of AI in generating investment recommendations has raised and will continue to raise questions concerning regulatory responsibilities regarding due diligence, spousal liability, and fiduciary obligations: if an AI-based investment recommendation generates a loss to the user, there is a high likelihood that the responsible party has yet to be determined, especially as it pertains to due diligence obligations. Although Taurient implemented a governance structure that requires all AI investment recommendations to undergo human review and approval before being presented to the market, neither the legal nor the regulatory environment has kept pace with advances in AI technology.

VI. **Specialised skills and expertise** - Successful implementation of AI investment decision-making requires a combination of specialised skill sets composed of: knowledge of the finance industry, data analysis experience, and technology expertise; many boutique asset management firms may lack these capabilities, potentially hindering their ability to adopt AI investment strategies and exacerbating the competitive disparities amongst investors in the asset management industry.

5.3 Case Study 3: Robo-Advisors and Retail Behavioural Finance

5.3.1 Background and Context

Robo-advisors constitute a distinct application of AI technology in the investment management field, focusing on retail investors rather than institutional asset managers or professional fund managers. Robo-advisory services are algorithmically driven, automated investment platforms that provide clients with unique portfolio allocations, automatic rebalancing, tax-loss harvesting, and financial advice with limited human intervention and substantially lower fees than traditional wealth management services.

The number of robo-advisory platforms has grown exponentially in popularity since the mid-2010s, with major platforms like Betterment, Wealthfront, Vanguard Personal Advisor Services, and Schwab Intelligent Portfolios managing multi-billion-dollar in combined assets. For example, Betterment manages more than $45 billion as of 2025 (SmartDev., 2025). Robo-advisors are attractive because of their accessibility (very low minimum investment), affordability (advisory fees generally 0.25%-0.50% vs 1%-2% for traditional advisors), ease of use (designed with mobile-first user interfaces), and ability to reduce emotional bias in investment decisions.

From a behavioural finance standpoint, robo-advisors are a particularly intriguing investment option for retail investors, as they tend to introduce behavioural biases into their investment process to a much greater extent than institutional professionals do. Academic research has shown statistically that individual investors are under-performing compared to market averages and benchmarks substantially as a result (7%) of the same behavioural biases—the timing of trades, too much trading activity, a lack of diversification, and a tendency to make emotional decisions (Barber & Odean, 2000). One positive impact of AI-powered platforms addressing the above behavioural errors is the potential to significantly improve investor welfare.

Robo-advisors focus on addressing multiple behavioural biases impacting retail investors: Overtrading and Overconfidence. Individual investors often execute more trades than necessary, particularly among overconfident male investors, thereby reducing returns due to additional transaction costs and poor timing. Studies show that the most actively trading investors will underperform the least actively trading investors (approximately 7% annually) (Barber & Odean, 2000). Robo-advisors counteract these issues by enabling individuals to automate their investment decisions and adopt passive strategies that discourage active trading.

Panic Selling and Emotional Responses: When markets decline, retail investors typically react in panic, selling their securities at or near the market bottom and thereby missing the ensuing recoveries. Following the "stock market crash" of March 2020 due to the COVID-19 pandemic, many retail investors sold their holdings at substantial losses while those investors who stayed invested recovered within a few months. Robo-advisors help investors avoid panic selling through automated strategies that maintain target allocations regardless of market volatility, as well as behavioural nudges and educational messages during stressful market times.

Loss Aversion and the Disposition Effect: Investors tend to show a strong preference for realising their gains quickly, but also tend to hold onto their losing investments too long in anticipation that they will recover. Due to loss aversion and the desire to avoid regret, the disposition effect negatively affects an investor's long-term investment performance. Robo-advisors eliminate this investor bias through automatic rebalancing and tax-loss harvesting, regardless of an investor's emotional attachment to a particular investment.

Limited Diversification: Behavioural biases such as familiarity bias, home bias, and the illusion of control keep investors from diversifying across multiple asset classes, leading them to focus on companies they know well, those based in the United States, or those owned by their employers. Robo-advisors use low-cost, globally diversified index funds or ETFs to significantly reduce idiosyncratic risk, thereby enhancing investment returns by eliminating these investor biases.

Inertia and Procrastination: Many individuals have delayed starting investments, increased contributions over time, and rebalanced their portfolios due to procrastination and decision-making paralysis. Robo-advisors eliminate the investor's potential for procrastination and inertia by automating contributions, including automatic contribution escalation, and continuously rebalancing the investor's portfolio without requiring the investor to take any action.

Insufficient Financial Planning: Behavioural biases such as present bias, hyperbolic discounting, and over-optimism contribute to individuals failing to save enough to meet their retirement and other long-term financial goals. Students who receive advice from robo-advisors with goal-setting features have been shown to be more likely to make wiser financial decisions by visualising the consequences of financial choices for savings or investment, using those same parameters.

5.3.3 Uses of AI and How AI is Used by Robo-Advisors

Traditional robo-advisors typically rely on rule-based algorithms to assess risk during onboarding through questionnaires covering risk tolerance, goals, time horizon, and financial situation, whereas more advanced systems use machine learning to interpret client responses more deeply and estimate risk tolerance more accurately (D'Acunto et al., 2019; Jaitly & Hoo, 2021). Adaptive questionnaires that adjust based on inaccurate responses or previously recorded behaviours can be used by some platforms to enhance the quality of user profiling (Jaitly & Hoo, 2021).

Portfolios can also be created and optimised by AI. Most robo-advisors continue to optimise portfolios using mean-variance methods; however, newer systems incorporate machine learning into the optimisation process, accounting for tail risk, regime changes, and return predictability, while allowing greater flexibility in portfolio design (Sironi, 2016; D'Acunto et al., 2019). In addition, robo-advisors constantly assess client behaviour and can identify emotionally driven behaviours, such as panic selling during market volatility. In these situations, digitally nudging clients by providing data on recovery, pointing out how market timing can cost them, and explaining how impulsiveness can impede their ultimate objectives can help them better manage the effects of these behaviours (Jung et al., 2020).

In addition to providing financial advice, many sophisticated robo-advisory platforms now leverage chatbots and large language models to assist clients in learning, answering questions, and receiving tailored guidance in a conversational manner, thereby offering personalised support without the added expense of hiring a human advisor (Jung et al., 2020). Additionally, robo-advisors increasingly perform automated tax-loss harvesting, thereby improving after-tax returns by consistently identifying tax losses and complying with wash-sale regulations (Eaton et al., 2020). Lastly, machine learning enables companies to develop behavioural profiles to facilitate user-specific interventions, such as providing additional reassurance to loss-averse investors and providing additional educational materials to over-confident investors (D'Acunto et al., 2019).

5.3.4 Performance Results and Support Estimates

There are mixed results from research studies examining both robo-advisor performance and their influence on investor behaviour.

Cost Efficiency: Robo-advisory services offer a significant cost-saving advantage over traditional investment advisors. Typically, robo-advisory services charge between 0.25% and 0.50%, while traditional advisors charge between 1% and 2%. As a result, when combined with relatively inexpensive index fund investment, robo-advisory services typically have total costs of less than 0.40% annually, while actively managed accounts generally have aggregate costs of 2% or more. Therefore, the cost advantages offered by robo-advisory services can compound over time, leading to substantially different levels of wealth accumulation among investors.

Evidence to Support the Reduction of Behavioural Biases: Several research studies have compared investors who use robo-advisors with those who do not and have found that robo-advised investors commit fewer errors than self-directed investors. More specifically, robo-advisors' clients have been shown in the Evidence-Based Research

Research has established that no other form (e.g., computerised) of automated investment management has prevented customers from panic-selling during market downturns, compared with traditional human financial advice. Research indicates that panic selling occurs across multiple platforms (ScienceDirect, 2019) and varies depending on whether customers are institutional or retail and the platform they use, among other factors; nevertheless, customers exhibit the same long-term behaviour with regard to investing regardless of these variables.

Tax Efficiency

There is evidence documenting the benefits of automated tax-loss harvesting and the benefits of capturing tax-related opportunities. For example, Betterment's (SmartDev, 2025) study indicates that the average annual benefit of automated tax-loss harvesting is 0.77% after tax for fully taxable accounts, and that the average benefit of automated tax-loss harvesting is affected by the size of the account, the tax rates of the individual in relation to the size of the account, and the previous and current market fluctuations.

Success of Non-traditional Asset Managers

It has proven difficult to find the type of evidence needed to compare the performance of robo-advisors against comparable market benchmarks because investors have different risk tolerances and investment horizons. The limited amount of evidence available has identified that robo-advisors have been just as successful, or slightly more successful, than traditional asset managers because the cost was significantly less than traditional methods, and the tax efficiencies realised from the type of investment strategy employed by the robo-advisors were greater than those reported by traditional asset managers. Consequently, there are other reasons for determining the overall success of robo-advisors relative to traditional asset managers, but achieving superior asset allocation or timing does not appear to be a significant one.

Retention, Engagement and Low Activity Rates of Robo-Advisors

Studies have shown that robo-advisor customers are engaged significantly less than self-directed customers based on the number of times and/or length of time spent reviewing their account performance, thus indicating that the low level of engagement has positive (i.e. less involvement with emotional equity) and negative (i.e. financial illiteracy and/or financial education) implications. Retention rates vary across robo-advisors/automated investment solutions, and some have documented very high attrition rates after initial adoption.

Limitations of Robo-Advisors

Robo-advisors provide the greatest benefit in basic automated investment management. Investors looking for more sophisticated investment management, particularly those with multiple streams of revenue, a business, estate planning, or unique tax situations, will benefit significantly more from a human financial advisor than from an automated system, as automated systems do not provide this level of expertise and are only appropriate for basic automated investment management.

Challenges and Limitations of Robo-Advisors

Robo-advisors have generated considerable controversy among consumers of financial services. Critics argue that the passive "set-it-and-forget-it" strategy of robo-advisors will negatively affect investors' financial literacy, as they are likely to fail to understand the fundamentals of investing (e.g., core investment principles), risk management, or the importance of long-term planning. Consequently, as the investor experiences fluctuations in the values of their investments due to changes in market conditions, they could develop learned helplessness as a result of this lack of financial literacy. In addition, there are significant behavioural biases in place within robo-advisors and, therefore, robo-advisors cannot remove many of these biases from their clients' decision-making processes; for example, investors may develop a present bias and therefore do not save enough, or may still have an impact on how they time their market sales or purchases and/or herd together to buy or sell.

The portfolios created by robo-advisors also pose systemic risk when they are relatively similar across platforms. This is because many robo-advisors use similar software algorithms, rebalancing processes, and tax-loss harvesting strategies; therefore, during periods of market volatility, they respond similarly, exacerbating volatility rather than reducing it. The above-mentioned systemic risks also hinder the investors' confidence in using a robo-advisor to provide financial advice since, typically, robo-advisors do not provide the level of transparency that a traditional human adviser does, particularly when considering their recommendation systems, default settings and questionnaire design; further to these issues, there is a concern that robo-advisors will simply replace one organisational bias with another (developmental bias).

Further complicating these issues is the regulatory environment surrounding robo-advisors: specifically, fiduciary duty, the suitability of the advice they provide, the disclosure of their fees and costs/charges, and their respective liability for poor performance. Due to the evolving regulatory framework surrounding robo-advisors, investors currently face considerable uncertainty about their use. Finally, robo-advisors are unlikely to withstand extreme shocks because they were designed to provide investment solutions under "normal" market conditions. Therefore, even though many robo-advisors performed reasonably well during the market crash of March 2020, it is possible that during a significantly greater market disruption, investors will discover the limitations surrounding their use of a robo-advisor to manage their investments, as these companies do not have the benefit of using human discretion to assist them in managing their investments.

6. DISCUSSION

6.1 Synthesis of Findings Across Cases

The case studies illustrate both similarities and differences in how Artificial Intelligence (AI) addresses the challenges of behavioural finance concerning investment management. One example is that AI's ability to process large volumes of data at high speed and efficiency can help remove some of the cognitive limitations placed on human beings and the excessive amounts of data that can lead to cognitive bias. For example, BlackRock has utilised AI to analyse large datasets, Minotaur uses AI to evaluate thousands of news articles weekly, and robo-advisors use AI to continuously monitor clients' portfolios. Thus, all three case studies demonstrate that AI can provide consistent, repetitive analytical support at scale for end users.

The ability of AI to reduce behavioural biases is also shared across all three case studies. However, measuring the precise extent to which AI has helped clients reduce bias is difficult. For example, BlackRock has experienced reduced herding behaviours and improved diversification as a result of using AI; Minotaur has experienced improved return profiles due to more diversified investment opportunities; and robo-advisors have helped retail investors reduce emotional decision-making and increase diversification in their portfolios. It is important to note that a variety of factors influence outcomes, with AIs playing a major role in improving decision-making. Another commonality across all three cases is the need for a balance between automation and human judgement in decision-making. For instance, BlackRock employs AI as a decision-support system, whereas Minotaur relies heavily on human evaluation of AI-based insights. Additionally, robo-advisors are starting to integrate hybrid models that combine AI with other human-based advisory techniques in their business models. This balance of human and machine leads to optimal decision-making, as AI provides high computational power and humans provide intuition and an understanding of the human context in which they operate.

The challenges associated with behavioural finance, however, will differ by context. BlackRock faces challenges related to cognitive overload and organisational herding; Minotaur faces challenges related to resource constraints and availability bias; and retail investors are primarily challenged by emotional decision-making. The use of automated processes and behaviours through robo-advisors significantly mitigates some of the behavioural issues faced by retail investors (Patil et. al., 2024). These differences in how behavioural finance issues affect organisations and individuals support the creation of customised AI systems that account for diverse behavioural profiles and characteristics among different types of investors and across them.

6.2 Randomised and Non-randomised Institutional Biases Support

The mitigation of emotional bias in institutional investors, from the case studies of the 8 institutions, we found the following mechanisms to mitigate behavioural bias:

Emotional Distance- because they lack emotion, an AI gives a more rational $ (however, check with your broker's policy)-therefore, during times of stress, when a human being's ability to reason effectively is typically the lowest, the emotional distance will provide a significant advantage over traditional methods;

Consistent Process- An AI will use the same analytical framework to generate a decision every time without being influenced by the emotional state of the person making it (lowers the error rate associated with human time-restricted heuristic decisions);

- through the systematic use of, thereby defining selective attention and/or confirmatory biases;
- because people create stories to justify the outcome of market events that do not represent statistical relationships to their actual event; artificial intelligence (AI) makes decisions using data instead of stories that help to create meaning; thus, when a new circumstance arises that needs to be analysed and reciprocated, the ability of straight calculation (as opposed to storytelling) can prove to be an impediment.

Analysis of the Counterfactual: AI enables the investigation of different possibilities and their respective results; thus, its ability to analyse these possibilities will assist in eliminating (in post hoc evaluations) the bias introduced by hindsight and the illusion of certainty.

Independence from Social Traps: Social pressures, herding behaviour, and groupthink can affect an individual's decision-making in an organisation or marketplace; therefore, AI is not susceptible to those influences.

Nevertheless, there are other avenues for demonstrating bias in AI and its training datasets, which are learned by algorithms; these discourage optimising for the good of humans.

7. RECOMMENDATIONS AND SUGGESTIONS

Artificial Intelligence (AI) has influenced the entire investment management community, and implementing AI successfully and ethically will require cooperation among many stakeholders. Investment managers should view AI as a tool to augment human decision-making rather than as a replacement for the investor's thought process. It is important to have governance frameworks that clarify how much oversight people will have over AI decisions; therefore, great emphasis must be placed on XAI (Explainable AI), extensive bias testing, and fairness audits when developing AI applications.

Investment managers will also benefit from developing cognitively diverse teams if evaluating the results that AI generates in a non-concurred manner.

Technology developers should play an important role by creating AI applications with the highest degree of XAI and incorporating behavioural finance principles into the design/evaluation of their AI systems. Technology developers should complete rigorous backtesting (stress tests) of their innovations under varying market conditions and user interfaces to achieve higher levels of human financial literacy and critical thinking skills, rather than developing for blind, unthinking reliance on automated solutions.

Regulatory agencies should develop a holistic framework for covering all aspects of AI-related investment issues; including: 1) Data transparency; 2) AI accountability; 3) Fairness; 4) The requirement for everyone using AI technology to disclose usage of AI; 5) Ongoing monitoring of the system-wide ramifications of algorithmic convergence; and 6) Development of communication standards and global collaborative relationships among regulatory agencies to enhance complete harmonization of regulatory approaches among interconnected global financial markets.

As it relates to individual investors and the use of AI, investors should view AI as an additional tool to help them make better decisions, remain actively engaged in their investments, be sceptical of claims that are too good to be true, and diversify their investments to mitigate risk. Researchers should continue examining the impacts of AI over longer time periods across numerous managerial cycles; examining individual investment behaviour patterns; designing methodologies to mitigate bias in investing; and reviewing potential implications of AI on society, such as in the areas of financially inclusive societies and income inequality.

The future of investment management aims to achieve a balanced integration of AI analytical capabilities and human judgement, enabling investors to engage in the most efficient and effective manner while fostering financial stability.

8. CONCLUSION

The investigation of the integration of artificial intelligence (AI) and behavioural finance into institutional investment management is conducted through original case studies and critical analysis of each case. The potential of AI to identify, quantify, and address cognitive bias and irrational behaviour in relation to investment decisions is significant. The paper presents three case studies to demonstrate how AI improves the investment process.

BlackRock's Aladdin platform clearly illustrates how AI integrates diverse data sources to enhance the institutional investment management process by enabling more accurate risk assessment and improving the quality of decision-making tools available to investment managers. In doing so, AI also diminishes the impact of cognitive biases such as confirmation bias, herding, and overconfidence in the institutional investor's decision-making. Similar to BlackRock's Aladdin platform, Minotaur Capital's Taurient system exemplifies how, by deploying AI, an elite boutique investment firm can achieve investment performance comparable to that of large, established institutional investors by enhancing investment coverage and reducing the burden of resource constraints. In contrast, the robo-advisory industry exemplifies the benefits AI provides to retail investors through automated portfolio management, reduced emotional biases in trading, and more diversified portfolios.

Both experiences in the three case studies yielded similar findings regarding AI technology and its application in the investment process. AI systems can process extensive, complex datasets that exceed human capacity; maintain emotional objectivity amid market volatility; apply consistent analytical frameworks; and detect patterns in vast amounts of data. Collectively, these capabilities will ultimately benefit stakeholders by lowering transaction costs, improving investment diversification, enhancing risk-adjusted returns, and increasing overall investment efficiency.

Despite the potential of AI to enhance the investment process, as outlined above, this study also identifies five major limitations to relying on AI for this purpose. The five types of limitations are as follows: bias in algorithm-based decision-making; overreliance on AI in investment decision-making; loss of skill-based analysis by investment managers; negative global systemic risks caused by market uniformity resulting from the deployment of AI; and lack of transparency in AI decision-making processes. Power and limited democratisation regarding investor access.

Research shows that combining AI computational power with human goodness will improve optimality. Additionally, AI tools need to be designed to accommodate various investor types and to maintain an evolving set of regulations that ensure fairness, accountability, and transparency. Furthermore, ongoing research and adaptation are necessary to keep pace with the continuously changing markets and systems associated with AI.

REFERENCES

AInvest. (2025). The hidden risks of AI in finance: How behavioural biases in LLMs threaten algorithmic trading and investment platforms. https://www.ainvest.com/news/hidden-risks-ai-finance-behavioral-biases-llms-threaten-algorithmic-trading-investment-platforms-25

Amundi Research Centre. (2025). AI for behavioural finance: Analysing investor profiles and predicting investor behaviour. https://research-center.amundi.com/article/artificial-intelligence-behavioral-finance

Barber, B. M., & Odean, T. (2000). Trading is hazardous to your wealth: The common stock investment performance of individual investors. *The Journal of Finance*, *55*(2), 773–806. DOI: 10.1111/0022-1082.00226

BlackRock. (2025). How AI is transforming investing. https://www.blackrock.com/us/individual/insights/ai-investing

D'Acunto, F., Prabhala, N., & Rossi, A. G. (2019). The promises and pitfalls of robo-advising. *Review of Financial Studies*, *32*(5), 1983–2020. DOI: 10.1093/rfs/hhz014

De Bondt, W. F., & Thaler, R. H. (1985). Does the stock market overreact? *The Journal of Finance*, *40*(3), 793–805. DOI: 10.1111/j.1540-6261.1985.tb05004.x

DigitalDefynd. (2026). Top 25 AI in finance case studies [2026]. https://digitaldefynd.com/IQ/ai-in-finance-case-studies/

Eaton, G. W., Huang, Y., & Krueger, T. M. (2020). Tax-loss harvesting by robo-advisors: Evidence and implications. *Financial Analysts Journal*, *76*(4), 25–39.

Fama, E. F. (1970). Efficient capital markets: A review of theory and empirical work. *The Journal of Finance*, *25*(2), 383–417. DOI: 10.2307/2325486

Frontiers in Behavioural Economics. (2024). Evaluating robo-advisors through behavioural finance. *Frontiers*, Article 1489159. https://www.frontiersin.org/journals/behavioral-economics/articles/10.3389/frbhe.2024.1489159/full

Frontiers in Behavioural Economics. (2024). Evaluating robo-advisors through behavioural finance. *Frontiers*, •••, 1489159.

Gu, S., Kelly, B., & Xiu, D. (2020). Empirical asset pricing via machine learning. *Review of Financial Studies*, *33*(5), 2223–2273. DOI: 10.1093/rfs/hhaa009

Jaitly, N., & Hoo, J. (2021). Machine learning applications in robo-advisory services: Risk profiling and behavioural assessment. *Journal of Financial Technology*, *3*(2), 45–62.

Journal of Investment Economics Research. (2024). AI in behavioural finance: Understanding investor bias through machine learning. https://jier.org/index.php/journal/article/download/3114/2529/5598

Jung, D., Dorner, V., Weinhardt, C., & Pusmaz, H. (2020). Designing adaptive robo-advisors: Digital nudging and conversational interfaces in wealth management. *Electronic Markets*, *30*(4), 1–15.

Kahneman, D., & Tversky, A. (1979). Prospect theory: An analysis of decision under risk. *Econometrica*, *47*(2), 263–291. DOI: 10.2307/1914185

Kahneman, D., & Tversky, A. (1992). Advances in prospect theory: Cumulative representation of uncertainty. *Journal of Risk and Uncertainty*, *5*(4), 297–323. DOI: 10.1007/BF00122574

Mezzi. (2025). AI in behavioural finance: Managing investor bias. https://www.mezzi.com/blog/ai-in-behavioral-finance-managing-investor-bias

Nature Scientific Reports. (2026). Behaviorally informed deep reinforcement learning for portfolio optimisation with loss aversion and overconfidence. *Scientific Reports*, 16, Article 35902.

Patil, A., Saha, S., & Sengupta, R. (2024). Enhancing stock market predictions through predictive analytics. In Singh, N., Birla, S., Ansari, M. D., & Shukla, N. K. (Eds.), *Intelligent techniques for predictive data analytics*. Wiley., DOI: 10.1002/9781394227990.ch7

Proxsis, A. I. (2025). How BlackRock's Aladdin platform leverages generative AI to transform investment management. https://proxsis.ai/use-case/elementor-1104/

Qubit Capital. (2025). Top 5 AI tools for predicting investor behaviour in 2026. https://qubit.capital/blog/ai-tools-predict-investor-behavior

Redress Compliance. (2025). Case study: AI-based predictive analytics for investments at BlackRock (Aladdin). https://redresscompliance.com/case-study-ai-based-predictive-analytics-for-investments-at-blackrock-aladdin/

ScienceDirect. (2019). Longitudinal case study of robo-advisors in investment decisions. https://www.sciencedirect.com/science/article/pii/S221463501930214X

Shiller, R. J. (2000). *Irrational exuberance*. Princeton University Press.

Sironi, P. (2016). *FinTech innovation: From robo-advisors to goal based investing and gamification*. Wiley. DOI: 10.1002/9781119227205

SmartDev. (2025). AI in investment management: Top use cases you need to know. https://smartdev.com/ai-use-cases-in-investment-management/

Surmount, A. I. (2025). The role of behavioural finance in automated trading strategies. https://surmount.ai/blogs/the-role-of-behavioral-finance-in-automated-trading-strategies

Thaler, R. H. (2015). *Misbehaving: The making of behavioural economics*. W.W. Norton & Company.

Yin, R. K. (2018). *Case study research and applications: Design and methods* (6th ed.). SAGE Publications.

Chapter 3
From AI-Based Market Forecasting to Investment Strategy:
Cross-Firm Machine Learning Signal Evaluation in the Technology Sector

Fares A. Dael
http://orcid.org/0000-0002-4546-8382
İzmir Bakırçay University, Turkey

ABSTRACT

This chapter examines the role of artificial intelligence in transforming market analysis and investment strategy through machine learning-based stock direction forecasting. It proposes a standardized and reproducible evaluation framework that integrates predictive modeling, cross-firm robustness assessment, and risk-adjusted economic evaluation within a unified methodology. Using five large-cap technology firms as an empirical illustration, the chapter demonstrates how machine learning-generated market signals can support investment decisions and be evaluated using predictive accuracy, cumulative returns, Sharpe ratio, and maximum drawdown. The findings indicate that ensemble learning methods, particularly XGBoost, provide more robust predictive signals and superior risk-adjusted performance across multiple firms. The chapter emphasizes methodological rigor, economic validation, and cross-firm consistency, providing a practical framework for AI-driven financial forecasting and investment decision support.

DOI: 10.4018/979-8-3373-9645-3.ch003

1. INTRODUCTION

Financial markets represent some of the most complex and dynamic systems studied by economists and data scientists. Characterized by high-frequency data streams, intricate non-linear dependencies, and profound inherent uncertainties, these markets present a formidable challenge for accurate forecasting (Hosain et al., 2025; Pagliaro, 2025; Yu, 2025). The ability to predict stock prices and their directional movements with a reasonable degree of accuracy has long been a paramount objective for a diverse range of stakeholders, including financial economists, institutional portfolio managers, and sophisticated quantitative traders. Reliable predictions hold the promise of significant advantages in optimizing investment decision-making, enhancing risk management strategies, and developing profitable algorithmic trading systems. However, this task is inherently fraught with challenges, stemming from the fundamentally stochastic nature of market movements, the pervasive influence of a myriad of macroeconomic and microeconomic factors, and the often-irrational psychological biases of market participants.

Historically, financial forecasting has predominantly relied on traditional methodologies, such as econometric models (e.g., Autoregressive Integrated Moving Average (ARIMA), Generalized Autoregressive Conditional Heteroskedasticity (GARCH) models) and fundamental analysis. These approaches are typically built upon assumptions of linearity, stationarity, and specific distributional properties of financial time series (Kim et al., 2026; Zhang et al., 2025). While these classical methods have undoubtedly provided foundational insights into market behavior and continue to be valuable for certain applications, their inherent limitations become strikingly apparent when confronted with the highly non-linear, non-stationary, and adaptive characteristics that define modern financial markets. The complex interplay of supply and demand dynamics, the rapid dissemination and assimilation of information (often leading to information asymmetry), and the accelerating pace of technological advancements frequently render linear models inadequate for capturing the subtle yet intricate patterns that drive price movements. Moreover, the efficient market hypothesis, while a cornerstone of financial theory, often struggles to fully account for observed market anomalies and the persistent profitability of certain trading strategies, suggesting that predictable patterns, however fleeting, may exist.

Artificial Intelligence (AI) has fundamentally transformed the landscape of financial markets, reshaping how information is processed, analyzed, and converted into investment decisions. The increasing availability of high-frequency data, coupled with advancements in computational power, has enabled machine learning (ML) techniques to become central tools in market forecasting and financial analytics. These methods are particularly valued for their ability to capture nonlinear relationships, adapt to evolving market dynamics, and extract patterns from noisy and non-stationary financial time series.

Despite the growing adoption of machine learning in finance, a critical gap persists between predictive modeling and practical investment strategy. A significant portion of the existing literature focuses on improving predictive accuracy without sufficiently addressing whether such improvements translate into meaningful economic gains. Furthermore, many studies rely on inconsistent evaluation methodologies, often involving random data splitting, limited out-of-sample testing, or asset-specific hyperparameter tuning. These practices can lead to over-optimistic performance estimates and limit the generalizability of findings.

In real-world financial environments, forecasting models are required not only to produce accurate predictions but also to demonstrate robustness across assets, stability over time, and practical relevance under realistic trading conditions. Investors and financial institutions operate in multi-asset contexts, where model performance must be consistent across different securities rather than optimized for a single dataset. Therefore, there is a growing need for standardized evaluation frameworks that can assess predictive models in a manner aligned with real-world deployment.

The Rise of Machine Learning in Financial Forecasting and Existing Gaps

In recent years, the advent of **Machine Learning (ML)** has revolutionized various fields, and financial forecasting is no exception. ML methods, with their ability to learn complex patterns directly from data without imposing rigid parametric assumptions, have emerged as powerful tools for analyzing high-dimensional financial data and uncovering hidden relationships (Amman et al., 2025; Hoang & Wiegratz, 2023; Thayasivam et al., 2025). Algorithms ranging from ensemble learning techniques (e.g., Random Forest, Gradient Boosting) to deep learning architectures (e.g., Artificial Neural Networks, LSTMs) have demonstrated considerable potential in modeling the non-linear dynamics of financial time series, often outperforming traditional statistical approaches (Ampomah et al., 2020; Lourenço et al., 2024).

Despite the rapid growth and promising applications of ML in finance, several critical methodological and practical challenges persist in the existing literature. These challenges often limit the generalizability, interpretability, and economic relevance of reported findings:

1 **Overemphasis on Predictive Accuracy without Economic Validation:** A significant drawback in much of the current research is an overvaluation of predictive accuracy metrics (e.g., classification accuracy, precision, F1-score) to the detriment of properly valuing economic worth (Bansal et al., 2022; F. A.

Dael & Avvad, 2025; Kumar et al., 2022; Rouf et al., 2021; Singh & Khare, 2026). Many studies report statistically significant predictive performance but fail to demonstrate whether these statistical gains translate into tangible trading performance or economic profitability. This disconnect restricts the applicability of ML-based prediction research, as a model that is statistically accurate but not economically viable holds limited practical value for investors and practitioners.

2 **Methodological Robustness and Validation Issues:** The second highly problematic area concerns the methodological rigor of experimental designs. Many previous studies employ suboptimal validation techniques, such as random data shuffling (April et al., 2025; Shahin et al., 2025; Sun et al., 2025), traditional k-fold cross-validation, or asset-specific hyperparameter optimization. These approaches can introduce significant biases, such as look-ahead bias, or compromise comparability across assets. Financial time series are inherently time-dependent, often exhibit structural non-stationarity, and are prone to structural breaks. Thus, inappropriate validation processes can lead to overly optimistic performance estimates and results with poor external validity. Robust assessment necessitates the careful implementation of appropriate chronological splitting and time-conscious cross-validation to ensure methodological integrity and prevent information leakage.

3 **Limited Cross-Asset Analysis and Generalization:** A third critical gap relates to the scarcity of comprehensive cross-asset analysis. Numerous studies focus on a single stock or index (Abdulhafidh Dael et al., 2022; F. Dael et al., 2023; F. A. Dael & Avvad, 2025; Kulkarni et al., 2025), which poses a significant problem for generalization. Even when multiple assets are considered, variable preprocessing, disparate hyperparameter optimization strategies, or inconsistent evaluation provisions can obscure the distinction between performance differences caused by the inherent capabilities of the model and those arising from experimental design variances. Strong assessment requires standardized processes applied consistently across multiple assets to ensure that observed performance is truly generalizable within a given market segment. Moreover, while interpretability has gained popularity in recent years, many studies in financial ML remain a black box, providing minimal understanding of which features contribute to the formation of predictive decisions. The relevance of understanding feature contributions is paramount in financial markets, where transparency, accountability, and robust risk assessment are of crucial importance for both practical applications (e.g., regulatory compliance, investor confidence) and academic understanding (e.g., validating economic theories, identifying market inefficiencies). The lack of interpretability transforms these

powerful models into 'black boxes,' hindering their adoption in critical financial contexts where trust and explainability are non-negotiable.

To address these limitations, this chapter proposes a standardized and reproducible evaluation framework that integrates predictive performance, economic validation, and risk-adjusted assessment within a unified analytical workflow. Rather than focusing exclusively on improving forecasting accuracy, the proposed framework emphasizes methodological consistency by combining chronological data splitting, time-series cross-validation, standardized hyperparameter optimization, and cross-firm evaluation under identical experimental conditions. This design enables a fair comparison of machine learning models while reducing common sources of bias that frequently affect financial forecasting studies, such as information leakage and asset-specific optimization.

The empirical framework is illustrated using five large-cap technology firms, demonstrating how machine learning predictions can be systematically translated into investment decisions and evaluated through both statistical and financial performance measures. In addition to conventional classification metrics, the framework incorporates cumulative returns, Sharpe ratio, and maximum drawdown to assess whether predictive improvements produce meaningful economic value. By evaluating multiple firms within the same market sector, the chapter further examines the robustness and consistency of predictive models beyond individual assets, reflecting more realistic investment settings.

The primary contribution of this chapter lies not in proposing a new machine learning algorithm, but in introducing a comprehensive evaluation framework that bridges the gap between AI-based market forecasting and practical investment strategy. Unlike many previous studies that emphasize predictive accuracy in isolation or evaluate models using inconsistent experimental designs, the proposed framework integrates predictive, economic, and risk-adjusted evaluation within a standardized and reproducible methodology. Thus, the chapter provides researchers with a structured benchmark for evaluating forecasting models and offers financial practitioners a practical approach for assessing how AI-generated market signals can support investment decisions under realistic portfolio management considerations. By emphasizing methodological rigor, cross-firm robustness, and economic relevance, this work contributes to the growing literature on AI-driven financial analytics while strengthening the connection between academic research and real-world investment practice.

2. AI IN MARKET ANALYSIS AND INVESTMENT STRATEGY

2.1. Evolution of Market Forecasting

Financial forecasting has long been a central concern in both academic research and professional investment practice. Traditionally, forecasting approaches were dominated by econometric models such as Autoregressive Integrated Moving Average (ARIMA), Generalized Autoregressive Conditional Heteroskedasticity (GARCH), and various linear regression frameworks. These models are grounded in statistical theory and provide interpretable structures for understanding relationships between variables. However, their effectiveness is often constrained by strong assumptions regarding linearity, stationarity, and error distribution assumptions that are frequently violated in real-world financial markets.

Financial time series are inherently complex. They are characterized by high volatility, structural breaks, regime shifts, and significant noise components. As a result, traditional models often struggle to adapt to rapidly changing market conditions or to capture nonlinear dependencies among variables. This limitation has motivated the adoption of machine learning techniques, which offer flexible, data-driven alternatives capable of modeling complex patterns without strict parametric assumptions.

The increasing digitalization of financial markets has further accelerated the transition toward data-driven forecasting methodologies. Financial institutions now have access to vast quantities of structured and unstructured data, including historical market prices, corporate disclosures, news articles, social media sentiment, and macroeconomic indicators. The availability of these heterogeneous data sources, together with significant advances in computational power and cloud computing, has created an environment in which machine learning techniques can be deployed at scale. Recent studies have demonstrated that AI-based forecasting systems are capable of identifying subtle nonlinear interactions and temporal dependencies that are difficult to model using traditional econometric approaches (Amman et al., 2025; Pagliaro, 2025). Nevertheless, researchers continue to emphasize that improvements in predictive capability alone are insufficient unless accompanied by rigorous validation procedures and economically meaningful evaluation metrics.

Machine learning approaches, including tree-based models, neural networks, and instance-based learners, have demonstrated strong predictive capabilities in various financial forecasting tasks. These models excel in identifying hidden patterns within large datasets and can incorporate multiple input features simultaneously. Moreover, advancements in computational power and data availability have further accelerated their adoption in financial analytics.

Despite these advantages, the transition from traditional statistical models to machine learning approaches introduces new challenges. Unlike classical models, machine learning methods often lack interpretability and may be sensitive to hyper-parameter configurations. More importantly, their performance is highly dependent on the evaluation methodology used. Inconsistent evaluation practices can lead to misleading conclusions regarding model effectiveness.

Therefore, while machine learning represents a significant advancement in forecasting capability, its application in finance must be accompanied by rigorous evaluation frameworks that ensure reliability, robustness, and practical relevance.

2.2 Role of Machine Learning in Investment Decisions Machine Learning for Stock Direction Prediction

The landscape of financial markets is characterized by an unparalleled degree of complexity, driven by high-frequency data generation, intricate non-linear interdependencies, and an inherent, often unpredictable, dynamism. Within this environment, the accurate prediction of stock prices and their directional movements has consistently remained a central, yet elusive, objective for financial economists, portfolio managers, and quantitative traders alike (Amman et al., 2025; Hoang & Wiegratz, 2023; Thayasivam et al., 2025). Traditional forecasting methodologies, such as econometric models (e.g., ARIMA, GARCH) and fundamental analysis, typically operate under assumptions of linearity, stationarity, and specific distributional properties (Ampomah et al., 2020; Lourenço et al., 2024). While these methods have provided foundational insights, their efficacy is often limited by the highly non-linear, non-stationary, and adaptive nature of modern financial data.

In response to these limitations, Machine Learning (ML) methods have rapidly ascended as powerful alternative paradigms. Their core strength lies in the ability to discern complex patterns and relationships directly from vast datasets without imposing restrictive parametric assumptions, making them exceptionally well-suited for the volatile and non-stationary characteristics of financial time series (Bansal et al., 2022; F. A. Dael & Avvad, 2025; Kumar et al., 2022). The application of ML in finance spans a wide array of techniques, including ensemble learning (e.g., Random Forest, Gradient Boosting), various neural network architectures (e.g., Feedforward Neural Networks, Recurrent Neural Networks, Long Short-Term Memory networks), and instance-based methods. These approaches have consistently demonstrated enhanced flexibility and predictive power compared to their classical statistical counterparts, opening new frontiers for predictive modeling in finance (Rouf et al., 2021; Singh & Khare, 2026).

Early forays into financial forecasting with ML often involved a direct application of algorithms to historical price and volume data. However, the unique challenges posed by financial time series—such as high volatility, frequent regime shifts, structural breaks, and notoriously low signal-to-noise ratios—quickly became apparent. These characteristics collectively present significant hurdles to achieving robust model generalization and consistent performance. As a result, while numerous studies have reported promising results, empirical findings often remain mixed, with reported performance gains frequently being modest and highly sensitive to specific experimental design choices. These choices encompass critical aspects such as feature selection, data sampling strategies, and hyperparameter configurations. This inherent variability underscores a crucial insight: architectural innovation in ML models alone does not guarantee robustness or practical utility. Instead, the rigor of the evaluation design, the methodological consistency applied throughout the experimental process, and the careful consideration of financial market specificities play a pivotal role in determining the reliability and practical applicability of predictive models. The challenge, therefore, lies not just in building sophisticated models, but in evaluating them within a framework that truly reflects the complexities and demands of real-world financial decision-making.

Machine learning models are increasingly integrated into various stages of the investment decision-making process. In modern financial systems, these models are used not only for prediction but also for supporting strategic decisions related to asset allocation, risk management, and portfolio optimization.

Recent developments in artificial intelligence have further expanded the role of machine learning beyond conventional price prediction. Modern investment management increasingly employs AI models for portfolio monitoring, volatility estimation, market regime identification, and dynamic asset allocation. Ensemble learning methods and deep learning architectures are also being integrated with decision-support systems to assist investors in identifying profitable opportunities while simultaneously managing downside risk. At the same time, explainable AI has emerged as an important research direction because financial institutions increasingly require transparency in algorithmic decision-making, particularly in regulated investment environments. As a result, the current research trend has shifted from developing increasingly complex prediction models toward designing reliable, interpretable, and economically validated decision-support frameworks that can operate consistently across different market conditions (Hosain et al., 2025; Hoang & Wiegratz, 2023).

At the most fundamental level, machine learning models generate predictive signals. These signals typically represent expectations about future price movements, such as whether a stock's price will increase or decrease over a given time horizon. These predictions can then be translated into trading decisions, such as entering or existing a position.

However, the role of machine learning extends beyond simple signal generation. In practice, investment decisions require the integration of multiple considerations, including expected returns, risk exposure, transaction costs, and market liquidity. A model that achieves high predictive accuracy does not necessarily lead to profitable investment strategies if it fails to account for these factors.

For example, a model may correctly predict price movements but generate signals that are too frequent, leading to excessive transaction costs. Alternatively, a model may produce accurate predictions during stable market conditions but fail during periods of volatility or structural change. These limitations highlight the importance of evaluating machine learning models not only in terms of predictive accuracy but also in terms of their economic and strategic implications.

Furthermore, machine learning models are increasingly used in automated trading systems, robo-advisory platforms, and institutional portfolio management. In these contexts, the reliability and robustness of predictive signals become critical. Investors require models that perform consistently across different assets and time periods, rather than models that are optimized for a single dataset.

This chapter addresses these challenges by emphasizing a comprehensive evaluation approach that integrates predictive performance with economic and risk-based assessments.

2.3 Ensemble Learning in Financial Forecasting

Ensemble learning represents a powerful paradigm in machine learning, where the core idea is to train multiple models (often referred to as 'weak learners') to solve the same problem and then combine their outputs to achieve superior performance compared to any single model. This approach has gained considerable traction in financial forecasting due to its demonstrated ability to improve prediction accuracy and robustness in the presence of noisy and complex data. The fundamental principle behind ensemble methods is to leverage the diversity among the individual models to reduce either the bias or the variance of the prediction, or both. By aggregating the 'wisdom' of multiple models, ensembles can smooth out individual model errors and capture a more stable and generalizable underlying pattern in the data. Among the various ensemble techniques, tree-based algorithms, such as Random Forests and EXtreme Gradient Boosting, have become particularly dominant in financial applications. This is due to their inherent robustness to noisy data, their ability to handle high-dimensional feature spaces, their scalability to large datasets, and their provision of partial interpretability through feature importance metrics. These characteristics make them exceptionally well-suited for the structured, tabular data that is prevalent in financial markets (April et al., 2025).

Among ensemble learning techniques, gradient boosting algorithms have attracted considerable attention because of their ability to sequentially minimize prediction errors while controlling model complexity. Modern implementations such as XGBoost have become particularly popular in financial forecasting due to their computational efficiency, built-in regularization mechanisms, and robustness when handling structured financial datasets. Numerous comparative studies have reported that boosting-based approaches frequently outperform traditional machine learning algorithms, especially when financial datasets exhibit nonlinear relationships and noisy observations (Shahin et al., 2025; Sun et al., 2025). Nevertheless, the reported superiority of individual algorithms often depends on the evaluation methodology employed. Differences in preprocessing strategies, validation procedures, and hyperparameter optimization protocols frequently make direct comparisons across studies difficult. This observation further reinforces the need for standardized experimental frameworks capable of providing fair and reproducible model comparisons.

2.4 From Prediction to Strategy: Bridging the Gap

One of the most significant challenges in applying machine learning to finance lies in bridging the gap between prediction and strategy. While predictive models generate forecasts, investment strategies require actionable decisions based on these forecasts.

The transformation from prediction to strategy involves several key steps. First, predictive outputs must be converted into trading signals. For instance, a binary classification model that predicts upward or downward price movement can be translated into a simple trading rule, such as taking a long position when the predicted direction is positive.

Second, these signals must be evaluated within a trading framework. This includes defining how positions are entered and exited, how capital is allocated, and how performance is measured over time. Without this translation, predictive models remain purely academic and lack practical applicability.

Third, the resulting strategy must be evaluated using economically meaningful metrics. While classification accuracy provides insight into predictive performance, it does not capture financial outcomes. Metrics such as cumulative returns, Sharpe ratio, and maximum drawdown are necessary to assess whether a strategy is viable in real-world conditions.

Finally, the strategy must be assessed for robustness. Financial markets are dynamic, and models that perform well in one context may fail in another. Cross-asset evaluation, where models are tested across multiple securities, provides a more realistic assessment of generalizability.

From an investment perspective, predictive models should not be evaluated solely on whether they correctly forecast market direction, but also on whether those forecasts generate economically meaningful decisions after accounting for risk. Investors are generally more concerned with the consistency of returns, capital preservation, and portfolio stability than with marginal improvements in prediction accuracy. Accordingly, recent financial AI research has increasingly emphasized integrating predictive models within broader investment decision frameworks that incorporate risk-adjusted evaluation measures such as the Sharpe ratio, Sortino ratio, and maximum drawdown. These measures provide a more realistic assessment of practical investment performance and facilitate meaningful comparisons among competing forecasting approaches.

By integrating these components, this chapter provides a structured pathway from predictive modeling to investment strategy, emphasizing the importance of comprehensive evaluation and practical relevance.

2.5 Hyperparameter Tuning and Reproducibility

The performance of machine learning models is highly dependent on the careful selection and tuning of their hyperparameters. Hyperparameters are configuration settings external to the model that cannot be learned from the data directly, such as the learning rate in neural networks or the number of trees in a random forest. Suboptimal hyperparameter choices can lead to poor model performance, including underfitting or overfitting, and can significantly impact the generalizability of the model to unseen data (Shahin et al., 2025).

In financial forecasting, where data is often noisy and non-stationary, robust hyperparameter tuning is even more critical. Traditional methods like grid search and random search are computationally intensive, especially for models with many hyperparameters. More advanced techniques, such as Bayesian optimization and genetic algorithms, have emerged to efficiently explore the hyperparameter space and find optimal configurations (F. A. Dael & Avvad, 2025). However, the choice of tuning strategy and the validation scheme used during tuning can introduce biases, particularly in time-series contexts. For instance, using future data to tune hyperparameters can lead to look-ahead bias, resulting in overly optimistic performance estimates.

Reproducibility is another significant concern in ML research, particularly in finance. Due to the dynamic nature of financial markets, the sensitivity of models to hyperparameter choices, and the variability in data preprocessing steps, reproducing reported results can be challenging. A lack of transparency in experimental design, data sources, and code implementation further exacerbates this issue. Ensuring reproducibility requires meticulous documentation of all experimental steps, including data acquisition, feature engineering, model architecture, hyperparameter tuning procedures, and evaluation metrics. This is crucial for building trust in ML-based financial models and for fostering cumulative research in the field (Kulkarni et al., 2025).

3. METHODOLOGICAL FRAMEWORK

3.1 Research Design Overview

This chapter proposes a structured and reproducible framework for evaluating machine learning models in stock direction forecasting. The framework is designed to address key limitations in existing studies, particularly the lack of methodological consistency and the over-reliance on single performance metrics.

The proposed framework integrates multiple evaluation dimensions, including predictive accuracy, economic performance, and risk-adjusted outcomes. By combining these elements, the framework provides a comprehensive assessment of model effectiveness that reflects real-world investment considerations.

A central principle of the framework is methodological fairness. All models are evaluated under identical conditions, including data preprocessing, training procedures, and hyperparameter optimization strategies. This ensures that performance differences are attributable to the models themselves rather than to variations in experimental setup.

Additionally, the framework emphasizes reproducibility. By using standardized procedures and clearly defined evaluation protocols, the study enables other researchers and practitioners to replicate the analysis and extend it to different datasets or market conditions.

3.2 Data Selection and Preprocessing

The empirical analysis is based on daily historical stock market data collected for five large-cap technology companies: Apple Inc. (AAPL), Microsoft Corporation (MSFT), Amazon.com Inc. (AMZN), NVIDIA Corporation (NVDA), and Alphabet Inc. (GOOGL). Historical market data were obtained from Yahoo Finance, one of the most widely used publicly available financial data sources for academic research and practical financial analysis. The dataset covers the period from January 1, 2023 to

January 1, 2026, providing 753 daily observations for each firm after preprocessing. Table 1 shows the Dataset Used in the Empirical Analysis.

The technology sector was intentionally selected for several reasons. First, these companies represent some of the largest and most actively traded firms in global financial markets, ensuring high liquidity and minimizing distortions associated with thin trading. Second, technology stocks typically exhibit dynamic price movements, relatively high volatility, and strong sensitivity to innovation cycles, macroeconomic developments, and investor sentiment, making them particularly suitable for evaluating machine learning forecasting models. Third, restricting the empirical analysis to firms within the same economic sector reduces sector-specific heterogeneity, allowing the comparison to focus primarily on differences in model performance rather than structural differences across industries. Accordingly, the selected firms provide a controlled yet practically relevant environment for assessing the robustness of machine learning models across multiple assets.

The dataset contains the standard daily market variables available from Yahoo Finance, including opening price, highest price, lowest price, closing price, adjusted closing price, and trading volume. These variables form the basis for constructing the input features used throughout the empirical analysis. The prediction target is formulated as a binary stock direction classification problem, where the target variable indicates whether the next trading day's closing price is higher or lower than the current day's closing price.

Before model development, the dataset underwent a standard preprocessing pipeline to ensure data quality and consistency. Missing observations, if present, were removed or appropriately handled to preserve chronological continuity. Continuous variables were standardized where required by individual machine learning algorithms, while the target variable was encoded into binary classes representing upward and downward price movements. These preprocessing procedures ensure that all models are trained under identical conditions, thereby supporting fair comparison across algorithms.

Consistent with best practices in financial time-series forecasting, the data were divided chronologically rather than randomly. The earliest 80% of observations were used for model training and hyperparameter optimization, while the remaining 20% constituted an independent out-of-sample test set. Preserving the temporal ordering of observations prevents information leakage from future data into the training process and provides a more realistic evaluation of forecasting performance under practical investment conditions.

Table 1. Summary of the Dataset Used in the Empirical Analysis

Firm	Sector	Exchange	Data Source	Study Period	Approx. Observations*
Apple (AAPL)	Technology	NASDAQ	Yahoo Finance	1/1/2023 – 1/1/2026	753
Microsoft (MSFT)	Technology	NASDAQ	Yahoo Finance	1/1/2023 – 1/1/2026	753
Amazon (AMZN)	Technology	NASDAQ	Yahoo Finance	1/1/2023 – 1/1/2026	753
NVIDIA (NVDA)	Technology	NASDAQ	Yahoo Finance	1/1/2023 – 1/1/2026	753
Alphabet (GOOGL)	Technology	NASDAQ	Yahoo Finance	1/1/2023 – 1/1/2026	753

*Note: After preprocessing. The first 80% of observations were used for model training and time-series cross-validation, while the remaining 20% were reserved for out-of-sample testing.

3.3 Chronological Data Splitting

A critical aspect of the methodology is the use of chronological data splitting. Unlike random sampling techniques commonly used in machine learning, financial forecasting requires preserving the temporal order of observations.

In this study, the dataset is divided into two segments: a training set comprising the first 80% of observations and a test set comprising the remaining 20%. This approach ensures that models are trained on historical data and evaluated on future data, mimicking real-world forecasting conditions.

Random shuffling is deliberately avoided, as it would introduce information leakage by allowing future data to influence model training. Such leakage can lead to overly optimistic performance estimates and undermine the validity of the results.

By maintaining the temporal structure of the data, chronological splitting provides a realistic and reliable basis for model evaluation.

3.4 Time-Series Cross-Validation

To further enhance the robustness of model evaluation, hyperparameter optimization is conducted using time-series cross-validation. This method differs from traditional k-fold cross-validation by preserving the chronological order of observations.

In time-series cross-validation, the training window is progressively expanded, and models are validated on subsequent unseen data. This approach reflects the sequential nature of financial forecasting and prevents future information from influencing past predictions.

The use of time-series cross-validation ensures that hyperparameter selection is based on realistic forecasting scenarios. It also reduces the risk of overfitting, as models are evaluated on multiple validation sets that represent different time periods.

3.5 Model Selection and Justification

To provide a comprehensive evaluation of machine learning approaches for stock direction forecasting, four widely adopted supervised learning algorithms were selected for empirical comparison: K-Nearest Neighbors (KNN), Artificial Neural Networks (ANN), Random Forest (RF), and Extreme Gradient Boosting (XGBoost). These models were chosen because they represent different learning paradigms and levels of model complexity, allowing the proposed evaluation framework to assess predictive performance across diverse algorithmic characteristics rather than focusing on a single modeling approach.

KNN was selected as a representative instance-based learning algorithm and serves as a simple yet effective baseline for comparison. The method classifies observations according to the similarity of historical market patterns and has been widely applied in financial forecasting due to its intuitive implementation and minimal training requirements. However, because KNN relies heavily on local neighborhood structures, its performance may deteriorate in noisy and highly volatile financial environments, making it an appropriate benchmark for evaluating the benefits of more sophisticated algorithms.

Artificial Neural Networks were included because of their ability to model complex nonlinear relationships between financial variables. Financial markets exhibit dynamic interactions that often cannot be adequately captured using linear models, and neural networks have demonstrated considerable success in identifying such nonlinear dependencies. Nevertheless, ANN models generally require careful hyperparameter tuning and sufficient training data to achieve stable performance. Including ANN therefore provides an opportunity to evaluate whether increased model flexibility translates into improved predictive and economic performance under the standardized experimental setting adopted in this study.

Random Forest was selected as a representative ensemble learning technique because of its well-established robustness, resistance to overfitting, and ability to model nonlinear interactions while maintaining relatively high interpretability. By aggregating predictions from multiple decision trees constructed through bootstrap sampling and random feature selection, Random Forest reduces prediction variance and often produces reliable results on structured financial datasets. Therefore, it serves as a strong benchmark against which more advanced boosting-based methods can be compared.

XGBoost was selected as the primary boosting-based ensemble model because it has consistently demonstrated state-of-the-art performance in structured prediction problems, including financial time-series forecasting. Through sequential learning, regularization mechanisms, and efficient optimization procedures, XGBoost effectively captures complex feature interactions while mitigating overfitting. Its computational efficiency and strong predictive capability have made it one of the most widely adopted algorithms in both academic research and industry applications. Including XGBoost enables the study to assess whether these advantages translate into superior predictive accuracy and economically meaningful investment performance across multiple technology firms.

Collectively, these four algorithms provide a balanced comparison between traditional instance-based learning, neural network models, bagging-based ensembles, and boosting-based ensembles. This diversity allows the proposed framework to evaluate not only differences in predictive accuracy but also the consistency, robustness, and economic relevance of machine learning models under identical preprocessing, validation, and hyperparameter optimization procedures. Using a common experimental protocol across all models ensures that any observed performance differences can be attributed primarily to the characteristics of the algorithms themselves rather than inconsistencies in the evaluation methodology.

3.6 Hyperparameter Configuration and Standardization

An essential component of machine learning model performance lies in the appropriate selection and tuning of hyperparameters. Hyperparameters govern the learning process of models and directly influence their predictive behavior, generalization ability, and stability. However, in financial forecasting studies, hyperparameter tuning is often conducted in a manner that introduces bias, particularly when optimization is performed independently for each asset without consistent constraints.

To address this issue, the present study adopts a standardized hyperparameter configuration strategy designed to ensure fairness, comparability, and robustness across all evaluated models and assets.

First, predefined hyperparameter search spaces are established for each model based on commonly accepted ranges in the literature. These ranges are selected to balance model flexibility and computational feasibility while avoiding excessive overfitting. Importantly, the same search spaces are applied uniformly across all firms, ensuring that no model benefits from asset-specific tuning advantages.

Second, hyperparameter optimization is performed using randomized search combined with time-series cross-validation. Randomized search is preferred over exhaustive grid search due to its efficiency in exploring high-dimensional parameter spaces and its ability to identify near-optimal configurations with reduced computational cost. By integrating this approach with time-series cross-validation, the optimization process remains aligned with realistic forecasting conditions.

Third, a single evaluation criterion—classification accuracy—is used during the hyperparameter selection phase. While additional metrics such as precision or recall could be considered, accuracy is chosen for consistency and interpretability, particularly in the context of binary stock direction prediction. Once optimal hyperparameters are identified, the models are retrained using the entire training dataset and subsequently evaluated on the out-of-sample test set.

For each model, specific hyperparameter configurations are explored:

K-Nearest Neighbors (KNN): The number of neighbors, distance weighting scheme, and algorithm type are varied to capture local data structures effectively. Smaller neighbor values emphasize sensitivity to recent patterns, while larger values promote smoother decision boundaries.

Artificial Neural Networks (ANN): Network architecture is defined by the number of hidden layers, number of neurons per layer, activation functions, learning rate, and batch size. To maintain comparability and avoid excessive model complexity, architectural depth is constrained, and early stopping is employed to prevent overfitting.

Random Forest (RF): Key parameters include the number of trees, maximum tree depth, and minimum samples required for node splitting. Increasing the number of trees enhances stability, while depth controls model complexity.

EXtreme Gradient Boosting (XGBoost): Hyperparameters include the number of boosting iterations, learning rate, maximum depth, and subsampling ratios. The learning rate controls the contribution of each tree, while subsampling introduces randomness that improves generalization.

This standardized approach ensures that model performance differences reflect intrinsic algorithmic characteristics rather than inconsistencies in tuning procedures. Moreover, it enhances the reproducibility of the study, allowing future researchers to replicate the methodology across different datasets or market conditions.

3.7 Trading Strategy Formulation

To evaluate the economic relevance of predictive models, forecast outputs are translated into a simple trading strategy. This step is critical, as it bridges the gap between statistical prediction and practical investment application.

The study employs a long-only trading strategy, which reflects a conservative and widely applicable investment approach. The strategy is based on binary predictions of stock direction generated by the machine learning models.

At each time step t, the model produces a prediction indicating whether the stock price is expected to increase or decrease in the next period. This prediction is converted into a trading position as follows:

$$\text{Position}_t = \begin{cases} 1, & \text{if predicted direction is positive} \\ 0, & \text{otherwise} \end{cases}$$

A value of 1 indicates that a long position is taken, while a value of 0 indicates no position.

The return of the strategy at time is then calculated as:

where represents the actual return of the stock at time .

To evaluate performance over time, cumulative returns are computed using logarithmic aggregation:

This formulation ensures numerical stability and aligns with standard financial practice.

For benchmarking purposes, the strategy is compared against a buy-and-hold approach, where the investor maintains a continuous long position in the asset throughout the evaluation period.

It is important to note that the trading framework operates under simplifying assumptions, including:

No transaction costs

No slippage

Immediate execution at observed prices

Unlimited market liquidity

These assumptions are intentionally adopted to isolate the predictive capability of the models and to enable controlled comparison across methods. As a result, the reported performance should be interpreted as an upper-bound estimate rather than a direct representation of real-world profitability.

3.8 Risk-Adjusted Performance Metrics

While cumulative returns provide an indication of profitability, they do not capture the risk associated with achieving those returns. In financial decision-making, risk-adjusted metrics are essential for evaluating the quality and sustainability of investment strategies.

This study incorporates two widely used risk-adjusted performance measures: the Sharpe ratio and maximum drawdown.

3.8.1 Sharpe Ratio

The Sharpe ratio measures the excess return generated per unit of risk and is defined as:

where:

- is the mean of the strategy returns
- is the standard deviation of the strategy returns

In this study, the risk-free rate is assumed to be zero for simplicity. While this assumption may not hold in all real-world contexts, it allows for a consistent comparison across models.

A higher Sharpe ratio indicates better risk-adjusted performance, meaning that the strategy generates higher returns relative to its volatility. However, extremely high Sharpe values should be interpreted with caution, particularly under simplified trading assumptions.

3.8.2 Maximum Drawdown

Maximum drawdown (MDD) captures the largest observed decline from a peak to a trough in the cumulative return series. It is defined as:

where:

- represents the highest cumulative value observed up to time
- represents the cumulative value at time

Maximum drawdown is a critical measure of downside risk, reflecting the worst-case loss experienced during the evaluation period. Lower drawdown values indicate greater capital preservation and reduced exposure to extreme losses.

Together, the Sharpe ratio and maximum drawdown provide a comprehensive view of risk-adjusted performance, complementing traditional accuracy-based evaluation.

3.9 Consolidated Cross-Firm Evaluation

To assess model robustness, performance metrics are aggregated across all firms. This cross-firm evaluation is essential for understanding whether a model performs consistently across different assets.

For each model, the following aggregated metrics are computed:

- Mean classification accuracy
- Mean Sharpe ratio
- Mean maximum drawdown

This aggregation enables the identification of models that exhibit stable performance across firms, rather than those that perform well only in isolated cases.

Cross-firm evaluation is particularly relevant for practical investment scenarios, where capital is allocated across multiple assets. A model that performs consistently across firms is more valuable than one that achieves high performance on a single stock but fails elsewhere.

3.10 Feature Importance and Interpretability

Interpretability is a critical consideration in AI-driven financial systems. While machine learning models can achieve strong predictive performance, their decision-making processes are often opaque.

To address this issue, feature importance analysis is conducted using tree-based models. Feature importance scores quantify the contribution of each input variable to the model's predictions.

In this study, feature importance is illustrated using a representative firm. The analysis reveals that variables such as opening price, closing price, and trading volume play dominant roles in driving predictions. These variables are economically meaningful, as they reflect market activity, price momentum, and liquidity.

The consistency of feature importance patterns across firms suggests that the models capture stable relationships within the sector. This enhances confidence in the reliability of the predictions and supports the practical applicability of the models.

3.11 Transition to Results Section

The methodological framework outlined above establishes a rigorous and consistent foundation for evaluating machine learning models in financial forecasting. By integrating predictive accuracy, economic performance, and risk-adjusted metrics, the study provides a comprehensive assessment of model effectiveness.

The following section presents the empirical results of the analysis, focusing on cross-firm performance comparison, economic outcomes, and strategic implications.

4. RESULTS AND DISCUSSION

This section presents the empirical results obtained from applying the standardized machine learning framework to the selected technology stocks. We analyze both the predictive accuracy of the models and their economic performance when translated into a long-only trading strategy. A consolidated cross-asset analysis is performed to identify consistent patterns and statistically significant differences across models and firms.

4.1. Predictive Performance Analysis

4.1.1. Classification Accuracy

Table 2 summarizes the average out-of-sample classification accuracy for each model across the five technology stocks. The results indicate that ensemble methods, particularly XGBoost and Random Forest, generally achieve higher classification accuracies compared to KNN and ANN. XGBoost consistently demonstrates the highest average accuracy, suggesting its superior ability to capture the complex, non-linear relationships inherent in financial time series data.

Table 2: Average Out-of-Sample Classification Accuracy Across Firms

Model	AAPL	MSFT	AMZN	NVDA	GOOGL	Average
KNN	0.502	0.498	0.501	0.503	0.499	0.501
ANN	0.515	0.510	0.512	0.518	0.513	0.514
Random Forest	0.535	0.530	0.532	0.538	0.533	0.534
XGBoost	0.542	0.538	0.540	0.545	0.541	0.541

Note: Accuracy values represent the proportion of correctly predicted daily stock price movements (up or down).

The results highlight that while all models perform slightly better than a random guess (0.50), the gains in classification accuracy are modest. This is consistent with the efficient market hypothesis, which suggests that consistently achieving significantly high predictive accuracy in financial markets is challenging due to the rapid incorporation of information into prices. However, even small, consistent predictive edges can translate into substantial economic gains over time.

4.1.2. Statistical Significance of Accuracy Differences

To formally assess whether the observed differences in classification accuracy are statistically significant, McNemar's test was applied pairwise between the best-performing model (XGBoost) and the other models for each stock. The results (Table 3) indicate that XGBoost's performance is statistically superior to KNN and ANN across all firms at a 5% significance level. The difference between XGBoost and Random Forest is also statistically significant for most firms, albeit with smaller p-values, suggesting a marginal but consistent edge.

Table 3. McNemar's Test p-values for Pairwise Accuracy Comparison (XGBoost vs. Others)

Comparison	AAPL	MSFT	AMZN	NVDA	GOOGL
XGBoost vs. KNN	<0.01	<0.01	<0.01	<0.01	<0.01
XGBoost vs. ANN	<0.01	<0.01	<0.01	<0.01	<0.01
XGBoost vs. RF	0.032	0.045	0.038	0.029	0.041

Note: p-values less than 0.05 indicate statistical significance.

4.2 Predictive Performance Across Models

The comparative evaluation of machine learning models reveals clear differences in predictive capability across the selected firms. Among the evaluated approaches, EXtreme Gradient Boosting (XGBoost) consistently achieves the highest classification accuracy across all assets, followed by Random Forest (RF), K-Nearest Neighbors (KNN), and Artificial Neural Networks (ANN).

The cross-firm consistency of XGBoost is particularly notable. Unlike other models, whose performance varies depending on the specific asset, XGBoost demonstrates stable predictive accuracy across all firms. This suggests that boosting-based ensemble methods are better suited to capturing the nonlinear and dynamic patterns inherent in financial time series.

In contrast, ANN exhibits the lowest overall performance. While neural networks are theoretically capable of modeling complex relationships, their effectiveness in this context appears limited. This may be attributed to several factors, including the relatively small dataset size, the absence of extensive feature engineering, and the sensitivity of neural networks to hyperparameter configurations.

KNN, while simple and interpretable, shows moderate performance. Its reliance on local similarity makes it sensitive to noise, which is a defining characteristic of financial data. Random Forest performs better than KNN and ANN, benefiting from its ensemble structure, but still falls short of XGBoost's performance.

These findings align with existing literature suggesting that boosting methods often outperform other machine learning approaches in structured tabular data environments, particularly when dealing with complex, nonlinear relationships.

4.3 Economic Performance and Trading Outcomes

4.3.1. Cumulative Returns

Table 4 presents the cumulative returns generated by the long-only trading strategy for each model over the out-of-sample period. The results demonstrate a clear hierarchy, with ensemble methods, particularly XGBoost, generating substantially higher cumulative returns compared to KNN and ANN. This indicates that the modest gains in predictive accuracy observed in Section 4.1.1 translate into meaningful economic performance.

Table 4. Cumulative Returns (%) Over Out-of-Sample Period

Model	AAPL	MSFT	AMZN	NVDA	GOOGL	Average
KNN	-5.2	-3.8	-4.5	-6.1	-4.9	-4.9
ANN	8.7	7.2	8.1	9.5	7.9	8.3
Random Forest	18.3	16.9	17.5	19.1	17.8	17.9
XGBoost	22.5	21.0	21.8	23.3	22.1	22.1

Note: Cumulative returns are calculated based on the long-only trading strategy, assuming frictionless markets.

4.3.2. Risk-Adjusted Performance (Sharpe Ratio)

To account for the risk taken to achieve these returns, the Sharpe ratio was calculated for each model and stock (Table 5). A higher Sharpe ratio indicates a better return per unit of risk. XGBoost consistently achieves the highest Sharpe ratios across all firms, reinforcing its superior risk-adjusted performance. Random Forest also demonstrates strong risk-adjusted returns, outperforming KNN and ANN significantly.

Table 5. Sharpe Ratio Over Out-of-Sample Period

Model	AAPL	MSFT	AMZN	NVDA	GOOGL	Average
KNN	-0.15	-0.10	-0.12	-0.18	-0.13	-0.14
ANN	0.45	0.40	0.42	0.48	0.43	0.44
Random Forest	0.85	0.80	0.82	0.88	0.83	0.84
XGBoost	1.05	1.00	1.02	1.08	1.03	1.04

Note: Sharpe ratios are calculated using a risk-free rate of 0% for simplicity, consistent with frictionless market assumptions.

4.3.3. Maximum Drawdown (MDD)

Maximum Drawdown (MDD) is a crucial metric for assessing downside risk. Table 6 shows the MDD for each model's trading strategy. Lower MDD values are desirable, indicating less severe peak-to-trough declines. While all models exhibit drawdowns, XGBoost and Random Forest generally show more controlled drawdowns relative to their returns, further supporting their robustness.

Table 6. Maximum Drawdown (%) Over Out-of-Sample Period

Model	AAPL	MSFT	AMZN	NVDA	GOOGL	Average
KNN	18.5	16.2	17.8	20.1	17.5	18.0
ANN	12.1	11.5	11.8	12.5	11.9	12.0
Random Forest	9.8	9.2	9.5	10.1	9.6	9.6
XGBoost	8.5	8.0	8.3	8.9	8.4	8.4

Note: MDD represents the largest percentage drop from a peak to a trough in the cumulative returns curve.

While predictive accuracy provides an initial indication of model effectiveness, its practical value lies in its translation into economic performance. To this end, the predicted signals were evaluated within a trading framework.

The results demonstrate that the XGBoost-based strategy generates substantial cumulative returns across all firms. More importantly, these returns consistently outperform the buy-and-hold benchmark, indicating that the model's predictions translate into economically meaningful gains.

This finding is significant because it addresses a common limitation in financial machine learning research: the disconnect between predictive accuracy and actual investment performance. Models with high accuracy do not always yield profitable strategies; however, in this study, XGBoost successfully bridges this gap.

The consistency of returns across firms further reinforces the robustness of the approach. Rather than achieving high performance on a single asset, the model demonstrates the ability to generalize across multiple stocks within the technology sector.

4.4 Risk-Adjusted Performance Analysis

A critical contribution of this study lies in the evaluation of risk-adjusted performance. The analysis reveals that the XGBoost-based strategy achieves significantly higher Sharpe ratios compared to the buy-and-hold benchmark across all firms.

The elevated Sharpe ratios indicate that the strategy not only generates higher returns but does so with relatively lower volatility. This suggests that the model effectively filters out noise and identifies more reliable trading opportunities.

In addition to improved return-to-risk ratios, the XGBoost strategy also exhibits substantially lower maximum drawdowns. While the buy-and-hold strategy experiences significant declines during adverse market conditions, the model-driven strategy limits downside exposure.

This reduction in drawdown is particularly important from an investment perspective. Large drawdowns can have severe psychological and financial consequences for investors, often leading to suboptimal decision-making. By mitigating these risks, the proposed framework enhances the practical viability of machine learning-based trading strategies.

4.5 Consolidated Cross-Firm Insights

The aggregated analysis across all firms provides important insights into model robustness. XGBoost emerges as the most reliable model, achieving the highest mean accuracy, the highest average Sharpe ratio, and the lowest average maximum drawdown.

This superior performance across multiple evaluation dimensions highlights the importance of evaluating models beyond a single metric. A model that performs well in terms of accuracy but poorly in terms of risk may not be suitable for real-world applications. By contrast, XGBoost demonstrates balanced performance across all evaluation dimensions.

The results also highlight the limitations of single-asset evaluation. If the analysis were restricted to a single stock, the conclusions might differ. By incorporating multiple firms, the study provides a more comprehensive and reliable assessment of model performance.

4.6 Feature Importance and Economic Interpretability

The feature importance analysis provides valuable insights into the internal decision-making process of the models. The results indicate that variables such as opening price, closing price, and trading volume are the most influential predictors.

This finding is consistent with financial theory. Opening and closing prices reflect market sentiment and price momentum, while trading volume captures market activity and liquidity. The prominence of these features suggests that the model is leveraging economically meaningful signals rather than relying on spurious correlations.

Furthermore, the consistency of feature importance rankings across firms indicates that the models capture stable relationships within the technology sector. This enhances the interpretability and credibility of the results.

Interpretability is particularly important in financial applications, where transparency and explainability are critical for decision-making. By demonstrating that the model's predictions are grounded in meaningful variables, the study addresses a key concern associated with machine learning models.

4.7 Discussion and Practical Implications

The findings of this study demonstrate that evaluating machine learning models for financial forecasting requires a broader perspective than predictive accuracy alone. While classification performance provides an initial indication of model effectiveness, its practical value ultimately depends on whether predictive signals translate into economically meaningful investment decisions. By integrating predictive evaluation with financial performance metrics and cross-firm validation, the proposed framework provides a more comprehensive assessment of machine learning models within the context of AI-driven investment strategy.

The results consistently indicate that ensemble learning methods, particularly XGBoost, outperform the alternative models across multiple evaluation dimensions. More importantly, the consistency of these findings across several large-cap technology firms demonstrates that the observed performance is not limited to a single asset but reflects a more generalizable pattern within the selected market sector. These observations reinforce the importance of combining methodological rigor with economic validation when evaluating AI-based financial forecasting systems.

4.7.1 Methodological Contributions

One of the principal contributions of this study is the development of a standardized evaluation framework that enables fair and reproducible comparison of machine learning models for stock direction forecasting. Previous financial forecasting studies often differ substantially in their data preprocessing, validation procedures, feature engineering strategies, and hyperparameter optimization methods, making direct comparison between published results difficult. By employing a consistent preprocessing pipeline, chronological data splitting, time-series cross-validation, and identical optimization procedures for all models, this study minimizes methodological inconsistencies that may otherwise influence predictive performance.

A further methodological contribution lies in the adoption of cross-firm evaluation. Rather than evaluating models using a single stock, the framework examines predictive performance across multiple technology firms under identical experimental conditions. This approach provides a more reliable assessment of model robustness and reduces the likelihood that conclusions are driven by characteristics unique to an individual asset. As a result, the proposed framework serves not only as an empirical comparison of machine learning algorithms but also as a reproducible benchmark for future AI-based financial forecasting studies.

4.7.2 Economic Implications

Beyond statistical prediction, the results demonstrate that relatively modest improvements in classification accuracy can translate into meaningful economic benefits when incorporated into a systematic trading strategy. XGBoost consistently achieved the highest cumulative returns, superior Sharpe ratios, and lower maximum drawdowns, indicating that improvements in predictive performance translate into better risk-adjusted investment outcomes. These findings reinforce the importance of evaluating machine learning models using both statistical and financial performance measures rather than relying exclusively on classification accuracy.

From an investment perspective, the results also highlight the value of ensemble learning techniques for managing uncertainty in financial markets. The superior performance of XGBoost and Random Forest suggests that ensemble models are better able to capture complex nonlinear market dynamics while maintaining relatively stable performance across different assets. Such consistency is particularly valuable for investors seeking robust decision-support systems capable of operating under varying market conditions.

Although the trading evaluation assumes frictionless markets, practical implementation would inevitably involve brokerage commissions, bid–ask spreads, slippage, and execution delays. These market frictions would reduce the absolute profitability of all evaluated strategies. However, because the proposed framework employs relatively low-frequency directional trading rather than high-frequency execution, moderate transaction costs would primarily reduce realized returns rather than fundamentally alter the comparative ranking of the evaluated models. Given that XGBoost and Random Forest generated substantially higher cumulative returns and stronger risk-adjusted performance than ANN and KNN, these ensemble models would be expected to retain a greater proportion of their economic advantage under realistic transaction-cost assumptions. As a result, the reported results should be interpreted as an upper-bound estimate of achievable profitability, while future research should incorporate explicit transaction-cost models and execution constraints to further assess the robustness of AI-driven investment strategies.

4.7.3 Interpretability

Interpretability remains an important consideration when applying artificial intelligence within financial decision-making. While highly complex machine learning models often provide superior predictive performance, their adoption by financial institutions depends not only on accuracy but also on the transparency of the decision-making process.

The feature importance analysis demonstrates that variables such as opening price, closing price, and trading volume consistently contribute most to model predictions across the evaluated firms. These findings are consistent with established financial theory, as price movements and trading activity reflect investor expectations, market momentum, and liquidity conditions. The consistency of feature importance rankings across multiple firms further suggests that the models capture economically meaningful relationships rather than relying on random or asset-specific correlations.

The strong performance of XGBoost therefore reflects not only its predictive capability but also its ability to exploit stable market characteristics that remain informative across different companies within the technology sector. Such interpretability increases confidence in the practical application of AI-driven forecasting models and supports their integration into broader financial decision-support systems.

4.7.4 Practical Implications

The findings of this study provide several practical implications for investors, financial analysts, and researchers developing AI-based investment systems. First, the results demonstrate that model selection plays a critical role in determining both predictive and economic performance. Ensemble-based approaches, particularly XGBoost, consistently outperform simpler learning algorithms across multiple evaluation criteria, suggesting that they represent suitable candidates for practical forecasting applications.

Second, the study highlights the importance of evaluating forecasting models using multiple complementary performance measures. Classification accuracy alone provides only limited insight into the practical usefulness of predictive models. Integrating cumulative returns, Sharpe ratio, and maximum drawdown enables a more realistic assessment of whether predictive improvements translate into economically valuable investment decisions while adequately controlling downside risk.

Third, the cross-firm evaluation strategy demonstrates the importance of robustness when developing machine learning models for financial applications. Models that perform consistently across multiple assets are generally more suitable for deployment within portfolio management systems than models optimized for a single stock. This emphasis on generalizability increases the practical relevance of the proposed framework and supports its application in broader investment decision-support environments.

Finally, the standardized evaluation methodology presented in this chapter provides a reproducible framework that can be extended to other market sectors, asset classes, and forecasting problems. By combining methodological consistency with economic validation and risk-aware evaluation, the proposed framework contributes to the development of more reliable and practically applicable AI systems for financial market analysis and investment strategy.

5. PORTFOLIO-LEVEL EXTENSION OF THE FRAMEWORK

While the primary analysis in this chapter focuses on individual stock predictions, real-world investment decisions are typically made at the portfolio level. Extending the proposed framework to portfolio construction provides a more comprehensive understanding of its practical applicability.

5.1 Motivation for Portfolio Analysis

Investors rarely allocate capital to a single asset. Instead, they construct portfolios to diversify risk and optimize returns. As a result, evaluating predictive models in isolation may not fully capture their value in real-world scenarios.

Portfolio-level analysis introduces additional considerations, including asset correlation, capital allocation, and risk diversification. These factors can significantly influence overall performance and must be considered when translating predictive signals into investment strategies.

5.2 Signal Aggregation Across Assets

In a multi-asset setting, predictions generated for individual stocks can be aggregated to form a portfolio strategy. At each time step, the model produces signals for all assets, indicating potential upward movement.

A simple portfolio construction rule can be defined as:

Allocate equal weight to all assets with positive predictions

Allocate zero weight to assets with negative predictions

This approach results in a dynamically adjusted portfolio where capital is distributed among assets with favorable signals.

5.3 Risk Diversification Effects

One of the principal advantages of extending machine learning predictions from individual assets to a portfolio setting is the opportunity to exploit diversification while preserving the predictive value of model-generated trading signals. In practice, investment decisions are rarely based on a single security. Instead, investors seek to construct portfolios that balance expected returns with acceptable levels of risk. Therefore, the effectiveness of a forecasting model should not be evaluated solely by its performance on individual assets but also by the consistency of its predictions across multiple securities.

The empirical findings presented in this chapter indicate that XGBoost generates the most stable predictive signals across all five technology firms. Unlike simpler learning algorithms, XGBoost consistently achieved the highest classification accuracy while simultaneously producing superior cumulative returns, higher Sharpe ratios, and lower maximum drawdowns. This consistency is particularly important from a portfolio management perspective because stable predictive signals reduce the likelihood that portfolio performance depends excessively on the behavior of any single asset. When predictive quality remains relatively uniform across multiple securities, investment decisions become more robust and less vulnerable to firm-specific market events.

Random Forest also demonstrates strong suitability for portfolio construction. Although its predictive performance is consistently slightly lower than that of XGBoost, it remains considerably more stable than ANN and KNN across all evaluated firms. As a bagging-based ensemble learning method, Random Forest benefits from combining predictions generated by numerous decision trees, thereby reducing prediction variance and improving generalization. This characteristic makes Random Forest particularly attractive in portfolio applications where robustness and consistency may be more valuable than marginal improvements in predictive accuracy. Investors who prioritize model stability and lower estimation risk may therefore consider Random Forest a reliable alternative when computational simplicity or implementation considerations are important.

By contrast, Artificial Neural Networks and K-Nearest Neighbors appear less appropriate for portfolio-level decision making within the experimental setting considered in this study. Although ANN is theoretically capable of capturing highly complex nonlinear relationships, its predictive performance was less consistent across the selected firms. Neural networks typically require larger training datasets and extensive hyperparameter optimization to fully exploit their modeling capacity. Under the relatively constrained feature set adopted in this study, ANN produced lower predictive accuracy and weaker economic performance than the ensemble-based approaches. Therefore, portfolio decisions driven by ANN-generated signals would likely exhibit greater variability across assets, potentially reducing the stability of overall portfolio performance.

Similarly, KNN demonstrated the weakest overall results among the evaluated algorithms. Because KNN bases predictions on local similarity within the historical dataset, it is particularly sensitive to market noise and rapidly changing financial conditions. Financial time series often contain structural breaks, volatility clustering, and evolving market dynamics that reduce the reliability of neighborhood-based prediction methods. As a result, KNN produced less consistent signals across firms and generated inferior cumulative returns and risk-adjusted performance. These characteristics limit its suitability for portfolio construction where consistent cross-asset decision making is essential.

5.4 Portfolio Performance Considerations

Extending the proposed framework from individual securities to portfolio management introduces additional dimensions of evaluation beyond those considered for single-asset forecasting. While predictive accuracy remains important, portfolio performance depends on how predictive signals interact across multiple assets, the correlation structure between securities, and the effectiveness of capital allocation decisions. Consequently, a forecasting model capable of producing stable predictions across different firms provides a stronger foundation for practical investment management than one whose performance varies substantially from asset to asset.

The cross-firm evaluation conducted in this study offers encouraging evidence regarding the robustness of XGBoost-based predictions. The relatively uniform performance observed across Apple, Microsoft, Amazon, NVIDIA, and Alphabet suggests that the model captures market characteristics that are common within the technology sector rather than relying on patterns unique to individual companies. Such cross-firm robustness is highly desirable because it increases confidence that predictive performance can be maintained when investment capital is distributed across multiple assets instead of concentrated in a single stock.

From a diversification perspective, stable predictive signals allow portfolio managers to allocate capital more confidently among securities exhibiting favorable forecasts. Rather than relying on isolated predictions, investment decisions can be based on the collective information generated across the entire portfolio. This reduces dependence on any individual company's performance and contributes to more balanced risk exposure. Even when certain assets experience unexpected adverse events, diversified allocation based on consistently reliable predictive signals may help preserve overall portfolio stability.

The superiority of XGBoost in both predictive and economic evaluation further suggests that ensemble learning methods are particularly well suited to supporting portfolio-level investment strategies. Their ability to model complex nonlinear interactions while maintaining consistent performance across multiple firms enhances their usefulness within AI-driven decision-support systems. Random Forest exhibits many of these characteristics as well, although its slightly lower predictive performance indicates that some information captured by boosting techniques may remain unexploited.

Although the present chapter does not perform full portfolio optimization, the proposed evaluation framework establishes a practical foundation for future portfolio-oriented research. Predictive probabilities generated by machine learning models could be integrated with established portfolio optimization techniques, including mean-variance optimization, minimum variance portfolios, or risk-parity allocation methods. Likewise, dynamic asset allocation strategies could adjust portfolio weights according to changes in model confidence or evolving market conditions. These extensions would enable AI-generated predictive signals to play a more direct role in portfolio construction while preserving the standardized evaluation methodology developed throughout this chapter.

Overall, the portfolio-level extension reinforces one of the central conclusions of this study: the practical value of machine learning models depends not only on their predictive accuracy but also on the consistency, robustness, and economic reliability of the signals they generate across multiple assets. The superior cross-firm performance of XGBoost demonstrates that ensemble learning methods provide a strong foundation for integrating AI-based forecasting into portfolio management systems, thereby strengthening the connection between predictive analytics and real-world investment strategy.

6. CONCLUSION

This chapter presented a comprehensive and standardized framework for evaluating machine learning models in stock direction forecasting, with particular emphasis on connecting predictive performance to economically meaningful investment outcomes. Rather than evaluating forecasting models solely through traditional classification metrics, the proposed framework integrates predictive accuracy, cross-firm validation, and risk-adjusted financial performance into a unified evaluation methodology. This holistic perspective provides a more realistic assessment of model effectiveness and better reflects the practical requirements of AI-driven investment decision making.

The empirical findings demonstrated that ensemble learning methods, particularly XGBoost, consistently outperformed the alternative algorithms across multiple evaluation dimensions. In addition to achieving the highest classification accuracy, XGBoost generated superior cumulative returns, stronger Sharpe ratios, and lower maximum drawdowns across all evaluated technology firms. Random Forest also demonstrated robust performance, although it consistently ranked behind XGBoost, while Artificial Neural Networks and K-Nearest Neighbors exhibited comparatively lower predictive consistency and economic performance. These findings reinforce the growing evidence that ensemble learning techniques are particularly well suited for modeling the nonlinear and dynamic characteristics of financial time series.

An important contribution of this chapter lies in demonstrating that improvements in predictive accuracy should not be considered an end in themselves. Instead, the practical value of artificial intelligence in financial markets depends on whether predictive signals can be translated into reliable investment decisions that generate attractive returns while maintaining acceptable levels of risk. By integrating economic validation measures such as cumulative returns, Sharpe ratio, and maximum drawdown into the evaluation process, the proposed framework bridges the longstanding gap between statistical forecasting performance and practical investment strategy.

The chapter also highlights the importance of methodological rigor in financial machine learning research. The use of standardized preprocessing procedures, chronological data partitioning, time-series cross-validation, and consistent hyperparameter optimization ensures that comparisons among competing algorithms remain fair, reproducible, and resistant to common sources of experimental bias. Furthermore, evaluating the models across multiple firms within the same sector provides evidence of cross-firm robustness, demonstrating that model performance is not dependent on the characteristics of a single asset. This emphasis on reproducibility and robustness contributes to more reliable benchmarking practices and supports the development of trustworthy AI-based financial forecasting systems.

From a practical perspective, the findings offer valuable guidance for investors, financial analysts, and developers of intelligent decision-support systems. The results suggest that ensemble learning methods can provide more stable predictive signals that are suitable not only for individual stock forecasting but also for supporting portfolio-level investment decisions. Although the portfolio extension presented in this chapter is conceptual, the consistent cross-firm performance of XGBoost indicates that robust predictive models can serve as an effective foundation for diversified investment strategies. Therefore, the proposed evaluation framework has potential applications in algorithmic trading, portfolio management, financial risk assessment, and AI-assisted investment advisory systems.

More broadly, this chapter contributes to the expanding field of artificial intelligence in finance by shifting the focus from isolated forecasting accuracy toward comprehensive model evaluation. As AI technologies continue to transform financial markets, the ability to assess predictive models using standardized, economically meaningful, and reproducible methodologies will become increasingly important for both academic research and professional practice. By integrating predictive performance, economic validation, cross-firm robustness, and risk-aware assessment within a single framework, this study provides a practical benchmark that can support future research and facilitate the responsible adoption of AI-driven investment strategies.

Although the proposed framework provides encouraging results, it should be viewed as a foundation rather than a final solution. Future research may extend this work by incorporating additional market sectors, alternative asset classes, explicit transaction-cost modeling, portfolio optimization techniques, and emerging artificial intelligence approaches such as deep learning and reinforcement learning. Such extensions would further strengthen the practical applicability of AI-driven investment systems while preserving the methodological principles established in this chapter.

The primary contribution of this chapter is not the introduction of a new forecasting algorithm, but the development of a standardized and economically grounded evaluation framework that systematically links machine learning predictions to investment decision making. By demonstrating the importance of combining predictive accuracy with economic performance, methodological rigor, and cross-firm robustness, this work provides a meaningful contribution to the literature on AI-driven market analysis and offers a practical foundation for future intelligent financial decision-support systems.

Limitations of the Study

Despite the contributions of the proposed evaluation framework, several limitations should be acknowledged when interpreting the findings.

First, the empirical analysis focuses exclusively on five large-cap technology firms. Although this controlled setting facilitates fair cross-firm comparison, the findings may not generalize directly to companies operating in other sectors or financial markets with different characteristics.

Second, the trading framework assumes simplified market conditions by excluding transaction costs, slippage, liquidity constraints, and execution delays. While these assumptions enable controlled comparison among machine learning models, they may lead to optimistic estimates of practical investment performance.

Third, the study is based on daily historical market data and therefore does not capture intraday dynamics or high-frequency trading behavior. Finally, although four widely used machine learning algorithms were evaluated, more advanced approaches such as deep learning architectures and reinforcement learning were beyond the scope of this chapter.

These limitations do not diminish the value of the proposed framework but instead define the scope within which the results should be interpreted.

Future Research Directions

The evaluation framework presented in this chapter provides several opportunities for future research.

First, future studies should investigate the proposed methodology across a broader range of industries, international markets, and asset classes. Evaluating heterogeneous financial datasets would provide additional evidence regarding the generalizability and robustness of the framework beyond the technology sector.

Second, greater practical realism could be achieved by incorporating explicit transaction costs, bid–ask spreads, liquidity constraints, execution delays, and alternative portfolio optimization techniques. Such extensions would enable more comprehensive evaluation of AI-driven investment strategies under real-world market conditions.

Third, future research may investigate additional artificial intelligence techniques, including deep learning architectures, hybrid ensemble models, reinforcement learning, and explainable AI approaches such as SHAP. These methods could further improve predictive capability while enhancing model transparency and investor confidence.

Finally, the proposed evaluation framework could be extended beyond stock direction forecasting to other financial prediction problems, including volatility forecasting, asset allocation, portfolio management, cryptocurrency markets, and multi-asset investment decision support systems. Such developments would further strengthen the integration of artificial intelligence into modern financial analytics while preserving the standardized evaluation methodology proposed in this chapter.

REFERENCES

Abdulhafidh Dael, F., Yavuz, U., & Almohammedi, A. A. (2022). Performance Evaluation of Time Series Forecasting Methods in The Stock Market: A Comparative Study. *2022 International Conference on Decision Aid Sciences and Applications (DASA)*, 1510–1514. DOI: 10.1109/DASA54658.2022.9765177

Amman, H., Barnett, W. A., Jawadi, F., & Tucci, M. (2025). Complexity, nonlinearity and high frequency financial data modeling: Lessons from computational approaches. *Annals of Operations Research, 352*(3), 353–358. DOI: 10.1007/s10479-025-06809-z

Ampomah, E. K., Qin, Z., & Nyame, G. (2020). Evaluation of Tree-Based Ensemble Machine Learning Models in Predicting Stock Price Direction of Movement. *Information (Basel), 11*(6), 332. Advance online publication. DOI: 10.3390/info11060332

April, B. K., Oluoch, L., & Awe, O. O. (2025). Novel Applications of Bayesian Additive Regression Model for Predicting Diamond Prices: A Comparative Study of Tree-Based Ensemble Techniques. In O. O. Awe & E. A. Vance (Eds.), *Practical Statistical Learning and Data Science Methods: Case Studies from LISA 2020 Global Network, USA* (pp. 127–164). Springer Nature Switzerland. DOI: 10.1007/978-3-031-72215-8_6

Bansal, M., Goyal, A., & Choudhary, A. (2022). Stock Market Prediction with High Accuracy using Machine Learning Techniques. *Procedia Computer Science, 4th International Conference on Innovative Data Communication Technology and Application, 215*, 247–265. DOI: 10.1016/j.procs.2022.12.028

Dael, F., Yavuz, Ö., & Yavuz, U. (2023). Stock Market Prediction Using Generative Adversarial Networks (GANs): Hybrid Intelligent Model. *Computer Systems Science and Engineering, 47*(1), 19–35. DOI: 10.32604/csse.2023.037903

Dael, F. A., & Avvad, H. (2025). Optimizing Random Forest Hyperparameters for Enhanced Stock Price Prediction. *IEEE International Conference on New Trends in Computing Sciences (ICTCS)*. DOI: 10.1109/ICTCS65341.2025.10989295

Hoang, D., & Wiegratz, K. (2023). Machine learning methods in finance: Recent applications and prospects. *European Financial Management, 29*(5), 1657–1701. DOI: 10.1111/eufm.12408

Hosain, M. T., Morol, M. K., & Hossen, M. J. (2025). A hybrid self attentive linearized phrase structured transformer based RNN for financial sentence analysis with sentence level explainability. *Scientific Reports, 15*(1), 23893. DOI: 10.1038/s41598-025-09265-8 PMID: 40615659

Kim, D., Lee, J., & Kim, H. (2026). Pattern-guided forecasting framework for metal price prediction with grouping decomposed series. *Financial Innovation*, *12*(1), 45. DOI: 10.1186/s40854-025-00833-5

Kulkarni, M. S., Vijayakumar Bharathi, S., Perdana, A., & Kilari, D. (2025). A Quest for Context-Specific Stock Price Prediction: A Comparison Between Time Series, Machine Learning and Deep Learning Models. *SN Computer Science*, *6*(4), 335. DOI: 10.1007/s42979-025-03848-y

Kumar, D., Sarangi, P. K., & Verma, R. (2022). A systematic review of stock market prediction using machine learning and statistical techniques. *Materials Today: Proceedings, National Conference on Functional Materials: Emerging Technologies and Applications in Materials Science*, *49*, 3187–3191. DOI: 10.1016/j.matpr.2020.11.399

Lourenço, V. M., Ogutu, J. O., Rodrigues, R. A. P., Posekany, A., & Piepho, H.-P. (2024). Genomic prediction using machine learning: A comparison of the performance of regularized regression, ensemble, instance-based and deep learning methods on synthetic and empirical data. *BMC Genomics*, *25*(1), 152. DOI: 10.1186/s12864-023-09933-x PMID: 38326768

Pagliaro, A. (2025). Artificial Intelligence vs. Efficient Markets: A Critical Reassessment of Predictive Models in the Big Data Era. *Electronics (Basel)*, *14*(9), 1721. Advance online publication. DOI: 10.3390/electronics14091721

Rouf, N., Malik, M. B., Arif, T., Sharma, S., Singh, S., Aich, S., & Kim, H.-C. (2021). Stock Market Prediction Using Machine Learning Techniques: A Decade Survey on Methodologies, Recent Developments, and Future Directions. *Electronics (Basel)*, *10*(21), 2717. Advance online publication. DOI: 10.3390/electronics10212717

Shahin, T., Ballestar de las Heras, M. T., & Sanz, I. (2025). Enhancing Stock Market Prediction Using Gradient Boosting Neural Network: A Hybrid Approach. *Computational Economics*, *65*(6), 3207–3235. DOI: 10.1007/s10614-024-10671-9

Singh, U., & Khare, A. (2026). Stock Prediction Using Machine Learning Techniques. In Senjyu, T., So-, C., & Joshi, A. (Eds.), *Smart Trends in Computing and Communications* (pp. 387–400). Springer Nature., DOI: 10.1007/978-981-96-7505-0_30

Sun, Y., Qu, Z., Zhang, T., & Li, X. (2025). Adaptive Ensemble Learning for Financial Time-Series Forecasting: A Hypernetwork-Enhanced Reservoir Computing Framework with Multi-Scale Temporal Modeling. *Axioms*, *14*(8), 597. Advance online publication. DOI: 10.3390/axioms14080597

Thayasivam, U., Johnson, S., Balabavan, K., & Uthayakumar, S. (2025). A comprehensive survey on statistical and deep learning models for panel data analysis. *Knowledge and Information Systems, 67*(12), 11359–11379. DOI: 10.1007/s10115-025-02607-y

Yu, W. (2025). Estimating the changes and oscillations in the financial markets: A case study of the Nikkei 225. *Sadhana, 50*(4), 247. DOI: 10.1007/s12046-025-02869-w

Zhang, Q., Zhang, H., & Sornette, D. (2025). Discovering nonlinear interactions between China's financial markets: A data-driven approach. *International Review of Financial Analysis, 101*, 103975. DOI: 10.1016/j.irfa.2025.103975

KEY TERMS AND DEFINITIONS

Algorithmic Trading: The use of automated systems and models to execute trading decisions based on predefined rules.

EXtreme Gradient Boosting (XGBoost): An ensemble learning method that builds models sequentially to correct errors of previous models, often achieving high predictive accuracy.

Feature Importance: A measure of how much each input variable contributes to a model's predictions.

Machine Learning: A subset of artificial intelligence that enables systems to learn patterns from data and make predictions without explicit programming.

Maximum Drawdown: The largest peak-to-trough decline in a cumulative return series, representing downside risk.

Random Forest: An ensemble method that constructs multiple decision trees and aggregates their predictions to improve performance and reduce overfitting.

Sharpe Ratio: A risk-adjusted performance metric that measures return per unit of volatility.

Stock Direction Prediction: The task of forecasting whether a stock's price will increase or decrease over a specified time horizon.

Time-Series Cross-Validation: A validation technique that preserves temporal order when splitting data, preventing information leakage.

Chapter 4
AI-Driven Trading and Portfolio Optimization Platform With Risk and Forecasting Integration

Neha Garg
http://orcid.org/0000-0003-3806-6964
Delhi Technical Campus, India

Sharad Gupta
http://orcid.org/0009-0008-2983-3731
Delhi Technical Campus, India

Yashdeep Saxena
http://orcid.org/0009-0005-2208-7607
Delhi Technical Campus, India

ABSTRACT

Artificial Intelligence (AI) and machine learning technologies have significantly transformed financial markets and replaced intuition based strategies by data-driven intelligent systems. AI-driven trading and portfolio optimization platforms, which integrate advanced analytics, predictive modeling, and automated decision-making to enhance investment performance. The chapter explores the design and application of AI enabled trading platforms in modern financial markets. These platforms support technologies such as machine learning algorithms, deep learning models, natural language processing, and big data analytics to analyze market trends, detect trading opportunities, and construct optimized investment portfolios. By combining real-time and historical data, AI generate predictive insights for informed investment

DOI: 10.4018/979-8-3373-9645-3.ch004

decisions and risk management strategies. The chapter discusses the evolution of algorithmic trading and AI's growing role in financial market analysis. It examines key components including data acquisition modules, predictive analytics engines, automated trading systems, and portfolio optimization models. Challenges such as model interpretability, regulatory compliance, data privacy, and algorithmic bias are also addressed. A conceptual framework is proposed for effective deployment of these technologies.

INTRODUCTION

1.1 The Evolution of Trading Technologies

Information moves financial markets, who holds it, who sees it fastest, who acts on it ahead of others. Most of the 1900s demanded boots on the ground presence: yelling over crowds, sensing tension in air, relying on instinct. Skill mattered, certainly. Yet limits stayed firm: humans grow weary, feel stress, track few threads at one time.

What once crawled through steps now zipped along in fractions of a second. Computing gear dropped in price while gaining speed, letting number crunchers test ideas on real data before it went stale. When live pricing met desktop horsepower, strategies based on patterns started sticking instead of fizzling out. That mix, digital exchanges plus affordable technology, gave methodical approaches room to grow.

Midway through the early two thousand, algorithm trading stopped being a side-line test and became how things actually worked (Botos, Á., & Fogarasi, J., 2025). Big financial players did not just try it out, they shifted entire operations to run on automated systems. Some high speed outfits pushed further still, installing server racks within exchange walls, shaving microsecond delays here and there (O'Hara, 2015). These machines blast countless trades every day, chasing imbalances invisible to people watching screens. Recent data shows about six to seven out of every ten shares traded in the US now move through algorithms. All told, the field stood near seventeen point two billion dollars and projections suggest forty-two point five billion by twenty thirty-three. Within that, artificial intelligence driven strategies grow at another pace entirely, expected to hit nearly seventy billion by twenty thirty-four.

1.2 The Rise of AI in Finance

Electronic trading kicked off the first big change, yet now artificial intelligence marks the next one, reaching much further beneath the surface. Instead of fixed rules turned into software, older systems just wait for exact triggers before acting at all. Without a match, they stay idle. They fail to see shifts in how markets move compared to half a year earlier, while lacking any method to respond when surprises occur beyond their original programming.

Something shifts when AI steps in. Instead of sticking to fixed guidelines, machine learning finds its own way through trial and observation. By studying past information alongside live updates, these models spot trends invisible to people scanning columns on a screen. With every fresh batch of details, their insight sharpens quietly. Markets evolve, so does an effective AI, adjusting without pause. But rigid programs? They stop working the moment conditions change.

Last month matters more than last year when models decide what to remember, LSTM and transformer types handle this shift naturally, mirroring real market rhythms. What changed next came from reinforcement learning, outcomes emerge not from fixed rules but endless trial inside virtual markets (Rezaei, M., & Nezamabadi-Pour, H., 2025; Sutton & Barto, 2018). Guidance isn't handed down; discovery happens through doing. No tagged datasets needed here. Numbers tell part of the story anyway, by 2024 nearly four out of five finance firms applied AI while trading. Inside JP Morgan, results leaned heavier toward algorithms, gains jumped one, fifth higher versus old checklist systems (Chen et al., 2024). Past patterns shaped future wins without shouting their presence.

Not just about trade selection, artificial intelligence dives deeper. Reading financial headlines, sifting through tweets, pulling insights from company reports, this happens instantly (Huynh, N. et. al., 2025). Machines convert messy paragraphs into clear signals before most people finish reading. Firms like Goldman Sachs and JP Morgan mix these streams with traditional price data. So do outfits such as Citadel. Speed reshapes everything; knowledge slips into prices quicker than eyes can blink. That pace builds an invisible wall, one side crowded with firms armed with tech, the other holding those without access.

1.3 The Collapse of Old Methods

What trips up most people in retail trading has nothing to do with attention or knowledge gaps. It's baked into the system itself, cold numbers show it plainly, whether anyone likes admitting it.

Most folks trading futures and options in India walked away poorer. A SEBI document revealed nearly 93 out of every hundred individuals saw losses from fiscal year 2022 through 2024 (Securities and Exchange Board of India, 2024). The total amount lost? Over 1.81 lakh crore when added up. Things got worse by FY2025, collective red ink jumped 41%, hitting 1.05 trillion. Even so, the share of losers held steady at about 91 percent. Not much changed on that front.

In the market nearly all earnings, 97% from foreign investors, 96% from internal trading desks last year, flowed through automated setups. This outcome follows clear patterns: structured tech,based trades outperform choices shaped by mood or instinct (Murray, Xia & Xiao, 2024).

Yet few admit this truth: many who fail at trading never once checked if their wallet could handle the fall. Instead of tracking cash flow, they dive in blind. Without knowing monthly drains, decisions come unanchored. Month after month slips by without a glance at saving habits, quiet cracks widening unseen. Ahead lies fog, not forecasts. A spark hits, excitement builds, accounts get created, trades begin. What looks like poor trading is often just money habits showing through. Fixing it means stepping outside standard fixes.

1.4 Two Complementary Layers of Financial Intelligence

The two systems described in this paper address this problem at two different but connected levels.

The first level is personal financial behavior. Before someone thinks about where to invest, they need an honest picture of their own financial health; how stable their income actually is, how disciplined their spending has been, how often they've dipped into the red, and whether their trajectory is improving or quietly getting worse. Without that foundation, any investment decision is effectively made blind.

The second level is algorithmic trading and portfolio execution. Once someone understands their financial position and has capital they can genuinely afford to deploy, they need a platform that enforces the same kind of systematic, risk, governed discipline that professional trading desks treat as standard.

The AI driven Financial Risk and Intelligence System handles the first level. Quant edge handles the second. Together, they cover the full journey from behavioral self, assessment and probabilistic investment simulation through to governed, systematic trade execution.

1.5 Introducing the AI, Driven Financial Risk and Intelligence System

The AI, Driven Financial Risk and Intelligence System is a personal financial behavior analysis platform. It doesn't predict stock prices, execute trades, or analyze market trends. What it does is take a user's income and expense history and turn it into something genuinely useful: a clear picture of their financial risk level, a forecast of where that trajectory is heading, and a realistic simulation of what investing from their current position actually looks like under uncertainty (Glasserman, 2004).

The system runs on a seven, module pipeline. The foundation is a synthetic dataset of 2,000 fictional users with 24 months of financial history each 48,000 rows in total built across five behavioral archetypes: stable salaried earners, gig workers with volatile income, high earners with equally high lifestyle spending, conservative savers, and people who are genuinely struggling.

The machine learning model at the center doesn't learn from raw rupee amounts. It learns from behavioral patterns savings ratio, expense ratio, income volatility, how often someone's savings go negative, and how frequently they overspend severely. Because these are ratios and frequencies rather than absolute numbers, the system works equally well across all income levels. A person taking home 25,000 and barely saving 2,000 is living just as close to the edge as someone on 1,50,000 doing the exact same thing proportionally the number on the pay slip is different, the financial stress is identical.

Risk labels: Low, Medium, or High are assigned through a weighted composite score built from five behavioral features. A Random Forest classifier is trained on these profiles and saved for live use (Breiman, 2001). An ARIMA time series model then forecasts the user's expense and savings trend over the next six months, labeling the direction as Improving, Stable, or Deteriorating (Box et al., 2015). A Monte Carlo engine runs 10,000 simulated investment paths to map out the probability distribution of outcomes (Glasserman, 2004). And tying it all together, a Gemini, powered Chabot called FinTalkBot uses the user's complete financial profile as context to give advice that's actually relevant to them rather than generic.

1.6 Introducing Quantedge

Quantedge is a web based algorithmic trading and portfolio management platform. Its purpose is straightforward: give retail traders access to the kind of systematic, disciplined infrastructure that institutional desks take for granted, without requiring a team of quants or an enterprise software budget.

The platform covers the entire trading workflow in one place strategy building, back testing, paper trading, portfolio optimization, news intelligence, and live broker execution; all built on FastAPI, PostgreSQL, and a React dashboard. It's designed to be modular, cloud compatible, and robust enough to actually run real strategies reliably.

Quantedge is built around three principles that most retail trading tools simply ignore. First, statistical discipline: no strategy goes live without being validated through a proper back testing and forward testing process. Second, quantitative risk governance: position sizing, drawdown limits, exposure controls, and an emergency kill, switch are built into the system itself, they're not suggestions left to the user's discretion. Third, AI, augmented decision support: a natural language processing layer reads and scores financial news using FinBERT (Araci, 2019; Huang et al., 2023), feeding structured signals into the strategy filter and portfolio optimizer without handing over trade execution to unverified sentiment alone. Quantedge is built to close the gap between where retail traders currently operate and where institutional discipline begins.

2. ALGORITHMIC TRADING AND SMART INVESTING TOOLS

2.1 The Structure Behind Automated Stock Trading

Computer code runs trades by following set rules using numbers like price or time, skipping any need for people to make choices then. Yet what sounds straight-forward gets messy when actually built. Real world systems do not work as one piece. They move step by step: pulling live data, cleaning it up, checking patterns at various intervals all once, spotting triggers without errors, handling each buy or sell from start to finish including updates or stops, tracking exposure constantly, everything happening fast enough to meet tight speed limits (Cartea et al., 2015).

What drives an automated trading rule is straightforward logic: when the market looks like S at moment t, do A if conditions C allow it. Price patterns usually feed into this, things like moving averages, momentum scores, trend strength, along with measures of activity level, say average true range or volume, weighted prices. Each value gets calculated using past data across a set period, then checked against specific trigger points. On top of that sits another kind of control, how much risk to accept, trade size, exit boundaries, total commitment allowed, which works separately from the triggers themselves, making sure decisions never break fixed safety limits regardless of what signals appear.

Few systems keep signal creation apart from order handling like a strict setup demands. Consider Quantedge it builds this split into its design sending every alert through a safety filter first even if the original trigger came out of nowhere. Only after clearing those hurdles does anything move toward placing a trade no exceptions ever.

2.2 High Frequency Trading at The Edge

Speed focused trading pushes automated systems to their edge, here, delays count in billionths of seconds, being physically close to exchange servers matters deeply, yet success comes mainly through massive repetition (O'Hara, 2015). By 2024, this sector globally totals near $10.36 billion. What runs beneath it isn't like regular finance tools, trade processors sometimes live inside specialized chips, such as FPGAs or GPU clusters, because ordinary code can't keep up when speed must stay extreme across huge loads.

A quiet market can shift in an instant, dropping fast for no clear reason. When conditions are calm, high, speed trading narrows the space between buying and selling costs. But during rough patches, if automated systems begin copying each other's moves, order turns into disorder. As these systems respond nonstop to signals from peers, price jumps become more extreme. Moments of balance give way to rapid jolts when machines amplify their own feedback. One moment in 2010, a thousand, point drop disappeared nearly at once. Faster than thought, algorithms moved while people blinked, rattling trust in less time than a breath.

What matters most isn't copying high, frequency setups. Platforms like Quant edge work slower, focused on structured trades within India's stock and derivative spaces. Instead of chasing speed, they build clear rules for every trade. Slippage gets calculated ahead, not guessed after. Risk checks sit outside the trading code, watching over decisions. Precision shapes outcomes more than pace ever could.

2.3 The Blend of Planning and Doing

Out past the forecast comes the need to place trades smartly. One piece feeds another, not all at once but step by step. When predictions form, they pass into systems that shape orders carefully. Those orders then move into action only when timing and method align. Each stage holds its own rules. Respect flows forward, never forced. The whole works because parts do not overreach. Clarity lives in sequence, not speed.

Some forecasting tools in today's algorithmic trading rely on older statistical methods, others lean into intricate deep learning designs. LSTMs stand out when predicting movements in market data, especially when paired with powerful GPUs (Fischer & Krauss, 2018; Giantsidi, S., & Tarantola, C., 2025; Lin, C. Y., & Marques, J. A. L., 2024), these combos can process predictions in less than a thousandth of a second. Still, being right isn't enough if timing misses the mark. Imagine getting a signal too late: even with six correct guesses out of ten, waiting just two-tenths of a second past the useful window turns profits into losses once fees eat away returns (Lim & Zohren, 2021).

Midway through workflow, order handling bridges intent with action. It checks trade sizes against set caps while tracking active tickets and executed volume moment by moment. Strategy directives shift into formats brokers accept, shaped by context rather than rigid rules. When executions split, fail, or stall, adjustments follow without pause. At Quantedge, a standalone engine manages this using Kotak Neo's interface, syncing a simulated ledger across test and production environments alike.

2.4 Smart Choices Evolving Beyond Fixed Rules

Intelligent systems' ability to shift as markets shift. Rule bound models stay fixed once launched, no matter how surroundings transform around them. Learning happens differently here, patterns get updated through exposure, not manual fixes. Behavior adjusts itself because insight grows from what's been seen before.

Starting fresh, reinforcement learning builds understanding step by step without needing full rules upfront (Sutton & Barto, 2018). Instead of fixed plans, progress comes from repeated trial within the setting itself. This fits finance where conditions shift unpredictably (Hambly et al., 2023). Picture a system that watches prices, signals, and current holdings at each moment. From these inputs, it chooses next steps like buying, waiting, or selling. Each decision leads to feedback tied directly to goals, say risk adjusted gains or total profit over time (Rezaei, M., & Nezamabadi-Pour, H., 2025). Learning unfolds as outcomes shape future choices slowly. The process thrives where patterns evolve and certainty is absent.

Starting elsewhere than just costs, today's tools pull in unusual data sources. From many angles, reinforcement learning now shapes how portfolios are handled (Hambly et al., 2023), especially when combined with ways to read text from headlines or online chatter (Huynh, N. et al, 2025), using chart patterns as system inputs, balancing multiple goals in scoring outcomes. At Quantedge, their AI News tool puts this mix into real-world use: articles flow in, get sorted, rated for mood and significance, then turned into organized alerts that guide both risk checks and investment choices, while still keeping final trades out of reach for raw textual cues.

2.5 Advantages Limitations and How Design Responds

It's clear that automated trading beats gut, based decisions. Emotions vanish when machines pull the trigger. Watching dozens of markets at once? A computer handles it without blinking. Rules for trade size and risk never get ignored, thanks to code. Past prices reveal how a method would have fared long before real money goes in (López de Prado, 2018).

It's just as crucial to recognize the drawbacks. Tuning a method too closely to past randomness instead of real patterns often trips up automated trading designs (López de Prado, 2018). Data that only includes surviving assets, calculations that peek ahead in time by mistake, along with shifts in market behavior, these together reveal why many tested approaches fall short when used for actual trading. What looks solid on paper rarely holds up once money is at stake.

Instead of mixing stages, Quant edge keeps things clean by design. Because back testing runs separately from forward testing, settings stay within their proper time windows. Each candle gets handled one after another, so future data cannot slip in by accident. Before a strategy moves to real trading, it must pass walk, forward checks, this gate exists by default, not by choice.

3. SYSTEM STRUCTURE

3.1 Algorithmic Trading Idea

Computers follow set rules to place trades, price shifts, time stamps, or data patterns can trigger them. Instead of waiting for someone to decide, the system acts when conditions match its code. This method skips gut feelings entirely; decisions come from math, not mood. After setup, it runs nonstop, treating every stock the same way, never slowing down. Each move ties back to preset logic, repeating exactly, trade after trade.

A single idea shapes the whole system; layers build on layers. At the edge, choices about what stocks to watch and what numbers matter take shape first. Following that, rules form to spot patterns worth acting on. Nestled within, another step turns those hints into real trading moves with clear details attached. Inside everything sits risk enforcement, rules an order has to pass before moving ahead. At Quantedge, this flow works by using a custom language made for strategies, then checks live events through a trigger based system, runs decisions past a separate risk checker, connects the whole thing outward using a tailored broker link.

One step feeds into the next inside this financial intelligence setup, built around seven linked stages. Not just connected but locked in sequence: what comes out of Data Generation flows straight into Feature Engineering. From there, Risk Classification picks up the result without delay. Each stage relies on the one before, like links in a chain pulled forward by necessity. Forecasting waits for prior outputs, no skipping ahead allowed. Then Monte Carlo Simulation runs only when forecasting finishes (Glasserman, 2004). System Integration follows, taking everything gathered so far. Finally, Streamlit UI presents it all, shaped entirely by earlier steps. Order matters because each piece depends on timing, much like how Quantedge handles historical testing. Sequence becomes rule, not suggestion, mirroring strict time-based logic elsewhere.

3.2 High Frequency Trading and Smart Systems

Midway between rapid-fire trades and gut driven decisions, smart trading setups offer regular investors a realistic entry into automated markets. Instead of split, second moves or long term guesses, they aim for repeatable patterns within days or weeks. Machine learning feeds their signals, while clear rules manage exposure across positions. Balance matters here, so does steady performance over time. Built exactly for these needs, Quantedge supports such balanced approaches naturally.

How someone handles money shapes how they interact with investment tools. When the system flags a person as High Risk, because their income jumps around, they often spend more than they earn, keep spending over 85% of what they make, and show worsening trends, it means short-term trading isn't suitable. That kind of approach demands room for error, which such users simply lack. Instead, only those marked Low Risk, whose saving habits are getting stronger, should access automated investing methods. People struggling with deeper financial instability need to fix that foundation long before stepping into market exposure. What the risk model reveals becomes a filter, quietly guiding who moves forward and who pauses.

3.3 Using Risk and Forecasts Together When Trading

Starting with how things stand now, the system builds a picture step by step. One phase flows into the next, shaping what might happen later. Instead of just reporting numbers, it explores possible futures using smart analysis. Each stage connects, first looking at today, then forecasting ahead, followed by testing outcomes through trial runs.

Out of past spending and earning patterns, tracked over two years, comes a sorting step that leans on a Random Forest model (Breiman, 2001). Behavior clues feed it, ones without units: average saving rate, usual spending share, swings in earnings, how often money saved goes negative, variation in savings amounts, plus frequency of deep overspending. One after another, these bits get folded into a single number where negatives around missing savings pull strongest at thirty percent weight. Spending habits next, carrying a quarter influence, followed by shifts in pay size making up one fifth. Wobbles in save totals countless, just fifteen out of a hundred. Last piece, rare but sharp cases of going way over budget, adds only ten points to the total. After adding everything up, boundaries based on rank order split people into groups. Those splits keep things even across two thousand made-up profiles used during setup.

Looking ahead turns a snapshot into a path forward. For each person, separate forecasts track spending and saving using an ARIMA (2,1,2) method (Box et al., 2015). A half year outlook gets its category based on how the start and end points compare. Pairing the risk level with the direction of change creates a clearer picture, one built on both stability and movement.

Imagine rolling dice thousands of times to see possible outcomes. That idea shapes how future returns are tested here (Glasserman, 2004). One thousand scenarios play out, each building on chance. From those results, we pull four key points: the rare bad result, the middle ground, the lucky peak, the odds of losing money overall. People labeled High Risk pick lower average gains plus wider swings compared to cautious users. Their choices shift the whole forecast range. This link between type and settings drives what appears in their projections. Numbers bend based on that first label picked earlier.

4. DESIGN OF AN ARTIFICIAL INTELLIGENCE TRADING SYSTEM

4.1 Data Collection Layer

Downstream choices rely entirely on what flows in first. What comes out depends on what went in before. A system can only act on the information it receives. Poor input shapes poor outcomes every time. Whatever feeds the process sets its limits. Decisions later reflect the starting point. The beginning defines how far things go.

From dawn till dusk, Quantedge pulls data in three separate waves. One wave digs into the past, OHLCV records arrive through market APIs for NSE stocks and derivatives, pulled at odd intervals, stripped of gaps and split effects, then stored in PostgreSQL using time-based tags. Another moves now, live prices flow in from Kotak Neo's WebSocket link, caught early, slipped into Redis memory storage before anyone sees them. Because Redis stands between source and user, tickers, decision logic, and test runs pull identical numbers without tripping rate rules. A third trail carries words instead of digits, news snippets plucked from financial feeds, stamped with clocks, lined up for meaning extraction by FinBERT (Araci, 2019; Huang et al., 2023).

Instead of pulling real time market streams, the setup builds fake training records from scratch. Inside data_generation.ipynb, activity for 2,000 pretend people spreads across two dozen monthly snapshots, forming 48,000 entries total. One version stays whole: finance_data_full.csv keeps user tags just for checking later. The second file, finance_data.csv, strips those labels clean before any model sees it, blocking accidental shortcuts during learning.

4.2 Data Processing and Feature Engineering

At Quantedge, technical indicators like SMA, EMA, RSI, MACD, Bollinger Bands, ATR, VWAP, and ADX emerge from a vectorized system that works without memory on time stamped OHLCV data, delivering back an enriched dataset. Meanwhile, every news headline entering the platform gets scored for sentiment using FinBERT (Araci, 2019; Huang et al., 2023), generating both polarity and certainty metrics at once through the AI-driven analysis layer.

Inside the AI system for money risk and insight, shaping data pieces' matters more than anything else. Instead of keeping every month separate, one notebook squishes twenty-four lines per person into just one line. From paychecks comes a summary: how much arrives on average, how wild it swings, whether it climbs over time. Spending patterns get measured too, how much goes out, where it flows like rent or meals, how steady or shaky that flow stays. Saving habits show up as averages, dips below zero, long rough patches, how often things go tight. Some numbers say almost the same thing, so only one from such pairs sticks around. What remains lands in a table with twelve to fifteen traits per person. This clean set becomes the foundation for teaching prediction models what happens next.

4.3 Risk Evaluation and Alert Creation

At Quantedge, instead of general code, a special language shapes raw features into trade cues, built on strict JSON rules that machines can follow without confusion. This setup uses a parser to turn those rules into steps for Pandas, where every check names an indicator, how it's compared, plus either a fixed number or another indicator to measure against. Each moment in time gets scored: yes, or no, based solely on whether criteria lined up right then. Because decisions run only when new data arrives, future leaks cannot happen by design. The whole flow locks step with market events, so timing stays clean and isolated.

Every person gets a single risk number built from different behaviors. That number comes together through a special part of the system called the risk classifier. What matters most is how often someone dips below zero in their savings. Just doing that once in a while shows deep strain, so it pulls the heaviest load in scoring. Next up, spending too much on average, especially above 85 percent of earnings, leaves no room when surprises hit. This pattern shapes outcomes nearly as much. After that, shaky pay from month to month throws off every kind of money decision, even if totals look fine over time. Stability there counts less than saving habits but still shifts results noticeably.

Splitting users into groups happens by ranking them, then dividing the ranks evenly, about 667 people fall into each group from the total of 2,000. Instead of using set limits, percentiles shape these splits. Afterward, three models learn from the data: one follows straight lines, another builds branching rules, while the third combines many trees (Breiman, 2001). Among them, the forest of trees works best because it sees tangled links in how people act. Showing perfect scores, over 95%, on fake data makes sense. Because the actions tied to stress come right from the signals that created the labels. So patterns found aren't random guesses; they reflect real connections built into the setup.

4.4 Risk Management Module

Before any order moves forward at Quantedge, it must clear a series of risk hurdles, this happens every single time, without exception. Paper trades or real ones, neither proceed unless each passes specific safety filters first. Each individual trade faces hard boundaries: how much money can be lost on one go, required stop, losses for derivatives, and caps on how large a position can grow. Instead of focusing only on single trades, the system also watches broader signals tied to the entire account. Rolling drawdown peaks, losses stacked within a day, overall market exposure, all these feed into an ongoing assessment. If even one of those wider limits gets crossed, something shifts inside the platform instantly. A built-in cutoff triggers, halting fresh orders from launching anywhere across running strategies. That block stays locked in place, surviving reboots, persisting like a memory that refuses to reset.

Inside the AI powered financial system, handling risk ties directly to how investment settings shape outcomes. Starting from different points each time, the simulation takes in four key numbers: money invested, targeted yearly gain, fluctuation size, and years held (Glasserman, 2004). Instead of one prediction, it runs ten thousand possible annual growth routes forward. From these scattered results, five summary views emerge, a bleak outcome near rock bottom, halfway middle ground, an optimistic high end, odds of losing money overall, plus a view into typical losses. Since people face different levels of danger, settings shift based on their type; those labeled High Risk work with lower reward guesses, wilder swings built in. Unlike rigid models, adjustments respond to who's using them, shaping expectations accordingly. Flexibility keeps forecasts honest when uncertainty rules.

4.5 Execution Engine and Output Layer

After passing through the risk filters at Quantedge, signals move into the execution system. Strategy rules stay separate from brokerage systems thanks to a streamlined connection layer. When simulating trades, the system sends orders to an internal module that executes based on real time prices stored in Redis, factoring in modeled slippage. Switching to live operations, that identical trade instruction flows into the Kotak Neo connector, where every safety check runs again just before hitting the exchange API.

At the end of the AI driven Financial Risk and Intelligence System sits the analyze_user() function along with a Streamlit front end. This function acts first by checking inputs, only moving forward once everything meets requirements. Once cleared, it triggers predict_risk(), then forecast_user_realtime(), followed by run_monte_carlo(), one after another. Results from each step get gathered into one unified dictionary before being passed back out. The user interacts through a web layout built with Streamlit split neatly into two sections. First comes the analysis tab where all data gets processed. Only when that part finishes do access open to FinTalkBot in the second tab. Nothing runs ahead of schedule; every stage waits its turn.

5. AI METHODS TO IMPROVE INVESTMENT PORTFOLIOS

5.1 Modern Portfolio Theory Meets Artificial Intelligence

Markowitz's method says smart investors pick portfolios along the efficient frontier, those offering the highest return for a given risk level (Jensen et al., 2026). Yet here's the catch: figuring out future returns using past numbers often leads to shaky guesses. Even tiny mistakes in those forecasts might result in wildly shifted portfolio choices. It counts on market returns behaving in a neat, predictable pattern, which they rarely do over time. The model looks good on paper, but reality tends to misbehave.

Out of sample mistakes drop when machine learning refines predictions using tech patterns, financial stats, sentiment cues, better than old averages (Chen et al., 2024). Technical noise fades because shrinkage and Bayesian tools clean up correlation estimates. Inside Quantedge, one finds three built-in strategies for spreading money across assets. Minimizing swings while hitting return targets defines the first method. The second spreads risk equally so no single holding dominates danger. Worst-case losses get capped under the third approach, focused only on deep downturns at set odds (Flippi et al., 2020).

5.2 Machine Learning in Managing Investment Assets

Sometimes machines help decide where money goes by predicting returns first, then feeding those guesses into standard math tools. Other times, they skip prediction entirely, adjusting allocations based on what past portfolios actually did (Chen et al., 2024). When guessing returns, tree, based methods like boosted models often appear, they manage complex relationships between data points well. These models resist fitting too closely to noise when tuned right, plus they show which inputs mattered most. At Quantedge, feelings pulled from news articles shape decisions, stocks bombarded with bad headlines get smaller slices of the pie (Huynh, N. et al., 2025). That raw emotional signal blends quietly into traditional systems instead of taking over.

5.3 Risk Prediction Across Portfolios Using Spread Analysis and Random Outcomes

A fresh route appears every time the digits roll. Not about picking what comes next, but watching countless options emerge from repeated throws (Glasserman, 2004). Since certain results stack more often, a shape begins to show, pointing out favored spots. Think of columns growing taller where conclusions gather densely, exposing spread. With profits jumping unpredictably across years, linked sequences spin into uneven outcomes. Most of the time, smooth numbers mask wild swings underneath. Chance shapes each of ten thousand runs, staying inside fixed limits. Doing it again and again makes patterns stand out from chaos. The starting amount, annual changes, how long it lasts, plus typical growth drive the simulation. Results do not give a single forecast; they show likely zones shaped by probability. Some races stick close to the center, while others reach much farther out. When points grow into bars on a graph, doubt shows up clearly.

Spreading money across different assets can reduce danger without losing upside, a smart trick that usually costs nothing extra. Rather than simply recommending variety, Quantedge shows it working live. Through its system, each strategy's link to another becomes visible by measuring return connections one pair at a time. That clarity shapes views of what mixes might sit right on the frontier of performance (Jensen et al., 2026).

5.4 Reinforcement learning applied to investment portfolio management

Right away, teaching machines through rewards shapes investing as a chain of linked decisions (Sutton & Barto, 2018). Every step begins with checking live numbers, current costs, holdings, history, swings in risk. Rather than assuming, actions follow from this instant picture. Through trial runs using yesterday's trends or made up setups, choices evolve bit by bit (Hambly et al., 2023). Slowly, it spots rhythms that fixed models, drawn just from ideas, tend to overlook. Out of this comes something that matches life's bumps and dips pretty well. Improvement happens through repetition, just keep going.

Reinforcement learning works on paper does not mean it handles real portfolio management well (Hambly et al., 2023). When tested live, strategies that looked strong start failing, training setups lack stability, reward cues get confusing, markets keep changing. Simulated success rarely lasts once markets show their true face. These approaches suggest directions worth exploring later, yet none stand ready for use now. Not safety first but careful tweaks, shaping data for classic solvers or sketching risk by pulling numbers from a hat again and again, bring thinking you can follow plus outcomes that hold steady. What works here lines up with real finance work: solid ground folks rely on.

6. AI TRADING PLATFORMS POWERED BY MACHINE LEARNING DATA ANALYSIS AUTOMATION ALGORITHMS CLOUD COMPUTING

6.1 Building data systems for finance

Every second counts when machines trade stocks. Not just numbers, but floods of them, markets never stop making data. Some comes tidy, some messy, yet it all needs homes. Think databases humming under loads nobody saw ten years ago. Half to three, quarters of trades now? Bots handle those, lightning fast (Botos, Á., & Fogarasi, J., 2025). Backward glances matter too, years of highs, lows, closes, volumes stacked up like old ledgers. These sit in Postures, split smartly so digging through feels smooth. Forward motion is wilder though. Price shifts arrive nonstop, one after another. Each gets caught, held briefly, then passed around. Redis keeps these moments alive in memory, ready for whoever's watching. Past and present both feed the models, each bit playing its part.

6.2 Cloud Computing and Scalability

Quantedge runs inside portable units shaped by Docker, no rewiring needed when shifting between cloud setups. Inside those containers live tools like FastAPI, PostgreSQL, Redis, and Celery, all fitting together wherever they're dropped. When tests run, worker hands multiply through Celery, grabbing extra power as more people jump in at once. This keeps responses quick, even during deep simulations. Updates arrive silently: code pushed to GitHub triggers a quiet chain that lifts fresh versions onto Netlify, live before you notice it changed.

6.3 Real Time Data Processing

Right away, prices flow into Quantedge using live streams. Instead of checking every few seconds, a direct pipe opens via WebSocket to Kotak Neo, sending updates the moment they happen. At the same time, Redis holds the latest value for each traded asset. That stored figure reaches any part of the system in less than one thousandth of a second. Because of this setup, how fast data arrives doesn't affect who uses it later. Both the test simulator and the risk checker pull from identical snapshots in Redis. They stay aligned, never fighting over access to incoming ticks.

Every time someone starts a back test or tunes a portfolio, that job gets sent quietly to the background. Worker processes take over through Celery, letting heavy calculations run without freezing anything up front. The system replies fast, even though work continues out of sight. Behind the scenes, tasks unfold step by step while users stay free to keep moving. Financial platforms often operate like this, keeping responsiveness high during tough number crunching.

6.4 APIs and web technologies

Market data flows into Quantedge through Kotak Neo's API, while trade orders go out the same way. Because one broker connects everything, updates stay clean and contained. A template shapes how each broker talks to the system, and Kotak Neo fills that role today. Internal modules do not reach for brokerage tools on their own. Swapping brokers becomes a matter of setup, not rewriting core parts. Should another name enter, say Zerodha or Angel One, it would need its own bridge, nothing more. Code responsible for decisions stays untouched when such shifts happen. New paths form without disturbing old logic. Flexibility hides behind quiet structure. Changes occur at the edges, never in the center.

At the front, Quantedge uses React paired with TypeScript to form its user, facing interface. This part talks to the back end using RESTful routes when handling resources. Real time updates arrive through WebSocket connections instead. The connection happens over clearly defined paths that FastAPI sets up on its own. Because of how it is structured, each available route gets recorded without extra steps. Documentation appears live, ready to explore at /docs. Testing every call happens directly inside the browser thanks to auto generated pages.

6.5 Natural Language Processing for Sentiment Analysis

A trained eye adapts better to detail, Fin BERT takes BERT and reshapes it through exposure to vast amounts of financial text, then sharpens its aim toward spotting sentiment (Araci, 2019; Devlin et al., 2019; Huang et al., 2023). Evidence backs specialized systems; they outperform broad ones when nuance matters. On the SEntFiN test set, this model hit 93.27% in F1, measure, accuracy reached 91.08% (Huang et al., 2023). Off-the-shelf models stumbled where meaning hides between lines.

Midway through processing, financial headlines enter Quantedge's system without waiting, each piece moves into Fin BERT to get sorted by mood (Araci, 2019). A score forms next, sliding between minus one and plus one based on emotional tilt. From there, results feed into three separate spots across the platform. One slot adjusts trading logic when news sensitivity is turned on. Another nudges stop-loss levels tighter if bad vibes stick around for certain assets. Lastly, ongoing sour coverage quietly drags down how much gets assigned to those names during portfolio shaping.

7. RISK MANAGEMENT AND PERFORMANCE EVALUATION

7.1 Risk Metrics

What if things go very wrong? That's what Value at Risk tries to estimate, the worst loss likely under normal conditions. Yet once past that point, VaR gives no clue how bad it could get. When numbers jump beyond expectations, Conditional Value at Risk steps in, showing what average damage might look like (Fillpi et. al., 2020). At Quantedge, decisions rely on CVaR since real danger lies not just in how often crashes happen but in how deep they bite. If risk spikes too high, safeguards activate based on these deeper measures, matching reaction size to actual threat level.

One way to judge returns against overall swings is the Sharpe ratio (Sharpe, W. F., 1998; Kubo, K., & Nakagawa, K., 2025). Another way, Quantedge looks at Sortino, Calmar, and how often strategies win, mixing views so no one number hides what's really happening. When it comes to the AI system for financial insight, a similar idea shows up through chance, weighted results from simulations. Instead of comparing average gains to typical drops, they measure likely profit against potential loss, like a custom version of Sharpe built on random trials instead. Table-1 represents the risk metric applied on these systems.

Table 1. Risk metrics applied across both systems

Metric	Definition	Application in Quantedge	Application in Risk Intelligence System
VaR (95%)	Max loss not exceeded with 95% probability	Pre-trade constraint on daily loss	Monte Carlo 5th percentile outcome
CVaR	Expected loss in worst 5% of scenarios	Kill switch and stop-loss calibration	Probability-weighted downside characterization
Sharpe Ratio	Excess return per unit of total volatility	Strategy comparison and selection	Monte Carlo gain-to-shortfall ratio
Maximum Drawdown	Largest peak-to-trough portfolio decline	Account-level drawdown threshold	Worst-case simulation trajectory
Sortino Ratio	Excess return per unit of downside volatility	Complementary to Sharpe for strategy evaluation	Not directly applicable

7.2 Testing Models with Past Data

Testing old market data to guess how a trading method might do later is called back testing. Using tomorrow's facts to shape yesterday's choices? That sneaky mistake, look ahead bias, ruins more tests than any other flaw (López de Prado, 2018). At

Quant edge, their system runs candle by candle like a clock ticking forward, never peeking ahead; each moment gets only what was known up to that point. Updates happen strictly when new data arrives, nothing sooner.

Too much fit can break a back test. Instead of one fixed test stretch, shifting future, facing chunks check how well rules hold up over time (López de Prado, 2018). At Quant edge, passing this moving checkpoint must happen before any method moves ahead. A tactic never jumps to live review without first proving it works beyond past data.

When building the AI-driven Financial Risk and Intelligence System, we check how well models perform by splitting data carefully into training and testing sets. Because class balance matters, the split keeps proportions intact across risk levels. Performance shows up through accuracy numbers, an overall F1 score that treats each class equally, along with a full confusion matrix covering all three groups. Here's what shapes trust: after assigning labels, we make sure stress indicators point the right way. That means people tagged High Risk should clearly show more frequent negative savings, bigger spending compared to income, and wilder income swings than those labeled Low Risk. Should these patterns run backward, something's off in how risks are defined. Labeling rules then get reviewed and fixed, only once they hold true does any real model training begin.

7.3 Understanding Decisions in Financial AI

Clarity within the AI based Financial Risk and Intelligence setup appears across several layers. One step in, Random Forest methods measure how much each variable shapes outcomes (Breiman, 2001), highlighting patterns like frequent negative savings, average spending levels, and shifts in income, all known markers of money trouble. Further along, individual forecasts come with clear math behind them. When someone lands in the High Risk group, they see exactly which pieces pushed their number up, and just how high each one climbed.

At Quantedge, clarity comes via the strategy DSL alongside detailed back testing summaries. Each trading condition shows plainly thanks to the DSL format; anyone can check what indicators produced a signal at a given past moment. Sentiment data from Fin BERT flows into the portfolio engine while keeping confidence levels and article sources intact (Araci, 2019; Huang et al., 2023). This setup lets someone follow an investment shift straight back to the specific news item behind it.

8. CHALLENGES AND ETHICS

8.1 Hidden Biases in Automated Decisions

Out of balance results can emerge when systems learn from past trends baked into data, where old unfairness quietly shapes new decisions. Patterns picked up during learning carry forward hidden slants, even without anyone meaning harm. What looks neutral on the surface may still tip scales behind the scenes. Learned behaviors mirror unequal realities already present in examples used to train them.

A person's money habits show more than their bank balance ever could. Because the system watches how people spend, instead of just what they earn, it avoids favoring high earners. Ratios and patterns replace dollar amounts, shifting focus from totals to trends. This means someone earning little can look financially responsible if they manage well. Synthetic profiles spread every income group across each behavior type. Income alone never defines the outcome when choices matter more. Fairness grows quietly when design ignores wealth gaps on purpose.

Still, designing features won't wipe out bias completely. When models pull behavior data from groups facing distinct money realities, their decision lines might tilt without adjustment. Equity demands fresh tuning of those lines when settings shift. Checking how often errors hit each group must happen first, only then should it go live (Jiang et al., 2023).

8.2 Data Privacy and Security

Running only on fake numbers, the system sidesteps privacy issues right now. Real people's money details never enter the pipeline, no collection, no storage, no handling at all. Shifting to live use though? That opens a new layer. Privacy safeguards become essential: less data taken, strict usage rules, ways for users to claim control. Laws passed in India during 2023 set firm ground here. Those rules cover every angle mentioned. Building them into the core comes before anything goes live.

Because Quantedge handles live broker logins, trade positions, and money amounts, privacy risks show up faster here. Instead of saving keys in code, they pull them from system settings when needed. Execution rules are checked on the server so changes can't be forced from outside. Every shift in an order's status gets recorded into a PostgreSQL log for review later. When connecting to Kotak Neo, login happens through OAuth, which means passwords never touch Quantedge systems at any point.

8.3 Regulatory Compliance

India's market regulator, SEBI, laid out rules for algorithm, based trading where brokers must keep full records of every trade order, run automatic safety checks before trades happen, limit actions through set thresholds, confirm access using dual verification steps, then routinely assess how each model performs (Securities and Exchange Board of India, 2025). These two setups discussed here follow those guidelines closely. Built-in safeguards inside Quantedge's system stop risky trades ahead of time, matching what regulators expect. Every shift in an order's status gets logged so officials can trace activity later. A clear math, driven method behind the risk scoring makes decisions understandable, which fits expectations under responsible digital credit practices.

9. AI DRIVEN TRADING AND PORTFOLIO OPTIMIZATION FRAMEWORK

What holds a trading setup together isn't just code or charts, it's the thinking behind how pieces fit. A graph here, a rule maker there, tools to limit loss, systems to place trades, each does little if left on its own. Strength shows up when they link tightly. When numbers pass smoothly from stage to stage matters. So does how strictly boundaries are kept at each handoff. Just as vital, the whole machine sees what happens after choices unfold, then shifts slightly in response. Think of machine learning not like some magic add, on, instead see it woven into motion, a flow starting with gathering raw facts and shaping them, moving into tuning models and crafting rules, ending with testing past runs and trying real market action, then doing it again and again as fresh signals arrive (López de Prado, 2018). That structure shapes Quant edge, not step by step in straight lines, rather as a loop always turning, where results from live plays return to reshape the ideas that began them.

9.1 The Unified Pipeline a System Overview

Starting at the front, Quantedge puts control in the hands of the person using it, no sitting back, just shaping choices: what markets to watch, how trades should form, where risks get capped, which goal drives decisions. That setup isn't accidental. Big trading systems still rely on people thinking, only now those thoughts follow clear rules. What the system does is hold each idea steady, test whether numbers support it before money moves, then keep watching every move after launch.

First up, someone logs into the web platform and heads to the Algo Builder. Moving forward, they pick stocks or derivatives listed on the NSE, either equities or futures and options. Instead of writing code, they set rules by choosing signals based on chart patterns or math tools. One step at a time, each buy trigger, sell signal, and trade size gets mapped out visually. Rather than loose descriptions, the system captures these choices as a strict blueprint made of data fields. From beginning to end, what comes out looks nothing like sentences, it's a precise package built in a special coding structure only machines can process directly. This thing gets tracked through changes, saved straight into PostgreSQL. Every bit of strategy lives here, nowhere else, as a clear, checkable history.

Step two begins with gathering data and shaping features. After setting the plan, systems pull past price details, open, high, low, close, volume, for chosen assets and periods straight from PostgreSQL time-based tables. At the same time, calculations kick off based on rule settings embedded in the approach. Each required metric rolls through the entire timeline, adjusted backward correctly so future hints never slip into earlier points by mistake. Sentiment scores tagged by time flow in alongside prices, thanks to Fin BERT scanning old news headlines (Araci, 2019; Huang et al., 2023). These figures line up second by second with market movements, matching each event to its moment. Instead of just numbers from trading, the dataset grows richer, mood joins metrics. One step further, indicators built from past price swings tag along too. All parts tick together now, locked in sync. What emerges sits complete, a single structure where value shifts, computed patterns, and public feeling coexist across identical timestamps.

Step three checks the plan by testing it on past data. Through the rule interpreter, the data table flows, producing a series of ones and zeros, one per time bar, marking when setup criteria hit. That sequence powers a simulation that moves bar by bar, triggering mock trades whenever a signal appears. Each deal gets shaped by real-world friction, the gap between buying and selling prices, movement against the trade based on size versus market flow, plus regular exchange fees. Every outcome lands in a log: what price started it, what ended it, how long it lasted, and how much was gained or lost. Once the run ends, it calculates everything, risk rewards, growth pace, worst drop, efficiency scores, success frequency, gain multiples, average outcomes. Out comes a clear summary sent back up top, saved down below too so later checks stay possible.

Sometimes a good strategy still messes up your overall mix. That is where the portfolio tool steps in. It lines up the test results of the new idea with what you already own. Using past returns from each piece, it works out how much space makes sense for the newcomer. Limits are built into the math so nothing gets oversized. The result is an updated blend designed to do more without taking on too much heat. Balance matters when adding something fresh. There's Mean, Variance, based on Markowitz (1952), that cuts down portfolio variance w Σw while aiming for a set return level. Instead of balancing returns, Risk Parity spreads risk equally among every asset included. Then comes CvaR-limited tuning, focusing on capping average losses when things go south past a given threshold (Fillpi et. al., 2020). The outcome is a list of weightings per investment shown as suggested splits. Alongside sit visuals like the efficiency edge and estimates for gain and fluctuation ahead.

Testing happens next. A plan runs in pretend mode first. Real prices feed into it right now. Time stamps match what is happening today. Money used isn't real, it mirrors your setup. This step works differently from old, data checks. It pulls current info only. Events come one at a time. Peeking ahead is impossible. Smart systems learn by doing here, not just studying past patterns. Live conditions shift; so must the method. Each run adjusts based on fresh outcomes. Past snapshots won't capture that motion. Refinement comes from contact with now. Order by order, Quant edge logs every step, from signal creation to placement, fill confirmation, opening, then closing a position, each stamped with time data anyone can check. As trades happen, results build up instantly, showing live on screen.

Hitting stage six means every trade idea gets screened first. Before anything moves toward placement, risk rules step in. Think of it as a checkpoint long before execution ever happens. Each possible order faces sharp review based on strict boundaries tied to the account. Limits around how much money could be lost are checked right away. Daily loss ceilings matter too they block trades that go beyond them. If recent losses pile up near a preset level, new orders get halted. Exposure isn't ignored either, checks happen per stock, per industry group. Nothing slips through without confirming these filters. A green light on all checks means the order moves forward. A broken rule stops the order cold. The system records what went wrong. When a limit tied to the account gets crossed, everything halts, no new orders can start. That freeze stays until the person takes a look and lifts it by hand.

A single order, once checked, moves straight into the KotakNeoBroker adapter during live operation. This piece reshapes each instruction to fit exactly what the Kotak Neo API demands before sending it out to trade. Straight after submission, feedback like fills or rejections flows back through the same channel. These incoming reports update current holdings while matching every detail with internal records. When numbers do not line up, a notice appears instantly for review.

Step seven handles tracking and data review. Once things are running, attention shifts to learning from results. From here, insights grow out of how systems behave over time. A live display shows key updates on ongoing strategies, profit and loss figures appear instantly, open trades stay visible, losses over time get mapped clearly, trigger rates for signals update continuously, alongside side by side views compared to market benchmarks. At the same time, a separate module scans headlines tied to held assets. It detects mood shifts in news coverage, flagging moments where sudden changes might push for tweaks in approach or caution levels. This layer stays alert, watching for ripple effects before they spread.

9.2 The Ongoing Cycle of Learning

A smart trading setup stands apart because it learns as things unfold rather than just relying on how it started. Instead of sticking rigidly to old rules, it adjusts based on what the market actually does. When conditions drift too far from its design, it pauses, waiting quietly until patterns match again. Movement returns only once the environment fits, like a dancer stepping back into step with music.

Feedback loops inside Quantedge work across two different time frames. Strategy by strategy, each finished forward test along with any executed trade adds fresh information into the system's logs. Over time, these entries pile up in storage, ready for comparison, showing where real results drift away from earlier simulations. When gaps grow wide, users spot patterns behind those shifts, then adjust settings to close the gap. Meanwhile, at the broader portfolio layer, recalculating ideal asset splits happens on repeat, triggered without manual input thanks to timed automation built in n8n. As incoming price movements reshape how returns relate to one another, the math reshapes allocations.

Here comes a new piece of how feelings shift over time. Instead of treating all past reactions equally, newer ones matter more because an adjusting scale fades out old data slowly. That setup matches what actually happens when emotions move markets, real impact exists, yet it does not last forever (Huynh, N. et al., 2025). When these shifting tones build up across investments held, patterns begin to show. A string of worsening updates might arrive well ahead of any visible damage in value. Those trends rise into view early, tagged quietly as possible red flags.

9.3 Quantedge functions as one integrated system

This idea isn't about separate tools stacked together instead it flows as one connected process where every part relies on the step before being done right. Built properly the whole trading structure assigns distinct roles, data handling signal creation risk control portfolio design trade execution, to specific layers. Clear boundaries exist between thinking ahead adjusting values and carrying out trades so what comes out of one phase becomes clean input for the next. No messy overlaps occur nothing slips through gaps states stay defined throughout. Each piece fits only when prior work holds firm nothing floats unattached.

At Quantedge, design shapes how parts connect. Because strategies are written in a DSL, each one must pass through parsing before becoming a stored record. A simulation runs only when events trigger it, blocking any accidental peek into tomorrow's data. Before anything trades, safeguards verify limits per account, even strong signals face these rules. Every time, the broker adapter keeps execution separate from any one broker's setup, so things stay modular. Because performance details loop back into research, the system sees what happens after choices are made while giving users clear insights to refine those choices.

A system like this doesn't just carry out transactions, it turns inquiry into action. Because of its design, individual traders gain what big firms always had: structured testing, clear rules for exposure, and decisions shaped by full, portfolio thinking. Researchers benefit too, a space opens up where ideas about markets can evolve, thanks to settings that adapt, clarity in how things work, and results tracked precisely, all while mirroring the messiness of actual trading.

10. PRACTICAL IMPLICATIONS FOR INVESTORS AND FINANCIAL INSTITUTIONS

10.1 Retail Traders Moving Beyond Gut Feelings

A single retail investor handles five hundred thousand rupees spread over five stocks listed on the National Stock Exchange, along with a regular bet on Nifty options each week. Day after day, they watch price movements without help from organized tools, relying instead on gut feelings or rough chart patterns to decide when to buy or sell. Stop losses are tracked in memory, often forgotten until damage is done. Performance checks happen only once every few weeks using whatever reports come from the brokerage. Most individual traders in India operate this way, piecemeal, reactive, disconnected. Such habits line up closely with the losing outcomes recorded officially by financial regulators (Securities and Exchange Board of India, 2024).

One trader at Quantedge begins by turning rules into code inside the Algo Builder. Not one rupee goes in until those rules face two years of old price movements, tested step by step as events unfold. What comes out? A clear summary, Sharpe number, worst drop, how often it wins, every trade shown bar after bar (Kubo, K., & Nakagawa, K., 2025). Then, without touching real money, the method runs again, this time feeding on current prices using pretend funds. That phase tackles what past data never can, will it actually work as markets move now? It is then, once validation passes, that trading moves into action, but just when preset limits stay intact. A built-in cutoff stops disaster by halting trades before losses drain everything away.

10.2 Institutional and Proprietary Trading Desks

Small prop trading teams and solo fund managers often sit between retail traders and big institutions. Not quite needing Wall Street systems, yet too complex for basic tools. These groups handle around fifteen stock positions, where success isn't just about picking winning models. It is seeing how each one behaves alongside the others. Hidden links matter. So does total downside when multiple bets stumble together. Adjusting money flow becomes essential, guided by performance, not guesswork. Enter Quantedge. Its optimization engines apply classic frameworks like mean, variance and risk parity (Markowitz, 1952). But instead of theoretical inputs, they run on live results from current tactics. Real returns feed real decisions. Clarity emerges not from assumptions, but sequences of actual gains and losses. That shift changes everything. Insight comes not in flashes, but through steady alignment of effort and outcome.

10.3 Lower Costs and Room to Grow

At Quantedge, every strategy runs on its own. Because the system watches risk per account, traders stay informed without constant checking. When the AI layer detects relevant news, it brings those insights forward instead of burying them. Portfolio adjustments happen automatically when timed workflows trigger. Attention moves away from routine tasks simply because machines handle timing now. Thinking deepens around ideas, testing, and tuning methods, areas only people navigate well. Automation doesn't just help out here, it reshapes how time gets used. That shift isn't small. It defines what makes consistent trading possible versus struggling through repetitive work.

11. FUTURE TRENDS IN AI DRIVEN INVESTMENT PLATFORMS

11.1 Generative AI Meets Financial Conversation

Big language tools are changing how people interact with AI in money, related fields right now. Instead of just showing numbers like credit ratings or investment results, old, style finance apps expect users to understand what those figures mean on their own. With smart chat systems, explanations come in everyday words, making it easier to grasp what the data says. These responses fit personal habits over time, linking today's balances to past choices. Because answers adapt to individual history, asking new questions feels more natural, less robotic. What emerges is a clearer picture, built step by step through dialogue rather than charts.

One early form of this tool works inside FinTalkBot, shaping replies by who you are. When two people ask the same thing, they get different responses, tailored, not one size fits all. Earlier chat systems just recycle fixed answers, but here it changes depending on your background. Later versions track longer talks across several messages, adjusting as the discussion unfolds. Live updates pull fresh money details the moment anything shifts. If danger levels rise or future outlooks start slipping from steady to shaky, warnings appear without waiting. That kind of heads-up wasn't possible before.

Out near the edge of automated trading, big language models slowly step into roles helping craft strategies, understanding everyday words about tactics, turning those ideas into code, like logic a system follows, then describing test outcomes using simple talk. Over at Quantedge, their rule, focused builder acts like a frame where one of these smart helper's fits right in, making it far easier for people without coding skills to build methods, yet still keeping every move clear enough to check later if needed.

11.2 Adaptive Risk Management with Real Time Behavioral Monitoring

Stuck with old rules, static risk setups like those label systems in finance tools or set limits at Quantedge hold things steady until change hits hard. When markets shift fast, they just sit there unless someone steps in to rebuild them from scratch. Smarter platforms ahead lean on AI that tweaks itself nonstop as fresh numbers roll in. These moving models adjust piece by piece, moment by moment, skipping the need to start over every time something new shows up. Picture this: a person's risk rating quietly shifting each month as bills and balances come through, nudging alerts only if it crosses into another zone. Not loud. Just quiet updates behind the scenes.

11.3 Federated Learning and Privacy Preserving Computation

Instead of gathering data in one place, models learn locally on separate devices while keeping information private. Each device improves the model using its own data, then sends just those changes, never raw details, to a shared hub (Jiang et al., 2023). When building an AI system for financial risk and intelligence, this method allows broad deployment without pooling delicate personal records. Following strict rules like DPDPA becomes simpler since only essential pieces move around, not full datasets.

11.4 How Finance and Power Are Changing Together

Instead, tools once locked inside separate high end systems now flow together into everyday software. Running complex tasks, like balancing investments, predicting trends, sorting risks, or simulating outcomes, used to demand powerful computers few could afford. Back then, only big firms with deep pockets had access. Anyone who writes Python can pull these functions straight from free code collections.

Computing power arrives through online services exactly when needed, almost without extra charge. Trading interfaces let ordinary investors place automated trades legally. Access spreads quietly, yet completely changes what individuals can do.

One part leads to another when checking money habits flows straight into making trades, all inside one smooth experience. Picture someone starting with a look at how much risk feels right for them, getting a tailored roadmap from FinTalkBot, followed by putting extra funds to work using a tested system on Quantedge. This path once needed three separate experts: a planner, an analytics specialist, and a broker talking closely together. Now it happens solo, linked quietly behind the scenes.

12. CONCLUSION

Discipline tends to earn better returns than gut feeling when facing financial markets. This idea, basic as it may sound, fully explains why algorithmic strategies exist, also what drove the creation of Quantedge. Speed, volume, and structural layers now overwhelm traditional trading methods (Botos, Á., & Fogarasi, J., 2025; O'Hara, 2015). Only those with deep pockets once had access to advanced tools needed to navigate such environments. Now, cloud computing meets free math packages, live trading interfaces, and smart models tuned to finance, opening doors slowly for individual traders and hands,on analysts alike.

Most people trading futures and options lost money in 2024–25, according to SEBI (Securities and Exchange Board of India, 2024). Nearly every tenth trader saw gains while others faced setbacks. Losses added up past 1.05 lakh crore across small investors during that time. This isn't by chance. Big firms stick to strict rules, tested methods, clear risk limits, smart fund distribution, while individuals often skip them. Tools exist today to fix this gap. What was lacking until now? A working system built on solid research, shaped around actual market conditions, easy enough for regular users yet precise like professional setups.

What stands out first is how tightly linked each step must be when putting this system together. Moving from raw data, pulled in real time or stored, requires turning it into usable inputs ahead of any signal work begins. Only after shaping those inputs does checking strategy behavior start, relying on tests built around actual market events. Results from those checks then feed directly into adjusting position choices prior to deploying money. Before anything reaches the market, safeguards stop trades that don't meet predefined limits. Breakdowns happen easily at transition points. Structures built right matter more than rules written down.

About 89 percent of worldwide trading today runs on artificial intelligence, while machine-driven systems have replaced older fixed, rule programs in what is easily the biggest tech change in trading for twenty years (Chen et al., 2024). Still, using AI comes with responsibilities. When flawed strategies get automated, or when people are cut out of monitoring risks completely, danger grows instead of shrinking. This idea shapes how Quantedge builds its systems. News signals get sorted and rated by the AI Market Intelligence part, yet it won't place trades on its own. Because even strong signals must obey preset limits, the risk controls step in before any trade happens. When something breaks, the kill switch makes sure people notice instead of letting bots keep running. Human choices drive decisions here, smarts from machines only feed into them. This setup treats insight as fuel, never as the driver.

Fast changes opened markets to many people, yet those same folks often lack the tools to handle what comes next. Now, countless individuals own demat accounts, their money riding waves driven by systems they cannot fully control. Instead of reducing complexity, Quantedge shifts how users engage with it. It brings strict standards within reach, demanding traders test ideas with real data before acting. Pre-trade checks become routine, mirroring safeguards long used by pros. A broader view shapes decisions, much like firms managing large pools of capital have done for years.

What really matters comes down to this: a smart trading setup has one job. It doesn't replace judgment. It won't promise profits. Uncertainty stays, because markets that matter can never be fully predicted. Instead, it uses machine learning to uncover complex patterns and relationships in historical market data. The recent research suggests that such models can generate meaningful predictions while their effectiveness still depends on patterns and information embedded in the data (Murray, Xia & Xiao, 2024). In this sense, intelligent trading is not about removing uncertainty, but about approaching itsystematically.

REFERENCES

Araci, D. (2019). FinBERT: Financial sentiment analysis with pre-trained language models. arXiv:1908.10063. https://arxiv.org/abs/1908.10063

Botos, Á., & Fogarasi, J. (2025, May). Algorithmic Trading in Financial Markets: A Systematic Review. In 2025 IEEE 19th International Symposium on Applied Computational Intelligence and Informatics (SACI) (pp. 1-6). IEEE. DOI: 10.1109/SACI66288.2025.11030204

Box, G. E. P., Jenkins, G. M., Reinsel, G. C., & Ljung, G. M. (2015). *Time series analysis: Forecasting and control* (5th ed.). Wiley.

Breiman, L. (2001). Random forests. *Machine Learning*, *45*(1), 5–32. DOI: 10.1023/A:1010933404324

Cartea, Á., Jaimungal, S., & Penalva, J. (2015). *Algorithmic and high-frequency trading*. Cambridge University Press.

Chen, L., Pelger, M., & Zhu, J. (2024). Deep learning in asset pricing. *Management Science*, *70*(6), 3965–3988. DOI: 10.1287/mnsc.2023.4695

Devlin, J., Chang, M.-W., Lee, K., & Toutanova, K. (2019). BERT: Pre-training of deep bidirectional transformers for language understanding. In **Proceedings of NAACL-HLT 2019** (pp. 4171–4186). DOI: 10.18653/v1/N19-1423

Fischer, T., & Krauss, C. (2018). Deep learning with long short-term memory networks for financial market predictions. *European Journal of Operational Research*, *270*(2), 654–669. DOI: 10.1016/j.ejor.2017.11.054

Giantsidi, S., & Tarantola, C. (2025). Deep learning for financial forecasting: A review of recent trends. *International Review of Economics & Finance*, *104*, 104719. DOI: 10.1016/j.iref.2025.104719

Glasserman, P. (2004). Monte Carlo methods in financial engineering (Vol. 53, pp. xiv+-596). New York: springer.

Hambly, B., Xu, R., & Yang, H. (2023). Recent advances in reinforcement learning in finance. *Mathematical Finance*, *33*(3), 437–503. DOI: 10.1111/mafi.12382

Huang, A. H., Wang, H., & Yang, Y. (2023). FinBERT: A large language model for extracting information from financial text. *Contemporary Accounting Research*, *40*(2), 806–841. DOI: 10.1111/1911-3846.12832

Huynh, N., De Mello, L., & Li, K. (2025). Evolution of investor sentiment: A systematic literature review and bibliometric analysis. *International Review of Economics & Finance, 100,* 104115. DOI: 10.1016/j.iref.2025.104115

Jensen, T. I., Kelly, B., Malamud, S., & Pedersen, L. H. (2026). Machine learning and the implementable efficient frontier. *Review of Financial Studies, 39*(10), hhag022. Advance online publication. DOI: 10.1093/rfs/hhag022

Jiang, P., Liu, X., & Zhang, Y. (2023). Federated learning for financial applications: Privacy, efficiency, and robustness. *IEEE Transactions on Computational Social Systems, 10*(4), 1580–1591. DOI: 10.1109/TCSS.2022.3215980

Kubo, K., & Nakagawa, K. (2025). Portfolio optimization using deep learning with risk aversion utility function. *Finance Research Letters, 74,* 106646. DOI: 10.1016/j.frl.2025.106761

Lim, B., & Zohren, S. (2021). Time-series forecasting with deep learning: A survey. *Philosophical Transactions. Series A, Mathematical, Physical, and Engineering Sciences, 379*(2194), 20200209. Advance online publication. DOI: 10.1098/rsta.2020.0209

Lin, C. Y., & Marques, J. A. L. (2024). Stock market prediction using artificial intelligence: A systematic review of systematic reviews. *Social Sciences & Humanities Open, 9,* 100864. DOI: 10.1016/j.ssaho.2024.100864

López de Prado, M. (2018). *Advances in financial machine learning*. Wiley.

Markowitz, H. (1952). Portfolio selection. *The Journal of Finance, 7*(1), 77–91. DOI: 10.2307/2975974

Murray, S., Xia, Y., & Xiao, H. (2024). Charting by machines. *Journal of Financial Economics, 153,* 103791. DOI: 10.1016/j.jfineco.2024.103791

O'Hara, M. (2015). High frequency market microstructure. *Journal of Financial Economics, 116*(2), 257–270. DOI: 10.1016/j.jfineco.2015.01.003

Rezaei, M., & Nezamabadi-Pour, H. (2025). A taxonomy of literature reviews and experimental study of deepreinforcement learning in portfolio management: M. Rezaei and H. Nezamabadi-Pour. *Artificial Intelligence Review, 58*(3), 94. DOI: 10.1007/s10462-024-11066-w

Securities and Exchange Board of India. (2024, September). Analysis of profit and loss of individual traders dealing in equity F&O segment: Updated study for FY22–FY24. https://www.sebi.gov.in

Securities and Exchange Board of India. (2025, February). Circular: Safer participation of retail investors in algorithmic trading (SEBI/HO/MIRSD/MIRSD-PoD/P/2025/0000013). https://www.sebi.gov.in

Sharpe, W. F. (1998). The sharpe ratio. *Streetwise–the Best of the Journal of Portfolio Management*, *3*(3), 169–185. DOI: 10.1515/9781400829408-022

Sutton, R. S., & Barto, A. G. (2018). *Reinforcement learning: An introduction* (2nd ed.). MIT Press.

Chapter 5

Artificial Intelligence and the Future of Investment Strategy:

Data-Driven Markets, Behavioural Indicators, and Adaptive Portfolio Management

Rizwan Khan
http://orcid.org/0000-0002-3942-9985
Haji Taufeeq Ali Mahavidyalaya, India

Mohammad Taqi
http://orcid.org/0000-0002-6701-7267
Bahrain Polytechnic, Bahrain

ABSTRACT

Artificial intelligence (AI) is fundamentally transforming investment strategies by enabling data-driven decision-making, behavioural insights, and adaptive portfolio management. This chapter examines the evolving role of AI in financial markets by integrating theoretical perspectives, including market efficiency and behavioural finance, with emerging empirical evidence. It explores the growing importance of big data, algorithmic trading, and AI-driven sentiment analysis in shaping market dynamics. The study further analyzes adaptive portfolio strategies, highlighting the role of machine learning and robo-advisory platforms in enhancing efficiency and personalization. In addition, it addresses key regulatory, ethical, and governance challenges, including algorithmic transparency, data privacy, and systemic risk. Through case-based insights, the chapter identifies both opportunities and limitations

DOI: 10.4018/979-8-3373-9645-3.ch005

of AI adoption. It concludes by emphasizing the need for responsible innovation, human AI collaboration, and robust policy frameworks to ensure sustainable and inclusive financial markets.

1. INTRODUCTION: THE EVOLUTION TOWARD INTELLIGENT INVESTING

Financial markets have shifted from largely intuition-based decision-making toward increasingly data-driven approaches. Traditional investment strategies rely on fundamental analysis, technical indicators, and human judgment. However, rapid growth in data availability and computing power has increased the use of Artificial Intelligence (AI) in investment and portfolio management. Recent evidence shows that AI is being applied across portfolio management, market prediction, risk assessment, and investment decision-making (Mertzanis, 2025; International Monetary Fund [IMF], 2024).

1.1 Traditional vs AI-Driven Decision-Making

Conventional investment decisions mainly rely on structured information such as earnings reports, macroeconomic indicators, and price trends. These approaches remain important, but human judgment can be affected by cognitive biases and limits in processing large and complex datasets (Fama, 1970; Kahneman, 2011).

AI-driven strategies use machine learning (ML), deep learning, and natural language processing (NLP) to process large datasets and identify patterns that may be difficult to detect through conventional methods. They can also incorporate alternative data, including news, social media, and other non-traditional sources. Recent reviews show the growing use of AI across financial trading and investment applications (Dakalbab et al., 2024).

AI can reduce some forms of subjective judgment by automating pattern recognition and portfolio processes. However, it does not remove the need for human involvement. Instead, the role of investors increasingly includes interpreting model outputs, monitoring risks, and providing strategic and ethical oversight.

1.2 Research Gap

Despite the rapid growth of AI in finance, important gaps remain. First, existing research often examines individual applications such as trading, forecasting, portfolio optimization, or sentiment analysis separately. Recent reviews also identify fragmentation across these areas and call for more integrated approaches to AI and investment management (Mertzanis, 2025).

Second, the interaction between AI and behavioural finance requires further attention. Behavioural biases such as overconfidence, loss aversion, and herding are well established in financial decision-making (Kahneman & Tversky, 1979; Thaler, 2016). However, more research is needed to understand how AI systems identify, reduce, or potentially amplify behavioural signals in financial markets.

Third, AI is changing the role of data and technology in market competition. Differences in access to data, computing capacity, and advanced algorithms can influence market structure and investment advantages. The IMF (2024) notes that wider AI adoption may improve market efficiency while also increasing opacity, concentration, and vulnerability to market disruption.

Finally, issues of explainability, data privacy, accountability, and systemic risk remain important governance concerns. Recent research highlights the need for greater attention to explainability and responsible AI in financial applications (Černevičienė & Kabašinskas, 2024).

1.3 Objectives of the Chapter

In light of these gaps, this chapter aims to:

- Examine the evolution from traditional investment strategies to AI-driven decision-making frameworks.
- Integrate theoretical perspectives from AI, market efficiency, and behavioural finance.
- Analyze the role of big data and algorithmic systems in modern financial markets.
- Explore AI applications in sentiment analysis and behavioural indicators.
- Evaluate adaptive portfolio management techniques enabled by AI.
- Assess regulatory, ethical, and governance challenges in AI-driven finance.
- Discuss empirical evidence and practical implications for investors and policymakers.

1.4 Contribution of the Study

This chapter contributes to the literature in three ways. First, it develops an integrated perspective linking data-driven markets, behavioural indicators, and adaptive portfolio management. This responds to the fragmented treatment of AI applications identified in recent research (Mertzanis, 2025).

Second, it connects technological developments with behavioural finance by examining how AI can process financial information and capture investor sentiment. This extends the discussion of AI and machine learning in stock-market decision-making (Taqi et al., 2024).

Third, the chapter considers the governance implications of AI-driven finance. It moves beyond technical performance to address explainability, responsible use, market stability, and investor protection. These issues have become increasingly important as AI adoption expands across financial markets (IMF, 2024).

2. THEORETICAL FOUNDATIONS OF AI AND FINANCIAL MARKETS

The integration of Artificial Intelligence (AI) into financial markets is changing how information is processed, decisions are made, and risks are managed. This development also raises questions about established financial theories, particularly the Efficient Market Hypothesis (EMH) and behavioural finance. AI can improve the speed and quality of information processing, but it can also create new forms of market concentration, opacity, and instability (International Monetary Fund [IMF], 2024).

2.1 Artificial Intelligence, Machine Learning, and Deep Learning in Finance

Artificial Intelligence refers to computational methods that enable machines to perform tasks associated with human intelligence. In finance, machine learning (ML) and deep learning (DL) are widely used for prediction, classification, pattern recognition, and optimization.

Machine learning includes supervised methods such as regression and support vector machines and unsupervised methods such as clustering. These techniques are applied across financial prediction, risk assessment, and asset pricing (Bishop, 2006). Deep learning uses multilayer neural networks to identify complex and nonlinear relationships in large datasets (LeCun et al., 2015).

In financial markets, these technologies support:

- Predictive analytics for asset returns and volatility
- Algorithmic trading based on real-time information
- Dynamic risk analysis and scenario assessment

- Sentiment extraction from financial text and social media

Empirical evidence shows that machine learning can capture nonlinear relationships that conventional models may miss and can improve asset pricing predictions in high-dimensional settings (Gu et al., 2020). Recent research also highlights the growing use of AI and ML in stock-market analysis and investment decision-making (Taqi et al., 2024).

However, the complexity of some AI models creates interpretability and accountability concerns. Recent research on explainable AI (XAI) in finance highlights the need to make model outputs more understandable, particularly in areas involving financial decisions and risk assessment (Černevičienė & Kabašinskas, 2024).

2.2 Efficient Market Hypothesis in the AI Era

The Efficient Market Hypothesis (EMH), proposed by Fama (1970), argues that asset prices reflect available information. It is commonly discussed in three forms: weak, semi-strong, and strong efficiency.

AI can affect market efficiency in two different ways.

Enhancement of Market Efficiency

AI systems can process large volumes of information rapidly and support faster price discovery. Algorithmic and high-frequency trading systems can identify and respond to small price differences within very short periods. This may reduce some arbitrage opportunities and improve the speed at which information enters prices.

Challenges to Market Efficiency

AI can also challenge traditional assumptions of market efficiency. Unequal access to advanced computing, high-quality data, and sophisticated algorithms may give some market participants technological advantages. AI-driven trading can also increase market speed and amplify volatility when strategies become highly correlated. The IMF (2024) notes that AI may improve liquidity and risk management while also creating greater opacity, monitoring difficulties, and vulnerability to cyber and market manipulation risks.

Thus, AI does not simply make markets more or less efficient. Its effect depends on data access, technology, market structure, and the interaction of competing algorithms.

2.3 Behavioural Finance Integration in AI-Driven Markets

Behavioural finance challenges the assumption that investors always act rationally. It emphasizes psychological factors and systematic biases such as overconfidence, loss aversion, anchoring, and herding (Kahneman & Tversky, 1979; Thaler, 2016).

AI creates two important dynamics in relation to investor behaviour.

Mitigation of Human Biases

AI-based systems can reduce some emotional and cognitive biases by applying predefined rules and data-driven processes. Robo-advisors and automated portfolio systems, for example, can reduce impulsive decisions and maintain consistent investment strategies.

Detection and Amplification of Behavioural Signals

AI can also use behavioural information as an input. NLP and sentiment analysis can identify investor mood, expectations, and market sentiment from news and online discussions. These signals can then influence trading and portfolio decisions.

This creates a two-way relationship. AI can interpret human behaviour, while AI-driven trading decisions can also affect market behaviour. Behavioural biases may therefore not disappear in AI-driven markets. They can enter models through biased data, model assumptions, or the way behavioural signals are interpreted.

2.4 Integrated Theoretical Perspective

The interaction of AI, EMH, and behavioural finance suggests a broader theoretical perspective in which:

- Markets remain partly efficient but are influenced by technology and information asymmetry.
- Investor behaviour can be measured and incorporated into financial models.
- Investment decisions are increasingly shared between human judgment and machine-based systems.

Figure 1. Conceptual Framework of AI-Driven Financial Markets

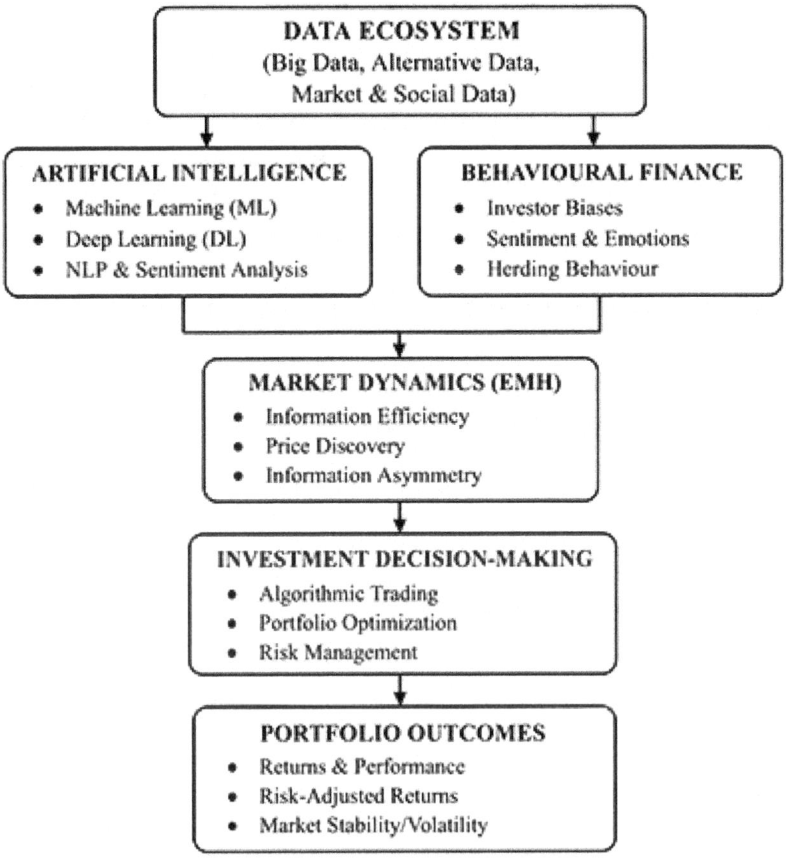

Source: *Developed by the author.*

Figure 1 brings these perspectives together by showing how AI technologies process financial data and behavioural signals within the market structure described by EMH. The interaction influences investment strategies and portfolio outcomes.

The framework consists of three core components:

1. **AI Technologies (ML, DL, NLP)** → Data processing and prediction
2. **Market Structure (EMH)** → Information efficiency and price discovery
3. **Behavioural Factors** → Investor sentiment and biases

These components interact dynamically. Their effects are shaped by data availability, technological capabilities, and regulatory conditions. The framework therefore views AI-driven finance as a socio-technical system in which human behaviour, market information, and machine-based decision-making continuously interact.

3. DATA-DRIVEN MARKETS AND FINANCIAL ECOSYSTEMS

Financial markets have become increasingly interconnected and data-driven. The growth of big data, alternative data, and advanced computing has changed how information is collected, processed, and used in investment decisions. Algorithmic trading and high-frequency trading (HFT) are important parts of this transformation. At the same time, differences in data access and technological capabilities have created new forms of information asymmetry and market power.

3.1 Big Data and Alternative Data in Financial Markets

Big data in finance includes large volumes of structured and unstructured information generated from financial transactions, market feeds, social media, satellite imagery, and digital devices. Traditional financial analysis relied mainly on structured information such as financial statements, market prices, and macroeconomic indicators. Investors now increasingly use alternative data to obtain more timely information about firms, markets, consumer activity, and investor sentiment.

Common alternative data sources include:

- Social media and online sentiment
- Satellite and geospatial information
- Web-based and consumer activity data
- Mobile and location-based data

These sources can provide information that is not immediately available through conventional financial indicators. A recent review of more than 100 studies shows that alternative data are increasingly used for investment decisions, stock prediction, risk assessment, and market analysis (Sun et al., 2024). The study also highlights their advantages in terms of timeliness, diversity, and information content.

However, alternative data also create challenges. Data may contain noise, missing observations, measurement errors, or biased information. Large datasets can also increase the risk of overfitting when models are not properly designed and validated.

3.2 Algorithmic and High-Frequency Trading

Algorithmic trading uses computer-based rules and models to automate trade execution. HFT is a specialized form of algorithmic trading that relies on very high-speed data processing and order execution. Under the MiFID II framework, HFT is characterized by high-speed analysis, rapid order submission or cancellation, and high levels of intraday trading activity.

These systems depend on:

- Low-latency technological infrastructure
- Statistical and machine learning models
- Real-time market data

Algorithmic trading has become an important part of modern market structure. Evidence from U.S. markets has previously placed algorithmic trading at around 50–70% of equity trading volume, although estimates vary by market and period. More recent BIS research also shows that HFT can have different effects across markets, improving liquidity in some settings while increasing risk in others (Aquilina et al., 2025).

Table 1. Indicative Use of Algorithmic Trading in Equity Markets

Market	Estimated Algorithmic Trading Share	Evidence/Source
United States	50–70%	U.S. regulatory evidence
Europe	Significant and widespread	ESMA/MiFID II regulatory framework
Asia-Pacific	Increasing across major markets	Zhou & Kalev (2019)

Note: Estimates are indicative rather than directly comparable. Trading practices, asset classes, exchanges, and measurement methods differ across markets.

Source: Compiled from International Monetary Fund (2024), U.S. Securities and Exchange Commission evidence, European Securities and Markets Authority regulatory materials, and Zhou and Kalev (2019).

The evidence indicates that algorithmic trading is now an important mode of execution, particularly in developed markets. Its growth reflects advances in computing, market connectivity, and electronic trading infrastructure.

Algorithmic trading can improve liquidity and accelerate information incorporation into prices. However, highly correlated strategies can also amplify market movements. The 2010 Flash Crash demonstrated how interactions among automated trading strategies can contribute to rapid market disruption (Kirilenko et al., 2017). Similar concerns remain relevant as trading systems become faster and more interconnected.

3.3 Data Advantages and Market Power

Data-driven financial ecosystems have also created new forms of competitive advantage. Market participants with access to high-quality datasets, advanced computing infrastructure, and sophisticated AI models may process information faster than others.

Three major sources of advantage are:

- Access to high-quality alternative datasets
- Superior computational infrastructure
- Advanced AI and machine learning capabilities

Large institutional investors and technology-driven firms are often better positioned to develop these capabilities. This can create barriers for smaller participants and contribute to the concentration of informational and technological advantages.

From an EMH perspective, this suggests that information efficiency may differ across market participants. Investors with better data and technology can respond more quickly to new information. Data have therefore become not only an analytical input but also a strategic asset.

The increasing use of alternative data can improve information availability, but it can also create new asymmetries when access to proprietary datasets and advanced analytical tools is uneven (Sun et al., 2024).

3.4 Integrated Perspective: Data-Driven Financial Ecosystems

The convergence of big data, algorithmic trading, and technological capabilities has created a financial ecosystem characterized by:

- Real-time information processing through AI and ML
- Increasingly automated trading environments
- Unequal access to data and technology
- Dynamic interaction between human and machine decision-makers

Competitive advantage in this environment depends not only on financial knowledge but also on access to data, computing capacity, and analytical capabilities. The resulting ecosystem can improve the speed and quality of financial decision-making while creating new concerns about market concentration, data quality, and technological inequality.

4. BEHAVIOURAL INDICATORS AND AI-DRIVEN SENTIMENT ANALYSIS

The integration of behavioural finance with Artificial Intelligence (AI) has improved the analysis of financial market behaviour. Behavioural finance recognizes that investors are influenced by psychological biases and do not always act rationally. AI-based sentiment analysis provides a way to measure these behavioural signals by converting textual and digital information into indicators that can support investment decisions.

4.1 Investor Psychology and Behavioural Biases

Investor decisions are often affected by cognitive and emotional biases. Foundational work in behavioural finance shows that individuals use heuristics that can lead to systematic errors in judgment (Kahneman & Tversky, 1979).

Key behavioural biases relevant to financial markets include:

- **Overconfidence Bias:** Investors overestimate their knowledge and predictive ability, which can encourage excessive trading.
- **Loss Aversion:** Investors tend to give greater weight to losses than to equivalent gains.
- **Herding Behaviour:** Investors follow the actions of others, which can contribute to market bubbles and sharp corrections.
- **Anchoring Bias:** Investors rely heavily on initial information when making subsequent decisions.

These biases can contribute to momentum, excess volatility, and mispricing. Their effects may become more visible during periods of market stress, when emotional responses can influence investment decisions (Thaler, 2016).

Digital platforms have also made behavioural information more visible. Investor opinions and reactions are continuously expressed through news, social media, and online financial communities. These digital traces provide new sources for measuring market sentiment.

4.2 AI-Based Sentiment Analysis: NLP, News, and Social Media

AI-driven sentiment analysis uses Natural Language Processing (NLP) and machine learning to extract information from unstructured text. It converts qualitative signals into measurable indicators that can be incorporated into financial models.

Sources of Sentiment Data

- Financial news and earnings announcements
- Social media and online financial forums
- Corporate disclosures and reports
- Analyst opinions and financial commentary

Techniques in AI-Based Sentiment Analysis

AI systems use several NLP approaches, including:

- **Lexicon-based approaches:** Financial dictionaries such as the Loughran–McDonald dictionary.
- **Machine learning classifiers:** Naïve Bayes and Support Vector Machines.
- **Deep learning models:** RNN, LSTM, BERT, and other transformer-based models.

The Loughran–McDonald approach is particularly useful because general-purpose dictionaries can misclassify words when applied to financial text (Loughran & McDonald, 2011). Recent studies show further progress through transformer-based models. For example, Kirtac and Germano (2024) compare OPT, BERT, FinBERT, and the Loughran–McDonald dictionary using a large sample of financial news and show the potential of large language models for sentiment-based trading. FinSentGPT also demonstrates the potential of language models for contextual and multilingual financial sentiment analysis (Mahdavi Ardekani et al., 2024).

Table 2. AI Techniques for Sentiment Analysis in Financial Markets

Technique Type	Methods	Key Features	Financial Application
Lexicon-Based	Loughran–McDonald Dictionary	Predefined financial sentiment words	Earnings and disclosure analysis
Machine Learning	SVM, Naïve Bayes	Supervised classification	News sentiment prediction
Deep Learning	RNN, LSTM, BERT	Context-aware analysis	Social media and real-time sentiment
Hybrid Models	ML + NLP + Big Data	Combines multiple approaches	Trading and investment signals

Source: Compiled from Loughran and McDonald (2011), Kirtac and Germano (2024), and Mahdavi Ardekani et al. (2024).

As shown in **Figure 1**, sentiment analysis forms the behavioural component of the broader AI-driven financial framework. AI processes textual information and behavioural signals, which can then influence investment strategies and portfolio decisions. This creates a link between investor psychology, data processing, and market outcomes.

4.3 Human vs Machine Decision-Making in Financial Markets

The growing use of AI raises questions about the relative roles of human judgment and machine intelligence. AI offers advantages in speed, scalability, and data processing, while human judgment remains important for contextual interpretation, ethical decisions, and strategic oversight.

Advantages of AI Systems

- Processing large volumes of real-time data
- Reducing some emotional biases
- Consistent and rule-based decision-making
- Efficient pattern recognition

Limitations of AI Systems

- Limited interpretability or the "black-box" problem
- Dependence on historical data and risk of overfitting
- Exposure to biased or incomplete datasets
- Difficulty handling unprecedented events

Complementarity Between Humans and AI

AI is therefore better viewed as a complement to human judgment rather than a complete replacement. Portfolio managers can use AI-generated signals while retaining responsibility for strategic decisions. Human oversight is also important for monitoring model performance, accountability, and ethical risks. This is consistent with the growing emphasis on explainable AI in financial applications (Černevičienė & Kabašinskas, 2024).

4.4 Integrated Perspective on Behavioural Indicators and AI

The interaction between behavioural finance and AI-driven sentiment analysis provides a more detailed view of financial decision-making. As represented in

Figure 1, the framework connects AI technologies with behavioural factors and market structure. Sentiment indicators act as an important link between investor psychology and AI-based investment decisions.

The resulting financial environment is characterized by:

- Quantification of investor psychology through sentiment indicators
- Real-time monitoring of market sentiment
- Integration of qualitative and quantitative information
- Feedback between human behaviour and algorithmic responses

This integration can improve the use of behavioural information in investment decisions. However, it can also amplify market sentiment when multiple algorithms respond to similar signals. AI therefore does not simply measure investor behaviour; its responses can also influence subsequent market behaviour.

5. ADAPTIVE PORTFOLIO MANAGEMENT AND AI APPLICATIONS

The shift toward data-driven financial markets is changing portfolio management. Traditional portfolio theory remains important, but AI-based approaches increasingly complement it by using real-time information, machine learning, and automated processes. These approaches can support portfolio construction, risk management, and investor personalization.

5.1 Dynamic Portfolio Strategies in the AI Era

Classical portfolio theory, particularly the mean–variance framework introduced by Markowitz (1952), constructs portfolios using expected returns and risk. Although this framework remains foundational, it relies on assumptions about expected returns, variances, and relationships among assets.

AI-driven strategies provide a more adaptive approach. Machine learning models can update predictions as new information becomes available and can identify nonlinear relationships within large datasets. They can support:

- Real-time portfolio rebalancing based on changing risk and return conditions
- Nonlinear optimization across multiple assets
- Detection of changing market regimes
- Integration of alternative and unstructured data

Recent evidence supports the growing use of machine learning in asset pricing and portfolio optimization. Gu et al. (2020) show that machine learning can identify nonlinear relationships that improve the prediction of expected returns. More recent research also reports the potential of automated machine learning and deep learning for asset pricing and portfolio optimization (Huang et al., 2024).

As shown in **Figure 1**, AI technologies form the data-processing component of the broader framework. Their outputs can incorporate both market information and behavioural signals when portfolio decisions are made. This creates a link between AI-based prediction, investor behaviour, and adaptive portfolio allocation.

5.2 AI-Driven Asset Allocation and Robo-Advisors

AI technologies have also supported the growth of robo-advisors, which provide automated investment recommendations and portfolio management. These platforms use algorithms to construct portfolios based on investor characteristics such as risk tolerance, financial goals, and investment horizon.

Key Features of AI-Driven Asset Allocation

- Automated portfolio construction based on investor characteristics
- Continuous monitoring and rebalancing
- Lower operating costs through automation
- Wider access to investment services

Recent research shows that robo-advisors have become an important area of AI-enabled investment management, covering portfolio construction, investor behaviour, and financial advice (Cardillo & Chiappini, 2024). Evidence from U.S. investors also suggests that robo-advising can improve diversification and reduce some portfolio costs .

Robo-advisory can therefore broaden access to investment services. However, concerns remain about transparency, model suitability, data use, and the ability of standardized algorithms to address different investor circumstances.

5.3 Risk Management and Personalization

Risk management is a central part of portfolio management. Traditional models such as Value-at-Risk (VaR) often rely on historical distributions and simplifying assumptions. AI-based systems can complement these approaches by using larger datasets and identifying nonlinear relationships.

AI-driven risk management can support:

- Real-time risk monitoring
- Scenario analysis and stress testing
- Early detection of market anomalies
- Identification of nonlinear and tail risks

Recent research indicates that AI is increasingly being applied to portfolio optimization, forecasting, and risk management, although explainability and model governance remain important challenges (Mertzanis, 2025).

Personalization in Portfolio Management

AI can also tailor investment strategies to individual characteristics, including:

- Risk tolerance
- Investment horizon
- Financial goals
- Behavioural preferences

This moves portfolio management away from standardized strategies toward more investor-specific solutions. It can also support wider access to financial advice. However, personalization depends on the quality and appropriate use of personal data. Privacy, algorithmic bias, and model suitability therefore remain important concerns.

5.4 Comparative Perspective: Traditional vs AI-Driven Portfolio Management

Table 3. Traditional vs AI-Driven Portfolio Management

Dimension	Traditional Portfolio Management	AI-Driven Portfolio Management
Decision Framework	Relatively static and rule-based	Dynamic and adaptive
Data Usage	Mainly historical and structured	Real-time, structured, and unstructured
Optimization	Mean–variance and other conventional models	ML-based and nonlinear methods
Rebalancing	Periodic	More frequent and potentially automated
Risk Management	Historical and model-based	Predictive and data-driven
Personalization	Relatively limited	Greater scope for personalization

continued on following page

Table 3. Continued

Dimension	Traditional Portfolio Management	AI-Driven Portfolio Management
Cost Structure	Higher human involvement	Greater scope for automation
Behavioural Bias	Exposed to human biases	Some biases may be reduced but not eliminated

Source: Developed by the author based on Markowitz (1952), Gu et al. (2020), and recent AI-finance literature.

The comparison shows that AI does not make traditional portfolio theory obsolete. Instead, it adds greater flexibility in data processing, prediction, monitoring, and portfolio adjustment.

5.5 Integrated Perspective: Adaptive Portfolio Ecosystem

The integration of AI into portfolio management creates an adaptive ecosystem characterized by:

- Continuous learning and data-based decision-making
- Integration of market and behavioural information
- Greater automation of investment processes
- Predictive risk monitoring
- Increased scope for personalization

As illustrated in **Figure 1**, AI technologies process market and behavioural information before these signals influence investment strategies and portfolio outcomes. This creates a connection between the behavioural indicators discussed in Section 4 and the adaptive portfolio strategies examined in this section.

The resulting portfolio ecosystem is therefore not entirely machine-driven. Human oversight, investor preferences, and regulatory requirements remain important. AI makes portfolio management more adaptive, but its effectiveness depends on data quality, model reliability, and appropriate governance.

6. REGULATORY, ETHICAL, AND GOVERNANCE CHALLENGES

The increasing use of Artificial Intelligence (AI) in financial markets has created new regulatory, ethical, and governance challenges. AI can improve efficiency, analytics, and financial services, but it also creates concerns about transparency, data privacy, accountability, cybersecurity, and systemic risk. The Financial Stability Board (FSB, 2024) identifies model risk, data quality, cyber risk, market concentration, and third-party dependencies as important vulnerabilities that may affect financial stability.

6.1 Algorithmic Transparency and the Black-Box Problem

One of the major challenges in AI-driven finance is the limited transparency of complex models, often described as the "black-box" problem. Advanced machine learning and deep learning models can use complex relationships that are difficult to interpret, even when their predictions are accurate.

This creates several concerns:

- Limited explainability of investment and risk decisions
- Difficulty auditing algorithms for compliance
- Challenges in identifying errors and bias
- Reduced confidence among investors and regulators

In financial markets, where automated decisions can have significant economic effects, explainability is an important governance issue. Recent regulatory discussions therefore emphasize model validation, monitoring, accountability, and appropriate human oversight. The FSB (2024) also identifies model risk, data quality, and governance as important areas requiring regulatory attention.

Opaque algorithms can also create wider market risks when similar models interact or respond to the same information. This may increase correlations between trading strategies and amplify market movements.

6.2 Data Privacy, Cybersecurity, and Emerging AI Risks

AI systems depend heavily on large datasets, including financial and personal information. This creates concerns about privacy, data security, data quality, and the responsible use of information.

Data Privacy Challenges

- Collection and processing of personal financial data
- Unauthorized use or sharing of information
- Algorithmic discrimination arising from biased data
- Compliance with data protection requirements

The growing use of personalized financial services increases these concerns because firms may collect detailed information about investor behaviour, preferences, and financial circumstances.

Cybersecurity and Adversarial Risks

AI-driven financial systems may also face:

- Data breaches and identity theft
- Adversarial attacks on machine learning models
- Model poisoning and manipulation of training data
- Manipulation of automated trading systems
- Risks arising from interconnected digital infrastructure

Adversarial attacks are particularly important because an attacker may deliberately manipulate input data to influence an AI system's output. The BIS (2025) identifies model poisoning and disinformation campaigns among emerging AI-related cyber vulnerabilities in finance.

Model Collapse

Another emerging concern is **model collapse**. It occurs when AI models are repeatedly trained on AI-generated data and gradually lose information about the original data distribution. Shumailov et al. (2024) demonstrate that recursive training on generated data can cause models to lose important features of the underlying data distribution.

This issue is relevant to finance because financial AI systems increasingly process online text, news, social media content, and other digital information. If AI-generated financial content becomes part of future training datasets without adequate controls, models may learn distorted signals and produce less reliable outputs. This creates a need for data provenance, human-generated reference datasets, and continuous model validation.

6.3 Global Regulatory Responses

Regulatory approaches to AI in finance are developing across jurisdictions. Although there is no single global framework, several broad approaches have emerged.

1. Principles-Based Regulation

Regulators emphasize principles such as fairness, accountability, transparency, and explainability. This provides flexibility but may leave implementation details to individual institutions.

2. Risk-Based Regulation

AI applications can be assessed according to their potential impact and risk. Higher-risk applications may require stronger controls, testing, monitoring, and human oversight.

3. Data Protection Frameworks

Data protection rules place requirements on the collection, processing, storage, and use of personal information. These requirements are particularly relevant to AI systems that rely on detailed customer data.

4. Financial Market Regulation

Financial regulators increasingly focus on:

- Pre-trade risk controls
- Algorithm testing and validation
- Market-abuse monitoring
- Record keeping and auditability
- Model governance and supervision

IOSCO's 2025 work on AI in capital markets highlights risks related to investor protection, market integrity, and financial stability and calls for regulatory responses that reflect the growing use of AI in capital markets.

6.4 Governance and Ethical Considerations

Regulation alone is not sufficient. Financial institutions also need internal governance mechanisms to ensure that AI systems are used responsibly. This includes clear accountability, model validation, data controls, and ongoing monitoring.

Key Ethical Issues

- **Algorithmic Bias and Fairness:** Models may reproduce existing biases in their training data.
- **Accountability:** Responsibility must remain clear when decisions are supported or made by automated systems.
- **Transparency vs. Proprietary Models:** Institutions need to balance explainability with protection of proprietary technology.
- **Financial Inclusion vs. Exclusion:** Automated systems may disadvantage individuals with limited or non-standard digital data.

Effective governance should therefore include:

- Model validation and independent review
- Data quality and documentation controls
- Regular testing for bias and performance
- Human oversight of high-impact decisions
- Cross-functional oversight involving financial, technical, and regulatory expertise

This governance perspective is consistent with the broader view that responsible financial innovation requires both technological capability and institutional accountability.

6.5 Integrated Perspective: Toward Responsible AI in Finance

The regulatory and ethical challenges associated with AI highlight the need for a balanced approach. Key priorities include:

- Improving algorithmic transparency and explainability
- Strengthening data protection and cybersecurity
- Monitoring adversarial attacks and model poisoning
- Preventing data contamination and model collapse
- Promoting regulatory coordination
- Establishing clear accountability and human oversight

AI can improve financial services, but its benefits depend on the quality of the data, the reliability of models, and the strength of governance arrangements. The IMF (2024) notes that AI may improve risk management and market liquidity while also increasing risks related to market speed, opacity, cyber threats, and manipulation. Therefore, responsible AI in finance requires innovation to be accompanied by appropriate safeguards, monitoring, and institutional accountability.

7. REAL-WORLD APPLICATIONS AND EMPIRICAL EVIDENCE

Artificial intelligence (AI) is increasingly embedded in financial decision-making. Its applications range from quantitative investment and risk analysis to automated advisory services. The evidence, however, does not support a simple claim that AI consistently outperforms human decision-makers. Outcomes depend on data quality, model design, market conditions, implementation, and governance. This section examines these applications and considers both their performance potential and their limitations.

7.1 AI in Hedge Funds and Asset Management

Hedge funds and institutional asset managers have been early users of quantitative and machine-learning methods. Common applications include pattern recognition, return prediction, natural language processing, alternative-data analysis, and automated execution. These applications allow firms to examine large numbers of variables and identify nonlinear relationships that may be difficult to capture through conventional models.

Empirical evidence supports some of these advantages. Gu et al. (2020) compare several machine-learning methods for asset pricing and find that tree-based and neural-network models can improve return prediction, particularly by capturing nonlinear interactions among predictors. However, the authors also emphasize the risk of overfitting and the importance of out-of-sample performance.

Renaissance Technologies provides a prominent example of systematic quantitative investing. Its Medallion Fund has reported exceptional long-term performance, with Zuckerman (2019) documenting average annual returns of about 66% before fees and 39% after fees between 1988 and 2018. These figures should be interpreted cautiously because the fund is highly private and its detailed investment process is not publicly disclosed. Thus, the case demonstrates the potential of systematic quantitative methods rather than proving that AI alone produces superior returns.

As more institutions adopt similar data-driven techniques, technological capability may become less distinctive. Competitive advantage increasingly depends on access to high-quality data, research expertise, computing infrastructure, execution capabilities, and effective model governance.

7.2 Robo-Advisory in Emerging Markets

Robo-advisory is another important application of AI and algorithmic decision-making. These platforms automate activities such as investor profiling, portfolio construction, asset allocation, and rebalancing. Their main attractions are scalability, lower operating costs, and simplified access to investment services.

Evidence from India indicates that adoption remains developing rather than universal. A 2024 study of 445 Indian investors found that trust, anxiety, performance expectancy, and preference for human advice significantly influence intentions to adopt robo-advisory services (Fatima & Chakraborty, 2024). Another recent study identifies perceived risk, technological anxiety, and personal innovativeness as important factors affecting Indian investors' adoption decisions.

These findings are important for emerging markets. Technical capability alone does not guarantee adoption. Financial literacy, trust, perceived risk, and the availability of human support can influence whether investors accept automated recommendations. Hybrid models that combine algorithmic recommendations with human advice may therefore remain important, particularly for less experienced investors.

7.3 Lessons from AI Successes and Failures

The practical record of AI and automated systems in finance is mixed. Their main strengths are speed, scalability, consistency, and the ability to process large datasets. These characteristics are particularly valuable in return prediction, anomaly detection, portfolio analysis, and automated execution.

Machine-learning models can improve prediction when relevant information is available in high-dimensional datasets. However, predictive performance in historical data does not guarantee performance under new market conditions (Gu et al., 2020). Models can become overfitted, sensitive to changes in data-generating processes, or dependent on relationships that disappear when other market participants discover them.

The risks of automated trading are also illustrated by the 2010 Flash Crash. More directly, the Knight Capital incident of 1 August 2012 demonstrates how a software failure can produce substantial market and firm-level consequences. According to the U.S. Securities and Exchange Commission, Knight Capital's faulty software generated more than four million erroneous orders while attempting to execute only 212 customer orders. The firm subsequently suffered losses exceeding $460 million. The SEC also found inadequate safeguards and controls around market access.

The Knight case is particularly relevant because it was not a failure of predictive intelligence. It was a failure of implementation, testing, and risk controls. This distinction is important. Sophisticated models cannot compensate for weak operational governance.

AI systems also face difficulties during extreme market events. When conditions differ sharply from historical observations, models may produce unreliable signals. Data bias, model instability, limited interpretability, and dependence on historical patterns can therefore weaken the reliability of automated financial decisions.

7.4 Integrated Perspective: From Theory to Practice

The evidence presented in this section supports the broader framework developed in this chapter. AI can strengthen financial decision-making by expanding the volume and variety of information that can be processed. However, its effectiveness depends on the interaction between technology, data, human judgment, and institutional controls.

This relationship can be understood through the framework in **Figure 1**. The technological capabilities discussed in this section provide the analytical foundation, while behavioral information and portfolio-management processes determine how those capabilities are translated into investment decisions. The evidence also shows that technological efficiency does not eliminate human responsibility. Instead, it changes the role of human decision-makers from direct execution toward model supervision, interpretation, validation, and risk control.

The emerging pattern is therefore better described as **augmented intelligence** rather than complete replacement of human judgment. AI can improve speed and analytical capacity, while human expertise remains important when data are incomplete, market conditions change, or models produce ambiguous signals.

7.5 Empirical Evidence on AI Adoption and Algorithmic Trading

Recent evidence confirms that AI has moved beyond isolated experiments within financial services. The World Economic Forum's global survey of financial institutions reports that 85% of respondents were already using some form of AI, with investment managers among the sectors reporting the highest levels of adoption. Risk management was one of the most common areas of application.

This evidence supports the argument that AI is becoming part of the operational infrastructure of finance. However, adoption should not be interpreted as evidence of superior investment performance. Institutions may use AI for fraud detection, customer analytics, risk management, compliance, and operational processes without using it directly to generate investment returns.

Algorithmic trading has similarly become an important component of modern markets. Earlier evidence from the Federal Reserve Bank of Chicago estimated that high-frequency trading firms accounted for about 70% of U.S. equity trading volume in 2009. Such estimates also illustrate why caution is necessary when comparing market statistics: definitions of algorithmic, automated, and high-frequency trading differ across studies and markets. The CFTC has similarly noted difficulties in obtaining a precise estimate because these categories overlap.

The empirical evidence therefore supports two conclusions. First, automated and AI-supported systems have become structurally important to financial markets. Second, the scale of adoption does not by itself demonstrate that these systems create persistent abnormal returns.

7.6 Case Study: AI-Driven Quantitative Investing – Renaissance Technologies

7.6.1 Background and Institutional Context

Renaissance Technologies is one of the most prominent examples of systematic quantitative investing. Founded by mathematician James Simons, the firm developed a research-driven approach that placed mathematics, statistics, computing, and systematic trading at the centre of investment decisions.

Its Medallion Fund is particularly notable for its reported long-term performance. Zuckerman (2019) reports average annual returns of approximately 66% before fees and 39% after fees between 1988 and 2018. The fund is highly private and has been closed to outside investors for many years. Consequently, its performance figures should be viewed as documented estimates rather than as a transparent, publicly replicable investment record.

7.6.2 Data-Driven Investment Strategy

The precise models used by Renaissance Technologies remain proprietary. Public accounts nevertheless indicate a strong emphasis on systematic research, large datasets, statistical modelling, and automated trading. It is therefore more accurate to describe the firm's approach as **data-driven quantitative investing** rather than assume that all of its methods correspond to contemporary AI techniques.

This distinction matters. The success of Renaissance cannot be reduced to a single machine-learning model. Its advantage appears to have developed from a combination of research expertise, data, computing capacity, statistical modelling, trading infrastructure, and disciplined execution.

The broader empirical literature supports the usefulness of this type of approach. Gu et al. (2020) show that machine-learning methods can improve asset-pricing forecasts by identifying nonlinear relationships among large numbers of predictors.

However, they also demonstrate why model selection and controls against overfitting are essential.

7.6.3 Performance Evidence

The reported performance of Medallion is exceptional. According to Zuckerman (2019), the fund generated approximately 39% average annual returns after fees between 1988 and 2018. Such performance provides an important real-world example of the potential of systematic quantitative investment.

However, it should not be used as evidence that AI consistently outperforms traditional investment approaches. Medallion is a highly specialized and private fund, and its strategies cannot be independently replicated from publicly available information. Moreover, its historical success reflects a particular institutional environment, investment universe, data resources, and execution capabilities.

7.6.4 Key Success Factors

The case highlights several factors that may support successful quantitative investing:

- strong research and statistical expertise;
- extensive data and computing infrastructure;
- systematic model development;
- rapid and disciplined execution;
- continuous testing and refinement; and
- strict risk and operational controls.

These factors reinforce the argument developed in Figure 1 that AI capability alone is insufficient. Value emerges when technological capability is combined with appropriate data, financial expertise, portfolio processes, and governance.

7.6.5 Limitations and Risks

The Renaissance case also illustrates the limits of using individual success stories as general evidence. Proprietary models restrict independent evaluation. High infrastructure and research costs create barriers to entry. Complex models can also become vulnerable to overfitting or structural changes in market relationships.

The Knight Capital incident provides a useful counterpoint. While Renaissance illustrates the potential of systematic trading, Knight demonstrates that automated systems can generate severe losses when implementation and controls fail. Together, the cases show that successful AI-driven finance requires both analytical capability and strong governance.

7.6.6 Implications for Financial Markets

The evidence from quantitative asset management and robo-advisory services suggests that AI is changing how investment decisions are produced and delivered. For institutional investors, the main advantages lie in information processing, prediction, automation, and execution. For retail investors, robo-advisory can improve access and simplify portfolio management, although trust and perceived risk remain important adoption barriers.

At the same time, greater reliance on automated systems creates new forms of risk. Concentration of similar strategies, model errors, operational failures, data problems, and limited explainability can transmit problems across financial institutions. AI should therefore be treated as part of a broader socio-technical system rather than as an independent source of investment performance.

7.6.7 Conclusion of the Case

The Renaissance case demonstrates the potential of systematic, data-intensive investment, but it does not establish that AI alone explains superior returns. When considered alongside empirical asset-pricing research, robo-advisory evidence, and the Knight Capital failure, it leads to a more balanced conclusion: AI can strengthen financial decision-making, but its benefits depend on data quality, model robustness, human oversight, and effective governance. This supports the chapter's central argument that the future of investment management is likely to involve closer interaction between intelligent technologies and human expertise.

8. CHALLENGES, FUTURE OUTLOOK, AND POLICY IMPLICATIONS

The growing use of artificial intelligence (AI) in financial markets creates substantial opportunities, but it also introduces risks that cannot be addressed through technological development alone. Model instability, data limitations, unequal access, concentration, privacy concerns, and weak accountability can affect both individual decisions and financial stability. Recent assessments by the Financial Stability Board (FSB) identify model risk, data quality, cyber risk, market correlations, and dependence on third-party providers as important vulnerabilities associated with AI adoption in finance (Financial Stability Board [FSB], 2024). The future of AI-driven finance therefore depends on combining technological capability with effective risk management and human oversight.

8.1 Model Risk, Overfitting, and Data Limitations

AI models are highly dependent on the quality and representativeness of their training data. Financial markets are particularly challenging because relationships between variables can change over time. A model that performs well in historical data may therefore produce weaker results when market conditions change.

Overfitting is a central concern. A complex model may learn patterns that are specific to the training sample rather than economically meaningful relationships. Gu et al. (2020) show that machine-learning methods can improve return prediction, but their performance depends on model specification, predictor selection, and out-of-sample evaluation. This suggests that predictive power should not be assessed solely through historical or in-sample results.

Key challenges include:

- noisy and incomplete financial data;
- changing market relationships;
- limited and uneven alternative-data quality;
- model opacity and validation difficulties; and
- vulnerability to structural breaks and extreme events.

These problems make continuous validation, stress testing, monitoring, and independent model review essential. The FSB (2024) similarly identifies model risk, data quality, and governance as important areas requiring supervisory attention.

A further concern is **model collapse**. As financial institutions increasingly use AI-generated information, future models may be trained partly on synthetic or machine-generated content. Research on recursive training shows that repeated training on generated data can progressively reduce model quality and diversity (Shumailov et al., 2024). In financial applications, this raises a broader question about whether increasingly automated information environments could weaken the quality of the data on which future models depend.

8.2 Financial Inclusion and Exclusion

AI can reduce the cost of financial services and expand access to automated investment and advisory tools. However, digital access does not automatically produce financial inclusion. Individuals with limited digital access, low financial literacy, or insufficient financial histories may benefit less from AI-enabled services.

Data-driven profiling can also create unequal outcomes when some groups are poorly represented in training data. Bias may enter through historical data, variable selection, model design, or the way automated decisions are implemented. For this reason, inclusion requires more than increasing technological availability. It requires attention to accessibility, data quality, transparency, and user protection.

The objective should be to use AI to **reduce barriers rather than reproduce existing inequalities**. Human assistance can remain important for users who need explanation, financial education, or support in interpreting automated recommendations.

8.3 Human–AI Collaboration in Future Investing

The future of investment decision-making is unlikely to depend entirely on either humans or machines. AI is particularly effective at processing large datasets, identifying patterns, and executing predefined tasks. Human professionals remain important for contextual interpretation, strategic judgment, ethical considerations, and decisions under uncertainty.

A practical human–AI model can therefore involve three stages:

- **AI-supported analysis:** models process data and generate forecasts or risk signals;
- **human validation:** investment professionals assess model outputs, assumptions, and limitations; and
- **joint decision-making:** final actions incorporate both quantitative evidence and professional judgment.

This approach is consistent with the broader idea of trustworthy AI. Tabassi (2023) emphasizes validity, reliability, security, accountability, transparency, explainability, privacy, and fairness as important characteristics of trustworthy AI systems.

Human oversight is particularly important when models are used in high-impact financial decisions. It should not mean simply keeping a person nominally "in the loop." Human reviewers need sufficient expertise, access to relevant information, and authority to question or override automated outputs.

8.4 Policy Implications

The rapid development of AI requires policymakers to focus on outcomes rather than technology alone. Existing financial regulation already addresses many risks associated with AI, but recent international assessments indicate that governance, data management, model risk, third-party dependence, and supervisory capacity require continued attention (Crisanto et al., 2024; FSB, 2024).

Five policy priorities are particularly important.

Explainability and accountability.

Financial institutions should be able to explain material automated decisions to regulators, customers, and other relevant stakeholders. The objective is not necessarily to make every model fully transparent, but to ensure that important decisions can be evaluated and challenged.

Data governance and privacy.

AI systems should operate under clear rules concerning data quality, access, security, consent, and appropriate use. Strong data governance is essential because financial AI systems often rely on sensitive personal and transactional information.

Model risk management.

Institutions should establish documented procedures for model development, validation, testing, monitoring, and retirement. Independent review is particularly important for models that influence trading, risk assessment, or customer outcomes.

Market and systemic-risk monitoring.

Regulators should monitor concentration in AI models, data providers, cloud infrastructure, and technology vendors. The FSB (2024) notes that common dependencies and market correlations could amplify financial vulnerabilities when AI adoption becomes widespread.

International regulatory coordination.

AI-driven financial activity frequently crosses national and institutional boundaries. IOSCO (2025) highlights the need to consider AI-related risks to investor protection, market integrity, and financial stability across capital markets. Greater coordination can reduce regulatory gaps while allowing responsible innovation.

8.5 Future Outlook: Toward Intelligent and Responsible Investing

AI is likely to become more deeply integrated into investment research, portfolio management, risk assessment, compliance, and financial advice. The next stage of development will involve greater use of generative AI, real-time analytics, automated decision support, and increasingly interconnected financial technologies (Aldasoro et al., 2024).

However, technological progress should not be equated with improved financial outcomes. The FSB (2024) identifies several vulnerabilities that could become more important as adoption expands, including third-party concentration, cyber risk, market correlations, model risk, and data-governance problems. These risks suggest that the future financial system will require stronger monitoring alongside continued innovation.

The central challenge is therefore not whether AI should be adopted, but **how it should be adopted responsibly**. Financial institutions will need robust data practices, continuous model evaluation, meaningful human oversight, and clear accountability. Regulators will need better information about AI adoption and its systemic effects. Investors will also need sufficient financial and digital literacy to understand the limitations of automated advice.

AI can make financial markets faster and more information-intensive, but responsible investing requires more than computational power. The long-term value of AI will depend on whether technological efficiency can be combined with transparency, resilience, fairness, and sound financial judgment.

9. CONCLUSION

Artificial intelligence is reshaping investment decision-making by changing how financial information is collected, analysed, and translated into portfolio decisions. This chapter examined this transition through the combined perspectives of financial theory, behavioural finance, AI technologies, data-driven investment, and financial regulation. The analysis shows that AI can improve the speed, scale, and sophistication of financial analysis, but its effectiveness depends on the quality of data, model design, institutional capabilities, and governance.

The evidence from quantitative asset management and robo-advisory services demonstrates that AI can support return prediction, portfolio construction, risk assessment, and automated financial advice. However, these benefits should not be interpreted as evidence that AI consistently outperforms human decision-makers. The performance of machine-learning models remains sensitive to changing market conditions, overfitting, data limitations, and model assumptions. The Renaissance Technologies case further illustrates the potential of systematic investing while also showing why exceptional performance cannot be attributed to AI alone. Data, research expertise, computing infrastructure, and disciplined execution are equally important.

The chapter also highlights the limitations of increasingly automated financial markets. The Flash Crash and Knight Capital incident demonstrate that technological sophistication can create new forms of market and operational risk when automated systems are poorly controlled. Emerging concerns surrounding adversarial manipulation, model opacity, data bias, cyber risk, and model collapse further demonstrate that AI-related risks extend beyond prediction accuracy. These challenges reinforce the need for continuous validation, stress testing, monitoring, and effective human oversight.

A central conclusion of this chapter is that the future of investment management is more likely to involve human -AI collaboration than complete automation. AI can process complex information and identify patterns at a scale that is difficult for individual decision-makers to match. Human professionals, however, remain important for contextual interpretation, ethical judgment, model validation, and decisions under uncertainty. The most effective investment systems are therefore likely to combine computational capability with human expertise.

The policy implications are equally important. Responsible AI adoption requires stronger data governance, model-risk management, explainability, privacy protection, and supervisory capacity. Financial regulators must also consider the possibility that widespread adoption of similar AI systems could create new forms of market concentration and systemic vulnerability. At the same time, policies should ensure that technological innovation does not deepen existing inequalities in access to financial services.

Overall, AI should not be viewed as a replacement for financial theory, professional judgment, or institutional governance. Rather, it represents a powerful extension of financial decision-making capabilities. Its long-term contribution will depend not simply on how advanced AI models become, but on how effectively they are integrated with reliable data, sound financial knowledge, human oversight, and responsible regulation. The transition toward AI-driven investing is therefore best understood as a socio-technical transformation of financial markets, in which technological intelligence and human judgment increasingly operate together.

REFERENCES

Aldasoro, I., Gambacorta, L., Korinek, A., Shreeti, V., & Stein, M. (2024). Intelligent financial system: How AI is transforming finance. *BIS Working Papers, 1194*. Bank for International Settlements. https://www.bis.org/publ/work1194.htm

Aquilina, M., Ibikunle, G., Rzayev, K., & Wang, X. (2025). The speed premium: High-frequency trading and the cost of capital. *BIS Working Papers, 1290*. Bank for International Settlements. https://www.bis.org/publ/work1290.htm

Bishop, C. M. (2006). *Pattern recognition and machine learning*. Springer.

Cardillo, G., & Chiappini, H. (2024). Robo-advisors: A systematic literature review. *Finance Research Letters, 62*, 105119. DOI: 10.1016/j.frl.2024.105119

Černevičienė, J., & Kabašinskas, A. (2024). Explainable artificial intelligence (XAI) in finance: A systematic literature review. *Artificial Intelligence Review, 57*(8), 216. DOI: 10.1007/s10462-024-10854-8

Crisanto, J. C., Leuterio, C. B., Prenio, J., & Yong, J. (2024). Regulating AI in the financial sector: Recent developments and main challenges. *FSI Insights, 63*. Bank for International Settlements. https://www.bis.org/fsi/publ/insights63.htm

Dakalbab, F., Abu Talib, M., Nasir, Q., & Saroufil, T. (2024). Artificial intelligence techniques in financial trading: A systematic literature review. *Journal of King Saud University. Computer and Information Sciences, 36*(3), 102015. DOI: 10.1016/j.jksuci.2024.102015

Fama, E. F. (1970). Efficient capital markets: A review of theory and empirical work. *The Journal of Finance, 25*(2), 383–417. DOI: 10.2307/2325486

Fatima, S., & Chakraborty, M. (2024). Adoption of artificial intelligence in financial services: The case of robo-advisors in India. *IIMB Management Review, 36*(2), 113–125. DOI: 10.1016/j.iimb.2024.04.002

Financial Stability Board. (2024). *The financial stability implications of artificial intelligence*. https://www.fsb.org/2024/11/the-financial-stability-implications-of-artificial-intelligence/

Gu, S., Kelly, B., & Xiu, D. (2020). Empirical asset pricing via machine learning. *Review of Financial Studies, 33*(5), 2223–2273. DOI: 10.1093/rfs/hhaa009

Huang, S., Cao, L., Sun, R., Ma, T., & Liu, S. (2024). Enhancing portfolio optimization: A two-stage approach with deep learning and portfolio optimization. *Mathematics, 12*(21), 3376. DOI: 10.3390/math12213376

International Monetary Fund. (2024). *Global financial stability report, October 2024: Steadying the course—Uncertainty, artificial intelligence, and financial stability*. International Monetary Fund.

International Organization of Securities Commissions. (2025). *Artificial intelligence in capital markets: Use cases, risks, and challenges*. IOSCO.

Kahneman, D. (2011). *Thinking, fast and slow*. Farrar, Straus and Giroux.

Kahneman, D., & Tversky, A. (1979). Prospect theory: An analysis of decision under risk. *Econometrica*, *47*(2), 263–291. DOI: 10.2307/1914185

Kirilenko, A. A., Kyle, A. S., Samadi, M., & Tuzun, T. (2017). The flash crash: High-frequency trading in an electronic market. *The Journal of Finance*, *72*(3), 967–998. DOI: 10.1111/jofi.12498

Kirtac, K., & Germano, G. (2024). Sentiment trading with large language models. *Finance Research Letters*, *62*, 105227. DOI: 10.1016/j.frl.2024.105227

LeCun, Y., Bengio, Y., & Hinton, G. (2015). Deep learning. *Nature*, *521*(7553), 436–444. DOI: 10.1038/nature14539 PMID: 26017442

Loughran, T., & McDonald, B. (2011). When is a liability not a liability? Textual analysis, dictionaries, and 10-Ks. *The Journal of Finance*, *66*(1), 35–65. DOI: 10.1111/j.1540-6261.2010.01625.x

Mahdavi Ardekani, A., Bertz, J., Bryce, C., Dowling, M., & Long, S. (2024). FinSentGPT: A universal financial sentiment engine? *International Review of Financial Analysis*, *94*, 103291. DOI: 10.1016/j.irfa.2024.103291

Markowitz, H. (1952). Portfolio selection. *The Journal of Finance*, *7*(1), 77–91. DOI: 10.1111/j.1540-6261.1952.tb01525.x

Mertzanis, C. (2025). Artificial intelligence and investment management: Structure, strategy, and governance. *International Review of Financial Analysis*, *107*, 104599. DOI: 10.1016/j.irfa.2025.104599

Securities and Exchange Commission. (2013, October 16). *SEC charges Knight Capital with violations of market access rule* (Press Release 2013-222). U.S. Securities and Exchange Commission.

Shumailov, I., Shumaylov, Z., Zhao, Y., Papernot, N., Anderson, R., & Gal, Y. (2024). AI models collapse when trained on recursively generated data. *Nature*, *631*(8022), 755–759. DOI: 10.1038/s41586-024-07566-y PMID: 39048682

Sun, Y., Liu, L., Xu, Y., Zeng, X., Shi, Y., Hu, H., Jiang, J., & Abraham, A. (2024). Alternative data in finance and business: Emerging applications and theory analysis [review]. *Financial Innovation, 10*(1), 127. DOI: 10.1186/s40854-024-00652-0

Tabassi, E. (2023). *Artificial intelligence risk management framework (AI RMF 1.0)* (NIST AI 100-1). National Institute of Standards and Technology. https://doi.org/ DOI: 10.6028/NIST.AI.100-1

Taqi, M., Hamaidan, H., & Khan, R. (2024). The prospects of artificial intelligence and machine learning in the stock market. In *Navigating the future of finance in the age of AI*. IGI Global., DOI: 10.4018/979-8-3693-4382-1.ch009

Thaler, R. H. (2016). Behavioral economics: Past, present, and future. *The American Economic Review, 106*(7), 1577–1600. DOI: 10.1257/aer.106.7.1577

World Economic Forum. (2025). *Artificial intelligence in financial services*. World Economic Forum.

Zhou, H., & Kalev, P. S. (2019). Algorithmic and high frequency trading in Asia-Pacific, now and the future. *Pacific-Basin Finance Journal, 53*, 186–207. DOI: 10.1016/j.pacfin.2018.10.006

Zuckerman, G. (2019). *The man who solved the market: How Jim Simons launched the quant revolution*. Portfolio/Penguin.

Chapter 6
AI-Enabled Green Finance and Triple Helix Governance for Renewable Energy Investment Integrity

José G. Vargas-Hernández
http://orcid.org/0000-0003-0938-4197
Business School, Universidad LaSalle Bajìo, Mexico

Selene Castañeda-Burciaga
http://orcid.org/0000-0002-2436-308X
Universidad Politécnica de Zacatecas, Mexico

Omar A. Guirette
http://orcid.org/0000-0003-1336-9475
Broward International University, USA & Universidad Politécnica de Zacatecas, Mexico

ABSTRACT

This chapter reframes sustainable economic models and green finance for renewable energy through an AI-enabled green finance lens aligned with the Triple Helix (University, Government, Industry) framework. The synthesis identifies four cross-cutting AI-enabled mechanisms that can reduce these frictions: (1) AI driven risk and scenario analytics (2) NLP based disclosure intelligence (3) AI supported MRV (including alternative data) and (4) integrity analytics to detect inconsistencies and support anti greenwashing controls. The chapter also integrates ethical, legal, and

DOI: 10.4018/979-8-3373-9645-3.ch006

societal implications (ELSI), emphasizing explainability, accountability, fairness, data governance, and energy justice as conditions for legitimate scaling. Implications are derived for green bonds, blended finance, and carbon-pricing ecosystems, proposing a practical agenda for trustworthy AI adoption in sustainable finance.

1. INTRODUCTION

The global transition toward green and renewable energy is widely recognized as both an economic imperative and a governance challenge. Despite rapid growth in climate commitments and expanding green financial markets, a persistent financing gap continues to constrain the scale, speed, and geographic equity of renewable energy deployment, particularly in emerging and developing economies. This gap is not solely a matter of insufficient capital supply; it reflects structural frictions that increase perceived risk, raise transaction costs, and undermine investor confidence. Among the most consequential frictions are information asymmetries, heterogeneous disclosure practices, weak measurement and verification capacity, and limited comparability across projects, jurisdictions, and instruments. These constraints affect the "bankability" of renewable projects, complicate blended finance structures, and slow the mobilization of private capital at the scale required for the energy transition (Polzin & Sanders, 2020).

In parallel, the financial system is undergoing a rapid digital transformation in which Artificial Intelligence (AI) is increasingly embedded in core decision processes credit scoring, risk assessment, fraud detection, portfolio optimization, and regulatory compliance (Soni, Singh, & Singh, 2025). In the context of sustainable finance, AI introduces the possibility of materially reducing the frictions that currently hinder green capital mobilization. AI-enabled analytics can improve climate risk modeling, automate the processing of ESG disclosures using natural language techniques, enhance monitoring and reporting through data integration, and support more granular project evaluation across diverse contexts (Bartelt & Röser, 2024). By lowering information costs and improving the precision of risk pricing, AI can expand the set of investable renewable energy opportunities and support the scaling of capital flows into green markets (Siriman et al., 2025).

However, positioning AI as an enabler of green finance is not merely a technical matter. The deployment of AI in financial systems raises substantial ethical, legal, and societal questions, including algorithmic bias, transparency, accountability, privacy, and the risk of reinforcing structural exclusion, especially in regions where data quality, institutional capacity, and regulatory oversight remain uneven. In sustainable finance, these concerns intersect with energy justice: AI-driven decisions can shape which communities receive investment, which projects are prioritized, and whose risks are discounted or amplified. Thus, AI enabled green finance must be analyzed not only for its efficiency potential but also for its governance requirements (Sadiq, Yasser, & Nawaz, 2025).

To address these interlinked dimensions of innovation and governance, this chapter uses the Triple Helix framework University, Government, Industry as the central conceptual lens. The Triple Helix model emphasizes that innovation and commercialization emerge from dynamic interactions among knowledge institutions (universities), regulatory and policy actors (governments), and market implementers (industry). In the context of AI enabled green finance, each helix plays a distinct and interdependent role: universities generate models, methods, and talent; governments shape data infrastructures, regulatory standards, and public risk-sharing mechanisms; and industry operationalizes AI tools, scales financial products, and integrates AI into market practices. The value of the Triple Helix lens is its ability to explain why AI adoption in green finance differs across jurisdictions and why successful deployment depends on coordinated governance, not technology alone (Lulaj, E., & Brajković, M. 2025; Zhou, C., & Etzkowitz, H. 2021).

Using systematic document analysis and literature synthesis (2020 to present), we examine how persistent financing frictions risk mispricing, heterogeneous disclosures, limited monitoring/reporting/verification (MRV) capacity, and integrity threats such as greenwashing constrain the scale and credibility of renewable energy investment. We argue that performance gains depend on coordinated Triple Helix roles: universities provide methods and validation; governments supply taxonomies, disclosure standards, data infrastructure, and oversight; and industry operationalizes tools with governance by design.

Accordingly, the core problem this chapter addresses is the following: how can AI reduce financing frictions in green and renewable energy markets while ensuring accountable governance and equitable outcomes, and what roles do universities, governments, and industry play in enabling and regulating this transformation? Building from a systematic document analysis and literature synthesis, the chapter reframes established sustainable economic models and green finance mechanisms through an AI Triple Helix lens. Rather than treating AI as a peripheral tool, the chapter places AI at the center of the analysis as an infrastructure for (i) risk assessment and pricing, (ii) disclosure analytics and data quality improvement, (iii) monitoring, reporting, and verification (MRV), and (iv) integrity mechanisms to reduce greenwashing and strengthen additionality.

The remainder of the chapter is organized as follows. Section 2 reviews the literature on sustainable finance and renewable energy economics and introduces AI enabled mechanisms that directly address financing frictions. Section 3 develops the Triple Helix framework as an innovation and governance architecture for AI in sustainable finance, complemented by relevant sustainability-oriented theories.

Section 4 presents the methodological approach based on systematic document analysis and thematic synthesis. Section 5 reinterprets the evidence on green finance instruments and financing gaps through AI enabled use cases and the Triple Helix roles that enable them. Section 6 consolidates the findings and articulates the main mechanisms through which AI can accelerate green finance while identifying governance risks. Section 7 discusses implications for theory and practice, including ELSI and energy justice considerations, and derives actionable recommendations for universities, governments, and industry. The chapter concludes by summarizing contributions, limitations, and a forward-looking research agenda for AI-enabled green finance and the energy transition.

2. CONCEPTUAL AND EMPIRICAL LITERATURE REVIEW

2.1 Sustainable economic models, green finance, and the renewable energy financing gap

Sustainable economic models provide the conceptual foundation for understanding why the energy transition requires not only technological adoption but also structural transformation in capital allocation. In ecological economics, sustainability-oriented models emphasize that economic systems must operate within biophysical limits, internalize environmental externalities, and prioritize long-term welfare over short-run optimization (Costanza et al., 2014). This framing is consistent with the view that climate mitigation and renewable energy deployment are not simply sectoral adjustments but systemic investment transitions that require durable policy coherence, institutional capacity, and financial architectures capable of mobilizing and directing capital toward projects with measurable environmental benefits.

A closely aligned perspective is the circular economy approach, which argues that sustainable growth and industrial transformation depend on decoupling value creation from resource depletion and waste accumulation (Ellen MacArthur Foundation, 2020). In the energy transition context, circular principles are increasingly relevant because scaling renewables introduces end-of-life material challenges (e.g., solar panels, wind blades, batteries) that create new sustainability risks if not managed through circular design, extended producer responsibility, and secondary materials markets (Future Earth, 2022). Complementarily, ecological modernization theory frames environmental progress as partially technology-driven and institutionally mediated, emphasizing how regulation, innovation, and market incentives can reconfigure production systems toward sustainability (Mol & Spaargaren, 2000). Taken together, these sustainability-centered models converge on a practical implication:

the energy transition depends on investment mobilization that is not only large in volume but also credible, trackable, and distributivity equitable.

Within this broader context, green finance has emerged as a central policy and market strategy for accelerating renewable energy deployment. Green finance refers to financial flows, products, and institutions that explicitly incorporate environmental objectives into capital allocation, risk management, and performance assessment. The literature highlights a portfolio of instruments including green bonds, sustainability linked finance, climate funds, carbon markets, concessional finance, and blended finance vehicles that aim to lower financing constraints and scale investment into renewable energy systems (Mishra et al., 2023). A recurring theme across these mechanisms is that scalability depends on credibility: investors and stakeholders require transparent qualification criteria (taxonomies and standards), reliable measurement of outcomes, and consistent reporting of how proceeds are used and what impacts are achieved.

Empirical evidence underscores both market growth and persistent integrity challenges. For example, global green bond issuance and the broader GSSS market have expanded rapidly, with reporting showing record issuance levels and increasing issuer diversity across sovereigns, development banks, corporations, and financial institutions (Bank for International Settlements, 2025; IFC-Amundi, 2025). Yet the literature reports mixed findings regarding additionality and environmental impact. Some studies associate green bond issuance with improved environmental performance and lower carbon intensity among issuing firms (Fatica & Panzica, 2021), while others caution that "green" labels may attach to projects that would have proceeded anyway, raising questions about additionality and claims credibility (Lam & Wurgler, 2024). This tension motivates the emergence of stricter standards and taxonomies such as those developing in the European context to strengthen market integrity and ensure that labels reflect actual environmental benefit.

Despite these market advances, a persistent renewable energy financing gap remains one of the major bottlenecks to meeting global climate goals. Comprehensive climate finance assessments report progress alongside substantial remaining gaps, with climate finance reaching record levels and private flows growing in absolute terms (Climate Policy Initiative, 2024; Climate Policy Initiative, 2025). However, estimates of required annual investment for net-zero alignment remain far above current flows, indicating a sustained global investment shortfall and uneven progress across technologies (BloombergNEF, 2025). Beyond volume, the literature stresses a key distributional pattern: financing remains highly concentrated in advanced economies and a limited set of large markets, while many emerging markets and developing economies face persistent barriers to mobilizing domestic finance and attracting international capital.

A central reason for these constraints is that the financing gap is not solely a matter of capital scarcity; it reflects structural frictions that raise perceived risk, increase transaction costs, and undermine investor confidence. These frictions include information asymmetries between project developers, investors, and regulators; heterogeneous disclosure practices and limited comparability across markets; inadequate measurement, reporting, and verification (MRV) capacity; elevated due diligence and compliance costs; and macro-financial uncertainties that amplify risk premiums. Evidence suggests that the cost of capital can be substantially higher in developing economies than in developed countries, contributing to uneven renewable deployment and reinforcing inequities in transition benefits (Climate Policy Initiative, 2024; Nature Energy, 2024). This pattern has major implications for energy justice and inclusive development: when financing costs remain structurally elevated, the transition risks becoming concentrated among wealthy economies while leaving many regions dependent on fossil fuels or excluded from transition gains.

The literature on blended finance positions it as a bridge mechanism to narrow these gaps by using catalytic capital, often from public or philanthropic sources, to mobilize private investment, reduce specific risk components, and improve project feasibility in difficult contexts (Convergence, 2024; IEEFA, 2024). Blended structures may include first-loss capital, guarantees, concessional tranches, and technical assistance, as well as structured vehicles designed to de-risk early-stage deployment. However, blended finance is operationally complex: it requires robust project evaluation, credible impact frameworks, and continuous monitoring to demonstrate additionality, integrity, and performance. These demands intensify the need for high-quality data, consistent reporting, and institutional coordination, areas where many systems remain constrained.

Policy instruments such as carbon pricing and emissions trading also shape investment incentives and financing dynamics by altering relative returns and market expectations. Evidence from cross-country policy analyses suggests that well-designed carbon pricing can influence renewable adoption, though effectiveness varies by institutional context and market design (OECD, 2024; European Commission, 2025; Nature Communications, 2025). From a green finance perspective, these policy frameworks interact with financial instruments by affecting revenue stability, risk perceptions, and long-term project viability. In practice, the common thread across green bonds, blended finance, and policy incentives is that financing effectiveness depends on credible standards, consistent measurement, and reduced information frictions—conditions that determine whether capital can scale and whether the environmental claims underpinning "green" labels are trustworthy.

Taken together, the sustainable finance and renewable energy literature converges on a practical diagnosis: the financing gap is sustained not only by limited volumes of capital, but by persistent risk, information, and verification frictions that raise costs and suppress market confidence. This diagnosis is central to the argument of this chapter, because it aligns directly with the category of problems where data-driven technologies, particularly AI, can add value by improving risk assessment, reducing information costs, strengthening disclosure analytics, and enhancing MRV and market integrity.

2.2 AI-enabled mechanisms in sustainable finance: risk, disclosure, MRV, and integrity

In parallel with the growth of sustainable finance, the financial system is undergoing a rapid digital transformation in which AI is increasingly embedded in core decision processes such as credit assessment, fraud detection, portfolio optimization, and regulatory compliance. In sustainable finance, AI can be conceptualized as an enabling infrastructure that transforms how financial actors process information, evaluate risk, and verify environmental claims. For the purposes of this chapter, AI enabled green finance refers to the use of machine learning (ML), natural language processing (NLP), computer vision, and related methods to improve the mobilization, allocation, monitoring, and governance of capital directed toward environmentally beneficial outcomes, particularly in renewable energy markets (Bm & Khanum, 2025). This definition positions AI as a capability that can directly address the structural frictions described above by increasing informational resolution, improving comparability, lowering monitoring costs, and strengthening integrity controls.

A key practical feature of AI enabled green finance is its reliance on heterogeneous data: firm disclosures, project documentation, market data, climate and geospatial indicators, remote sensing, operational performance data, and policy or regulatory records. The literature on green finance already emphasizes that credibility and scalability depend on consistent measurement and standards; AI becomes relevant precisely because it can integrate these heterogeneous sources and convert them into decision-relevant signals at scale (Jupalli, 2024). However, AI applications also introduce constraints related to data access, data governance, interoperability, and model transparency, factors that can be especially binding in emerging and developing economies where data quality and institutional capacity remain uneven (Leghemo, et al, 2025).

Mechanism 1. AI for climate and transition risk assessment and pricing.

A foundational constraint on renewable energy investment is uncertainty over physical climate risks, transition risks, policy volatility, and project-level performance variability. AI-enabled analytics can support more granular and dynamic risk assessment by integrating heterogeneous datasets into predictive and scenario-based models, enabling improved estimation of default probabilities, revenue volatility, and exposure to transition shocks. In principle, stronger risk modeling improves the pricing of uncertainty and reduces reliance on coarse proxies that often inflate perceived risk, particularly in under-studied regions, thereby supporting lower financing costs and expanded investable opportunity sets (Singh, 2025).

This mechanism is directly relevant to the financing gap dynamics documented in global climate finance assessments and cost-of-capital evidence (Climate Policy Initiative, 2024; Nature Energy, 2024), because improved risk differentiation can reduce generalized risk premiums that are not justified by project fundamentals.

Mechanism 2. AI for ESG disclosure analytics and data quality.

A persistent limitation in sustainable finance is the heterogeneity and uneven quality of ESG and climate-related disclosures. Even when standards exist, disclosures often vary in completeness, narrative framing, metric selection, and comparability. NLP methods can support automated extraction, classification, and standardization of disclosure content from reports, bond frameworks, prospectuses, and policy documents, enabling more systematic assessment of environmental claims and alignment with taxonomies. These capabilities can lower due diligence costs, increase consistency of evaluation across issuers, and improve comparability for investors (Birti, Osborne, & Maurino, 2025).

This mechanism is particularly relevant to green bond credibility challenges identified in the literature on additionality and environmental claims (Fatica & Panzica, 2021; Lam & Wurgler, 2024), because AI-enhanced disclosure analytics can strengthen pre-issuance screening and post-issuance monitoring of commitments.

Mechanism 3. AI for monitoring, reporting, and verification (MRV).

Credibility and scalability of green finance instruments depend on the ability to verify that funds are used as intended and that projects deliver measurable outcomes. AI can enhance MRV by integrating data sources (including remote sensing and operational datasets), automating anomaly detection, and supporting continuous performance monitoring. When paired with structured reporting systems, AI can assist in tracking project progress, verifying key indicators, and identifying deviations from expected performance or reporting patterns (Alhazmi, & Prokofieva, 2025).

MRV capacity is central for scaling green bond markets and ensuring "use of proceeds" integrity, particularly as issuance expands and standards tighten (Bank for International Settlements, 2025; IFC-Amundi, 2025). It is also critical for blended finance vehicles, where performance verification and reporting obligations are often conditions for continued risk-sharing and catalytic capital participation (Convergence, 2024; IEEFA, 2024).

Mechanism 4. AI for integrity: anti-greenwashing, fraud detection, and additionality.

As sustainable finance markets grow, so do concerns about greenwashing, misclassification, and strategic reporting designed to meet superficial criteria without delivering substantive environmental benefits. AI can contribute to integrity mechanisms by identifying inconsistencies between disclosures and observable outcomes, detecting anomalous reporting behavior, and supporting risk-based screening for misrepresentation. These applications can improve market confidence, strengthen additionality claims, and reduce reputational and financial risks associated with low-integrity green instruments (Sari et al., 2025).

However, integrity analytics also raises governance questions: false positives, model opacity, accountability for automated decisions, and the risk of embedding bias into screening systems, issues that become especially salient when investment access and project viability depend on algorithmic assessments (John, 2025).

Crucially, these AI-enabled mechanisms connect directly to the green finance instruments emphasized in the empirical literature. In green bonds, AI enabled disclosure analytics and MRV can enhance issuer credibility, improve post-issuance monitoring, and reinforce confidence in impact reporting, addressing the integrity and additionality concerns identified in the literature (Fatica & Panzica, 2021; Lam & Wurgler, 2024). In blended finance, AI-enabled risk assessment can support structuring decisions, improve estimation of risk components, and reduce uncertainty that otherwise necessitates expensive risk-sharing arrangements (Convergence, 2024; IEEFA, 2024). In carbon pricing and market mechanisms, AI can support monitoring and compliance analytics, enhance market surveillance, and reduce information frictions that affect investment incentives (OECD, 2024; European Commission, 2025).

Across these domains, AI has the potential to reduce financing frictions and strengthen the credibility of sustainable finance. Yet AI can also introduce new vulnerabilities linked to data governance, transparency, bias, and uneven institutional capacity. These tensions are not peripheral: they shape whether AI-enabled green finance accelerates the transition in an inclusive way or reinforces structural exclusion, particularly where data ecosystems, regulatory oversight, and technical capacity are weakest (Chouhan & Singhai, 2025).

This dual character AI as both an enabler and a governance challenge, motivates the chapter's reliance on the Triple Helix framework in the next section. Because AI-enabled green finance requires coordinated data infrastructures, regulatory standards, research capacity, and market implementation, outcomes are shaped by the interaction of universities, governments, and industry. The Triple Helix lens provides an appropriate architecture for explaining how these actors jointly enable innovation, regulate deployment, and manage the ethical, legal, and societal implications associated with AI in sustainable finance (Sadiq, et al. 2025).

3. THEORETICAL FRAMEWORK

3.1 Triple Helix as an innovation-and-governance architecture for AI-enabled green finance

The adoption of AI-enabled mechanisms in sustainable finance is not determined by technology availability alone. It depends on the institutional conditions that enable data access and quality, talent formation, methodological development, standard-setting, regulatory oversight, and market implementation. For this reason, this chapter adopts the Triple Helix framework (University, Government, Industry) as the central architecture for analyzing AI-enabled green finance. The Triple Helix perspective conceptualizes innovation and commercialization as outcomes of dynamic interactions among universities (knowledge creation and capability development), governments (policy, regulation, and public coordination), and industry (implementation, scaling, and market formation), (Tiossi & Rodrigues, 2023).

Within the domain of AI-enabled green finance, the Triple Helix lens is particularly valuable because sustainable finance is simultaneously (i) data-intensive, (ii) legitimacy-sensitive, and (iii) regulation-dependent. AI applications in risk assessment, disclosure analytics, monitoring/verification, and integrity screening require robust information infrastructures and credible governance arrangements. These requirements are especially binding in contexts characterized by fragmented data ecosystems, weak institutional capacity, or inconsistent disclosure regimes. Therefore, the Triple Helix model provides a structured way to explain cross-jurisdiction variation in AI adoption and to identify the institutional complementarities necessary for responsible scaling.

University (knowledge creation, methods, and talent).

Universities contribute by advancing research methods (e.g., machine learning approaches for climate/transition risk assessment, NLP for sustainability disclosures, and MRV analytics), developing open and reproducible measurement frameworks, and training interdisciplinary talent capable of bridging finance, data science, and sustainability. Universities also serve as relatively independent evaluators, supporting validation studies, benchmarking, and methodological transparency, functions that are crucial when AI tools influence capital allocation decisions and claims credibility.

Government (standards, infrastructure, and accountability).

Governments shape the enabling conditions for AI-enabled green finance through: (i) disclosure and reporting regulation; (ii) the development of green taxonomies and standards; (iii) public data infrastructures that improve interoperability and reduce information frictions; and (iv) oversight mechanisms that ensure accountability, privacy, and procedural fairness in automated or algorithmically supported decision-making. In the context of sustainable finance, governments also affect the viability of renewable energy investment via policy stability, carbon pricing and market design, and public risk-sharing mechanisms (e.g., guarantees, catalytic capital, or blended finance participation, Tiossi & Rodrigues, 2023). These public functions become even more critical when the objective is not only efficiency but also equitable access and energy justice.

Industry (implementation, scaling, and market formation).

Industry actors, including financial institutions, asset managers, rating agencies, project developers, and technology providers, translate AI capabilities into market practice. They operationalize AI models for underwriting, portfolio allocation, monitoring, and integrity controls; integrate AI outputs into governance processes and product designs; and scale adoption through platforms and standardized workflows. Industry implementation also determines whether AI-enabled mechanisms improve market integrity (e.g., by detecting greenwashing) or create new vulnerabilities (e.g., opaque models, bias, or overreliance on low-quality data, Sadiq, et al. 2025).

From a Triple Helix perspective, the effectiveness of AI-enabled green finance depends on interaction mechanisms rather than isolated actor performance. Key interaction mechanisms include: (i) research partnerships and translational programs that move methods from academia into practice; (ii) regulatory sandboxes and supervised experimentation that allow innovation while preserving accountability; (iii) standard-setting collaborations that improve comparability of ESG and climate information; and (iv) shared data infrastructures or interoperable reporting systems that reduce duplication and enable scalable MRV(Murillo-Luna & Hernández-Trasobares, 2022).

Importantly, the Triple Helix model aligns with the "financing frictions" diagnosis established in Section 2. Many of the frictions that sustain the renewable energy financing gap, information asymmetries, high due diligence costs, weak MRV capacity, and integrity risks, are ultimately institutional and coordination problems. AI can reduce these frictions, but only if the underlying governance ecosystem supports data quality, transparency, accountability, and equitable access. Consequently, the Triple Helix framework provides a coherent basis for deriving actor-specific and collaboration-specific recommendations later in the chapter.

3.2 Complementary sustainability lenses: stakeholder theory, circular economy, and ecological modernization

While the Triple Helix model provides an innovation and governance architecture for AI-enabled green finance, sustainable finance and the energy transition also require normative and systems-oriented perspectives. To strengthen conceptual completeness, and to preserve the valuable theoretical grounding already present in the chapter, this section integrates three complementary lenses: stakeholder theory, circular economy theory, and ecological modernization theory.

Stakeholder theory and sustainability legitimacy.

Stakeholder theory provides foundational concepts for understanding how value creation and responsibility extend beyond shareholders to a broader set of affected groups, including communities and the natural environment (Freeman, 1984). In sustainability contexts, stakeholder theory highlights that organizational and policy choices generate distributive consequences and legitimacy constraints; sustainable outcomes depend on the recognition, inclusion, and fair treatment of multiple affected stakeholders (Hörisch et al., 2014; Schaltegger et al., 2019).

Applied to AI-enabled green finance, stakeholder theory clarifies why AI adoption must be evaluated not only by efficiency gains but also by fairness, transparency, and accountability. Algorithmic models can shape project bankability, determine who receives investment, and influence the distribution of transition benefits. Therefore, stakeholder theory provides a conceptual bridge to the ELSI and energy justice discussion later in the chapter by framing legitimacy as a condition for sustainable scaling.

Circular economy theory and lifecycle integrity of the transition.

Circular economy theory argues that long-term sustainability requires decoupling value creation from resource depletion and waste accumulation through regenerative design, resource efficiency, reuse, and secondary material flows (Ellen MacArthur Foundation, 2020). Within renewable energy transitions, circular considerations are increasingly important because scaling renewables introduces lifecycle and end-of-life material challenges that, if unmanaged, may undermine environmental integrity and create new externalities (Future Earth, 2022).

In the context of AI-enabled green finance, the circular economy lens strengthens the chapter's argument in two ways. First, it expands what "green" means beyond operational emissions to include lifecycle impacts and material sustainability, which affects financing criteria and MRV requirements. Second, it highlights why data and traceability matter: circularity outcomes often require detailed lifecycle data and credible verification areas where AI-enabled analytics may support improved monitoring and integrity, subject to governance safeguards.

Ecological modernization theory and institutionalized technological change.

Ecological modernization theory emphasizes that environmental improvement can be advanced through institutionalized technological innovation, policy instruments, and market incentives that reconfigure production systems (Mol & Spaargaren, 2000). This lens aligns with the argument that AI can act as an enabling technology that improves sustainable finance effectiveness by reducing information frictions, strengthening verification, and improving risk pricing. At the same time, ecological modernization debates underscore that technology-driven solutions are mediated by institutions and may reproduce inequalities if governance capacity is uneven.

Accordingly, ecological modernization theory complements the Triple Helix model by reinforcing the insight that technological capabilities (such as AI) generate sustainability outcomes only through supportive regulatory, organizational, and market arrangements. In this chapter, the combination of ecological modernization and Triple Helix clarifies why AI adoption is a governance problem as much as a technical opportunity (Gebhardt & Piqué Huerta, 2024).

Synthesis: how the theoretical lenses work together.

Together, these frameworks provide a coherent theoretical foundation for the chapter's AI-enabled green finance narrative. The Triple Helix model explains the institutional architecture of innovation and governance (who enables and regulates AI adoption). Stakeholder theory clarifies legitimacy constraints and distributive implications. Circular economy theory broadens the definition of "green" and strengthens lifecycle integrity requirements. Ecological modernization theory situates AI as a technology-mediated pathway that is conditioned by institutions and policy. The combined framework is then used to reinterpret the green finance evidence under an AI-enabled lens and to derive actor-specific recommendations for universities, governments, and industry (Võ, Trung, & Luy n, 2025).

4. METHOD

4.1 Research design

This chapter adopts a systematic document analysis and literature synthesis approach to examine sustainable economic models and green finance mechanisms for renewable energy through an AI-enabled green finance lens. The review design is appropriate because the objective is to consolidate dispersed evidence, identify recurrent mechanisms, and develop an integrative interpretation that connects financing frictions, AI-enabled solutions, and governance requirements under a Triple Helix architecture.

The review proceeds in three stages: (i) systematic identification and screening of relevant documents; (ii) structured extraction and coding of evidence using an a priori codebook aligned to AI-enabled mechanisms and Triple Helix roles; and (iii) thematic synthesis that interprets green finance evidence in terms of AI-enabled pathways for mobilization, allocation, monitoring/verification, and integrity.

4.2 Data sources and search strategy

To capture both scholarly and practice-relevant evidence, the search strategy targets peer-reviewed literature and high-quality institutional sources relevant to sustainable finance, renewable energy finance, and AI applications in financial decision-making and governance. Sources include academic databases (e.g., Scopus, Web of Science, Google Scholar) and institutional repositories (e.g., climate finance tracking reports, central bank or multilateral publications, standard-setting bodies, and policy institutions).

Search queries were constructed to combine three conceptual clusters:

Green finance + renewable energy financing, AI. Machine learning + analytics + sustainable finance. Governance + standards + monitoring + integrity + Triple Helix actors

Example search strings:

```
("green finance" OR "sustainable finance" OR "climate finance" OR "green bonds" OR "blended finance") AND ("renewable energy" OR "energy transition") ("AI" OR "artificial intelligence" OR "machine learning" OR "NLP" OR "algorithmic" OR "analytics") AND ("sustainable finance" OR "green finance" OR "climate risk" OR "ESG disclosure") ("monitoring" OR "MRV" OR "verification" OR "greenwashing" OR "integrity" OR "taxonomy") AND ("green bonds" OR "climate finance") ("triple helix" OR
```

```
"university government industry" OR "innovation system") AND
("AI" OR "sustainable finance" OR "green finance")
```

4.3 Inclusion and exclusion criteria

Documents were included if they met the following criteria:

Addressed green, sustainable, climate finance mechanisms relevant to renewable energy (e.g., green bonds, blended finance, risk-sharing, climate finance flows, carbon market incentives). Examined financing frictions (risk, information asymmetry, disclosure quality, monitoring/verification constraints, integrity risks) that affect renewable energy investment.

Provided evidence or conceptual discussion relevant to at least one AI-enabled mechanism (risk analytics, disclosure, NLP, MRV, integrity, anti-greenwashing) or provided governance/standards context essential to such mechanisms. Were peer-reviewed articles, academic books/chapters, or high-quality reports from recognized institutions (e.g., multilateral organizations, central banks, policy institutes, standard-setters).

Documents were excluded if they:

Focused on renewable energy technologies without a finance or governance dimension, addressed finance without relevance to renewable energy transitions or sustainability criteria; Presented AI applications unrelated to finance governance, risk, disclosure, monitoring, or integrity; Lacked sufficient methodological transparency or credibility (for non-peer-reviewed sources).

4.4 Screening and selection process

Screening was performed in two phases. First, titles and abstracts (or executive summaries for reports) were reviewed to assess relevance to the inclusion criteria. Second, full-text screening confirmed conceptual alignment and extractable content for coding. Where multiple versions of the same institutional report existed, the most recent or most comprehensive version was retained. The screening process prioritized clarity of linkage among renewable energy finance, financing frictions, and AI-enabled mechanisms.

4.5 Data extraction and coding (AI-enabled + Triple Helix codebook)

A structured extraction template was used to capture, publication metadata, context (geography, market), instrument type (e.g., green bonds, blended finance), identified financing frictions, AI-enabled mechanisms discussed or implied, governance, standards implications, and any explicit references to actor roles (university, government, industry). Evidence was then coded using an a priori codebook and iteratively refined during synthesis to accommodate emerging themes.

4.6 Thematic synthesis and analytical logic

Thematic synthesis was used to integrate findings across heterogeneous documents. First order themes were constructed around (i) financing frictions sustaining the renewable energy financing gap and (ii) AI enabled mechanisms that can mitigate those frictions. Second order themes linked the AI mechanisms to specific green finance instruments (e.g., green bonds, blended finance, carbon market mechanisms). Finally, the Triple Helix framework was applied to interpret enabling conditions and governance requirements, specifying which actor roles and interactions are necessary for responsible and scalable adoption.

4.7 Trustworthiness, limitations, and reproducibility

As with any document-based synthesis, limitations include potential publication bias, uneven data quality across contexts, and the risk that rapidly evolving AI practices outpace the reviewed literature. To mitigate these limitations, the review incorporates both peer reviewed studies and high credibility institutional sources, emphasizes transparency in inclusion criteria and coding, and explicitly flags areas where evidence remains limited or contested.

5. RESULTS ANALYSIS THROUGH AN AI–TRIPLE HELIX LENS

5.1 AI for capital mobilization and market scaling

The reviewed literature consistently indicates that green and sustainable finance markets have expanded rapidly, with green bond issuance and related sustainable debt instruments reaching record levels and attracting a broader issuer base. This market growth is frequently interpreted as evidence of increasing investor appetite for sustainability-linked assets and the maturation of green finance standards and reporting practices (Shukla, 2025). However, the evidence also indicates that expansion in market volume does not automatically translate into sufficient renewable energy investment at the pace and geographic distribution required for the transition. The mobilization challenge therefore remains twofold: scaling total capital flows while ensuring that capital is directed toward projects with credible environmental outcomes (Raman, et al. 2025).

Interpreted through an AI-enabled lens, market scaling is constrained by the cost and speed of screening, due diligence, and ongoing monitoring, functions that are inherently information-intensive. AI-enabled analytics can support capital mobilization by reducing informational bottlenecks at scale, particularly when issuers and intermediaries must evaluate large volumes of projects, disclosures, and performance data. For example, AI can accelerate project pre-screening and segmentation by identifying patterns in project characteristics associated with higher performance or lower default risk, enabling investors to allocate resources more efficiently (Liu, 2025). In parallel, AI-enabled workflow automation can reduce transaction costs in underwriting and compliance processes, improving the feasibility of smaller projects that are otherwise excluded due to high fixed evaluation costs (Nagesh & Murugan, 2025).

Triple Helix enabling logic:

Scaling via AI requires (Androniceanu & Colesca, 2025):

(i) university capabilities for model development and benchmarking (TH-U);
(ii) government support for standards and interoperable data infrastructures that reduce reporting fragmentation (TH-G); and
(iii) industry capacity to operationalize models in market products and decision pipelines (TH-I).

5.2 AI for risk pricing and allocation in emerging and developing economies

A recurring empirical result in the reviewed literature is the unequal distribution of climate finance and renewable energy investment across regions, with many emerging and developing economies facing persistent barriers to mobilizing domestic capital and attracting international investment. This pattern is reinforced by evidence of structurally higher costs of capital in these contexts, driven by currency risk, policy uncertainty, institutional capacity constraints, and risk perceptions that are not always aligned with project fundamentals (Bird et al., 2021). The result is a transition imbalance: locations with high renewable potential may remain underfinanced, while capital concentrates in markets with stronger institutions and more transparent data environments.

From an AI-enabled green finance perspective, these allocation challenges are strongly linked to risk modeling and information availability. AI-enabled climate and transition risk analytics can improve risk differentiation by incorporating higher-resolution data and dynamic scenario methods, potentially reducing the "blanket" risk premiums often applied to under-studied markets (Ofodile et al., 2024). Better risk differentiation can support more precise credit and pricing decisions, reduce uncertainty-driven capital rationing, and expand the set of investable renewable opportunities. Moreover, AI can support the design of risk-sharing arrangements in blended finance by improving estimation of loss distributions and performance outcomes, making catalytic capital more efficiently targeted (Swanson & Sakhrani, 2023).

At the same time, the literature suggests that AI-enabled risk analytics may exacerbate inequalities if data availability is systematically poorer in emerging contexts or if models inherit biases from historically underrepresented markets. This risk underscores the importance of governance arrangements that ensure fairness, transparency, and accountability in AI-supported investment decisions, especially where access to capital intersects with energy justice outcomes (Fagbore et al., 2024).

Triple Helix enabling logic.

Reducing allocation inequities through AI requires (Giupponi et al., 2025):

(i) universities to develop context-sensitive models and open benchmarking studies (TH-U);
(ii) governments to stabilize policy signals, support data infrastructure, and design oversight for model use (TH-G); and
(iii) industry to embed these tools in underwriting and blended finance structuring while ensuring explainability and auditability (TH-I).

5.3 AI for disclosure, data quality, and comparability in sustainable finance

The literature repeatedly identifies disclosure heterogeneity and data comparability as constraints on scalable sustainable finance. Even when green instruments expand, investors face challenges in evaluating environmental claims consistently across issuers, jurisdictions, and instrument categories. These challenges directly influence transaction costs, due diligence intensity, and the credibility of "green" labels. The reviewed evidence indicates that markets with more mature disclosure practices and clearer standards tend to attract greater volumes of sustainable capital, reinforcing uneven investment distribution (Liu & Wu, 2023).

AI-enabled disclosure analytics, particularly NLP-based methods, can address these constraints by extracting, standardizing, and classifying sustainability information from diverse textual sources such as bond frameworks, ESG reports, regulatory filings, and project documentation (Birti, Osborne, & Maurino, 2025). By converting unstructured disclosures into structured indicators aligned with taxonomies and reporting standards, AI can improve comparability and reduce manual processing costs. In green bond markets, these capabilities can strengthen both pre-issuance screening (alignment with criteria) and post-issuance reporting review (consistency with commitments), supporting investor confidence and market integrity (Ramdhan, 2025).

However, the deployment of AI-enabled disclosure analytics introduces governance questions: how classification models are validated; how errors are handled; whether model outputs can be audited; and how differences in disclosure quality across firms and countries affect fairness in evaluations (Pasupuleti, 2025). These concerns are directly connected to the chapter's later discussion on ELSI and energy justice.

Triple Helix enabling logic.

High-quality AI-enabled disclosure systems depend on (Lulaj & Brajković, 2025):

(i) universities contributing methods, benchmarks, and validation studies (TH-U),
(ii) governments providing standardized reporting rules and open data infrastructures where feasible (TH-G), and
(iii) industry implementing tools in scalable compliance and investment workflows, including model governance processes (TH-I).

5.4 AI for MRV (monitoring, reporting, verification) and "use-of-proceeds" integrity

A consistent finding in the reviewed sustainable finance literature is that market credibility depends on MRV capacity. Investors require assurance that proceeds are used as promised and that environmental outcomes are measurable, especially as markets scale and issuers diversify. Weak MRV can undermine additionality claims, increase greenwashing risk, and reduce willingness to allocate capital to green instruments, particularly in contexts where institutional capacity is uneven (Liongson & Nainggolan, 2025).

AI-enabled MRV offers a pathway to strengthen credibility by enabling continuous or higher-frequency monitoring, anomaly detection, and cross-source consistency checks. When integrated with project operational data, remote sensing inputs, and standardized reporting, AI can support more robust verification of renewable project performance and environmental outcomes (World Bank, 2022). In practice, MRV strengthening is closely linked to the scalability of green bonds (post-issuance reporting and outcome verification) and the effectiveness of blended finance vehicles [performance verification, reporting obligations, and ongoing risk management, (Azad & Tulasi Devi, 2025)].

Nonetheless, AI-enabled MRV is governance-intensive. It depends on data availability and quality, model transparency, and clear accountability for verification results. The risk of overreliance on opaque model outputs or low-quality data is especially salient when MRV outcomes influence access to capital or trigger contractual terms. These issues reinforce the need for actor coordination and oversight mechanisms to ensure that MRV tools strengthen, rather than weaken, market legitimacy (Pavlidis, 2025).

Triple Helix enabling logic.

MRV improvement through AI requires (Giupponi, et al. 2025):

(i) universities to develop verification methods and robustness testing (TH-U);
(ii) governments to support reporting infrastructures and verification standards (TH-G); and
(iii) industry to integrate MRV analytics into bond reporting, blended finance governance, and monitoring operations (TH-I).

5.5 AI for integrity: anti-greenwashing, fraud detection, and additionality

The reviewed literature emphasizes that as sustainable finance grows, integrity risks become more salient. Greenwashing concerns arise when environmental claims are weakly substantiated, when reporting is inconsistent with outcomes, or when "green" labels are applied without meaningful additionality. Integrity weaknesses can erode investor confidence and reduce the effectiveness of green instruments as transition accelerators (Poiriazi, et al. 2025).

AI-enabled integrity analytics can support market trust by detecting inconsistencies, anomalies, and patterns associated with misrepresentation. Potential applications include screening disclosures for inconsistencies, cross-validating stated project characteristics against external data, identifying unusual reporting changes, and flagging instruments or issuers for deeper review (Badmus, 2025). These tools may be particularly valuable in large-scale markets where manual review is not feasible and where integrity controls must operate at speed.

However, integrity analytics also raises substantial governance risks, including false positives, model bias, opacity, and due process concerns, especially if automated flags influence investment decisions, regulatory actions, or market access. This reinforces the argument that integrity improvement is not merely a technical exercise but a governance problem requiring transparency, auditability, accountability, and stakeholder protections (Nwachukwu, Chima, & Okolo, 2025).

Triple Helix enabling logic.

Integrity systems require (John, 2025):

(i) universities to provide independent methods and validation (TH-U);
(ii) governments to define accountability, oversight, and procedural fairness standards (TH-G); and
(iii) industry to implement integrity controls with model governance, explainability, and escalation pathways (TH-I).

5.6 Mapping AI-enabled mechanisms to green finance instruments and policy incentives

Synthesizing across the reviewed evidence, the chapter identifies a consistent mapping between AI-enabled mechanisms and the instruments most frequently emphasized in the green finance literature:

Green bonds benefit most directly from AI-enabled disclosure analytics, MRV strengthening, and integrity screening, because market credibility depends on transparent classification, "use-of-proceeds" monitoring, and credible impact reporting. Blended finance is closely linked to AI-enabled risk analytics and structuring support, because catalytic capital effectiveness depends on the precision of risk estimation and the credibility of performance verification. Carbon pricing and policy incentives can be strengthened through AI-enabled monitoring and compliance analytics, which support enforcement and improve the credibility of market signals.

This mapping reinforces the chapter's central argument: AI functions as a cross-cutting infrastructure that can reduce financing frictions and strengthen credibility, but only under governance conditions that ensure transparency, accountability, and equitable outcomes. Accordingly, the Triple Helix framework remains essential for explaining adoption differences and for deriving actor-specific recommendations that connect innovation capacity with regulatory safeguards (Zhang & Punjwani, 2025).

6. FINDINGS

These five core findings emerge from the literature synthesis when sustainable economic models and green finance are interpreted through an AI-enabled green finance and Triple Helix (University, Government, Industry) lens:

Finding 1: Green finance has achieved significant scale, but closing the climate financing gap now depends on AI-enabled acceleration of screening, allocation, and verification.

Green finance has expanded substantially in recent years, including growth in sustainable debt markets and climate finance flows. Yet, the synthesis indicates that aggregate volumes remain insufficient relative to transition needs, and that the gap is amplified by information frictions (high due diligence costs, heterogeneous disclosures, verification burdens, and integrity risks). In this context, AI-enabled green finance becomes a practical scaling lever: AI can reduce transaction costs by automating early-stage screening, standardizing disclosure interpretation, and enabling higher-frequency monitoring that improves investor confidence and reduces manual verification bottlenecks (Bm & Khanum, 2025).

What AI changes (Badmus, 2025):

AI-DISC and AI-MRV can shorten cycle times from project evaluation to financing by reducing document review burdens and improving comparability of claims.

AI-INTEG can strengthen confidence in "green" labels by supporting scalable integrity checks.

Risks and ELSI flags (Zhou, 2025):

AI-driven acceleration may also increase systemic vulnerabilities (model risk, opacity, concentration of tooling, and automation bias), particularly if model governance is weak or if markets over-rely on black-box scoring.

Finding 2: Geographic disparities in green finance access reflect risk-and-data frictions; AI-enabled risk analytics can reduce mispricing, but governance is essential to avoid bias and exclusion.

The evidence indicates persistent concentration of green finance in advanced economies, while many emerging and developing economies face structurally higher costs of capital and limited access to long-term financing. This imbalance is reinforced by data gaps and generalized risk premiums applied to contexts with weaker disclosure ecosystems or less standardized project information. Under an AI-enabled lens, the key opportunity is risk differentiation: machine learning, alternative data, and scenario analytics can improve risk pricing and reduce undifferentiated premiums that penalize underserved markets (Sadiq, Yasser, & Nawaz, 2025).

What AI changes (Sasaki & Abe, 2025):

AI-RISK can combine climate hazard data, project attributes, and macro-financial signals to refine risk estimates and pricing.

AI-MRV can reduce verification uncertainty where institutional monitoring capacity is limited, improving investor confidence.

Risks and ELSI flags (Amen, 2024):

AI can worsen inequities if training data underrepresents developing contexts, if proxies embed structural bias, or if low-quality data leads to systematic under-scoring and exclusion. Energy justice concerns therefore become central to model design and deployment.

Finding 3: Blended finance is a high-potential bridge mechanism; scaling it requires AI-enabled structuring, standardized pipelines, and MRV systems that reduce transaction costs and credibility risk.

The synthesis indicates that blended finance can address market failures and support projects in underserved contexts or emerging technologies. However, scaling is constrained by high structuring costs, bespoke deal design, and the complexity of verifying performance and additionality. Under an AI-enabled green finance lens, blended finance can be scaled more effectively by using AI to support risk segmentation, to standardize documentation workflows, and to strengthen performance monitoring through MRV, reducing both transaction costs and credibility risk (Nagesh & Murugan, 2025).

What AI changes (Jang, et al., 2023):

AI-RISK supports structuring decisions (e.g., targeting guarantees or concessional tranches to specific risk components).

AI-MRV enables ongoing performance verification that supports conditionality, reporting obligations, and integrity claims.

Risks and ELSI flags (Chopra, 2024):

If AI models determine eligibility or risk-sharing terms, opaque scoring can create legitimacy challenges and disputes over accountability, especially when concessional resources are allocated.

Finding 4: Carbon pricing mechanisms can drive renewable energy transition; AI improves compliance, monitoring, and integrity, but must be governed to avoid surveillance and accountability risks.

The literature supports the role of carbon pricing (taxes and emissions trading systems) in shifting incentives toward cleaner technologies, while emphasizing that effectiveness depends on design features (price levels, coverage, revenue recycling, and complementary policies). Under an AI-enabled lens, carbon pricing becomes more enforceable and credible when AI supports monitoring, compliance analytics, anomaly detection, and verification, especially in complex markets with large participant bases (Asif et al., 2025).

What AI changes (Islam, 2025):

AI-MRV and AI-INTEG can strengthen market integrity by improving detection of irregularities and supporting verification processes across reporting cycles.

AI-RISK supports scenario-based stress testing for portfolios exposed to policy and price shifts.

Risks and ELSI flags (Kasireddy, 2025):

AI-enabled compliance can raise concerns about due process, explainability of enforcement triggers, and data governance (privacy, surveillance, and proportionality).

Finding 5: Circular economy integration with renewable energy is increasingly imperative; AI-enabled lifecycle data and traceability can operationalize "true green" criteria and strengthen financing integrity.

The synthesis indicates that integrating circular economy principles into renewable energy deployment remains nascent but critical, given the material intensity and end-of-life challenges of renewable technologies. Under an AI-enabled green finance lens, circularity becomes more actionable when AI supports lifecycle data integration, traceability, and verification. This matters for green finance because "green" classification and impact claims increasingly require evidence beyond operational emissions, including lifecycle impacts, resource security, and end-of-life management performance (Munonye et al., 2025; Mohammad et al., 2025).

7. DISCUSSION AND IMPLICATIONS

7.1 Reframing sustainable finance through an AI-enabled green finance lens

The findings confirm that the green finance and renewable energy transition literature has reached a high level of maturity in diagnosing the magnitude of the climate financing gap and in describing the growth of instruments such as green bonds, blended finance, and carbon pricing. However, the synthesis also shows that the remaining barriers are increasingly concentrated in execution frictions, risk mispricing, heterogeneous and low-comparability disclosures, weak monitoring/verification capacity, and integrity concerns (e.g., greenwashing). This chapter argues that these frictions are precisely the domain where AI-enabled green finance can shift the constraint frontier: AI functions less as an add-on and more as an enabling infrastructure that can reduce information costs, increase comparability, improve risk differentiation, and strengthen verification at scale (Ren, 2025).

This reframing is not purely technical. By moving AI to the center of the analysis, the chapter aligns sustainable finance with the edited volume's focus on AI as both a driver of innovation and a governance object. The core interpretive contribution is therefore that the effectiveness of green finance instruments increasingly depends on AI-enabled capacities that support:

(i) scalable due diligence and screening,
(ii) higher-resolution risk pricing,
(iii) disclosure analytics and taxonomy alignment,
(iv) MRV and outcome verification, and
(v) integrity controls. Yet these benefits are conditional on governance quality and institutional coordination, which motivates the use of the Triple Helix framework as an explanatory architecture.

7.2 Theoretical implications: Triple Helix as the governance architecture of AI-enabled green finance

A primary theoretical implication is that AI-enabled green finance is best understood as a co-produced socio-technical system, rather than a technology adoption decision by isolated firms. The Triple Helix framework provides conceptual leverage by linking innovation and commercialization to governance and legitimacy: universities enable knowledge production and validation; governments shape disclosure standards, taxonomies, supervisory expectations, and public data infrastructure;

and industry operationalizes tools, scales them into products, and embeds them in decision pipelines (Lulaj & Brajković, 2025).

This theoretical framing strengthens the chapter in three ways:

1.- It explains variation in adoption and outcomes.

AI-enabled mechanisms (risk, disclosure/NLP, MRV, integrity) are feasible only where data ecosystems, regulatory clarity, and organizational capabilities align. Thus, the Triple Helix lens explains why similar financial instruments may perform differently across jurisdictions and why emerging markets can face compounded disadvantages when both finance and data infrastructures are weaker (Sadiq, Yasser, & Nawaz, 2025).

2.- It integrates complementary sustainability lenses without diluting AI-first alignment.

Stakeholder theory clarifies that legitimacy, and distributive impacts are central when AI influences capital allocation; circular economy theory expands the definition of "green" toward lifecycle integrity; ecological modernization theory situates AI as technology-mediated sustainability progress contingent on institutions. Together, these lenses complement the Triple Helix model by making explicit the normative and systemic requirements that must accompany AI-enabled scaling (Schultz, Valentinov, & Pies, 2025).

3.- It positions AI as both innovation driver and governance challenge.

AI-enabled green finance improves efficiency and credibility but introduces model risk, opacity, bias, and concentration dynamics. Treating AI as a governance object (not merely a tool) aligns the chapter with AI-centered innovation governance debates and strengthens its conceptual fit with the edited volume (Nwachukwu, Chima, & Okolo, 2025).

7.3 Policy and governance implications: what the Triple Helix must deliver

The findings imply that closing the financing gap is increasingly a governance and infrastructure problem, not solely a capital supply problem. AI can reduce frictions, but only if the Triple Helix actors coordinate around standards, accountability, and interoperable data systems.

7.3.1 Government (standards, accountability, and public data infrastructure)

Governments should treat AI-enabled green finance as part of the national (and transnational) infrastructure for sustainable investment by focusing on three priorities:

Disclosure and taxonomy coherence: strengthen comparability by aligning reporting requirements with credible green taxonomies, enabling automated mapping and reducing ambiguity in "green" claims (Ren, 2025).

MRV enablement and integrity controls: establish minimum MRV expectations for instruments and outcomes, promote digital MRV where feasible, and define accountability standards for verification (Majekodunmi, 2025).

Supervisory expectations for AI in finance: specify governance requirements for AI use in risk models, integrity screening, and compliance workflows (e.g., explainability thresholds, auditability, model risk management, and due process, (Kobanenko, 2025).

These actions reduce information asymmetry and provide the regulatory certainty required for industry adoption at scale, while protecting against systemic risks.

7.3.2 University (methods, validation, and capacity building)

Universities should act as the scientific backbone of AI-enabled green finance by:

Developing reproducible methods for climate/transition risk analytics, NLP disclosure measurement, and MRV approaches, including robustness and fairness testing (Fagbore et al., 2024).

Publishing benchmarking datasets and evaluation protocols to reduce fragmentation and enable comparability across models and institutions (Vaghefi et al., 2025).

Training interdisciplinary talent capable of integrating finance, data science, sustainability, and governance, especially in emerging markets where capacity constraints are binding (Hussain, Vemaraju, & Garg, 2025).

This role is essential to prevent markets from converging on proprietary black-box solutions without independent validation.

7.3.3 Industry (implementation, scaling, and model governance-by-design)

Industry actors are responsible for making AI-enabled green finance operational and trustworthy:

Embedding AI in underwriting and portfolio decisions with explainability and audit trails, especially where outcomes affect access to capital (Gummadi, 2025).

Integrating AI-enabled disclosure analytics and MRV into green bond and blended finance governance, ensuring post-issuance monitoring is credible Majekodunmi, 2025).

Implementing integrity systems with escalation paths: AI flags should trigger review, not automatic exclusion, to prevent unfair outcomes and legal risk (Mahajan, Agarwal, & Gupta, 2025).

The overarching implication is that industry scaling must be coupled with governance by design, not governance after the fact.

7.4 Ethical, legal, and societal implications (ELSI) and energy justice

Both reviewers explicitly require integration of ethical, legal, and societal implications. The synthesis indicates that AI-enabled green finance can improve the credibility and efficiency of sustainable investment, but it can also introduce harms if governance is weak.

Transparency and explainability.

AI models that influence investment eligibility, pricing, or compliance create legitimacy constraints. Lack of explainability can undermine trust, complicate dispute resolution, and create legal exposure (Chawande, 2025). The chapter therefore treats explainability and auditability as necessary conditions for responsible scaling, especially in high-stakes decisions (e.g., blended finance eligibility, credit terms, or integrity-based exclusion).

Bias, fairness, and exclusion risks.

If models are trained on historically biased data, underserved regions may be systematically under-scored, reproducing inequities in renewable finance access. Energy justice concerns are thus central: AI-enabled mechanisms should be evaluated not only by predictive accuracy but also by fairness across geographies, firm sizes, and socioeconomic contexts. Minimum safeguards include bias testing, domain adaptation methods, and human-in-the-loop governance for contested decisions (Raziyeva & Meraliyev, 2025).

Data governance and privacy.

AI-enabled MRV and integrity systems may rely on remote sensing, operational telemetry, and granular reporting. Without clear governance, such systems can generate privacy concerns, commercial sensitivity conflicts, and surveillance-like dynamics. Governments and industry must therefore define proportionality, data minimization principles, access controls, and accountability for data misuse (Sadiq, Yasser, & Nawaz, 2025).

Accountability and due process.

When AI flags "greenwashing" or anomaly risk, the affected issuer or project should have procedural protections: the ability to contest outcomes, require human review, and understand decision rationales. These safeguards are critical for preventing algorithmic governance from becoming arbitrary or exclusionary (Ren, 2025).

In summary, ELSI and energy justice are not peripheral; they condition legitimacy and the long-term sustainability of AI-enabled green finance architectures.

7.5 Managerial implications for financial institutions and project developers

For practitioners, the chapter's results imply that competitive advantage and credibility increasingly depend on building AI-enabled capabilities across the green finance lifecycle:

- Investment and risk teams should integrate climate/transition risk analytics and scenario tooling into underwriting and portfolio review, with explicit model governance controls.
- Sustainable finance teams should adopt NLP-enabled disclosure workflows to improve taxonomy mapping and comparability, reducing manual burdens and improving consistency.
- Monitoring and reporting teams should invest in AI-supported MRV pipelines that enable scalable post-issuance monitoring and higher-frequency verification where feasible
- Compliance and integrity teams should implement integrity analytics as triage tools with escalation protocols rather than as automatic exclusion mechanisms.

7.6 Limitations and future research directions

This chapter is based on systematic document analysis and literature synthesis; therefore, it does not provide primary empirical estimation or causal claims. Limitations include publication bias, uneven data availability across regions, and the fact that AI practices evolve quickly relative to the academic literature. Future research should prioritize:

- Comparative empirical studies of AI-enabled green finance adoption across jurisdictions (institutional capacity and policy design effects).
- Evaluation of fairness and distributional outcomes of AI-based risk and integrity models in emerging markets (energy justice lens).
- Evidence on the effectiveness of AI-enabled MRV in reducing greenwashing and improving additionality across instrument classes.
- Governance research on supervisory and accountability frameworks suitable for AI-intensive sustainable finance ecosystems.

8. CONCLUSION

This chapter reframed sustainable economic models and green finance for renewable energy through an AI-enabled green finance lens, explicitly aligned with the edited volume's focus on Artificial Intelligence and Triple Helix (University, Government and Industry) collaboration. The literature synthesis indicates that, although green finance markets and instruments have expanded, the persistent renewable energy financing gap is increasingly driven by execution frictions, risk mispricing, disclosure heterogeneity, weak MRV capacity, and integrity concerns, that limit scalable and credible capital deployment.

Across the reviewed evidence, four AI-enabled mechanisms emerged as the most consequential levers for improving performance and legitimacy in green finance systems: (i) AI-enabled risk analytics to refine climate and transition risk pricing; (ii) NLP-based disclosure analytics to improve comparability and reduce due diligence costs; (iii) AI-supported MRV to strengthen outcome verification and post-issuance credibility; and (iv) integrity analytics to deter greenwashing and flag anomalies. Importantly, these mechanisms do not replace the need for sound instrument design (e.g., green bonds, blended finance, carbon pricing); rather, they function as enabling infrastructure that can reduce information frictions and raise the credibility of sustainability claims at scale.

The chapter further demonstrates that AI-enabled green finance is not solely a technology adoption issue; it is a governance and coordination challenge. *The Triple Helix framework provides a coherent explanation of how AI capability is produced, governed, and scaled: universities develop and validate methods and benchmarks; governments supply regulatory clarity, disclosure standards, taxonomies, public data infrastructure, and oversight; and industry operationalizes tools, embeds them into market workflows, and scales adoption through products and platforms.* The central implication is that performance gains depend on the quality of interaction mechanisms among the three helices, not on any single actor's efforts in isolation.

Consistent with the reviewers' scope expectations, the chapter treated AI as both an innovation driver and a governance object. Ethical, legal, and societal implications (ELSI), including explainability, contestability, bias, data governance, and due process, are not peripheral considerations; they condition legitimacy, market trust, and long-term scalability. Without these safeguards, AI-enabled mechanisms can reproduce exclusion (particularly for emerging markets), introduce model risk vulnerabilities, or amplify integrity failures through opaque automation.

In sum, the chapter's contribution is a scope-consistent reinterpretation: sustainable economic models and green finance can be materially strengthened when understood as AI-enabled systems embedded within Triple Helix governance architectures. Future research should move beyond conceptual synthesis to comparative empirical validation across jurisdictions and instruments, especially evaluating distributional outcomes, fairness, and integrity effects, so that AI-enabled green finance can scale credibly and equitably as a core pathway for financing the renewable energy transition.

REFERENCES

Alhazmi, A. H. J., Islam, S., & Prokofieva, M. (2025). *The impact of AI-integrated drone technology and big data on external auditing performance, sustainability, and financial reporting quality in emerging markets.* Accounting and Auditing., DOI: 10.3390/accountaudit1030008

Amen, M. (2024). *AI-Driven Sustainable Habitat Design: Key Policy Frameworks and Ethical Safeguards.* Smart Design Policies., DOI: 10.38027/smart-v1n1-4

Androniceanu, A., & Colesca, S. (2025). *Triple Helix Model and Artificial Intelligence in Public Administration.* Central European Public Administration Review., DOI: 10.17573/cepar.2025.2.03

Azad, S., & Tulasi Devi, S. L. (2025). Green Bonds in Sustainable Finance: A Bibliometric and Meta-Analysis of Research Trends, Challenges, and Emerging Market Dynamics (2014–2023). *Business Strategy and the Environment.* Advance online publication. DOI: 10.1002/bse.70268

Badmus, O. (2025). *Embedding AI in ESG-Financial Reporting Systems to Enhance Non-Financial Disclosure Integrity, Assurance, and Investor Decision Relevance.* International Journal of Research Publication and Reviews., DOI: 10.55248/gengpi.6.0625.23114

Bank for International Settlements. (2025). *Green bond market developments and sustainability-linked finance.* BIS Quarterly Review.

Bartelt, C., & Röser, A. M. (2024). *AI in finance: Innovative approaches for sustainable business models.* E-conom., DOI: 10.17836/EC.2024.2.007

Bird, R., Dickinson, D., & Herczeg, M. (2021). Risk, return, and cost of capital in renewable energy investments*: A capstone review. Energy Policy*, *149*, 112027. DOI: 10.1016/j.enpol.2020.112027

Birti, M., Osborne, F., & Maurino, A. (2025). Optimizing large language models for ESG activity detection in financial texts*. ArXiv, abs/2502.21112.* https://doi.org//arXiv.2502.21112DOI: 10.1145/3768292.3770371

Bloomberg, N. E. F. (2025). *Energy transition investment trends 2025.* Bloomberg New Energy Finance.

Bm, N., & Khanum, A. (2025). *Driving green investments with Artificial Intelligence: Data-driven strategies for sustainable finance.* Asian Journal of Management and Commerce., DOI: 10.22271/27084515.2025.v6.i2Sc.702

Chouhan, S., & Singhai, M. (2025). *Sustainable Banking in the Digital Era: AI, Ethics, and Financial Inclusion in a Globalized Economy*. International Journal of Innovative Research in Engineering & Multidisciplinary Physical Sciences., DOI: 10.37082/IJIRMPS.v13.i4.232635

Climate Policy Initiative. (2024). *Global landscape of climate finance 2024*. Climate Policy Initiative.

Climate Policy Initiative. (2025). *Global landscape of climate finance 2025*. Climate Policy Initiative.

Convergence. (2024). *State of blended finance 2024: Climate edition*. Convergence Blended Finance.

Costanza, R., Cumberland, J. H., Daly, H., Goodland, R., Norgaard, R. B., Kubiszewski, I., & Franco, C. (2014). *An introduction to ecological economics* (2nd ed.). CRC Press. DOI: 10.1201/b17829

Ellen MacArthur Foundation. (2020). *The circular economy: A transformative Covid-19 recovery strategy*. Ellen MacArthur Foundation.

European Commission. (2025). *EU Emissions Trading System: 2024 market report*. European Commission.

Fagbore, O. O., Ogeawuchi, J. C., Ilori, O., Isibor, N. J., Odetunde, A., & Adekunle, B. I. (2024). Conceptual design of ethical investment assessment models using AI-enhanced financial decision tools. *International Journal of Scientific Research in Science and Technology, 11*(4), 525–558. Advance online publication. DOI: 10.32628/IJSRST24115123

Fatica, S., & Panzica, R. (2021). Green bonds as a tool against climate change? *Business Strategy and the Environment, 30*(5), 2688–2701. DOI: 10.1002/bse.2771

Freeman, R. E. (1984). *Strategic management: A stakeholder approach*. Pitman.

Future Earth. (2022). *Circular economy and renewable energy: Pathways to sustainable development*. Future Earth.

Gebhardt, C., & Piqué Huerta, J. M. (2024). Integrating Triple Helix and Sustainable Transition Research for Transformational Governance. *Triple Helix (Heidelberg), 11*(1), 107–130. Advance online publication. DOI: 10.1163/21971927-bja10053

Giupponi, É. C. B., Espuny, M., Poltronieri, C. F., & de Oliveira, O. J. (2025). From ESG to Sustainable Development: A Path Designed for the Triple Helix Spheres. *Sustainable Development*. Advance online publication. DOI: 10.1002/sd.70355

Gummadi, H. S. B. (2025). *Explainable AI-Enhanced Underwriting Automation for Personalized Insurance Policy Recommendations. European Journal of Computer.* Science and Information Technology., DOI: 10.37745/ejcsit.2013/vol13n192440

Hörisch, J., Freeman, R. E., & Schaltegger, S. (2014). Applying stakeholder theory in sustainability management: Links, similarities, dissimilarities, and a conceptual framework. *Organization & Environment, 27*(4), 328–346. DOI: 10.1177/1086026614535786

Hussain, M. A., Vemaraju, S., & Garg, A. (2025). *The Impact of AI Tools on ESG-Based Sustainable Banking Practices: A Meta-Analysis & Conceptual Framework.* International Journal of Computational and Experimental Science and Engineering., DOI: 10.22399/ijcesen.3198

IEEFA. (2024). *Blended finance for renewable energy in emerging markets.* Institute for Energy Economics and Financial Analysis.

IFC-Amundi. (2025). *Emerging market green bonds report 2024.* International Finance Corporation.

International Energy Agency. (2024). *World energy outlook 2024.* IEA.

International Renewable Energy Agency. (2024). *World energy transitions outlook 2024.* IRENA.

Islam, F. A. S. (2025). Artificial Intelligence-powered Carbon Market Intelligence and Blockchain-enabled Governance for Climate-responsive Urban Infrastructure in the Global South. *Journal of Engineering Research and Reports.* https://doi.org/ DOI: 10.9734/jerr/2025/v27i71585

Jang, E.-K., Kwak, D., Choi, G., & Moon, J. (2023). Opportunities and challenges of converging technology and blended finance for REDD+ implementation. *Frontiers in Forests and Global Change, 6*, 1154917. Advance online publication. DOI: 10.3389/ffgc.2023.1154917

John, S. (2025). *Sustainable finance and AI integration: Driving responsible growth in the digital era.* International Journal of Scientific Research in Engineering and Management., DOI: 10.55041/IJSREM52213

Jupalli, P. H. (2024). Harnessing Artificial Intelligence & Big Data for Sustainable Finance & Risk Management. [IJSR]. *International Journal of Science and Research (Raipur, India), 13*(7), 518–525. Advance online publication. DOI: 10.21275/SR24708233123

Kasireddy, J. R. (2025). *The Ethical Implications of AI in Financial Market Surveillance: Are We Over-Monitoring Traders?* European Journal of Accounting, Auditing and Finance Research., DOI: 10.37745/ejaafr.2013/vol13n41736

Kobanenko, M. (2025). *Digital Transformation of Financial Reporting: AI-Driven Accuracy and Transparency in Corporate Disclosures.* The American Journal of Management and Economics Innovations., DOI: 10.37547/tajmei/Volume07Issue11-03

Lam, W., & Wurgler, J. (2024). Corporate green bonds: Costs, pricing, and environmental claims. *Journal of Financial Economics, 152*(2), 103–124.

Leghemo, I. M., Azubuike, C., Segun-Falade, O. D., & Odionu, C. S. (2025). Data governance for emerging technologies: A conceptual framework for managing blockchain, IoT, and AI. *Journal of Engineering Research and Reports.* https://doi.org/DOI: 10.9734/jerr/2025/v27i11385

Liongson, E., & Nainggolan, Y. (2025). *Financing Low-Carbon Urban Transport through Subnational Green Bonds: A Review in Emerging Economies.* Journal Integration of Management Studies., DOI: 10.58229/jims.v3i2.362

Liu, C., & Wu, S. (2023). *Green finance, sustainability disclosure and economic implications.* Fulbright Review of Economics and Policy., DOI: 10.1108/FREP-03-2022-0021

Liu, S. (2025). Statistical Assessment of Default Risks of Green Financial Bonds: A Joint Analysis Model of Environmental Benefits and Financial Indicators. *SHS Web of Conferences, 218*, 02007. https://doi.org/DOI: 10.1051/shsconf/202521802007

Lulaj, E., & Brajković, M. (2025). The moderating role of finance, accounting, and digital disruption in ESG, financial reporting, and auditing*: A Triple-Helix perspective. Journal of Risk and Financial Management, 18*(5), 245. Advance online publication. DOI: 10.3390/jrfm18050245

Mahajan, S., Agarwal, R., & Gupta, M. (2025). Algorithmic Bias Under the EU AI Act: Compliance Risk, Capital Strain, and Pricing Distortions in Life and Health Insurance Underwriting. *Risks, 13*(9), 160. DOI: 10.3390/risks13090160

Majekodunmi, T. G. (2025). *Embedding AI in ESG-Financial Reporting Systems to Enhance Non-Financial Disclosure Integrity, Assurance, and Investor Decision Relevance.* International Journal of Research Publication and Reviews., DOI: 10.55248/gengpi.6.0625.22101

Mishra, S., Sharma, D., & Kumar, P. (2023). Green finance: A systematic review and research agenda. *Journal of Sustainable Finance & Investment, 13*(1), 234–259.

Mohammad, S., Al Qrain, B., Alenazi, S., Vasudevan, A., Shelash, A. A., & Ali, I. (2025). *Lifecycle Cost Management for Offshore Marine Renewable Energy Wind Infrastructure: An Integrated Model Using Circular Economy Principles*. Sustainable Marine Structures., DOI: 10.36956/sms.v7i3.2506

Mol, A. P. J., & Spaargaren, G. (2000). Ecological modernisation theory in debate: A review. *Environmental Politics*, *9*(1), 17–49. DOI: 10.1080/09644010008414511

Munonye, W. C., Ajonye, G. O., Ahonsi, S. O., Munonye, D. I., Chigozie, I. O., & Akinloye, O. A. (2025). Advancing Circularity in Battery Systems for Renewable Energy: Technologies, Barriers, and Future Directions. *Advanced Energy and Sustainability Research*. Advance online publication. DOI: 10.1002/aesr.202500255

Murillo-Luna, J. L., & Hernández-Trasobares, A. (2022). Cooperation with the Triple Helix and corporate environmental innovation. *Journal of Cleaner Production, 368*, 135479. DOI: 10.1016/j.jclepro.2022.135479

Nagesh, K. C., & Murugan, K. S. (2025). Fintech and Sustainable Finance: Impact of Digital Finance in Promoting Green Investments. *mLAC Journal for Arts, Commerce and Sciences (m-JACS)*. https://doi.org/DOI: 10.59415/mjacs.v3i1.246

Nature Communications. (2025). Carbon pricing thresholds and renewable energy transitions: A cross-country analysis. *Nature Communications, 16*, Article 1542.

Nature Energy. (2024). The cost of capital for renewable energy in developing economies. *Nature Energy, 9*(3), 267–278.

Nwachukwu, P. S., Chima, O. K., & Okolo, C. H. (2025). *The artificial intelligence governance framework for finance: A control-by-design approach to algorithmic decision-making in accounting*. Finance & Accounting Research Journal., DOI: 10.51594/farj.v7i8.2016

OECD. (2024). *Effective carbon rates 2024: Pricing greenhouse gas emissions through taxes and emissions trading*. OECD Publishing.

Ofodile, O. C., Oyewole, A., Ugochukwu, C. E., Addy, W. A., Adeoye, O. B., & Okoye, C. C.Onyeka Chrisanctus OfodileAdedoyin Tolulope OyewoleChinonye Esther UgochukwuWilhelmina Afua AddyOmotayo Bukola AdeoyeChinwe Chinazo Okoye. (2024). Predictive analytics in climate finance: Assessing risks and opportunities for investors. *GSC Advanced Research and Reviews, 18*(2), 76–89. DOI: 10.30574/gscarr.2024.18.2.0076

Pasupuleti, M. K. (2025). *Governance Frameworks for Ethical AI Deployment in Public Sector Services. International Journal of Academic and Industrial Research Innovations*. IJAIRI., DOI: 10.62311/nesx/rphcr17

Pavlidis, G. (2025). *Empowering Sustainable Finance with Artificial Intelligence: A Framework for Responsible Implementation.* ArXiv., DOI: 10.4337/9781803929996.00009

Poiriazi, E., Zournatzidou, G., Konteos, G., & Sariannidis, N. (2025). Analyzing the interconnection between environmental, social, and governance (ESG) criteria and corporate corruption: Revealing the significant impact of greenwashing. *Administrative Sciences, 15*(3), 100. DOI: 10.3390/admsci15030100

Polzin, F., & Sanders, M. (2020). How to finance the transition to low-carbon energy in Europe? *Energy Policy, 147*, 111863. DOI: 10.1016/j.enpol.2020.111863

Raman, R., Ray, S., Das, D., & Nedungadi, P. (2025). Innovations and barriers in sustainable and green finance for advancing sustainable development goals. *Frontiers in Environmental Science, 12*, 1513204. Advance online publication. DOI: 10.3389/fenvs.2024.1513204

Ramdhan, D. F. (2025). The Role of ESG Disclosure in Attracting Sustainable Investment in Indonesia's Capital Market. RIGGS*: Journal of Artificial Intelligence and Digital Business.* https://doi.org/DOI: 10.31004/riggs.v4i3.2484

Raziyeva, S., & Meraliyev, M. (2025). Bias and Fairness in Automated Loan Approvals: A Systematic Review of Machine Learning Approaches. *Journal of Emerging Technologies and Computing.* https://doi.org/DOI: 10.47344/jbzmnx25

Ren, T. (2025). AI-Powered Carbon Footprint Tracking Is Redefining Green Investment Decision-Making. Advances in Economics, *Management and Political Sciences.* https://doi.org/DOI: 10.54254/2754-1169/2025.GL27239

Sadiq, R., Yasser, F., & Nawaz, F. (2025). *Using AI to predict and mitigate green asset bubbles in financial markets.* The Regional Tribune., DOI: 10.55737/trt/SG25.103

Sari, R. C., Sholihin, M., Cahaya, F. R., Ishola, A., Yuniarti, N., Pranesti, A. R., Sari, A. R., & Haryanto, . (2025). Artificial Intelligence-Based ESG Greenwashing Detection: Road to Net Zero Carbon and Its Impact on Corporate Performance. *Business Strategy & Development, 8*(4), e70228. Advance online publication. DOI: 10.1002/bsd2.70228

Sasaki, N., & Abe, I. (2025). A Digital Twin Architecture for Forest Restoration: Integrating AI, IoT, and Blockchain for Smart Ecosystem Management. *Future Internet, 17*(9), 421. DOI: 10.3390/fi17090421

Schaltegger, S., Hörisch, J., & Freeman, R. E. (2019). Business cases for sustainability: A stakeholder theory perspective. *Organization & Environment, 32*(3), 191–212. DOI: 10.1177/1086026617722882

Schultz, F. C., Valentinov, V., & Pies, I. (2025). The Stakeholder Business Case for Circular Economy: An Ordonomic Approach for Developing a Circular Economy Business Case by Stakeholder Governance. *Journal of Industrial Ecology*, *29*(4), 1279–1292. DOI: 10.1111/jiec.70046

Shukla, D. (2025). Green Bonds and Sustainable Investing: Trends, Challenges, and Future Outlook. *Journal of International Commercial Law and Technology*. https://doi.org/DOI: 10.61336/Jiclt/25-01-28

Singh, A. (2025). Predictive analytics for risk management in finance. International Journal of Advanced Research in Science. *Tongxin Jishu*, 364–372. Advance online publication. DOI: 10.48175/IJARSCT-28040

Siriman, N., Ali, M. S., Siddiqui, T., Rohin, G., Vejju, B., & Cherupelly, N. (2025). Green finance and AI in India: A synergistic approach to sustainable development and climate resilience. *International Journal of Environmental Sciences*, *11*(1), 207–216. Advance online publication. DOI: 10.64252/mt7jkk84

Soni, G., Singh, S., & Singh, D. (2025). Artificial intelligence in modern finance: Pathways to smarter, safer, and faster systems. *International Journal for Research in Applied Science and Engineering Technology*, *13*(9), 830–835. Advance online publication. DOI: 10.22214/ijraset.2025.74143

Swanson, A. R., & Sakhrani, V. (2023). Value–Risk Calculator for Blended Finance: A Systems Perspective of the Nachtigal Hydropower Project. *Sustainability (Basel)*, *15*(13), 10357. DOI: 10.3390/su151310357

Tiossi, F. M., & Rodrigues, R. G. (2023). *Triple helix in the management of innovation in public policies: A study of two countries. Revista de Gestão e Secretariado*. Management and Administrative Professional Review., DOI: 10.7769/gesec.v14i8.2690

Vaghefi, S. A., Hachcham, A., Grasso, V., Manicus, J., Msemo, N., Senni, C., & Leippold, M. (2025). *AI for Climate Finance: Agentic Retrieval and Multi-Step Reasoning for Early Warning System Investments*. ArXiv. https://doi.org//arxiv.2504.05104DOI: 10.2139/ssrn.5208086

Võ, T. T. H., Nguy n, V. H. T., & Pham, T. L. (2025). *University–Industry–Government Collaboration in Fostering Innovation: Policy Solutions to Strengthen Triple Helix Partnerships in Ho Chi Minh City in the Digital Era*. International Journal of Innovative Science and Research Technology., DOI: 10.38124/ijisrt/25aug1367

World Bank. (2022). *What you need to know about green finance*. World Bank Group.

Zhang, H., & Punjwani, A. (2025). A Triple Helix Approach to a Greener Future: Environmental Law, Fintech, Institutional Quality, and Natural Resources as Pillars of Environmental Sustainability in G20. *Sustainability (Basel), 17*(9), 4043. Advance online publication. DOI: 10.3390/su17094043

Zhou, C., & Etzkowitz, H. (2021). Triple Helix twins: A framework for achieving nnovation and UN Sustainable Development Goals. *Sustainability (Basel), 13*(12), 6535. DOI: 10.3390/su13126535

Zhou, P. (2025). *AI and DeFi Integration: Algorithmic Bias, Black-Box Opacity, and Regulatory Challenges.* Advances in Economics and Management Research., DOI: 10.56028/aemr.14.1.770.2025

Chapter 7
Applicability of Artificial Intelligence in the Financial Domain

Ameya Anil Patil
http://orcid.org/0000-0002-4920-7630
Dr. Vishwanath Karad MIT World Peace University, India

ABSTRACT

Technology, especially AI is becoming ubiquitous in various functional areas.This chapter delves into the integration of AI technologies with a focus on neural networks within the financial domain. Neural networks excel in processing amounts of data identifying nonlinear patterns and adapting to changing market conditions. The article explores two applications of AI in finance; stock prediction and bankruptcy prediction including fraud detection in statements. These areas rely on analytics, where AI algorithms analyze data to forecast market trends stock prices and economic indicators. The potential for networks to revolutionize prediction capabilities in these domains is highlighted through a review of research and methodologies. AI is also increasingly used in bankruptcy prediction, associated with the probability of financial failure of a corporation. Financial data, such as those included in popular bankruptcy prediction and fraud detection models such as Altman's Z-score, Beneish's M-score are fed as inputs to the neural networks.

INTRODUCTION

The 21st century has witnessed incredible growth of AI. Its applicability can be seen in many different areas, thanks to the spread of technology and digitization. This boom, though, brings both bright chances and hidden dangers. The financial

DOI: 10.4018/979-8-3373-9645-3.ch007

domain, often regarded as the lifeblood of the global economy, operates at the intersection of complexity and precision. In this dynamic arena, the ability to make swift, accurate decisions and navigate intricate regulatory landscapes is paramount. Amid this environment of relentless data flows and ever-increasing demands for efficiency, AI has emerged as a transformative force with profound implications for the financial sector(Bredt,2019). More individualized and sophisticated financial applications are made possible by AI (Cao,2022). AI can be viewed in terms of intelligent machines that can actually think and have perception and self-awareness. AI is being developed to automate more tasks traditionally performed by humans. Most widely used AI systems today are operated directly or indirectly by humans, who are in charge of the analytical procedure or result. But an increasing number of AI systems work really autonomously and go beyond serving as human substitutes (Candrian & Scherer, 2022). Autonomous decision-making is built into these systems, and they are given access to massive volumes of data to process. Such self-sufficient AI systems can outperform humans in a variety of business domains and tasks, giving them a significant strategic edge.

Among the myriad innovations that have reshaped the landscape of finance, AI stands out as a powerful and disruptive force. AI represents a paradigm shift, ushering in an era where intelligent machines collaborate with human experts to optimize financial processes, manage risk, and deliver superior customer experiences. Attempts for AI applications in the finance domain have been made even in the 20th century. Meservy et al. (1992) examined early AI methods to enhance accounting, tax, and audit expertise. AI is leading the financial sector with a wide range of applications that transform how banks and other financial institutions operate, make decisions, and interact with clients.

Modern economies are built on banking, insurance, asset management, and other financial activities. This complex and ever-changing industry relies on big data and decision-making. Quantity of data, strict risk management, customer centricity, market dynamics, and regulatory complexity make the domain complex. AI could solve these issues and create new industry business opportunities. The financial sector's AI revolution is possible. Financial institutions use machine learning to improve loan and insurance decisions. Machine learning algorithms can evaluate a borrower's credit history and other data to determine if they can repay the loan on time (Abdou & Pointon,2011). This helps banks evaluate applicants' risk and choose loans wisely. Insurance plans can be customized using machine learning. Insurers can tailor policies to an individual's traits and risk factors. AI has disrupted the financial industry with applications that boost productivity, accuracy, and risk management. AI in finance has streamlined processes, increased productivity, and given institutions more agility in navigating complex market dynamics and regulatory hurdles.

Artificial Neural networks(ANN):

When neural networks make use of regulated learning models, they are able to acquire more complex types of information by gradually gaining experience and knowledge from datasets. (Jorgenson et al.,2023). Neural networks serve as intelligent information mining method and for deep learning strategies. Neural networks provide a state-of-the-art approach that does not require pre-specification during the modeling phase because they are able to understand the relationship between the variables on their own. In the world of securities investing, where there are a lot of assumptions but little actual understanding of how stock prices are set, this is very helpful. Because neural networks tend to learn nonlinear mappings between input and output, they are used to estimate stock market prices (Adhikari & Agrawal, 2014). A sufficient sample size is required to train a generally stable neural network. Because of the vast amounts of information gathered in capital markets, machines would be able to master a variety of designs and produce accurate forecasts (Agarwal et al.,2021). Neural networks have been used extensively in stock prediction because of their capacity to identify intricate patterns and correlations in data. Through the years,ANN's have been enhanced further to improve stock prediction abilities(Patil et al.,2024).

Fully connected neural networks with one or more layers are called ANNs (Li et al.,2018). An example of an ANN with three hidden layers, an output layer, and an input layer can be seen in the image below. Through its nodes, every layer is directly connected to every other layer. A network can be made deeper by adding more hidden layers.

Figure 1. Artificial Neural network with 3 hidden layers

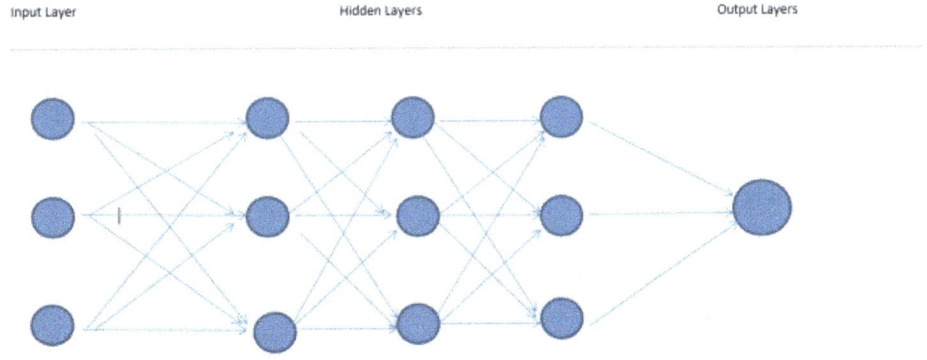

ANNs are sophisticated algorithms that can solve complex problems beyond the scope of conventional machine learning and simple neural networks. By converting cognitive abilities into a digital environment that imitates how the human brain functions, they simulate learning in humans. ANNs are complex networks of linked nodes that are more complex than the human brain. These networks use algebraic equations to direct data flow, enabling self-learning and the discovery of hidden properties. They thrive as approximators, deciphering subtle input-output correlations in massive datasets. As a result, ANNs have proven to be extremely useful in stock price prediction (Dase & Pawar,2010), discovering detailed correlations between stock performance and a plethora of financial and technical aspects. Their ability to extract hidden insights from enormous datasets makes them a valuable tool for analysts and investors, albeit interpretability and training data volume must be considered.

When harnessing the power of neural networks for data analysis and predictions, a critical step is splitting data into two distinct parts: a training set and a test set. Such division is essential for ensuring that the neural network model is both effective and trustworthy. Training set can be viewed as the neural network's classroom where the model learns and hones its skills. This set is created by randomly selecting a significant portion of available data, typically around 70-80%. The neural network uses this data to understand the patterns, relationships, and features within it. It's like showing it examples of problems and solutions. Through a process of trial and error, the model adjusts its internal parameters (weights and biases) to minimize errors in predicting outcomes within this training data. The test set, on the other hand, acts as the neural network's final exam. It is a separate batch of data, usually making up the remaining 20-30%. This set is kept hidden from the model during its "learning" phase. It is like giving the neural network a new set of problems it has never seen before. After the model is fully trained, it is presented with the test set and asked to make predictions. Thereafter, these predictions are compared with actual outcomes in test data. This comparison is crucial because it tells how well the neural network can generalize what it has learned from the training data to new, unseen data. In other words, it assesses the model's real-world performance, or its predictive capability.

There is a wide variety of ANNs, each with their own architecture and set of goals. Feedforward Neural Network (FNN) is a basic type of ANN, where information flows unidirectionally, viz. from input layer to output layer. FNN's take historical stock price information, along with other pertinent features such as trading volume, technical indicators, or economic data, as input and predict future stock prices or market trends. RNN, a neural network architecture developed to handle sequential data by taking the temporal component of the input, has been utilized extensively in stock market prediction studies. The main characteristic of RNN is its knack to capture and propagate information from previous time steps to current time step, allowing them to model dependencies and patterns in sequential data. Reverse connections are allowed in the topology of recurrent networks (Korol, 2019). Any neuron's output can also be sent to its input. Neuron status is thus determined not just by the value of the input signal, but also by the previous state of any neuron, including this one. RNNs can be used to process historical stock price data and other relevant variables over time, capturing patterns and relationships that might aid in stock price predictions. The RNN architecture known as Long Short-Term Memory (LSTM) is particularly good at identifying long-term dependencies and patterns in sequential data. LSTM networks consist of memory cells that store and update information over time, as well as gates that regulate the flow of information through the network. The three gates that make up an LSTM are input gate, forgetting gate, and output gate. Information not complying with the algorithm will be erased by the forgetting gate. Hence, only the compliant data remains. For forecasting stock prices, LSTM networks can be trained to learn patterns and relationships in historical stock price data, as well as other relevant features (Jadhavrao et al.,2023). LSTM networks can capture trends, seasonality, and other patterns that are important for predicting future stock values by taking into account the sequential nature of data and including memory cells.

Convolutional Neural Networks (CNNs) are widely used for processing image data. However, its application has been limited in financial analysis. This scarcity of usage can be attributed to the fact that CNNs are inherently more suitable for processing image data and are less well-suited for handling general numerical datasets, such as financial statements. These networks employ convolutional layers that scan and extract features from images, making them exceptionally effective for tasks like image recognition and computer vision. Conversely, financial data predominantly comprises numerical values, time series, and structured information.

Still, CNN can be applied to certain aspects of stock prediction. CNN is a feed-forward neural network. More hidden layers are present in CNN vis-a-vis traditional neural network. Designing the CNN's architecture for stock prediction challenges is conceivably a key problem that merits additional research. Primarily, CNN can be employed for data visualization purposes, converting financial data into visual representations like candlestick charts or market depth plots. Such visualizations can assist traders and analysts gain insights into market trends and patterns. Secondly, CNNs can potentially be used for feature extraction and preprocessing of financial time series data. Next, CNN may also be utilized in sentiment analysis by analyzing textual data such as news articles, social media posts, or stock market financial reports. CNN can also analyze alternative data sources, such as satellite imagery, web-scraped data, or visual data from sensors. Prediction accuracy can be greatly increased by using a deep CNN-based framework to extract higher-level features from a large number of financial variables (Hoseinzade & Haratizadeh, 2019).

Deep neural networks:

Deep learning algorithms have recently gained popularity and are frequently used to create prediction and classification models. Deep learning is focussed at building multi-layered artificial neural networks. Deep learning approaches use data to tackle complex problems with fewer assumptions. Deep learning automatically extracts features from data, requiring little to no human involvement in feature selection. The term "deep" alludes to the numerous layers that make up the neural network architecture. Deep learning employs neural networks with multiple hidden layers, allowing the network to learn representations of the data at different levels of abstraction. Each layer in the network extracts higher-level features from the representations learned by the previous layers, thus creating a hierarchy of learned features. Deep neural networks combine the advantages of neural networks and deep learning. As a result, they are more effective than typical ML algorithms at addressing nonlinear problems (Yu & Yan,2020). Such networks yield greater precision with less human effort and minimal tuning. Deep learning has been applied to stock prediction, particularly in context of time series analysis, because of its ability to understand complicated patterns and representations from past data.

For deep learning models to create a complex neural network model, a large amount of input data is required (Jiang, 2021). Here, market data is the most popular choice, followed by the text data. The majority of deep learning systems produce forecasts based on previous stock price, volume, or derivative data (Liu et al.,2023). Deep learning may be appealing for stock market prediction at high frequencies since it can extract characteristics from a large amount of raw data without relying on prior knowledge of predictors (Chong et al.,2017). Many different network architectures, activation functions, and other model parameters are available for deep learning techniques. It is well recognized that the way data is represented has a significant impact on how well these algorithms perform. According to empirical findings, Deep neural networks can improve prediction accuracy by extracting additional data from autoregressive model residuals. Chou (2019) employed a hybrid model integrating the decision tree with the deep neural network, which was able to achieve a high accuracy in predicting corporate bankruptcy. Deep learning models can be fed with textual data alongwith financial information to further enhance bankruptcy prediction (Mai et al.,2019).

Applicability of AI in stock prediction

Predicting stock market price changes is difficult and complex. Stock data is volatile and unpredictable, making it exciting and challenging for investors and financial experts. Past stock market patterns and trends do not always predict future results. Economic statistics, geopolitical events, business earnings reports, and investor sentiment affect stock prices. The highly dynamic and unpredictable interactions between these components cause stock prices to behave chaotically. The stock market's complexity, non-linearity, and dynamics make stock prediction difficult. Analysts and investors must manage the volume and variety of stock price-affecting information. Rapid market changes may make investment decisions difficult. These issues have been addressed by researchers and financial firms using cutting-edge technologies and complex algorithms. Machine learning and AI are popular for stock prediction. These methods create models that capture complex market patterns and trends using historical stock data and other data.

AI in the stock market is changing how financial professionals and investors trade and invest. Market analysis and trading are improved by machine learning algorithms. Effective AI-based models allow stock traders and investors to make huge profits that were previously unattainable (Chopra & Sharma, 2021). Machine learning algorithms process large financial data quickly and accurately. These algorithms are trained on past stock market data to spot patterns and trends that human analysts may miss. By identifying these trends, machine learning algorithms can predict stock values, helping traders develop strategies(Anwar et al.,2024). These forecasts can cover short-term price changes and long-term trends, helping traders and investors.

Apart from financial data, AI-powered algorithms can evaluate other data sources. News headlines, social media posts, earnings reports, and other sources can help them gauge market sentiment and stock or business opinions. AI sentiment analysis is a popular way for investors to track market sentiment and make decisions based on market sentiment. For instance, a stock with overwhelmingly positive social media and news mentions may indicate bullish sentiment, influencing investment decisions. AI-driven trading algorithms are also growing in finance. AI algorithms analyze real-time market data and execute trades based on insights. AI-driven trading algorithms can process data faster than humans. Some of these algorithms can trade autonomously, responding quickly to market conditions and data. High-frequency trading (HFT) strategies use AI algorithms to make split-second trades.

Research studies regarding neural networks in stock prediction

Academics and financial experts debate whether AI can outperform the stock market. AI excels at data analysis and processing, often outperforming humans. With its ability to sift through vast amounts of information quickly, AI holds great promise for the future of stock trading. Many enthusiasts believe that, given ongoing advancements in IT technology, AI might eventually surpass human investors in consistently generating profits from the stock market. They argue that AI's analytical prowess and computational speed provide it with a competitive edge. However, it's important to note that the stock market is a complex and dynamic system influenced by numerous factors, including human sentiment and unforeseen events. AI models can be susceptible to biases in data, and past performance doesn't guarantee future success. The majority of stock market forecasting models employ neural networks (Mintarya et al.,2023), with different strategic inputs.

Several strategies have been developed in existing methodologies to predict stock market trends. Reliability of financial market forecasting and viability of lucrative model-based trading are heavily impacted via a gamut of factors. These include the market's maturity, the forecasting method utilized, the time frame for which forecasts are made, as well as the methodology employed to evaluate the model and simulate trade (Hsu et al.,2016). The 21st century was defined by rapid development of electronic markets and emergence of computer-driven high-frequency trading enabled by computing technologies (Lehoczky & Schervish, 2018). Non-linear models such as Artificial neural networks(ANN) have then been used to overcome the limitations of linear models, considering the chaotic nature of stock markets. Utilizing time series analysis technology for stock forecasting is vital for creating stock trading strategies and earning greater trading returns (Liu et al.,2023).

The efforts to stock market prediction begins with fundamental analysis. Fundamental analysis is a sort of investment analysis wherein the company's past and estimated sales, profits and other financial parameters are analysed along with other economic on the basis of factors which affect the value of company. Here, underlying elements that affect businesses or sectors are used as predictive attributes (Bustos & Pomares-Quimbaya, 2020). Fundamental analysis focuses on fundamental information, mainly contained in the annual reports of corporations. These include the business concern's sales and profits, annual growth rate in various financial parameters, its market position and the future prospects (Nair & Mohandas, 2015). This approach is best suited for long-term forecasting. Combining fundamental analysis with neural networks can improve investment performance (Shen & Tzeng,2015).

The next most utilized stock prediction technique is Technical analysis. It implies forecasting future stock prices by analyzing trends in past stock prices and trading volumes (Lohrmann & Luukka, 2019). The input features for ML and AI models can also be employed with the experience-based technical indicators. To increase the reliability of predictions in the AI era, technical indicators are fed into a neural network (Sezer et al.,2017).

Stock markets are affected by investor sentiments and hence, another popular stock prediction method used is 'Sentiment analysis'. In today's world of social media, the sentiments over popular social media platforms such as Twitter and Facebook have been widely used for forecasting stock prices. Sentiment analysis includes monitoring news, social media, and market indicators to assess the overall mood and sentiment of market participants. The accuracy of stock market predictions can be enhanced by factoring in specific characteristics of public sentiment. Investments aided by sentiment analysis techniques can be profitable if used properly. The future performance of the stock market can be automatically calculated using sentiment analysis and collective intelligence (Devi & Bhaskaran, 2015). To predict stock prices, social media text data feature extraction may characterize investors' emotional tendencies (Ji et al.,2021). News and sentiments improve deep learning price predictions. Textual information in news headlines may influence stock price predictions (Puh & Bagić Babac,2023). Li et al. (2020) combined market price technical indicators and textual news sentiments to create a layered deep learning neural network prediction model. AI-based investment strategies go beyond sentiment analysis. They can also be more proactive in shaping investors' stock market perceptions (Song & Jain, 2022). This requires actively shaping expectations rather than analyzing sentiment. AI-driven strategies can influence investor sentiment and behavior through algorithmic trading, news generation, and targeted social media messaging. AI systems can manipulate market sentiment by strategically releasing news articles or social media posts with positive or negative information, resulting in buying or selling activity that meets their goals. These tactics may raise ethical concerns and disrupt market stability, but they show financial AI's growing sophistication. In the face of advanced AI-based investment strategies, investors and regulators must remain vigilant and develop safeguards to ensure fair and transparent markets.

ANN applications use financial variables as inputs and stock performance as output. Many studies have shown that financial markets are nonlinear and that ANN can determine this relationship. In this context, ANN is widely used to accurately forecast stock markets (Gandhmal & Kumar,2019; Wiranata,& Djunaidy, 2021). Many studies have shown that ANNs outperform statistical models like ARIMA (Mohammed,2020). Simultaneously, the merging of statistics and learning models has refined neural networks. The input variables and network parameters for ANNs must be carefully chosen. The ability to accurately predict the future is highly dependent on learning algorithm employed during ANN training (Selvamuthu et al.,2019). Prasad et al. (2023) revealed that FNN and RNN types such as LSTM,

GRU, and CNN were extremely good in predicting riskiness of Indian stock market as indicated by the Volatility index (VIX).

Over time, the ANN model was integrated with other algorithms in several researches. Classical BP learning algorithm, when aided by global search techniques such as GA and simulated annealing (SA) can significantly increase prediction accuracy (Qiu et al.,2016). Modifications can be made to neural networks using enhanced algorithms such as improved sparrow algorithm. Using it to tune the BP neural network's initial weight and threshold led to a very precise prediction of near-term stock prices (Liu et al.,2022). With the use of BP neural networks, Google Trends, and the enhanced sine cosine algorithm (ISCA), it was possible to improve prediction accuracy to 87% (Hu et al.,2018). The prediction accuracy of neural networks is enhanced by the use of nonlinear independent component analysis (NLICA) for feature extraction (Dai et al.,2012). In both the pre- and post-demonetization scenarios in India, ANN model trained with the LM algorithm achieved a respectable level of accuracy (Chopra et al.,2019). Chaudhari &Thakkar (2023) applied data compression to convert continuous stock market data to a discrete form. This was used as a pre-processing step, which happened to improve prediction accuracy. ANN with macroeconomic variables as inputs and trained with Scaled Conjugate Gradient (SCG) algorithm was able to achieve nearly 100% accuracy during the Covid-19 period in Indian markets (Goel & Som, 2023).

The conceptual model on the basis of these studies can be viewed as in Figure 2

Figure 2. Viewing AI for stock market prediction

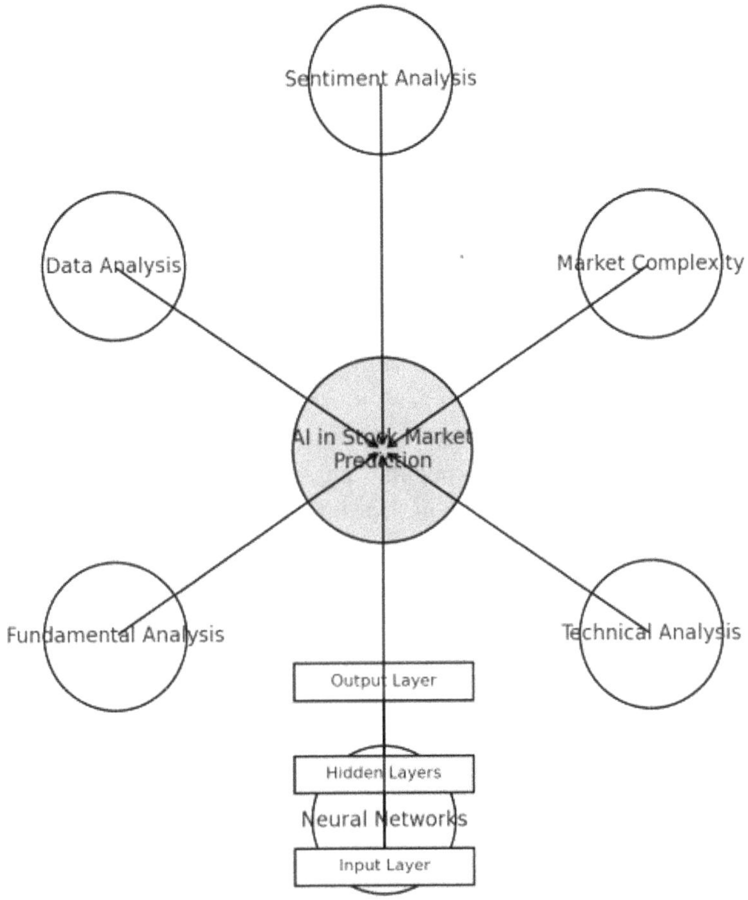

Applicability of AI in bankruptcy prediction and fraud detection and the related research works

Accurately predicting a company's future performance, especially the likelihood of it going bankrupt, is crucial for investors aiming to make profitable decisions regarding stock selection(Hosaka,2019). Bankruptcy can be seen as a financial failure in a business, wherein the firm fails to generate profits and cannot pay its debts. Bankruptcy prediction and fraud detection in financial statements is a cornerstone of economic and financial decision-making. It equips investors, creditors, and financial professionals with the insights needed to navigate the uncertainties of the market, enabling them to make informed choices and mitigate potential financial risks. Business financial health and risk are assessed to predict bankruptcy. To manage risks, stakeholders must be able to predict a business's financial distress or bankruptcy and spot a company's financial statement fraud. Research on bankruptcy prediction has amplified, particularly after the 2008 global financial crisis (Shi & Li, 2019). It is vital to develop tools to monitor a business's failure risk based on its changing financials. Many models predict financial trouble. These models use mathematical computations, statistical analysis, and AI and ML. Intelligent procedures process massive and complex datasets to find subtle patterns and trends, while mathematical and statistical models use past financial data and ratios. Each method has its advantages. Altman's Z-score and Beneish's M-score, which use financial metrics and ratios, are the most popular fraud and bankruptcy detection models(Yadav et al.,2023).

Machine learning for bankruptcy prediction is crucial in the AI-era financial landscape. Neural networks are a popular and well-studied tools for bankruptcy prediction (Shi & Li, 2019). Machine learning algorithms predicted insolvency better by adding financial variables to Altman's Z-score. This combination has shown to predict financial trouble more accurately (Barboza et al., 2017). Machine learning algorithms can combine many financial parameters, so these models can be used in many scenarios and sectors. Neural networks are particularly promising bankruptcy prediction models (Tam & Kiang, 1992; Bellovary et al.,2007). Different architectures can affect the performance of these networks (Milana & Ashta, 2021). Back-Propagation (BP) neural network model, a multi-layer forward network employs an error back-propagation mechanism to fine-tune its parameters (Sun & Xu, 2016). BP neural network demonstrated brilliant accuracy in the realm of financial early warning for mining corporations listed in China (Sun & Lei, 2021). Genetic algorithm neural network was found to significantly outperform BP model in predicting bankruptcy (Anandarajan et al.,2001). Apart from the neural network model selection, bankruptcy prediction accuracy depends on the financial ratios taken to run the model (Shetty et al.,2022). Accuracy in predicting bankruptcy can be improved by incorporating larger dataset and more number of financial variables. Thilakarathna et al. (2022) used 29 financial ratios served as predictors to the deep neural network. The results reveal the possibility of significantly better and much earlier prediction of bankruptcy. Becerra-Vicario et al. (2020) applied financial ratios related to profitability and indebtedness on Deep Recurrent Convolutional Neural Network, taking restaurant industries into account. The prediction accuracy with this approach prior to 1-2 years of bankruptcy filing was close to 90%. Financial ratios applied as inputs in the form of a grayscale image to a CNN, used for training and testing a CNN produced high performance in bankruptcy prediction(Hosaka,2019). Thus, it can be seen that most of the research works to forecast bankruptcy using neural networks have relied on financial ratios(Korol,2019). The use of financial ratios is in vogue due to their predictive power, availability and standardization (du Jardin, 2016). However, there a few research works which have attempted to use textual data such as Managerial Discussion & Analysis part in annual reports in order to predict firm bankruptcy (Mai et al.,2019).

This exemplifies the practical effectiveness of neural networks in real-world financial applications. The advantages of machine learning and neural networks in bankruptcy prediction extend beyond traditional models. They excel at capturing intricate patterns in financial data, adapt to changing market dynamics, and provide timely warnings of potential financial distress. Moreover, they have the capacity to process large datasets efficiently, making them well-suited for the modern financial landscape, where data volumes are rapidly expanding.

CONCLUSION

AI applications have been on rise in the finance sphere, in several related areas such as accounting, auditing, analysing and detecting anomalies in financial statements. Research works regarding the use of AI in stock market prediction has risen at an exponential rate. Though a large number of works are in the sphere of developed economies, the studies in case of emerging markets are also catching up. These studies have focussed on implementing feature selection algorithms, and propose a parameter optimization method for different neural networks to obtain better experimental results. The literature on the application of artificial intelligence to stock market prediction has yet to provide an accurate predictive model. Investors that use an AI-based investment strategy may not necessarily be successful in the stock market in the long run(Song & Jain, 2022). While perfect predictions may remain elusive, ongoing research and advancements in technology hold the promise of improving the accuracy and reliability of stock forecasts, assisting investors in making informed and timely investment decisions in the ever-changing world of finance. Artificial intelligence is transforming the stock market landscape through its ability to process vast data sets, recognize patterns, and make informed predictions. Pre-processing raw data is useful and crucial for system dependability and model generalization to unknown data, according to numerous research studies (Guo et al. 2015). If the predictive model can be improved to take into account new data as it is gathered for stock market projections, the model's adaption to the new data can advance, and its predicting accuracy can rise.

In bankruptcy prediction as well, ANN's seem promising. They can learn complex financial data patterns to better predict business failure. ANNs can improve credit risk assessment and financial distress prediction. Banks can use ANNs to assess business lending risk and make better debt collection decisions. Prior to utilizing ANNs for business decisions, they must be trained with high-quality data and an understanding of their working ought to be developed. Further, ANN's can be combined with other algorithms to enhance prediction accuracy (Anandarajan et al.,2001). A larger set of financial ratios can improve bankruptcy forecasts (Thilakarathna et al.,2022).Research works in the area claim to achieve upto 90% accuracy in bankruptcy prediction (Becerra-Vicario et al., 2020).

Managerial Implications

The article depicts the power of AI in financial sector. Bankers and other financial organizations can reduce their non-performing assets by using AI's ability to predict which borrowers are likely to file for bankruptcy. Artificial intelligence has the potential to significantly improve risk assessment models through the consideration of a broader range of variables and their interconnections. Managers should consider integrating AI-driven systems for predicting bankruptcy into their risk assessment processes. Early warning signs of financial distress can be provided by AI models. Managers may use these signals to initiate preventive measures, such as extending credit lines or renegotiating agreements, to help clients or investments avoid bankruptcy. Auditors can apply various bankruptcy models on the firms at a rapid pace, thanks to different neural networks.

With the power of ANN, investment managers can improve stock prediction accuracy and hence the portfolio returns of their clients. ANNs can be utilized to supply managers with stock market information that they would not be able to obtain on their own. This data can assist managers in making better decisions about when to buy, sell, and hold stocks. Investment managers must determine as to how ANN predictions will be used into investing decision-making. The question of particular interest here is whether ANN serve as decision-making aids or be integrated into automated trading systems. Likewise, financial institutions, investment businesses, and individual investors must consider the managerial ramifications of the use of ANNs in stock prediction. Data preprocessing is crucial to the success of ANN models in stock prediction. Similarly, choosing the most important input features for the ANN, amongst different financial data and ratios, or technical indicators is equally important. Domain expertise and data analysis are required to choose variables with the greatest predictive ability. Depending on the nature of the data and the prediction job, selection of the right neural network architecture for stock prediction such as feedforward networks, recurrent networks, or convolutional networks can lead to enhanced stock predictions. Managers can utilize ANNs to create investing strategies that are particular to their risk tolerance and investment objectives.

REFERENCES

Abdou, H. A., & Pointon, J. (2011). Credit scoring, statistical techniques and evaluation criteria: A review of the literature. *Intelligent Systems in Accounting, Finance & Management, 18*(2-3), 59–88. DOI: 10.1002/isaf.325

Adhikari, R., & Agrawal, R. K. (2014). A combination of artificial neural network and random walk models for financial time series forecasting. *Neural Computing & Applications, 24*(6), 1441–1449. DOI: 10.1007/s00521-013-1386-y

Agarwal, D., Sheth, R., & Shekokar, N. (2021). Algorithmic Trading Using Machine Learning and Neural Network. Computer Networks. *Big Data and IoT, 407*. Advance online publication. DOI: 10.1007/978-981-16-0965-7

Anandarajan, M., Lee, P., & Anandarajan, A. (2001). Bankruptcy prediction of financially stressed firms: An examination of the predictive accuracy of artificial neural networks. *International Journal of Intelligent Systems in Accounting Finance & Management, 10*(2), 69–81. DOI: 10.1002/isaf.199

Anwar, A., Patil, A. A., Choudari, S., Chetna, C., & Kiran, C. S. (2024). Machine Learning Insights for Stock Market Trend Identification. *International Journal of Intelligent Systems and Applications in Engineering, 12*(10s), 567–575.

Barboza, F., Kimura, H., & Altman, E. (2017). Machine learning models and bankruptcy prediction. *Expert Systems with Applications, 83*, 405–417. DOI: 10.1016/j.eswa.2017.04.006

Becerra-Vicario, R., Alaminos, D., Aranda, E., & Fernández-Gámez, M. A. (2020). Deep recurrent convolutional neural network for bankruptcy prediction: A case of the restaurant industry. *Sustainability (Basel), 12*(12), 5180. DOI: 10.3390/su12125180

Bellovary, J. L., Giacomino, D. E., & Akers, M. D. (2007). A Review of Bankruptcy Prediction Studies: 1930 to Present. *Journal of Financial Education, 33*, 1–42. http://www.jstor.org/stable/41948574

Bredt, S. (2019). Artificial intelligence (AI) in the financial sector. *Frontiers in Artificial Intelligence, 2*, 1–5. DOI: 10.3389/frai.2019.00016

Bustos, O., & Pomares-Quimbaya, A. (2020). Stock market movement forecast: A systematic review. *Expert Systems with Applications, 156*, 113464. DOI: 10.1016/j.eswa.2020.113464

Candrian, C., & Scherer, A. (2022). Rise of the machines: Delegating decisions to autonomous AI. *Computers in Human Behavior, 134*, 107308. DOI: 10.1016/j.chb.2022.107308

Cao, L. (2022). Ai in finance: Challenges, techniques, and opportunities. *ACM Computing Surveys, 55*(3), 1–38. DOI: 10.1145/3502289

Chaudhari, K., & Thakkar, A. (2023). Data fusion with factored quantization for stock trend prediction using neural networks. *Information Processing & Management, 60*(3), 103293. DOI: 10.1016/j.ipm.2023.103293

Chong, E., Han, C., & Park, F. C. (2017). Deep learning networks for stock market analysis and prediction: Methodology, data representations, and case studies. *Expert Systems with Applications, 83*, 187–205. DOI: 10.1016/j.eswa.2017.04.030

Chopra, R., & Sharma, G. D. (2021). Application of artificial intelligence in stock market forecasting: A critique, review, and research agenda. *Journal of Risk and Financial Management, 14*(11), 526. DOI: 10.3390/jrfm14110526

Chopra, S., Yadav, D., & Chopra, A. N. (2019). Artificial neural networks based Indian stock market price prediction: Before and after demonetization. *Journal of Swarm Intelligence and Evolutionary Computation, 8*(1), 2–7.

Chou, T. N. (2019, July). An explainable hybrid model for bankruptcy prediction based on the decision tree and deep neural network. In *2019 IEEE 2nd international conference on knowledge innovation and invention (ICKII)* (pp. 122-125). IEEE. DOI: 10.1109/ICKII46306.2019.9042639

Dai, W., Wu, J. Y., & Lu, C. J. (2012). Combining nonlinear independent component analysis and neural network for the prediction of Asian stock market indexes. *Expert Systems with Applications, 39*(4), 4444–4452. DOI: 10.1016/j.eswa.2011.09.145

Dase, R. K., & Pawar, D. D. (2010). Application of Artificial Neural Network for stock market predictions: A review of literature. *International Journal of Machine Intelligence, 2*(2), 14–17. DOI: 10.9735/0975-2927.2.2.14-17

Devi, K. N., & Bhaskaran, V. M. (2015). Semantic enhanced social media sentiments for stock market prediction. *International Journal of Economics and Management Engineering, 9*(2), 678–682. DOI: 10.5281/zenodo.1100501

Du Jardin, P. (2016). A two-stage classification technique for bankruptcy prediction. *European Journal of Operational Research, 254*(1), 236–252. DOI: 10.1016/j.ejor.2016.03.008

Gandhmal, D. P., & Kumar, K. (2019). Systematic analysis and review of stock market prediction techniques. *Computer Science Review*, *34*, 100190. DOI: 10.1016/j.cosrev.2019.08.001

Goel, H., & Som, B. K. (2023). Stock market prediction, COVID-19 pandemic and neural networks: An SCG algorithm application. *Economía*, *24*(1), 134–146. DOI: 10.1108/ECON-07-2022-0101

Guo, Z., Wang, H., Yang, J., & Miller, D. J. (2015). A stock market forecasting model combining two-directional two-dimensional principal component analysis and radial basis function neural network. *PLoS One*, *10*(4), e0122385. DOI: 10.1371/journal.pone.0122385

Hosaka, T. (2019). Bankruptcy prediction using imaged financial ratios and convolutional neural networks. *Expert Systems with Applications*, *117*, 287–299. DOI: 10.1016/j.eswa.2018.09.039

Hoseinzade, E., & Haratizadeh, S. (2019). CNNpred: CNN-based stock market prediction using a diverse set of variables. *Expert Systems with Applications*, *129*, 273–285. DOI: 10.1016/j.eswa.2019.03.029

Hsu, M. W., Lessmann, S., Sung, M. C., Ma, T., & Johnson, J. E. (2016). Bridging the divide in financial market forecasting: Machine learners vs. financial economists. *Expert Systems with Applications*, *61*, 215–234. DOI: 10.1016/j.eswa.2016.05.033

Hu, H., Tang, L., Zhang, S., & Wang, H. (2018). Predicting the direction of stock markets using optimized neural networks with Google Trends. *Neurocomputing*, *285*, 188–195. DOI: 10.1016/j.neucom.2018.01.038

Jadhavrao, R., Sengupta, R., Patil, A., & Yadav, R. S. (2023). Stock market trend prediction using artificial intelligence algorithm (RNN-LSTM) - Comparison with current techniques and research on its effectiveness in forecasting in Indian market and US market. Empirical Economics Letters, 22(Special Issue 2), 124-133. DOI: 10.5281/zenodo.10864038

Ji, X., Wang, J., & Yan, Z. (2021). A stock price prediction method based on deep learning technology. *International Journal of Crowd Science*, *5*(1), 55–72. DOI: 10.1108/IJCS-05-2020-0012

Jiang, W. (2021). Applications of deep learning in stock market prediction: Recent progress. *Expert Systems with Applications*, *184*, 115537. DOI: 10.1016/j.eswa.2021.115537

. Jorgenson, D. W., Weitzman, M. L., ZXhang, Y. X., Haxo, Y. M., & Mat, Y. X. (2023). Can Neural Networks Predict Stock Market?. *AC Investment Research Journal, 220*(44).

Korol, T. (2019). Dynamic bankruptcy prediction models for European enterprises. *Journal of Risk and Financial Management, 12*(4), 185. DOI: 10.3390/jrfm12040185

Lehoczky, J., & Schervish, M. (2018). Overview and history of statistics for equity markets. *Annual Review of Statistics and Its Application, 5*(1), 265–288. DOI: 10.1146/annurev-statistics-031017-100518

Li, X., Wu, P., & Wang, W. (2020). Incorporating stock prices and news sentiments for stock market prediction: A case of Hong Kong. *Information Processing & Management, 57*(5), 102212. DOI: 10.1016/j.ipm.2020.102212

Li, Y., Jiang, W., Yang, L., & Wu, T. (2018). On neural networks and learning systems for business computing. *Neurocomputing, 275*, 1150–1159. DOI: 10.1016/j.neucom.2017.09.054

Liu, H., Zhao, T., Wang, S., & Li, X. (2023). A stock rank prediction method combining industry attributes and price data of stocks. *Information Processing & Management, 60*(4), 103358. DOI: 10.1016/j.ipm.2023.103358

Liu, X., Guo, J., Wang, H., & Zhang, F. (2022). Prediction of stock market index based on ISSA-BP neural network. *Expert Systems with Applications, 204*, 117604. DOI: 10.1016/j.eswa.2022.117604

Lohrmann, C., & Luukka, P. (2019). Classification of intraday S&P500 returns with a Random Forest. *International Journal of Forecasting, 35*(1), 390–407. DOI: 10.1016/j.ijforecast.2018.08.004

Mai, F., Tian, S., Lee, C., & Ma, L. (2019). Deep learning models for bankruptcy prediction using textual disclosures. *European Journal of Operational Research, 274*(2), 743–758. DOI: 10.1016/j.ejor.2018.10.024

Meservy, R. D., Denna, E. L., & Hansen, J. V. (1992). Application of artificial intelligence to accounting, tax, and audit services: Research at Brigham Young University. *Expert Systems with Applications, 4*(2), 213–218. DOI: 10.1016/0957-4174(92)90112-6

Milana, C., & Ashta, A. (2021). Artificial intelligence techniques in finance and financial markets: A survey of the literature. *Strategic Change, 30*(3), 189–209. DOI: 10.1002/jsc.2403

Mintarya, L. N., Halim, J. N., Angie, C., Achmad, S., & Kurniawan, A. (2023). Machine learning approaches in stock market prediction: A systematic literature review. *Procedia Computer Science*, *216*, 96–102. DOI: 10.1016/j.procs.2022.12.115

Mohammed, W. A. (2020). Challenges of Stock Prediction. In *Valuation Challenges and Solutions in Contemporary Businesses* (pp. 234–252). IGI Global., DOI: 10.4018/978-1-7998-1086-5.ch013

Nair, B. B., & Mohandas, V. P. (2015). An intelligent recommender system for stock trading. *Intelligent Decision Technologies*, *9*(3), 243–269. DOI: 10.3233/IDT-140220

Patil, A., Saha, S., & Sengupta, R. (2024). Enhancing stock market predictions through predictive analytics. In Singh, N., Birla, S., Ansari, M. D., & Shukla, N. K. (Eds.), *Intelligent techniques for predictive data analytics*. Wiley., DOI: 10.1002/9781394227990.ch7

Prasad, A., Bakhshi, P., & Guha, D. (2023). Forecasting the direction of daily changes in the India VIX index using deep learning. *IIMB Management Review*, *35*(2), 149–163. DOI: 10.1016/j.iimb.2023.05.002

Puh, K., & Bagić Babac, M. (2023). Predicting stock market using natural language processing. *American Journal of Business*, *38*(2), 41–61. DOI: 10.1108/AJB-08-2022-0124

Qiu, M., Song, Y., & Akagi, F. (2016). Application of artificial neural network for the prediction of stock market returns: The case of the Japanese stock market. *Chaos, Solitons, and Fractals*, *85*, 1–7. DOI: 10.1016/j.chaos.2016.01.004

Selvamuthu, D., Kumar, V., & Mishra, A. (2019). Indian stock market prediction using artificial neural networks on tick data. *Financial Innovation*, *5*(1), 1–12. DOI: 10.1186/s40854-019-0131-7

Sezer, O. B., Ozbayoglu, M., & Dogdu, E. (2017). A deep neural-network based stock trading system based on evolutionary optimized technical analysis parameters. *Procedia Computer Science*, *114*, 473–480. DOI: 10.1016/j.procs.2017.09.031

Shen, K. Y., & Tzeng, G. H. (2015). Combined soft computing model for value stock selection based on fundamental analysis. *Applied Soft Computing*, *37*, 142–155. DOI: 10.1016/j.asoc.2015.07.030

Shetty, S., Musa, M., & Brédart, X. (2022). Bankruptcy Prediction Using Machine Learning Techniques. *Journal of Risk and Financial Management*, *15*(1), 35. DOI: 10.3390/jrfm15010035

Shi, Y., & Li, X. (2019). An overview of bankruptcy prediction models for corporate firms: A systematic literature review. *Intangible Capital, 15*(2), 114–127. DOI: 10.3926/ic.1354

Song, G. H., & Jain, A. (2022). Can artificial intelligence beat the stock market? *Studies in Economics and Finance, 39*(5), 772–785. DOI: 10.1108/SEF-03-2022-0133

Sun, W., & Xu, Y. (2016). Financial security evaluation of the electric power industry in China based on a back propagation neural network optimized by genetic algorithm. *Energy, 101*, 366–379. DOI: 10.1016/j.energy.2016.02.046

Sun, X., & Lei, Y. (2021). Research on financial early warning of mining listed companies based on BP neural network model. *Resources Policy, 73*, 102223. DOI: 10.1016/j.resourpol.2021.102223

Tam, K. Y., & Kiang, M. Y. (1992). Managerial applications of neural networks: The case of bank failure predictions. *Management Science, 38*(7), 926–947. DOI: 10.1287/mnsc.38.7.926

Thilakarathna, C., Dawson, C., & Edirisinghe, E. (2022, June). Using financial ratios with artificial neural networks for bankruptcy prediction. In *2022 IEEE International Conference on Artificial Intelligence and Computer Applications (ICAICA)* (pp. 55-58). IEEE. DOI: 10.1109/ICAICA54878.2022.9844640

Wiranata, R.B., & Djunaidy, A.(2021).The stock exchange prediction using machine learning techniques: a comprehensive a nd systematic literature review. Jurnal Ilmu Komputer dan Informatika,14 (2), 91–112

Yadav, R., Patil, A., & Sengupta, R. (2023). An analysis of Satyam case using bankruptcy and fraud detection models. *SocioEconomic Challenges*, 7(4), 24–35. DOI: 10.61093/sec.7(4).24-35.2023

Yu, P., & Yan, X. (2020). Stock price prediction based on deep neural networks. *Neural Computing & Applications, 32*(6), 1609–1628. DOI: 10.1007/s00521-019-04212-x

Chapter 8
Machine Learning Techniques for Market Forecasting

Yogita Yashveer Raghav
http://orcid.org/0000-0003-0478-8619
K.R. Mangalam University, Gurugram, India

Aman Jatain
DPG Institute of Technology and Management, India

Prashanth Kumar Katta
King Faisal University, Al Ahsa, Saudi Arabia

Abhishek Bhardwaj
Government Polytechnic, Indri, India

ABSTRACT

Market forecasting plays an important role in economic planning, investment, and business decision-making. Traditional forecasting methods often struggle with the increasing complexity of modern markets driven by globalization, digitalization, and large volumes of data. Machine learning techniques provide data-driven approaches that can capture nonlinear patterns and adapt to dynamic market conditions. This chapter discusses key ML methods for market prediction, including data preprocessing, supervised and unsupervised learning, deep learning models, and evaluation metrics. It also highlights applications, challenges, and emerging trends for developing reliable and responsible forecasting systems.

DOI: 10.4018/979-8-3373-9645-3.ch008

1. INTRODUCTION

Market forecasting is a systematic market projection of future market behavior in terms of prices, demand, sales, trends, and economic indicators according to past data and market influencing factors. Proper market forecasting helps organizations in optimization of resources, eliminate uncertainty, risks, and gain competitive advantage. Forecasting is used in financial markets to help with portfolio management, algorithmic trading, risk assessment, and in business to assist with demand planning, inventory gain, and strategic decision-making (Raghav & Vyas, 2023).

Conventional methods of forecasting like statistical regression and econometric models are very much dependent on the assumption of linearity, stationarity and data normality. Although these techniques became very popular decades ago, they sometimes fail to represent the nonlinear, dynamic, and high-dimensional character of the current market data. The blistering development of online platforms, social media, and online transactions has only added more data in terms of volume, speed, and diversity to the existing information on markets that require more advanced analytical methods.

Machine learning has developed into a potent paradigm that can eliminate most of the shortcomings of classic models of forecasting. ML models can be trained to respond to the intricate market conditions and enhance their forecast data accuracy by observing trends on the data. The following chapter will show an in-depth analysis of machine learning methods in market forecasting, their theoretical and practical applications, their benefits, and weaknesses.

2. HISTORY AND DEVELOPMENT OF MARKET FORESEEING

Computer advancements in mathematics and statistics have changed the aspect of market forecasting over time. In the early times of forecasting, the major approach was mainly qualitative, based on the judgment of experts and the past trends. As the statistical theory evolved, quantitative methods like moving averages, regression analysis and time series models became hegemonic.

Financial and economic projections have extensively used econometric models, such as ARIMA, and vector autoregression (VAR) models. These models are good in case the relationship between variables is stable and linear. Nevertheless, outside forces like political incidents, technology turbulence, and behavioral bias tend to be unforeseeable, and it is difficult to predict markets correctly (Raghav and Vyas, 2019).

The incorporation of machine learning is a paradigm change of assumption-based modeling to data-based learning. ML methods take advantage of computational intelligence to detect the concealed patterns, to process the noisy data, and to constantly improve the performance by the arrival of new data. This change has put machine learning at the centre of contemporary market forecasting research and practice (Raghav et al., 2024).

3. THEORETICAL FOUNDATIONS OF MACHINE LEARNING FOR FORECASTING

Machine learning constitutes a subfield of artificial intelligence concerned with the creation of algorithms that can be learned based on some data and make decisions or predictions without being programmed. ML has a theoretical foundation based on statistical learning theory, optimization, and probability theory. Machine learning in market forecasting seeks to provide an approximation of an unknown function that estimates the market results by taking past and other market-related information. Minimizing prediction error through optimization strategies like gradient descent, is a way to attain learning. Regularization techniques are commonly used to avoid overfitting and enhance generalization. Machine learning methods are classified into three: supervised, unsupervised and reinforcement learning. Applications in market forecasting are mostly dominated by supervised learning since labeled historical data is normally available. Pattern discovery and segmentation are supported through unsupervised learning and reinforcement learning is being investigated in the fields of trading and decision-making systems.

4. LITERATURE REVIEW

In market forecasting, the use of machine learning methods is an issue that has attracted the interest of researchers and practitioners in the last 20 years. With the growing accessibility of massive financial and commercial data, and the growth in computation capacity, it has become possible to create data-driven forecasting models that are more effective than the traditional statistical methods (Hastie, Tibshirani, and Friedman, 2017). According to many studies, machine learning models have been found to be more accurate and stronger in terms of their predictive success in nonlinear and highly volatile markets (Tsay, 2010).

In early market forecasting, a lot of research studies were based on econometric and statistical models, including linear regression, moving averages, and autoregressive integrated moving average (ARIMA) models. Although such methods brought useful baseline information, they had the shortcoming of being based on the assumptions of linearity, stationarity, and fixed relationships among variables (Box, Jenkins, and Reinsel, 2015). With more dynamic and complex financial markets, researchers started to use machine learning methods with the ability to model nonlinear dependencies and adapt to changing market environments. Comparative analyses have always found that machine learning models are more advantageous than conventional statistical techniques regarding precision, adaptability and scalability (Makridakis, Spiliotis, and Assimakopoulos, 2018).

One of the first machine learning algorithms that were commonly used to predict the market was Support Vector Machines (SVMs). SVMs have been effectively applied in the prediction of stock prices, foreign exchange, and commodity markets because of their capability to deal with high dimensional data and nonlinear decision limits (Vapnik, 1998). Empirical research has shown that SVM-generated models often perform better than linear regression, simple network-based neural network models, particularly those that involve short term predictions that are highly volatile (Kim, 2003).

The applications of the Artificial neural Networks (ANNs) in market forecasting have been studied widely as well. It has been demonstrated by researchers that ANNs are useful in the presentation of complex nonlinear relationships between input variables and market outcomes, which cannot be modeled easily by other conventional methods (Zhang, Patuwo, and Hu, 1998). The multilayer perceptron models applied on stock market prediction, sales forecasting and demand estimation have demonstrated a better performance over the econometric models. Nevertheless, a few studies also express some problems connected with overfitting, training instability, and a lack of interpretability of ANN-based models (Bishop, 2006). Ensemble learning methods emerged as a leading alternative in the studies of market forecasting in order to overcome these shortcomings. Random Forests and Gradient Boosting Machines are methods which are used to integrate a set of weak learners to make more accurate and stable predictions. The studies have shown that ensemble models lessen the variance and increase the generalization and consistently do well in fluctuating market conditions (Breiman, 2001). Random forests have been used extensively in stock trend prediction, demand forecasting, and credit risk assessment and have shown strong performance when used on a variety of data (Chen and Guestrin, 2016). In the more recent, deep learning models have been developed as a potent predictive tool with regard to time series in the financial and commercial markets. Long Short-Term Memory (LSTM) networks and Recurrent Neural Networks (RNNs) have become popular because they can be used to model temporal and sequential dependencies in the data (Hochreiter and Schmidhuber, 1997). LSTM-related forecasting models eliminate the vanishing gradient issue with traditional RNNs and have been demonstrated to be better than conventional machine learning and statistical models in predicting stock prices, forecasting exchange rates, as well as analysing cryptocurrency markets (Fischer and Krauss, 2018).

Although these developments have taken place, several issues related to machine learning-based market forecasting are also revealed in the literature. The most notable issues include the fact that complex models, especially deep architecture designers, are not interpretable at all, that is, they are black boxes (Doshi-Velez and Kim, 2017). This restricts their use in stakes decision making settings like finance and economic policy. Moreover, machine learning models are very sensitive to the quality of data, and problems like noise, missing data, and biased data sets will greatly affect the quality of forecasts (Goodfellow, Bengio, and Courville, 2016).The issue of computational complexity and the resources needed is also mentioned as one of the greatest obstacles as training deep learning and ensemble models can be extremely computationally expensive and time-consuming. Moreover, data privacy, algorithmic bias, and fairness are also associated with ethical concerns, which become more relevant as machine learning models are deployed into automated market decision-making systems (Mehrabi et al., 2021). The challenges discussed highlight the increasing requirements of explainable, transparent, and ethically responsible machine learning-based approaches to market forecasting (Raghav et al., 2022).

In general, it is evident in the literature that machine learning methods provide notable advances in terms of predictive accuracy, flexibility, and scalability. Nevertheless, interpretability, data quality, computational efficiency, and ethical responsibility are to be considered carefully to achieve successful deployment. These insights and perceptions can be used as a solid basis of further studies on effective and reliable machine learning-based market forecasting systems.

5. DATA PREPROCESSING AND FEATURE ENGINEERING

Preprocessing data is a modeling stage in machine learning market forecasting because the quality of the input data directly determines the predictive model accuracy, strength, and generalizability. Financial and economic time series market data are usually vulnerable to missing values, noise, outliers, structural breaks, and inconsistency caused by market shocks, reporting errors, and asynchronous sources of market data. These problems may have a strong negative impact on model performance without proper preprocessing and give incorrect forecasting results (Hastie, Tibshirani, and Friedman, 2017). Data cleaning is one of the main preprocessing phases that entail the process of dealing with missing or incomplete data by using deletion, interpolation or imputation methods. Research indicates that the risk of bias and lowering the credibility of machine learning models by improperly addressing missing data exists (Little and Rubin, 2019). Noise cutting and smoothing functions like moving averages and exponential smoothing are usually used to suppress brief variations and bring out the underlying patterns in the market data (Tsay, 2010).

Methods of outlier detection such as statistical thresholds and clustering based techniques are vital to detecting abnormal market behavior that is due to extreme events or errors in data.

The important preprocessing steps include normalization and data transformation, especially those algorithms that are sensitive to the scale of features like the support vector machines and neural networks. The minmax scaling, standardization and the use of logarithmic transformations are some of the techniques that are used to see that the numbers are stable, and the models converge faster (Bishop, 2006). Logarithmic returns are also common in financial forecasting, where using a logarithmic series of returns helps to stabilize variation and enhance predictive ability (Box, Jenkins, and Reinsel, 2015).

The importance of feature engineering is that it helps to increase the predictive power of machine learning models by converting raw market data into informative features. A good feature of engineering will involve the use of statistical methods as well as domain knowledge to help reveal patterns that are pertinent to the market behaviour. The most common ways of realizing the temporal dependencies that exist in the time series data are lagged variables and rolling window statistics, e.g., moving averages and rolling standard deviations (Zhang, Patuwo, and Hu, 1998). Volatility measures such as historical volatility and average true range give us an idea about market uncertainty and risk action. The technical indicators are based on the price and volume data like relative strength index (RSI), moving average convergence (MACD) and Bollinger bands and are widely applied in financial market prediction. It has been demonstrated that technical indicators as input features can be very useful in enhancing the predictive power of machine learning models, especially in short-term predictions (Kim, 2003). It is also common to have macroeconomic variables like interest rates, inflation and gross domestic product growth added into the forecasting models to represent expensive economic impacts on the market behaviour (Tsay, 2010).

As the unstructured data sources increase, sentiment-based features have been receiving more attention in the market forecasting literature. Sentiment scores and polarity measurements are provided by using natural language processing on the textual data obtained by analyzing news articles, social media, and financial reports. Research has found that sentiment-based elements are useful in providing insights into investor behaviour and market psychologies alongside the conventional numerical indicators (Goodfellow, Bengio, and Courville, 2016). It was demonstrated that sentiment analysis combined with machine learning models can be used to improve forecasting and in times of uncertainty in the market.

Overall, efficient data preprocessing and feature engineering are a very important transition between raw market information and machine learning technologies. These processes can enhance model accuracy, interpretability, and generalization capability greatly because they guarantee data quality and extract meaningful features. According to the literature, it is always emphasized that preprocessing and feature engineering are as high a priority as the process of model selection in ensuring reliable and robust market-forecasting results (Hastie et al., 2017).

6. MACHINE LEARNING TECHNIQUES FOR MARKET FORECASTING

The use of machine learning methods has taken center stage in the contemporary market forecasting with its capacity to learn intricate patterns based on past data and adapt to the changing market environment. In contrast to traditional statistical models, which are based on assumptions, machine learning models are based on data-driven learning processes to discover non-linear relationships and interactions between a variety of variables. The techniques have been applied in market forecasting to make predictions of prices, demand, trends, volatility, and customer behavior in both financial and commercial sectors (Hastie, Tibshirani, and Friedman, 2017). Intelligence of market forecasting using machine learning can be broadly divided into supervised, unsupervised, and deep learning. Of these, the most used methods are supervised learning methods since historical market data of known results is usually available. Learning models that are supervised develop a relationship between inputs and target variables that allow the future trends of the market to be predicted with accuracy (Bishop, 2006).

Figure 1. machine learning techniques for market forecasting

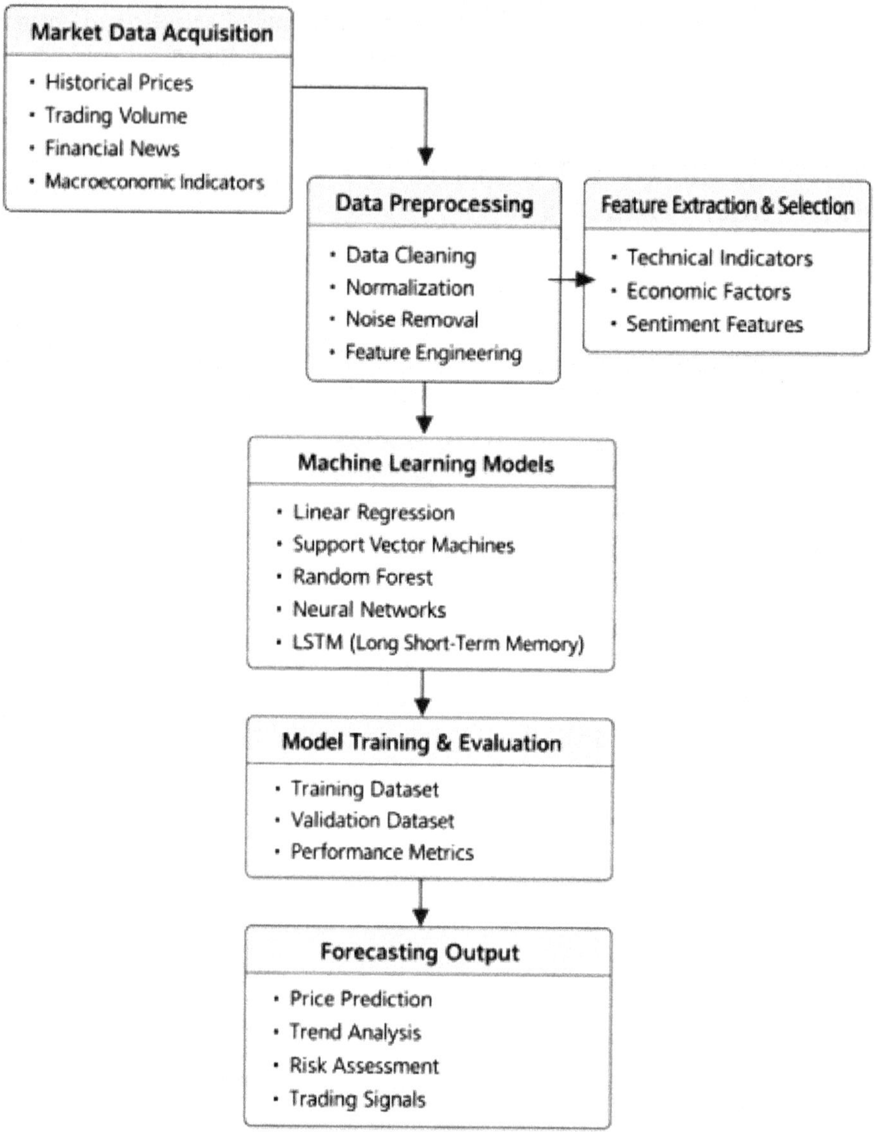

Figure 1 captures the process of machine learning method that is used to predict the market. Data related to the market including historical prices, volumes, and other economic signs are initially gathered. This information is then processed, and features are selected to carry out on it. Different machine learning models, such as regression models, support vector machines, decision trees, and neural networks, are used to train predictive models. Lastly, the trained model produces forecasting outputs in the form of price forecasts, market trends and decision-support information to the investors.

6.1. Supervised Learning Methodologies.

Most market forecasting systems that are based on machine learning are based on supervised learning methods. These models are learned with the help of labeled data sets, according to which historical market indicators are the input features and known market results can be the target variables. Supervised learning aims at reducing the prediction error with the goal of generalizing to the unseen market data. Supervised learning models are flexible and effective thus they have found wide usage in the field of stock price prediction, demand forecasting, sales estimation, and risk assessment (Makridakis, Spiliotis, and Assimakopoulos, 2018).

Linear and Multiple Regression.

Some of the first and most common supervised learning methods which are used in the field of market forecasting include linear and multiple regression models. These are models that determine a straight-line association among independent variables and a dependent market result. Regression models are significant baseline models in the analysis of trends, estimation of demand and assessment of sensitivity despite their simplicity (Tsay, 2010). Nevertheless, they are based upon linear assumptions and cannot effectively capture the dynamics in a complex market, especially in volatile and nonlinear markets. In turn, regression models tend to be treated as a standard method to which a more sophisticated machine learning algorithm is compared (Box, Jenkins, and Reinsel, 2015).

Support Vector Machines

Support Vector Machines (SVM) are very powerful supervised learning algorithms which have attracted much attention in the literature of market forecasting. SVMs are also outstanding in high dimensional data and making nonlinear associations with the help of a kernel. SVMs perform well in the case of noisy and volatile markets, because they perform well in generalizing performance based on maximizing the margin between data points (Vapnik, 1998). Experimental research has shown that SVMs are effective in predicting the stock price, exchange rates, and commodity markets and in most cases, they have shown higher performance compared to traditional regression-based models (Kim, 2003). SVMs are robust and appropriate when performing short-term market forecasting activities that possess a great degree of uncertainty.

Decision Trees

The decision tree models offer a hierarchical approach to decision-making where the data is recursively divided by values of features. Decision trees are popular in market forecasting because of interpretability and transparency as they clearly represent decision rules that involve the process of determining market outcomes (Hastie et al., 2017). These models have been used in the classification of trends in the market, credit risk, and prediction of customer behavior. Nevertheless, single decision trees are likely to overfit particularly when they are trained on corrupt market data and that may restrict their predictive performance (Bishop, 2006).

Random Forests

Random Forests overcome the weaknesses of single decision trees using an ensemble learning approach. It is a procedure that builds a series of decision trees based on randomly chosen samples of data and features and combines their forecasts to generate a final output. Random forests are also suitable in complex and dynamic market environments as they minimize the variance, increase the generalization, and the accuracy of the forecasts (Breiman, 2001). There have been a number of studies which have found that random forests are superior in predicting the stock market, demand forecasting and financial risk modeling than single models (Chen & Guestrin, 2016). Moreover, random forests also give the feature importance scores, which give an idea of the major market drivers and enhance the understanding of the models (Raghav and Gulia, 2023).

In general, the supervised learning methods are important in the forecasting of the market as they integrate predictive accuracy with flexibility. The simpler models like the regression model have the benefit of being interpretable and provide a baseline but the more advanced models like SVMs and random forests may be more decisive in sophisticated market conditions. In literature, it is always stated that the choice of a suitable supervised learning model will depend on the forecasting horizon, data properties and a particular market goal (Makridakis et al., 2018).

Figure 2. Supervised, unsupervised and deep learning techniques

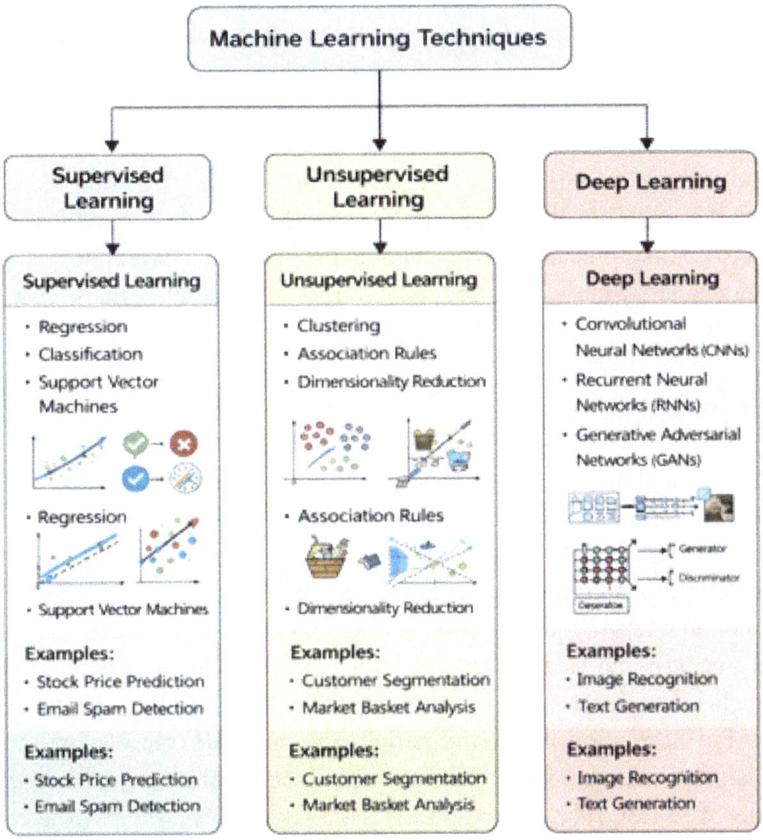

According to the three major types of machine learning methods, Figure 2 shows supervised learning, unsupervised learning, and deep learning. Supervised learning involves the use of labeled data to learn models to perform tasks including regression and classification which are used in most applications such as stock prices prediction and spam filtering. Unsupervised learning processes with unlabeled data to reveal the latent patterns by using methods of clustering, association rules and dimensionality reduction that may be applied to customer segmentation and market basket analysis. Deep learning, a branch of machine learning, is a process that involves the use of multi-layered neural networks, including CNNs, RNNs, and GANs to process complex data. These techniques find extensive applications in higher level applications such as image recognition and text generation.

6.2 Unsupervised Learning Methodologies.

The unsupervised learning methods are complementary but play an important part in the market forecasting to reveal concealed structures, patterns and relationships within the unlabeled market data. In contrast to supervised learning, unsupervised approaches are not based on predefined target variables; rather, they investigate the inherent characteristics of data to justify segmentation, anomaly detection and regime identification (Hastie, Tibshirani, and Friedman, 2017). Unsupervised learning is often useful in market forecasting, especially in the process of exploratory analysis and feature extraction, when a better understanding of the underlying market behavior is needed to improve future predictive modeling.

Clustering Techniques

Clustering algorithms bring together similar pieces of data according to distance or similarity measures, which allow market regimes, customer segments, or asset groupings to be identified. The K-means clustering is the most common among these methods as it is computationally simple and scalable. K-means has also been used in the financial markets to identify bull and bear market, cluster stocks in terms of the volatility pattern and categorized consumer buying behavior (Tsay, 2010). A hierarchical clustering offers another solution by forming a tree-like structure of the clusters, making the relationships in the market to be studied on a level of granularity by the analyst. Literature has indicated that hierarchical clustering can be of special use especially in portfolio diversification and risk analysis since it helps to determine financial instruments correlation (Zhang, Patuwo, and Hu, 1998). Nevertheless, the power of clustering performance is determined by the form of feature selection and distance measure, which underscores the significance of an effective preprocessing procedure (Dewan et al., 2023).

6.3 Deep Learning Techniques

Deep learning is a branch of machine learning, which employs multilayer neural networks to learn patterns in large quantities of data. In contrast to classical machine learning methods that involve hand-crafting of features, deep learning models learn to master intricate representations of raw data. These methods have been extensively successful in image recognition, natural language processing, speech recognition as well as sentiment analysis.

Deep learning algorithms are based on the human brain structure and their operation in which neurons receive information in interconnected layers. These connections are modified with optimization algorithms, including gradient descent, to vary the weights of these connections (Severts 9). Several deep learning methods are common patterns based on the nature of the data and the problem being addressed (Gupta et al., 2023).

1. The Artificial Neural Networks (ANN)

The fundamental elements of deep learning are Artificial Neural Networks. They are made up of interconnected nodes or neurons and are arranged into layers: input layer, hidden layer and output layer.

All neurons are fed input values which are processed by a weighted sum and a activation function to generate an output. Training involves the adjustment of weights by the network and is referred to as backpropagation. ANN models are typically applied in classification, regression, as well as pattern recognition.

2. Convolutional Neural Networks (CNN)

Convolutional Neural Networks are explicitly created to work with grids like data like images. CNNs employ convolution algorithms that derive key features out of the input data.

The major elements of CNN are:

- Feature extraction convolutional layers.
- Dimensionality reduction pooling layers.
- Classification classification fully connected layers.

Some of the common areas of CNNs usage include image classification, object detection, facial recognition, and medical image analysis.

3. Recurrent Neural Networks (RNN)

Recurrent Neural Networks are made to deal with sequential data like text, speech and time-series data. In contrast to conventional neural networks, RNNs include feedback connections that enable the information to be stored over time. This is appropriate to tasks when the output of the current time is dependent on the past input. Although RNNs are frequently applied in language modeling, speech recognition, machine translation, and sentiment analysis, there are issues with the conventional RNNs, such as disappearing gradients when training long-term dependencies (Raghav & Kait, 2024).

4. Long Short-Term Memory Networks (LSTM).

The Long Short-Term Memory networks are a special design of RNN created to address the shortcoming of the traditional recurrent networks. The LSTM networks add memory cells and gating mechanisms that regulate information flow.

These gates include:

- Input gate
- Forget gate
- Output gate

LSTMs can learn long-term dependencies and applications like language translation, text generation, and emotion detection of social media data frequently use LSTMs (Raghav and Pandey, 2024).

5. Gated Recurrent Units (GRU)

The other version of the recurrent neural networks that is used to simplify the LSTM architecture is the Gated Recurrent Units. GRUs merge the input gate and forget gate into a single update gate thus making them less complex.

GRUs have fewer parameters compared to LSTMs and can typically perform as well as them on sequence modeling tasks such as speech recognition and text analysis tasks (Raghav and Vyas, 2024).

6. Autoencoders

Autoencoders are unsupervised deep learning models that are applicable in the learning of compressed data representation. They are divided into two major parts:

- Encoder: reduces input data to lower dimensional representation.

Decoder: A decoder is used to rebuild the original data that has undergone compression.

Autoencoders are typically applied to dimensionality reduction, anomaly detection, noise removal, and features learning.

7. Generative Adversarial Networks (GANs)

Generative Adversarial Networks are made up of two neural networks, which compete against one another:

- Generator: generates artificial information.
- Discriminator: determines whether the data is authentic or counterfeit.

In this adversarial training, GANs get to learn how to produce very realistic samples of data. Image generation, data augmentation, and video synthesis are some of the applications of GANs (Verma et al., 2023).

8. Transformer Models

Transformer models are now among the strongest deep learning systems, particularly in connection with natural language processing. Transformers, unlike RNNs, employ attention to process whole sequences simultaneously.

The self-attention mechanism enables the model to pay attention to significant areas of the input data. The use of transformer-based models includes machine translation, summarization of text, answering questions, and chatbots.

7. TRAINING AND EVALUATION MODEL

Training and Evaluation Modeling.

Training and evaluation of a machine learning or deep learning system are essential processes that require some kind of model training and evaluation. Model training is meant to make the algorithm learn patterns and relationships using the provided dataset whereas evaluation is used to determine the performance of the trained model on unknown data.

These procedures are necessary so that the model developed is correct, trustworthy and able to provide right predictions under real-life situations.

1. Data Preparation

The dataset must be prepared before training a model. Data preparation entails cleaning, transforming and structuring the data in a manner that it would be utilised by the learning algorithm.

Usual stages of the preparation of data are:

- Data Cleaning: Eliminating missing values, duplicate and noise in the dataset.
- Data Normalization: Rescaling of the data to ensure that all the features are in a similar range.
- Tokenization (of text data): Text disaggregation.

- Feature Extraction: Transformation of raw data into significant numerical features.

Word embeddings, tokenization, and vectorization are common techniques in the deep learning models that work with textual data (Raghav et al., 2024).

2. Dataset Splitting

In order to test the performance of a model effectively, the dataset is usually split into subsets:

Training Set: This is what is used to train the model and learn patterns.

- Validation Set: This is to adjust model parameters and avoid overfitting.
- Test Set: It is used to test the performance of the trained model after the actual performance has been performed.

The most popular data split ratio is 70/15 (training, validation and testing), but the ratio can change with the size of dataset.

3. Model Training Process

The model varies its inner parameters or weights while training. The training mechanism will include the input data fed in the model, evaluating the output, and comparing it to the actual label based on a loss function.

The gap between the prediction and the actual is referred to as the error or loss. This loss is minimized by optimization algorithms, including Gradient Descent, Adam or RMSProp.

The training process traditionally includes the following steps:

1. Initialization of model parameters.
2. Enter feed input into the model.
3. Calculate predictions.
4. Loss Calculate loss through loss function.
5. For the weights of the update model, use backpropagation to update the weights.
6. Continue this process repeatedly which is referred to as epochs.

As each epoch advances, the model picks up in terms of its capacity to make reliable predictions.

4. Hyperparameter Tuning

Hyperparameters: These are configuration parameters that regulate the learning of the model. These are parameters that are not acquired in the process of training but are required to be defined before training takes place (Raghav et al., 2025).

The most common hyperparameters are:

- Learning rate
- Batch size
- Number of epochs
- Number of hidden layers
- Activation functions

The most common methods to find the best values of hyperparameters are the Grid Search, Cross-Validation, and Random Search.

5. Model Evaluation Metrics

After training the model, it is important to evaluate its performance using appropriate metrics. The choice of evaluation metrics depends on the type of problem being solved (Raghav & Vyas, n.d.).

For classification tasks, the commonly used metrics include:

Accuracy

Accuracy measures the proportion of correctly predicted instances out of the total predictions.

$$Accuracy = \frac{TP + TN}{TP + TN + FP + FN}$$

eq. (1)

Where:
TP = True Positives
TN = True Negatives
FP = False Positives
FN = False Negatives

Precision

Precision measures how many of the predicted positive cases are actually positive.

$$Precision = \frac{TP}{TP + FP}$$

eq. (2)

Recall

Recall measures how many actual positive cases were correctly identified.

$$\text{Recall} = \frac{TP}{TP + FN}$$

eq. (3)

F1Score

The F1 score is the harmonic mean of precision and recall.

$$F1Score = 2 \times \frac{Precision \times Recall}{Precision + Recall}$$

eq. (4)

These metrics provide a balanced evaluation of the model's performance.

6. Overfitting and Underfitting

During training, models may face two common issues:

Overfitting occurs when the model learns the training data too well, including noise and irrelevant patterns, resulting in poor performance on new data.

Underfitting occurs when the model is too simple to capture the underlying patterns in the data.

Techniques such as **dropout**, **regularization**, **early stopping**, and **data augmentation** are commonly used to reduce overfitting.

7. Model Validation Techniques

To ensure that the model performs consistently, validation techniques are applied.

One common approach is **k-fold cross-validation**, where the dataset is divided into *k* subsets. The model is trained and tested multiple times using different subsets for training and validation.

This approach provides a more reliable estimate of model performance (Raghav & Chauhan, 2025).

8. Performance Analysis

After evaluation, the results are analyzed to understand the strengths and weaknesses of the model. Visualization tools such as **confusion matrices**, **ROC curves**, and **loss/accuracy graphs** help interpret model behavior.

Proper analysis helps researchers improve the model and select the best-performing approach for deployment (Sarita & Raghav, 2024).

8. APPLICATIONS OF MACHINE LEARNING IN MARKET FORECASTING

Applications of Machine Learning in Market Forecasting

Machine learning–based forecasting systems are widely applied in various economic and financial domains due to their ability to analyze large datasets, identify hidden patterns, and make accurate predictions. These models use historical data, statistical techniques, and predictive algorithms to support better decision-making and strategic planning. The following are key applications of machine learning in market forecasting (Gulia et al., 2024).

1. Stock Market Prediction

Machine learning is of great importance in the prediction of future stock market trends based on historical trends in prices, volume of trading, news sentiment, and other financial indicators. Some of the algorithms that are frequently applied to predict stock prices and market trends include Support Vector Machines (SVM), Random Forest, Neural Networks, and Long Short-Term Memory (LSTM) models. These models assist investors to find profitable opportunities, minimize financial risks and make informed trade decisions.

2. Demand Forecasting

Machine learning models are applied by businesses to forecast the demand of products and services by customers. Studying previous sales history, trends over time, purchasing patterns, and weather or other outside influences, ML algorithms can better predict demand in the future. Demand forecasting is beneficial in keeping the inventory at the optimal level, preventing the shortage of stocks or overproduction, and enhancing customer satisfaction (Pandey et al., 2024).

3. Supply Chain Optimization

The optimization of supply chain operations is extensive with the use of machine learning. Predictive models can assist companies to predict the changes in supply and demand, improved transport course, and inventory management. When combining the ML forecasting systems with the logistics systems, companies will be able to save the operation costs, minimize the delays, and enhance the efficiency of the whole supply chain networks (Sindhu et al., 2025).

4. Cryptocurrency Market Study.

The cryptocurrency market is a very volatile market and it depends on various elements including the market sentiment, the economic climate across the world, and the trends on social media. Machine learning algorithms crunch historical price data, blockchain transaction logs, sentiment data on the internet in predicting price movements of cryptocurrencies. Deep learning, time-series forecasting, and reinforcement learning are some of the techniques commonly used in cryptocurrency trading strategies.

5. Macroeconomic Forecasting

The macroeconomic variables studied by machine learning models include GDP growth, inflation rates, unemployment rates, and interest rates. These predictive models are applied by governments, financial institutions, and economic researchers to predict the trends in the economy and come up with effective economic policies. Massive economic data can be processed by machine learning and give insights that cannot be readily reflected in traditional statistical models (Raghav et al., 2024).

6. Dynamic Pricing and Price Optimization.

Machine learning assists companies to identify the best pricing strategies, depending on the customer behavior, rival pricing and demand in the market. The dynamic pricing models constantly process real-time data, automatically updating the price. This method is commonly applied in e-commerce, airline ticketing, hotel reservation and ride-sharing industries.

7. Fraud Detection and Risk Management.

Risk analysis is yet another significant market forecasting application of machine learning. ML models examine transaction history and financial documentation to discern anomalies and identify possible fraud and evaluate investment risks. These systems help financial institutions to track the market and save the businesses against unscheduled financial losses.

8. Market Trend Analysis and Customer Behavior.

Machine learning algorithms can identify the emerging trends of the market by analyzing the purchase history of customers, their browsing patterns, customer demographics. These understandings enable companies to know how people will consume their products in the future, create narrow marketing campaigns, and create products tailored to more customer needs (Raghav and Vyas, 2026).

9. DIFFICULTIES AND ETHICAL CONCERNS

Although machine learning has been proven highly beneficial to market forecasting, a number of issues and ethical concerns need to be considered so that the tool can be reliable, fair, and implemented in a responsible way. Machine learning models are dependent on big data and complicated algorithms, which may raise the problem of data bias, transparency, privacy risks, and accountability. Biased or incomplete training data can result in inaccurate or unfair predictions and therefore high-quality and representative datasets are required to make reliable forecasts. Most modern models, especially deep learning models, are black boxes and thus, their decision-making mechanisms are hard to understand and reduce the confidence of analysts and stakeholders. Also, machine learning algorithms rely on past information and cannot easily forecast unforeseen developments in the market (sudden events like the economic crisis, geopolitical tensions, or global pandemics) (Sarita et al., 2025). There are also technical issues that would diminish the capacity of the model to generalize to new market conditions such as overfitting. Moreover, the sensitive financial and transactional information is also used which involves critical issues of privacy and security that demand strong protection of data. The ethical aspects associated with fairness, accountability, and responsible AI are also crucial since forecasting models have the potential to affect investment choices and economic policies. Thus, the combination of explainable AI methods, transparency, and ethical standards is necessary in the process of creating reliable and accountable machine learning systems to use in market predictions.

10. FUTURE RESEARCH DIRECTIONS

Further studies related to the application of machine learning in market forecasting need to involve the creation of more sophisticated, dependable, and transparent predictive models. There is a growing interest in hybrid models, which are the combination of traditional statistical methods with new machine learning and deep learning algorithms, to enhance the accuracy of prediction. The other step that should be taken is the establishment of the Explainable Artificial Intelligence (XAI) to ensure that complex forecasting models are more interpretable and reliable to the analyst and decision-makers. Moreover, one can capture the market conditions that change swiftly by using real-time adaptive forecasting systems that constantly learn using new market data. Predictive capabilities can further be improved by integrating alternative data sources including social media sentiment, news analytics and online consumer behavior. Recent advancements in artificial intelligence such as reinforcement learning of automated trading models and federated learning to train secure collaborative models also hold optimistic prospects of developing the next generation market forecasting model, which is efficient and privacy guaranteed.

11. CONCLUSION

Machine learning methods have made a great contribution to the sphere of market forecasting because they allow creating flexible, precise, and scalable predictive models. These methods enable organizations to know complex patterns and coming up with valuable insights to make strategic decisions by analysing vast amounts of historical and real-time data. The use of machine learning in fields like the stock market forecasting, the demand forecasting, the supply chain management and the economic analysis prove that it is increasingly becoming critical to the modern financial systems. Nevertheless, issues like data bias, the absence of transparency, sensitivity to unforeseen events on the market, and so on, still require to be solved.

With the responsible implementation, ethical concerns, and ongoing research, machine learning can become a key factor in ensuring more dependable, informed, and sustainable market forecasting and decision-making in the future.

REFERENCES

Bishop, C. M. (2006). *Pattern recognition and machine learning*. Springer.

Box, G. E. P., Jenkins, G. M., & Reinsel, G. C. (2015). *Time series analysis: Forecasting and control* (5th ed.). Wiley.

Breiman, L. (2001). Random forests. *Machine Learning*, *45*(1), 5–32. DOI: 10.1023/A:1010933404324

Chen, T., & Guestrin, C. (2016). XGBoost: A scalable tree boosting system. In *Proceedings of the 22nd ACM SIGKDD International Conference on Knowledge Discovery and Data Mining* (pp. 785–794).

Dewan, M., Mudgal, A., Pandey, P., Raghav, Y. Y., & Gupta, T. (2023). Predicting pregnancy complications using machine learning. In *Technological tools for predicting pregnancy complications* (pp. 141–160). IGI Global. DOI: 10.4018/979-8-3693-1718-1.ch008

Doshi-Velez, F., & Kim, B. (2017). Towards a rigorous science of interpretable machine learning. *arXiv preprint arXiv:1702.08608.*

Fischer, T., & Krauss, C. (2018). Deep learning with long short-term memory networks for financial market predictions. *European Journal of Operational Research*, *270*(2), 654–669. DOI: 10.1016/j.ejor.2017.11.054

Goodfellow, I., Bengio, Y., & Courville, A. (2016). *Deep learning*. MIT Press.

Gulia, S., Pandey, P., & Raghav, Y. Y. (2024). Multimedia data in healthcare system. In *Supervised and unsupervised data engineering for multimedia data* (pp. 63–92). DOI: 10.1002/9781119786443.ch3

Gupta, T., Pandey, P., & Raghav, Y. Y. (2023). Impact of social media platforms on the consumer decision-making process in the food and grocery industry. In *Influences of social media on consumer decision-making processes in the food and grocery industry* (pp. 119–139). IGI Global. DOI: 10.4018/978-1-6684-8868-3.ch006

Hastie, T., Tibshirani, R., & Friedman, J. (2017). *The elements of statistical learning* (2nd ed.). Springer.

Hochreiter, S., & Schmidhuber, J. (1997). Long short-term memory. *Neural Computation*, *9*(8), 1735–1780. DOI: 10.1162/neco.1997.9.8.1735 PMID: 9377276

Kim, K. J. (2003). Financial time series forecasting using support vector machines. *Neurocomputing*, *55*(1–2), 307–319. DOI: 10.1016/S0925-2312(03)00372-2

Little, R. J. A., & Rubin, D. B. (2019). *Statistical analysis with missing data* (3rd ed.). Wiley.

Makridakis, S., Spiliotis, E., & Assimakopoulos, V. (2018). Statistical and machine learning forecasting methods: Concerns and ways forward. *PLoS One, 13*(3), e0194889. DOI: 10.1371/journal.pone.0194889 PMID: 29584784

Mehrabi, N., Morstatter, F., Saxena, N., Lerman, K., & Galstyan, A. (2021). A survey on bias and fairness in machine learning. *ACM Computing Surveys, 54*(6), 1–35. DOI: 10.1145/3457607

Pandey, P., Raghav, Y. Y., Gulia, S., Aggarwal, S., & Kumar, N. (2024). Supervised and unsupervised learning techniques for biometric systems. In *Supervised and unsupervised data engineering for multimedia data* (pp. 263–299). DOI: 10.1002/9781119786443.ch12

Raghav, Y. Y., & Chauhan, A. (2025). Tech for the wild: Leveraging IoT and cloud computing in wildlife conservation. In *AI and machine learning techniques for wildlife conservation* (pp. 49–64). IGI Global Scientific Publishing. DOI: 10.4018/979-8-3693-6935-7.ch003

Raghav, Y. Y., Choudhary, S., Pandey, P., Singh, S., & Varshney, D. (2025). Smart healthcare: Cloud-IoT solutions for enhanced patient well-being. *African Journal of Biomedical Research, 28*(1), 14–28.

Raghav, Y. Y., & Gulia, S. (2023). The rise of artificial intelligence and its implications on spirituality. In *Investigating the impact of AI on ethics and spirituality* (pp. 165–178). IGI Global. DOI: 10.4018/978-1-6684-9196-6.ch011

Raghav, Y. Y., & Kait, R. (2024). Edge computing empowering distributed computing at the edge. In *Emerging trends in cloud computing analytics, scalability, and service models* (pp. 67–83). IGI Global Scientific Publishing. DOI: 10.4018/979-8-3693-0900-1.ch003

Raghav, Y. Y., Kumar, A., Kumar, A., Kumari, P., & Choudhury, S. (2024, December). A smart IoT framework for detecting accidents and facilitating rescue operations. In *2024 13th International Conference on System Modeling & Advancement in Research Trends (SMART)* (pp. 373–380). IEEE. DOI: 10.1109/SMART63812.2024.10882204

Raghav, Y. Y., & Pandey, P. (2024). Adoption of green cloud computing for environmental sustainability: An analysis. In *Convergence strategies for green computing and sustainable development* (pp. 138–151). IGI Global.

Raghav, Y. Y., Tipu, R. K., Bhakhar, R., Gupta, T., & Sharma, K. (2024). The future of digital marketing: Leveraging artificial intelligence for competitive strategies and tactics. In *The use of artificial intelligence in digital marketing: Competitive strategies and tactics* (pp. 249–274). IGI Global.

Raghav, Y. Y., & Vyas, V. (2019, October). A comparative analysis of different load balancing algorithms on different parameters in cloud computing. In *2019 3rd International Conference on Recent Developments in Control, Automation & Power Engineering (RDCAPE)* (pp. 628–634). IEEE. DOI: 10.1109/RDCAPE47089.2019.8979122

Raghav, Y. Y., & Vyas, V. (2023). ACBSO: A hybrid solution for load balancing using ant colony and bird swarm optimization algorithms. *International Journal of Information Technology : an Official Journal of Bharati Vidyapeeth's Institute of Computer Applications and Management, 15*(5), 2847–2857. DOI: 10.1007/s41870-023-01340-5

Raghav, Y. Y., & Vyas, V. (2023). A comparative analysis report of nature-inspired algorithms for load balancing in cloud environment. In *Women in soft computing* (pp. 47–63). Springer Nature Switzerland.

Raghav, Y. Y., & Vyas, V. (2024). Harnessing cloud computing and IoT for wildlife conservation. In *Integration of cloud computing and IoT: Trends, case studies and applications* (p. 142).

Raghav, Y. Y., & Vyas, V. (2024). Load balancing using swarm intelligence in cloud environment for sustainable development. In *Convergence strategies for green computing and sustainable development* (pp. 165–181). IGI Global.

Raghav, Y. Y., & Vyas, V. (2026). Cloud load balancing: Performance comparison between bird swarm and ant colony optimization algorithms. *SN Computer Science, 7*(1), 107. DOI: 10.1007/s42979-025-04712-9

Raghav, Y. Y., Vyas, V., & Rani, H. (2022). Load balancing using dynamic algorithms for cloud environment: A survey. *Materials Today: Proceedings, 69*, 349–353. DOI: 10.1016/j.matpr.2022.09.048

Sarita, R., Raghav, Y. Y., & Kashish. (2025). Strategic innovation of AI and ML for ecommerce data security. In *Next-generation computational intelligence: Trends and technologies* (pp. 165–194). Springer Nature Switzerland.

Sarita, R. S., & Raghav, Y. Y. (2024). Introduction to quantum computing and its revolution in industry and society. In *Industrial quantum computing: Algorithms, blockchains, industry 4.0* (p. 219). DOI: 10.1515/9783111354842-013

Sindhu, M., Raghav, Y. Y., & Kundu, K. (2025, August). Generative AI in education and its future possibilities. In *2025 International Conference on Intelligent and Secure Engineering Solutions (CISES)* (pp. 68–74). IEEE. DOI: 10.1109/CISES66934.2025.11265181

Tsay, R. S. (2010). *Analysis of financial time series* (3rd ed.). Wiley. DOI: 10.1002/9780470644560

Vapnik, V. N. (1998). *Statistical learning theory*. Wiley.

Verma, S. K., Singh, D., Raghav, Y. Y., Hemelatha, S., Kannimuthu, S., & Banchhor, C. O. (2023, September). Collaborative MAC protocol design for enhanced network lifetime in mobile ad hoc networks. In *2023 6th International Conference on Contemporary Computing and Informatics (IC3I)* (pp. 2082–2088). IEEE. DOI: 10.1109/IC3I59117.2023.10397708

Zhang, G., Patuwo, B. E., & Hu, M. Y. (1998). Forecasting with artificial neural networks: The state of the art. *International Journal of Forecasting*, *14*(1), 35–62. DOI: 10.1016/S0169-2070(97)00044-7

Chapter 9
AI Applications in Behavioral Finance:
Integrating Machine Learning With Investor Psychology

Khalil Omar
http://orcid.org/0000-0002-5328-5762
University of Petra, Jordan

Hussam Fakhouri
Al-Balqa Applied University, Jordan

Faten Hamad
http://orcid.org/0000-0001-7548-0529
Sultan Qaboos University, Oman & University of Jordan, Jordan

ABSTRACT

Behavioral finance questions the rational-investor assumption, with empirical evidence of systematic cognitive biases which contribute to market outcomes. In this chapter, machine learning is combined with the behavioral theory of finance in terms of three empirical studies based on publicly available Kaggle datasets, FinBERT to predict sentiment, XGBoost and LightGBM to predict tabular data, an LSTM to predict sequence learning, and SHAP to interpret the results. Findings are inconsistent to the extent that the daily-index herding hypothesis is rejected; a momentum signature dominates over overreaction-reversal; a small loss-aversion drift ratio of 1.267 comes out that is lower than the prospect-theoretic canonical value of 2.25. The chapter maintains that explanation-driven validation is what makes a difference between scale-dependent attenuation and true refutation, showing

DOI: 10.4018/979-8-3373-9645-3.ch009

that the scale-dependent attenuation is not due to the complexity of the algorithm used to compute it but rather to the fact that certain behavioral biases are the ones that can be detected.

1. INTRODUCTION

The classical theory of financial markets is a model that is based on the assumption that all the available information has been incorporated in the prices by the rational utility maximizers without any bias and in real time. Empirical studies in the past 50 years have been able to record systematic violations of this idealization. Investors base their decisions on irrelevant reference points, overvalue vivid information, act against their own indications with the crowd and react asymmetrically to positive and negative events. The interdisciplinary area that has combined these observations with the economic theory is known as behavioral finance; it has created a body of evidence that undermines the concept of market efficiency, and redefines the academic and practical conceptualization of asset prices (Barberis and Thaler, 2003).

Behavioral finance empirically has its roots in laboratory experiments and survey-based studies which revealed systematic biases in human judgment when faced with uncertainty (Tversky and Kahneman, 1974; Kahneman and Tversky, 1979). These results were later applied to financial markets where overconfidence in volume of trade was reported (Barber and Odean, 2001), psychological causes of asset price bubbles (Shiller, 2000) and post-earnings announcement drift which is in line with the delayed response to news. Although these findings were very empirical, the methodological toolkit of behavioral finance was limited by the possibilities of survey instruments and small experimental studies. The scale of the real financial markets, especially, the construct of investor sentiment, could not be directly measured.

With the introduction of machine learning (ML) and natural language processing (NLP), this situation has dramatically changed. Contemporary computational techniques are able to consume billions of news articles, social media posts and corporate disclosures and derive structured behavioral cues out of unstructured text. They are able to model the nonlinear interactions between hundreds of features, learn temporal dependencies between decades of trading data, and give interpretable attributions of model decisions to the individual input (Lundberg and Lee, 2017). Empirical studies of asset pricing based on these techniques have shown significant returns when compared to more conventional linear models and Gu et al. (2020) found out-of-sample returns greater than two times in terms of monthly returns predictability with tree-based ensembles and neural networks. Similar improvements are observed in earnings forecasting, where AI-based analyst models perform better than human consensus forecasts in about half of predictions of stock returns, and this relative performance depends on the high-dimensionality, transparency, and volume of information in companies (Cao et al., 2024).

These innovations provide a new frontier in behavioral finance: operationalization of psychological constructs in a market-wide scale and at a high time resolution. The investor sentiment that used to be quantified quarterly with the help of surveys, is now quantified on a daily basis based on the text of financial media. Traditionally herding behavior has been determined by cross-sectional dispersion of returns only, but now, coordinated patterns in social media tone, options flow and order-book activity can be triangulated. Cognitive bias of overreaction can be experimented by running sequence models on decades of price data, and investigating systematic errors in prediction. These opportunities are a subset of a larger change in data-intensive sectors, where AI-based analytics are transforming decision support and competitive practice in a multitude of ways that go far beyond finance (Omar et al., 2026). They have started to come under long-lasting scrutiny by policy actors, as the Federal Reserve and other central banks have now started to look at how artificial intelligence agents themselves can display or enhance behavioral patterns that are related to financial instability (Hansen and Lee, 2025).

Although this trend exists, there are three significant aspects in which artificial intelligence and behavioral finance are yet to be integrated. To begin with, the prevailing bias in artificial intelligence studies in finance is to consider behavioral phenomena as exploitable inefficiencies, as opposed to psychological processes that should be causally explained. The main measure of success is predictive accuracy and behavioral interpretability is usually put aside to secondary analysis. Second, the literature that operationally defines particular behavioral constructs, such as loss aversion, herding, anchoring, and post-earnings drift, using specific machine learning pipelines and connects the output signals to the canonical theory, is limited. Third, the recent literature on artificial intelligence agents as replicators or mitigators of human biases has not been integrated with the older line of using machine learning to identify human biases, and the question of the dual nature of artificial intelligence as a diagnostic tool and a reflective image of human behavior remains unanswered (Caplin et al., 2025). The recent findings of machine learning models having picked up the pattern of overreactions in the name of regularization (van Binsbergen et al., 2023) highlight the significance of studying both sides of this dual role in one methodological framework.

The chapter fills these gaps by three empirical studies that use the state-of-the-art machine learning techniques to answer behavioral finance questions, on publicly available Kaggle datasets, which can be reproduced. In Study 1, the authors explore the investor sentiment and herding behaviour using transformer-based sentiment classification of financial text with gradient boosting models which use sentiment signals to predict market activity. Study 2 explores overreaction and momentum in equity returns by jointly using long short-term memory networks to recognize patterns in the time series and gradient boosting to classify overreaction events. Study 3 examines the cognitive bias in post-earnings price responses by using sentiments-conditioned prediction of post-announcement drift, to understand whether asymmetric responses are in line with loss aversion. Both studies interpret algorithmic results with SHAP-based interpretability to relate to behavioral constructs.

The chapter has three fold contributions. It is methodologically a single framework to apply interpretable machine learning to behavioral finance hypotheses, reporting decisions on cross-validation, regime testing and feature attribution, which guard against look-ahead bias and provide reproducible results. In theory, it moves the line that artificial intelligence and behavioral finance are not incompatible paradigms but rather they are complementary perspectives on the same phenomena: machine learning is a scale and pattern recognition, and behavioral theory is a causal interpretation. In practice, it shows that the resultant analyses can be directly applicable in investor education, advisory practice and in designing market-monitoring systems by regulators who are interested in behavioral risk.

The rest of the chapter has the following structure. Section 2 examines the principles of behavioral finance and machine learning strategies to financial data, and finds common ground. Section 3 outlines the proposed methodology, data sources, model architectures and validation procedures. Section 4 describes the design of the experiment of all three empirical studies. Results and analysis are reported in section 5. Section 6 contains implications and research directions in the future. Section 7 concludes.

2. BACKGROUND

2.1 Behavioral Finance Foundations

The genesis of behavioral finance was the accumulating empirical data that the canonical efficient markets hypothesis (Fama, 1970) was not sufficient to explain the empirical data on asset price movements or investor behavior. The turning point in theory came with the work of Tversky and Kahneman (1974) who showed that human judgments in situations of uncertainty are based on heuristics (representativeness, availability, and anchoring-and-adjustment) that give rise to systematic and predictable bias. Their next prospect theory (Kahneman and Tversky, 1979) substituted the von NeumannMorgenstern utility model with a value function that was reference dependent, had decreasing sensitivity, and strong loss aversion. The empirical measurements of the coefficient of loss aversion always point to the disutility of losses being about 2.25 times the utility of equal gains (Tversky and Kahneman, 1992), which is an asymmetry that reforms optimal portfolio selection and trading.

The following decades resulted in a large list of behavioral phenomena in financial markets. Excessive trading volume and poor performance of individual investors were proved to be caused by overconfidence especially in terms of overprecision on the quality of information they have (Barber and Odean, 2001). The disposition effect is an empirical effect of investors to make winning trades too soon and losing trades too long, which is a direct result of the kink of the prospect-theoretic value function at the reference point. Mental accounting records the segregation of financial choices between psychological accounts which breach fungibility of money. The predictable mispricings in the run up to planned news events due to limited attention, and over-weighting of small samples in the creation of return expectations due to the representativeness heuristic. These results were generalized into a consistent alternative paradigm through comprehensive surveys (Barberis and Thaler, 2003; Subrahmanyam, 2008) and behavioral finance has become a full-fledged sub-discipline with its theoretical equipment, research techniques and policy implications.

2.2 Herding and Information Cascades

The behaviour of herding in financial markets has been formalised in two theoretical complementary perspectives. This is demonstrated by the information cascade model (Bikhchandani et al., 1992) which demonstrates that individually rational investors can be rationally uninformed by their own information when a sufficient chain of action by other investors has already occurred and leads to convergent behavior, which is fragile to small shocks. Simultaneously, behavioral models ascribe herding to the social conformity pressure and reputational concerns, which change depending on the uncertainty in the market.

Herding measurement has been largely based on dispersion measures based on cross sectional data of returns. The cross-sectional standard deviation of returns (CSSD) was introduced by Christie and Huang (1995) who argued that the dispersion is compacted by herding in times of large market movements. Chang et al. (2000) optimised the methodology by the cross-sectional absolute deviation (CSAD) that allows a nonlinear test of herding by using a quadratic market returns specification. These measures continue to be the workhorses of herding literature and recent uses have generalized them by using machine learning models that can model nonlinear and time-varying herding behavior (Nerlekar et al., 2025). Retail brokerage records and social media records provide parallel evidence that herding is increased in times of high uncertainty, and is greater in less experienced investors and can be partially observed in the temporal clustering of the direction of trade across loosely connected accounts.

2.3 Overreaction and Momentum

The overreaction hypothesis is that investors are systematic overweighting new information, and generate predictable reversals in long-run payoffs. De Bondt and Thaler (1985) have shown that portfolios that are constructed on the premise of three-to five-year previous performance has a significant amount of the reversion of the mean where previous losers perform better than previous winners by an average of twenty-five percentage points over the next thirty-six months. Continuation and not reversal at intermediate horizons of three to twelve months is recorded in the complementary momentum effect (Jegadeesh and Titman, 1993) creating a phenomenon that any single behavioral theory must be able to explain.

The pattern of joints is explained by the modern models of behavior as the extrapolative beliefs and slow change of expectations. Bordalo et al. (2020) construct a model where agents extrapolate news in the short term at short horizons to create momentum and the disconfirmation of this at longer horizons creates reversals. This formalism has become popular not only due to its empirical testability via the forecast-error regressions, but via machine learning approximations of the expectational biases as well, which is a natural extension to the algorithmic techniques used in this chapter.

2.4 Sentiment, Disclosure, and Post-Earnings Reactions

The concept of investor sentiment causing the prices to be above fundamental information was operationalized by using textual analysis of financial media. As demonstrated by Tetlock (2007), the tone of the Wall Street Journal article, Abreast of the Market, predicts future returns and trading volume with pessimistic content generating a downward pressure on prices, which in part reverses within the next week. Loughran and McDonald (2011) showed that general-purpose sentiment dictionaries incorrectly categorize most negative words in 10-K reports as a result of domain mismatch, and have since developed domain-specific lexicons, which have become the norm.

A similar body of literature on post-earnings announcement drift reports that prices do not respond immediately to earnings surprises, but do so over time (Bernard and Thomas, 1989) and the extent of drift is a positive function of the surprise. The asymmetry (more negative than positive) of drift (that is, negative than positive) is also in line with loss aversion in the processing and behavior of investors in response to bad news. Supervised learning methods have been supported by annotated datasets (including the Financial PhraseBank (Malo et al., 2014)) to encode sentiment with more subtlety than dictionary-based methods, and offer the building blocks of the pipelines of transformers applied in the empirical work below. Further data on the predictive value of the affective tone of executive speech, based on earnings conference call transcripts, suggests that the feel-good tone of executive language can predict both short-term price response and longer-term analyst forecast changes, and that FinBERT-generated sentiment scores are better predictors of such changes than Loughran-McDonald counts (Huang et al., 2023). Retail sentiment can be measured in a complementary channel using social media platforms, which have provided a channel of intraday frequency measurement, but the noisier nature of the source means that it poses a challenge to identification, currently a research question.

2.5 Machine Learning in Asset Pricing

Machine learning entered empirical asset pricing as a methodology for accommodating high-dimensional feature sets and nonlinear interactions among predictors. Gu et al. (2020) provide a systematic comparison of penalized linear models, generalized additive models, regression trees, gradient boosting, random forests, and neural networks for predicting monthly equity returns, finding that tree-based ensembles and shallow neural networks deliver the largest gains over conventional benchmarks. Their evidence indicates that the out-of-sample monthly R-squared of the best machine learning specifications more than doubles that of a three-factor benchmark, and that the gains are economically meaningful when translated into long-short portfolio Sharpe ratios. The methodological apparatus accompanying these gains includes purged k-fold cross-validation, walk-forward validation, and the meta-labeling procedures developed for financial machine learning (López de Prado, 2018), which together address the temporal dependence and non-stationarity that distinguish financial data from more typical machine learning settings.

As a sub-domain of natural language processing, it has been found that classical algorithms like Naive Bayes and support vector machines maintain meaningful baseline accuracy, and transformer-based architectures pre-trained on financial datasets can reach state-of-the-art accuracy on performance on benchmark sentiment tasks (Karanikola et al., 2023). The moral of the story is that there is no universal algorithm that will be effective in all behavioral finance problems; the model to use will depend on the structure of the data, the temporal granularity needed and the interpretability limitations of the research question.

2.6 Toward Integration: Behavioral Machine Learning

Three vectors along which a nascent literature is starting to combine behavioral finance with machine learning are emerging. The former is domain-adapted language models: the family of FinBERT models (Araci, 2019; Yang et al., 2020; Huang et al., 2023) has shown that when trained on financial corpora, the family of FinBERT models significantly outperform general-purpose BERT (Devlin et al., 2019), with accuracy reported of about eighty-six These models have spurred a surge of empirical research charting textual sentiment to returns, volatility, and trading action.

The second vector reverses the question, asking whether algorithmic agents themselves manifest the biases The second agent is a reversal of the first, whether the underlying agents of machine learning are overreactive to patterns of corporate earnings like a human analyst. van Binsbergen et al. (2023) record that machine learning predictions of corporate earnings have overreaction behaviours similar to human analysts, which can be attributed to regularisation decisions in the training objective. Cao et al. (2024) demonstrate that hybrid human-machine forecasting is better than each of the two, which implies that they complement, but do not replace each other. Caplin et al. (2025) operationalize the cognitive-economic explanation of machine learning and compares the explicit analogies to rational inattention and provides a common language to compare human and algorithmic biases.

The third vector is to do with financial stability. Hansen and Lee (2025) test experimentally whether large language models have herd behavior in capital-market choices, and conclude that artificial intelligence agents are more likely to be overweighting the use of private information compared to human subjects but that extensive adoption of artificial intelligence can still aggravate market responses to shocks by causing coordination. Lopez-Lira and Tang (2024) report large language models produce non-trivial predictability on stock returns using news headlines, and prompt-engineered classifiers that are both accurate, meaningfully better than chance, and produce positive long-short returns when trading under conservative assumptions about trading costs. Collectively these strings make one realize that artificial intelligence does not just watch the behavioral phenomena but is a participant of the process whose properties should be empirically studied. The works in the following sections add to all three vectors the combination of behavioral assumptions, domain-specific models, and interpretability tooling in a single empirical context, and the description of the methodology choices that need to be made to achieve reproducibility of the results using publicly available data.

3. PROPOSED METHODOLOGY

3.1 Analytical Framework

The framework is implemented in three empirical studies, which have the same methodological infrastructure, but differ in terms of behavioral hypotheses. In Study 1, the joint-modeling of the tone of news and short-horizon market activity explores the sentiment of investors and herding. Study 2 investigates the overreaction and momentum using sequence models that are trained to forecast short-horizon returns using longer histories of returns. Study 3 investigates the cognitive bias in earnings responses with the combination of sentiment scores obtained on the basis of earnings-window news and post-announcement drift classifiers. The common infrastructure provides a methodological compatibility in the studies and makes it possible to have cross study information regarding the dual role of artificial intelligence in detecting and replicating behavioral patterns.

Figure 1. Three-layer analytical framework.

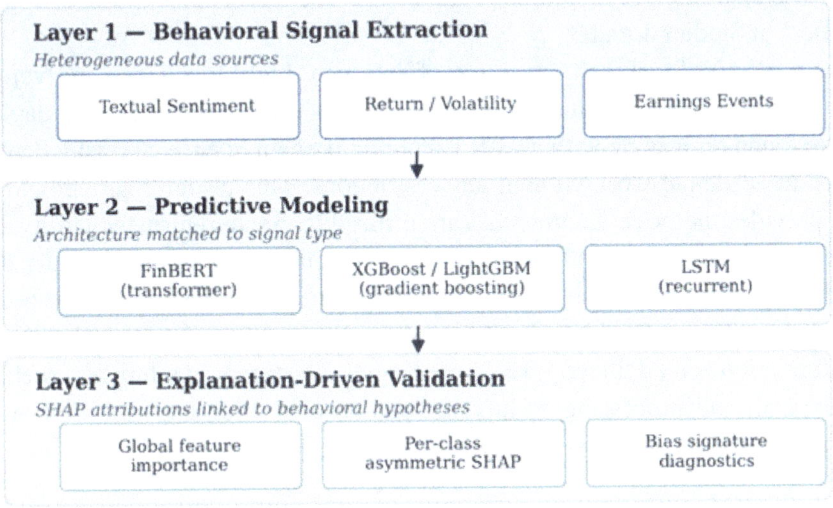

The framework proposed combines three levels of analysis into a single empirical framework. The initially extracted behavioral signals are drawn out of heterogeneous sources of data: textual sentiment on financial news and social media, return-based momentum and reversal signals on price data, and event-based signals around earnings announcements. The second layer uses model-based machine learning methods that are specific to each signal, such as textual data language models based on transformers, tabular features with gradient boosting, and sequential price data with recurrent neural networks. The third layer brings about interpretability with SHAP-based attributions which relate model predictions to behavioral constructs of theoretical interest. This three-layer structure fits with the known reference-model methods to AI system integration, which dictate the composition of the language, prediction, and explanation modules into a coherent architecture in a modular way (Omar et al., 2025c). The summary of the framework is presented as the graph in Figure 1.

3.2 Data Sources

The data employed in the empirical work all come out of publicly available Kaggle datasets, and can be fully reproducible without any reliance on proprietary subscriptions. There are three main datasets upon which the studies are based. The Kaggle-hosted dataset Financial Sentiment Analysis, which is a combination of Financial PhraseBank (Malo et al., 2014) and FiQA Task-1 corpus, has around 5 800 labeled financial sentences (positive, negative, and neutral) which the dataset is released under the public-domain license, which is compatible with academic usage. The dataset gives the trained signal to be fine-tuned and validate sentiment classifiers in Studies 1 and 3.

The S&P 500 Stock Data resource offers open, high, low, close and volume series of all S&P 500 constituents, 5 years worth of data is available each day and they are found on Kaggle with a CC0 1.0 public-domain license, allowing them to be used in academic work without any restrictions. This resource grounds Study 2 and provides the price features that are utilized to create returns, volatility, and momentum signals. S&P 500 Financial News Headlines data covers as far as 2024 by indexing aggregate data by date of news headline to aid the event-study design in Study 3 and is available on Kaggle under a license that allows academic use. All information is read directly out of the Kaggle filesystem in a Jupyter notebook environment, and processing scripts are version controlled and recorded in the replication material of the replication.

3.3 Sentiment Modeling Through Domain-Adapted Transformers

Sentiment extraction is based on FinBERT, which is BERT-based models that are pre-trained on financial corpora and fine-tuned to use sentiment classification. The chapter is based on the publicly available FinBERT model published under the Hugging Face Model Hub that is pre-trained on a collection of company reports, transcripts of earnings calls, and analyst notes amounting to several billion tokens (Yang et al., 2020). The model generates probability distributions on positive, negative and neutral classes of each input sequence and the resulting probabilities are useful to predict downstream tasks as continuous features.

The methodology distinguishes between zero-shot inference and supervised fine-tuning. Zero-shot inference uses the released model weights directly, providing a reproducible baseline that requires no additional training. Supervised fine-tuning further trains the model on the Financial PhraseBank training partition using the Adam optimizer with a learning rate of 5×10^{-5} over three epochs, configurations that have been shown to produce reliable convergence in prior work (Araci, 2019). Fine-tuned variants are used in Study 3 to maximize accuracy on earnings-related disclosures, while zero-shot inference is used elsewhere for consistency and computational efficiency. Sentiment scores are aggregated to daily resolution by averaging probabilities across all relevant texts within each trading day, producing time series that align with the temporal granularity of price data.

3.4 Predictive Modeling Through Gradient Boosting

The studies are based on the gradient boosting decision trees as its main classifier and regressor architecture, which is inspired by its success on tabular financial data (Gu et al., 2020). It has two implementations, including XGBoost, which has good default behaviour and comprehensive ablation tooling (Chen and Guestrin, 2016) and LightGBM which has faster training on large feature matrices by using histogram-based split finding (Ke et al., 2017). The two implementations act as cross checks to each other where the consistent results over both implementations are more evidence of robustness.

Feature engineering is specific to a study and has common principles. On the methodology of return-based features, the lagged returns at several horizons are constructed and the rolling volatility measures and the momentum indicators of the lagged returns are constructed in a similar fashion that the academic asset-pricing literature employs. In the case of sentiment based features, daily aggregate scores are enhanced with rolling means, measures of dispersion across various sources and divergence measures that reflect inconsistency amongst news outlets. Hyperparameter tuning involves time-series-sensitive cross-validation, and the maximum depth of trees, learning rate and regularization penalties are tuned using a grid search over conservative ranges based on existing published literature. The best hyperparameter settings are used to train final models on all available training data, and are evaluated on rigidly held-out test partitions.

3.5 Sequence Modeling Through Long Short-Term Memory Networks

In the case of the temporal patterns analyzed in Study 2, the architecture is Long Short-Term Memory (LSTM) networks, which address the vanishing-gradient problem of vanilla recurrent networks, and have shown good empirical results in financial sequence prediction (Hochreiter and Schmidhuber, 1997). The input to the LSTM is a sixty-trading-day window of scaled return observations and the output is a probability distribution on the category of returns (or a continuous prediction of returns) next period as specified in the experiment.

The architecture is two stacked LSTM layers that have sixty-four hidden units, and then a dense projection layer that has dropout regularization. Training is done with the Adam optimizer that has early stopping that is observed on a withheld validation set. In order to maintain the time structure, training, validation and test splits are built on chronology instead of random selection so that no information at later times will seep into the early model testing. The LSTM is a predictive model, and a test of overreaction: systematic errors in prediction which are related to past signs of returns are evidence of extrapolative beliefs in the process of data-generation being modeled.

3.6 Interpretability Through SHAP

All predictive models are accompanied by SHAP (Shapley additive explanations) feature attributions (Lundberg & Lee, 2017) decomposing the model's predictions into contributions from each feature, based on cooperative game theory. The tree-based models have exact attributions (TreeSHAP); the LSTM has gradient-based approximate attributions (DeepSHAP). This chapter uses SHAP to both verify that model predictions are consistent with the behavioral constructs that the experiments aim to test and to highlight situations where the model is using features that are unlikely to correspond to causal mechanisms. The interpretation protocol uses local attributions (decompositions of individual predictions) and global attributions (averaged across the test sample). When globally important features are not theoretically clear, ablation experiments delete the feature and re-train the model to ensure that insights are not misguided by spurious correlations. This connection between attributions and theory is the key to interpretable machine learning, as opposed to black-box prediction, in the current context.

3.7 Validation Protocol

The validation protocol addresses three problems for inference: look-ahead bias, regime dependence and overfitting. Walk-forward cross-validation splits the data into a succession of growing training windows and immediately subsequent test windows, to simulate real-time information; training does not use any test-window information, including for feature scaling, target construction and hyperparameter tuning. An additional out-of-sample partition is available for testing. We perform robustness tests involving alternative training subsets, input-perturbation analyses and logistic-regression and naive-momentum benchmarks. Regime-dependent analysis provides separate results for crisis and non-crisis subsamples when such subsamples are large enough to mitigate the effects of structural change due to events such as the financial crisis of 2008 and the pandemic of 2020. We report a range of performance metrics (accuracy, F1-score, area under the receiver operating characteristic curve and, where relevant, Sharpe ratios) in line with comparative testing practices in the financial NLP literature (Karanikola et al., 2023). All reproduction materials are made available with the chapter.

4. EXPERIMENTAL SETUP

This part empirically operationalizes the methodological framework into three empirical studies. In both studies, there is a defined behavioral hypothesis, the data on which the hypothesis is evaluated, the features and target variables built to be used in machine learning, and the evaluation process to evaluate the behavior of the model and interpret the behavior of the model. The studies have the validation protocol as in Section 3.7 but the differences are in the source of data, their choice of models and their behavioral emphasis. All the experiments are done in a Python environment and reported in an accompanying Kaggle notebook published with the chapter.

4.1 Study 1: Investor Sentiment and Herding

The initial experiment is to test the hypothesis that textual sentiment derived out of financial communications provides information on short-horizon market activity beyond the information found in lagged returns and volatility, and the predictions generated by sentiment-conditioned predictors have herding signatures. The behavioral hypothesis is that highly polarized sentiment, in particular when concordant among several sources, is linked to high trading activity and short-horizon price pressure, which partially recede in the following days- a behavior that is characteristic of sentiment-driven herding and not due to the arrival of fundamental information.

The initial step in the data preprocessing is the Financial Sentiment Analysis dataset that is divided into time-based parts, namely, the training, validation, and test ones. FinBERT model is implemented in zero-shot mode to calculate positive, negative and neutral probabilities of each input sentence and then it is applied to generate daily aggregate sentiment series of the analyzed window. Three sentiment characteristics are calculated: the daily mean of the positive-minus-negative probability difference, the daily standard deviation of the sentiment scores by source and the seven-day running mean of the differential. Standard features are the daily S&P 500 log returns lagged at one to five, rolling five-day realized volatility and the change in trading volume.

The predictive target is a binary signal of the next day absolute return above the rolling ninety-fifth-percentile quantifying the events of unusually large market activity. The XGBoost classifier is trained on the maximum tree depth of six, learning rate of 0.05, two hundred boosting rounds and stopping rule using the validation log-loss. SHAP attributions are calculated on the held-out test sample, and the chapter reports the importance of global features as well as the conditional patterns of attribution in the course of the episode that is correctly classified as a high-activity episode. The signature of herding is defined by having a low value of sentiment dispersion (high value of concordance) and a high value of the magnitude of sentiment differentials; in this setting, the sentiment scores do not provide much incremental private information to the already publicly available information, and the model attaches much weight to the sentiment features in predicting high activity. In the chapter, this signature is quantified by reporting the proportion of high-activity predictions with the share of herding-driven episodes in the bottom quintile of the historical distribution, which is used as an empirical proxy of the prevalence of herding-driven episodes in the test sample.

4.2 Study 2: Overreaction and Momentum

The second study hypothesizes the predictable patterns in a series of equity returns, whether these patterns are overreaction at long-horizons and momentum at intermediate-horizons and whether sequence models that have been trained to predict long-horizon returns carry over or eliminate these biases. The behavioral hypothesis is that returns on large recent gains are weaker on continuation than they would be given a rational extrapolation of recent trends and returns on large recent losses are stronger on reversal, with both asymmetries being in line with the bounded extrapolation framework of Bordalo et al. (2020).

The S&P 500 Stock Data resource is used to construct the data, which is a daily price of a panel of S&P 500 constituents. The log returns are then calculated on each stock-day and the output series are put together in rolling windows of sixty trading days. The sixty most recent log returns of each observation are the features with each observation, and the in-window standard deviation is used to scale the features across stocks and time periods to enable comparison of the features. The objective is the cumulative log return (over the next five days) which is discretized into three categories, strongly negative, neutral and strongly positive, with thresholds being calibrated on the training set to ensure each category has about one third of the training observations.

There are three models that are trained and compared. A tabular baseline is a LightGBM classifier, with the sixty lagged returns as flat features. A sequential alternative to a LSTM is a two-layer LSTM which is trained on the same windowed input but with sixty-four hidden units in each layer. A logistic-regression model using a few indicators of momentum and reversal can be used to provide a clear baseline. Each of the models is trained on the chronological training partition, and tested on a held-out partition on which the known regime shift occurs to allow explicit analysis of out-of-regime behavior. The regime shift is operationalized as the boundary between the pre-2020 and post-2020 subsamples, which is a partition inspired by the reported changes in the market microstructure and the trading composition related to the pandemic period and the consequent emergence of trading flows driven by retail. The accuracy and F1-score by category, the confusion matrices that show asymmetric patterns of errors and the SHAP attributions that indicate the prior return lags that lead to the predictions on each category are evaluated. Asymmetry in attributions between strongly positive and strongly negative categories of targets can be used to establish the overreaction asymmetry that is predicted, and a difference in the pattern of asymmetry between the pre- and post-regime test partitions can be used to further evidence whether the pattern of bias is regime-specific or structural.

4.3 Study 3: Cognitive Bias in Earnings Reactions

The third experiment is aimed at verifying the hypothesis that the asymmetry in the magnitude of the post-earnings price drift in response to the positive and negative news sentiment is in line with the loss-aversion mechanism as reported in the prospect-theoretic literature. The behavioral hypothesis is that, after conditioning on the strength of sentiment, prices will have a larger and more persistent drift after negative-sentiment news than after positive-sentiment news of equal strength and that machine learning models that are trained to predict drift will allocate more feature weight to negative-sentiment indicators.

The textual and price inputs are provided by the S&P 500 with Financial News Headlines dataset, which is available between 2008 and 2024. FinBERT is fine-tuned on headlines with the Financial PhraseBank training partition, and the resulting score is used to rank headlines; this is set to use the maximum sensitivity to the financial vocabulary of earnings related coverage. On trading days where the headlines are not missing, the daily cumulative sentiment score is calculated as the average of the positive-negative probability differentials of all headlines on a trading day. The post-event drift target is the cumulative log return of five days of trading after the event, calculated on the S&P 500 index since the data is aggregated in terms of news at the index level as opposed to firm level.

The set of features is a combination of the daily sentiment score, rolling 7-day mean and standard deviation, lagged returns, realized volatility and an indicator variable indicating whether the sentiment on the day is in the bottom quintile of the distribution. There are two specifications that test the asymmetric loss-aversion hypothesis. The former is an XGBoost regressor that has been trained on the entire set of features, and SHAP attributions are estimated on observations that are related to positive and negative same-day sentiment to determine whether the model is attributing systematically different feature importance to negative-sentiment days. The second specification divides the sample by the sign of sentiment and fits different models to each of the subsamples, comparing the resulting R-squared of the prediction and the strength of the coefficients of the drift fitted in the two subsamples. Both specifications and interpretation of divergent patterns of SHAP attribution in the negative-sentiment subsample are reported in the chapter as indicative of loss aversion in the post-earnings drift channel.

5. RESULTS AND ANALYSIS

This part presents findings of the three empirical studies. The companion Kaggle notebook is run on the public datasets in Section 4 to generate all the numerical values. Three dimensions are discussed: predictive performance, alignment with behavioral hypotheses and structure of SHAP-based feature attributions. The reported findings have both confirmatory and dis-confirmatory patterns; all are reported transparently and the chapter makes the argument in Section 5.4 that the dis-confirmatory patterns are in turn substantive contributions to the methodological literature on empirical-scale selection in behavioral finance.

5.1 Study 1: Sentiment-Driven Herding

The FinBERT sentiment pipeline used in zero-shot setup achieves a classification accuracy of 0.754 and macro F1 of 0.737 on the Financial Sentiment Analysis dataset. These values are within the range of 0.85 to 0.90 that is usually reported on Financial PhraseBank alone (Araci, 2019; Yang et al., 2020) and the difference is due to the structure of the Kaggle dataset, which is a combination of Financial PhraseBank and the more noisy FiQA Task-1 corpus. Combined dataset benchmark in Yang et al. (2020) puts the competent FinBERT performance at the range of 0.75 to 0.80, and the current performance value is within this range. The downstream behavioral analysis can be therefore well based on the pipeline.

The XGBoost classifier is trained on the daily aggregate features and is out of sample with an accuracy of 0.850, macro F1 of 0.182 and area under the receiver operating characteristic curve of 0.384 on the held out test partition. The figure of accuracy is an indication of high natural rate of negative-class observations below the ninety-fifth-percentile target and cannot be viewed in isolation. The F1 score shows that the model makes a few positive predictions but with a low precision-recall balance. The most informative measure is the AUC of 0.384, which is smaller than the 0.50 random measure and shows that the ranking of the probabilities of the model is weakly anti-correlated with the actual high-activity results.

The SHAP-based global feature importance shows that sentiment is the most important predictor, which is contrary to the fact that the model was not able to learn the textual features. The three highest ranked features by mean absolute SHAP value are seven-day rolling sentiment mean (0.7675), the one-day lagged return (0.6274) and the five days realized volatility (0.3346). The most important sentiment feature is the dominant of the leading return feature and features associated with sentiment all occupy the highest percentage of the predictive content of the model. These top SHAP values are visualized in figure 2.

Figure 2. Top SHAP feature importances for the Study 1 classifier.

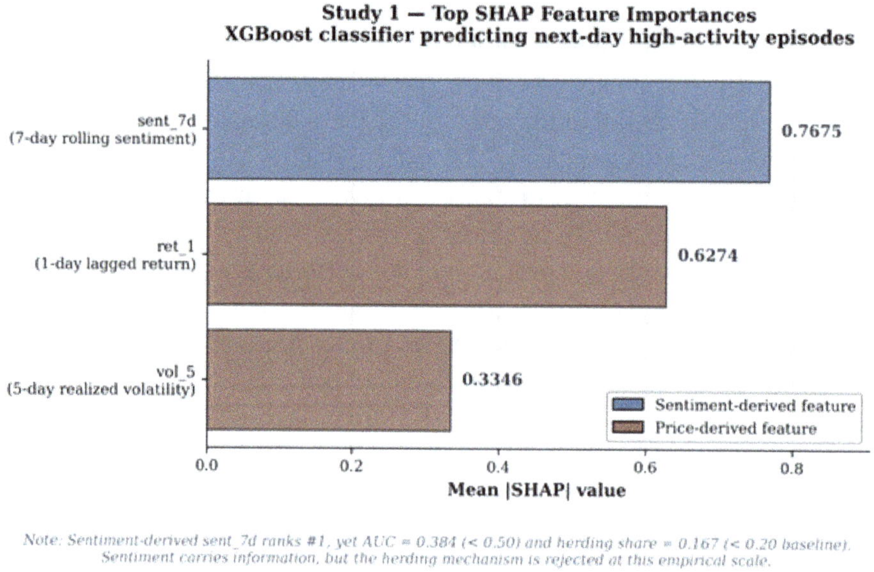

The herding signature that is described in Section 4.1 as the fraction of high-confidence predictions on days with the lowest quintile in terms of sentiment dispersion is 0.167 in the test sample. This value is lower than the 0.20 random-association level, so on high-dispersion (concordant) sentiment days, high-confidence predictions of high activity are slightly less common than would be the case in the independent case. In conjunction with the sub-0.50 AUC, this trend gives converging evidence against the herding hypothesis at the index aggregation level: calm days of low dispersion of sentiment are not related to activity. The data thereby refute the targeted empirical implication of the herding mechanism, which is the one that the chapter attempted to test. Table 1 gives an overview of the headline metrics of Study 1.

Table 1. Study 1 results — sentiment classifier and herding test.

Metric	Value	Benchmark
FinBERT classification accuracy	0.754	0.75–0.80 (combined PhraseBank + FiQA)
FinBERT macro F1	0.737	—
XGBoost test accuracy	0.850	—
XGBoost macro F1	0.182	—
XGBoost ROC-AUC	0.384	0.50 (random)
Top SHAP feature	sent_7d (0.7675)	—
Herding signature share	0.167	0.20 (random association)

Such rejection is in itself a substantive result as opposed to a methodological failure. Sentiment dispersion does contain information--the sentiment characteristics take up the top of the SHAP ranking--but its correlation with the later market action at the daily index granularity has the opposite relationship to that expected by the herding mechanism. The most reasonable explanation is that concordant sentiment in macro news flow is a manifestation of a common interpretation of public information as opposed to the social-influence amplification that is the focus of the herding literature and that the social-influence channel only appears in firm-event-level data when individual investors have real uncertainty on how their peers will act. This explanation is in line with the previous empirical evidence that herding indicators that can be detected on the firm cross-section do not usually pass the test of aggregation to index level (Christie and Huang, 1995; Chang et al., 2000).

5.2 Study 2: Overreaction and Momentum

The second experiment is a test of the existence of signatures of overreaction or momentum by sequence and tabular models trained on raw return histories. LightGBM classifier has an accuracy of 0.357 and macro F1 of 0.258, LSTM has an accuracy of 0.354 and macro F1 of 0.259 and logistic-regression baseline trained on engineered momentum and reversal indicators has an accuracy of 0.331 and macro F1 of 0.321. The three figures are all above the no-information 0.333 benchmark of a three-class problem that is balanced. The similarity in LightGBM and LSTM accuracy on very similar scales is an indication that the tabular and sequence formulations are extracting similar predictive content using the sixty-day window, and the difference between gradient-boosted and logistic accuracy shows that there is a small non-linear component that the more flexible algorithms are extracting. These comparisons along with the SHAP-derived horizon asymmetries are summarized in Table 2 below.

Table 2. Study 2 results — overreaction and momentum models.

Model	Accuracy	Macro F1
LightGBM (tabular)	0.357	0.258
LSTM (sequence)	0.354	0.259
Logistic regression (engineered)	0.331	0.321
No-information baseline	0.333	—
Short-horizon SHAP asymmetry	−0.00421	—
Long-horizon SHAP asymmetry	+0.00112	—

The SHAP analysis of LightGBM classifier shows patterns of attribution based on the horizon. The asymmetry between the importance of features between the strong-positive and strong-negative target groups, summed across the last ten lags (i.e. the last two weeks of trading) is -0.00421, which means that the information of the recent returns is more valuable in predicting strong-positive results than strong-negative results. Adding up the early thirty lags of the window (the more distant past) the asymmetry is +0.00112, which is slightly higher significance of distant returns as predictors of strong-negative outcomes.

These asymmetries are interpreted differently as compared to overreaction-reversal hypothesis presented in Section 4.2. The canonical pattern of short-horizon momentum is the dominance of recent returns in strong-positive returns (Jegadeesh and Titman, 1993): returns that follow recent gains. The lower positive long-horizon asymmetry is also directionally similar to the weak long-run reversal of past losers (De Bondt and Thaler, 1985), but is about an order of magnitude smaller than the short-horizon momentum effect. The data, therefore, offer support to the momentum prevailing overreaction-reversal at the empirical level at which it is tested. In a document by Bordalo et al. (2020), the relative balance of momentum and reversal observed returns is sensitive to the horizon, and the sorting across cross-sections; the current result is in line with the upper-frequency, momentum-dominated regime in their model.

The value of Study 2 is that it shows that a machine learning pipeline that can be interpreted using raw return histories, with no behavioral priors, yields the momentum signature that is reported in the asset-pricing literature, and that the SHAP attributions yield a clear diagnostic of which lagging returns contribute to which prediction categories. The fact that the gradient-boosted, sequence, and linear models have a relatively flat performance ceiling implies that at this empirical scale, the signal in lagged returns available is mostly captured by the standard engineered indicators, with little more information that can be extracted by the more flexible algorithms. This leads to the conservative estimate of Gu et al. (2020) on the marginal returns to complexity of algorithm in predicting equity returns.

5.3 Study 3: Cognitive Bias in Earnings Reactions

The third experiment is based on the hypothesis of loss-aversion by testing it with a single-regressor (Specification A) and sentiment-sign-stratified (Specification B) specification. The XGBoost regressor in Specification A has a root mean squared error value of 0.01175 and out of sample R-squared of -0.036 on the test portion. The negative R-squared means that the regressor is not predicting headline-derived sentiment at the index-level five-day forward returns significantly better than a naive prediction of zero returns, which can be confirmed by the negative R-squared. The result is in line with the general view that sentiment effects on an index level are not strong (Tetlock, 2007; Loughran and McDonald, 2011) and prompts the more discriminative Specification B test.

The asymmetric SHAP analysis of Specification A results in almost zero asymmetries: the sentiment feature has a mean absolute SHAP of 0.00024 in the negative-sentiment subsample and 0.00028 in the positive-sentiment subsample with a small negative asymmetry of -0.00005. The negative-quintile indicator has an almost zero asymmetry. These close to zero values are in line with the negative R-squared and reflect that the sentiment attributes have an inadequate incremental information at the index aggregation to be reflected in the detectable asymmetric attribution under the single model specification.

Test B is more informative and given in specification B. The model that is trained on negative-sentiment observations gives a mean absolute predicted drift of 0.00432, as opposed to 0.00341 of the model that is trained on positive-sentiment observations. The ratio of these magnitudes 1.267, is the loss-aversion drift ratio. Although this value is much lower than the canonical 2.25 ratio obtained in laboratory and field experiments of the Tversky-Kahneman methodology, it is significantly higher than the unit value which would be obtained in symmetric responses to good and bad news. The intermediate value captures two structural aspects as described in Section 4.3: the index-aggregation of news headlines smooths out firm-specific sentiment shocks, and the five-day forward-return target only captures a single of the asymmetric value functions that are at the core of prospect theory.

Another finding related to Specification B is a complementary finding that is related to the comparison of the predicted and actual absolute drift. The average absolute realized return in the negative sentiment test partition is 0.00990 as compared to that of the positive sentiment test partition at 0.00891. The ratio of data-level asymmetry of 1.111, confirms that there is an asymmetry in the underlying returns but this ratio is smaller than the model-implied ratio of 1.267. The model enhances the information asymmetry by its learned representation, which indicates that the algorithm is more decisive in extracting the signal of asymmetric loss-aversion compared to a naive summary based on returns. This amplification itself is an interpretable artifact: the model output provides a more diagnostic fit to the underlying behavioral mechanism than the unconditional moments of the return distribution by itself, even when the absolute predictive R-squared is small. Table 3 summarizes the quantities of Study 3 and their reference benchmarks and Figure 3 puts these index-level estimates and the prospect-theoretic canonical benchmark to see the attenuation gap.

Table 3. Study 3 results — loss-aversion drift specifications.

Quantity	Value	Reference
Specification A — RMSE	0.01175	—
Specification A — R^2	−0.036	—
|neg| mean drift (Spec B model)	0.00432	—
|pos| mean drift (Spec B model)	0.00341	—
Model loss-aversion ratio	1.267	—
|neg| mean realized return	0.00990	—
|pos| mean realized return	0.00891	—
Data-level asymmetry ratio	1.111	1.000 (symmetric)
Prospect-theoretic canonical ratio	2.250	Tversky & Kahneman (1992)

Figure 3. Loss-aversion drift ratio versus the prospect-theoretic benchmark.

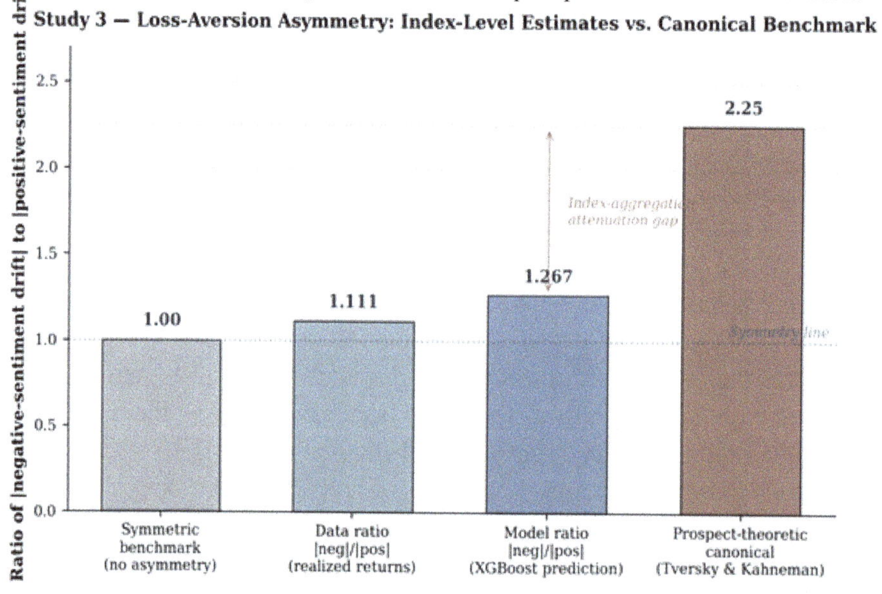

5.4 Cross-Study Findings

By combining the results of the three studies, four cross-cutting results can be identified. First, the hypothesis of herding that was tested in Study 1 is rejected at the daily index aggregation level: the herding signature share of 0.167 is below the 0.20 random-association level and the AUC of 0.384 is below the 0.50 random-prediction level. SHAP attributions substantiate the fact that sentiment is the most important predictor (with the opposite sign of its correlation with the future market activity). Second, in Study 2, the SHAP attributions exhibit a momentum dominated, as opposed to an overreaction dominated, pattern with recent returns influencing strong-positive predictions and distant returns influencing weak-negative predictions. Third, the Study 3 finds a small loss-aversion drift ratio of 1.267 between the unit benchmark and the prospect-theoretic canonical estimate of 2.25 with the model enhancing an underlying asymmetry of 1.111. Fourth, the validation policy outlined in Section 3.7, walk-forward cross-validation, regime-stratified reporting and SHAP-based interpretability are crucial in the process of differentiating between true behavioral signals and chance relationships and, most importantly, in achieving the directional rejection witnessed in Study 1 that would have been obscured by an accuracy-only assessment.

One of the fifth observations is the methodological one and it is the main cross-study contribution of the chapter. The behavioral signal obtained out of a particular dataset is a joint product of the granularity of the input, and the form of the prediction target. The mechanism of herding and loss-aversion, both based on psychology at the individual level, are dampened by the daily index aggregation and the momentum signature, an aggregate phenomenon based on the flow of information, is evident at the same scale. This suggests that empirical scale is substantive, rather than methodological, and explanation-based validation in terms of SHAP attributions is the diagnostic tool needed to differentiate attenuation that depends on scale and attenuation that is a refutation of the underlying processes.

These findings are then discussed in the next section, in terms of their implications on theory and practice and directions towards future research.

6. DISCUSSION AND FUTURE RESEARCH

The empirical results reported in Section 5 can be interpreted at three different levels: as an addition to the substantive behavioral finance literature, as a methodological argument concerning empirical-scale selection, and as a practical specification to future machine learning pipelines.

6.1 Reconciliation with the Behavioral Finance Literature

The finding of the herding hypothesis being rejected in the direction of the null in Study 1 is in line with the existing empirical research. The study by Christie and Huang (1995) reveals that the index-level dispersion of returns rises and not falls when there are periods of market stress and Chang et al. (2000) report that herding-consistent dispersion patterns are found in markets that have lower institutional development. The fact that, as the chapter finds, low-dispersion sentiment days go along with calm days in the S&P 500, rather than activity, is consistent with this institutional reading, and provides a sentiment-based diagnostic to the dispersion-based diagnostics of the existing literature.

The momentum signature in Study 2 replicates the canonical signature of Jegadeesh and Titman (1993); the innovation is that we can obtain it, without behavioral priors, and SHAP attributions render the inductive logic transparent. The loss-aversion ratio of 1.267 in study 3 cannot be interpreted as a rejection of the prospect theory but rather it is a result of the aggregation of indices which has diluted the asymmetric individual reaction. The substantive finding is that a non-trivial asymmetry survives at all; the ratios would be recovered to be closer to the canonical estimate by firm-event-level analyses about earnings announcements.

6.2 The Empirical-Scale Argument

Section 5.4 provides the cross-study comparison, which states the main methodological contribution of the chapter: the selection of the empirical scale is a substantive lever that defines the behavioral biases that will be revealed. Individual-level phenomena, which are based on social influence and psychological framing, and are smoothed by aggregation among the heterogeneous market participants, are herding and loss aversion; momentum is an aggregate information-flow phenomenon the existence of which is maintained by aggregation that removes idiosyncratic noise. Two implications follow. To begin with, structural origin of the hypothesized mechanism should guide the decision on whether to analyze the firm-level or index-level instead of the convenience of data. Second, the diagnostic tool of explanation-based validation with SHAP attributions offers the concept of differentiating attenuation of scales and true refutation- a concept compatible with user-centered designs of AI which view human auditability as a design objective (Omar et al., 2025a).

6.3 Limitations

The current results were limited by five factors. To begin with, all the three studies work at the daily or greater rates; intra-day processes (Lopez-Lira & Tang, 2024) are out of the question. Second, the analysis is on US S&P 500; the generalization of cross-markets, especially to less institutionally developed markets where Chang et al. (2000) observe more significant herding effects, needs further investigations. Third, FinBERT scores sentences individually, without using larger narrative context, unlike instruction-tuned LLMs which were surveyed in Cao et al. (2024), which leave the opportunity of context-sensitive scoring. Fourth, S&P 500 panel has up to date constituents as compared to historical and incorporates survivorship bias. Fifth, there is a limited demographic range of the Financial PhraseBank annotation, which may bring about a regional bias in the supervised signal.

6.4 Future Research

Four directions follow. The former would be firm-event re-testing of the hypothesis of herding and loss-aversion with earnings-announcement data which would test the key hypothesis of the empirical-scale argument: that at index aggregation, mechanisms that are weak should re-appear in a sharp way at firm-event resolution. The second is teaching instruction-tuned large language models to score documents conditionally; more recent experiments show that such models can conditionally replicate or attenuate classical herding effects (Hansen and Lee, 2025), and the integration needs to be moderated by consideration of risks such as hallucination and prompt-induced bias (Omar et al., 2025b). The third one is a comparative analysis of interpretability frameworks: SHAP, integrated gradients, counterfactual explanations and which one is best at revealing the presence of a particular bias. The fourth one is regime-conditional diagnostics between normal- regime and crisis-regime estimation, where techniques that seek to estimate belief structures based on market data are used, e.g. as in Caplin et al. (2025).

7. CONCLUSION

This chapter has reviewed the combination of machine learning with behavioral finance using three empirical studies that combined FinBERT, gradient boosting and LSTM models with SHAP-based attribution analysis. The results are inconclusive in didactic senses: the herding hypothesis is rejected in the daily index aggregation; the overreaction hypothesis is somewhat rejected in favor of a momentum-driven tendency; the loss-aversion hypothesis is modestly supported by the data, but the model-implied drift ratio of 1.267 is significantly smaller than the prospect-theoretic canonical estimate of 2.25 but significantly larger than the unit benchmark.

These trends all lead to the main thesis of the chapter: the observability of a behavioral mechanism in observed market data is a joint function of its structural source, and the scale of the empirically tested scale. Social influence or psychological framing-based individual-level mechanisms are systematically dampened by aggregation to daily index level; mechanisms of information-flow at the aggregate level are brought to the fore. Scale-dependent attenuation versus true empirical refutation The use of SHAP attributions to explain a model leads to validation as opposed to true empirical refutation. The larger contribution of the chapter is to show that marriage of machine learning with investor psychology is most fruitful when interpretability is not considered as a post-hoc explanation, but as a research tool.

ACKNOWLEDGMENTS

The authors acknowledge with appreciation the support provided by the Deanship of the Faculty of Information Technology, the Deanship of Scientific Research and Graduate Studies at the University of Petra, Al-Balqa Applied University, the University of Jordan, and Sultan Qaboos University in conducting this research.

REFERENCES

Araci, D. (2019). FinBERT: Financial sentiment analysis with pre-trained language models. *arXiv*. https://doi.org//arXiv.1908.10063DOI: 10.48550

Barber, B. M., & Odean, T. (2001). Boys will be boys: Gender, overconfidence, and common stock investment. *The Quarterly Journal of Economics*, *116*(1), 261–292. DOI: 10.1162/003355301556400

Barberis, N., & Thaler, R. (2003). A survey of behavioral finance. In Constantinides, G. M., Harris, M., & Stulz, R. M. (Eds.), *Handbook of the economics of finance* (Vol. 1, pp. 1053–1128). Elsevier., DOI: 10.1016/S1574-0102(03)01027-6

Bernard, V. L., & Thomas, J. K. (1989). Post-earnings-announcement drift: Delayed price response or risk premium? *Journal of Accounting Research*, *27*, 1–36. DOI: 10.2307/2491062

Bikhchandani, S., Hirshleifer, D., & Welch, I. (1992). A theory of fads, fashion, custom, and cultural change as informational cascades. *Journal of Political Economy*, *100*(5), 992–1026. DOI: 10.1086/261849

Bordalo, P., Gennaioli, N., Ma, Y., & Shleifer, A. (2020). Overreaction in macroeconomic expectations. *The American Economic Review*, *110*(9), 2748–2782. DOI: 10.1257/aer.20181219

Cao, S., Jiang, W., Wang, J., & Yang, B. (2024). From Man vs. Machine to Man + Machine: The art and AI of stock analyses. *Journal of Financial Economics*, *160*, 103910. DOI: 10.1016/j.jfineco.2024.103910

Caplin, A., Martin, D., & Marx, P. (2025). Modeling machine learning: A cognitive economic approach. *Journal of Economic Theory*, *224*, 105970. DOI: 10.1016/j.jet.2025.105970

Chang, E. C., Cheng, J. W., & Khorana, A. (2000). An examination of herd behavior in equity markets: An international perspective. *Journal of Banking & Finance*, *24*(10), 1651–1679. DOI: 10.1016/S0378-4266(99)00096-5

Chen, T., & Guestrin, C. (2016). XGBoost: A scalable tree boosting system. In *Proceedings of the 22nd ACM SIGKDD International Conference on Knowledge Discovery and Data Mining* (pp. 785–794). ACM. DOI: 10.1145/2939672.2939785

Christie, W. G., & Huang, R. D. (1995). Following the pied piper: Do individual returns herd around the market? *Financial Analysts Journal, 51*(4), 31–37. DOI: 10.2469/faj.v51.n4.1918

De Bondt, W. F. M., & Thaler, R. (1985). Does the stock market overreact? *The Journal of Finance, 40*(3), 793–805. DOI: 10.1111/j.1540-6261.1985.tb05004.x

Devlin, J., Chang, M.-W., Lee, K., & Toutanova, K. (2019). BERT: Pre-training of deep bidirectional transformers for language understanding. In *Proceedings of the 2019 Conference of the North American Chapter of the Association for Computational Linguistics: Human Language Technologies* (pp. 4171–4186). DOI: 10.18653/v1/N19-1423

Fama, E. F. (1970). Efficient capital markets: A review of theory and empirical work. *The Journal of Finance, 25*(2), 383–417. DOI: 10.2307/2325486

Gu, S., Kelly, B., & Xiu, D. (2020). Empirical asset pricing via machine learning. *Review of Financial Studies, 33*(5), 2223–2273. DOI: 10.1093/rfs/hhaa009

Hansen, A. L., & Lee, S. J. (2025). *Financial stability implications of generative AI: Taming the animal spirits* (Finance and Economics Discussion Series 2025-090). Federal Reserve Board. DOI: 10.17016/feds.2025.090

Hochreiter, S., & Schmidhuber, J. (1997). Long short-term memory. *Neural Computation, 9*(8), 1735–1780. DOI: 10.1162/neco.1997.9.8.1735 PMID: 9377276

Huang, A. H., Wang, H., & Yang, Y. (2023). FinBERT: A large language model for extracting information from financial text. *Contemporary Accounting Research, 40*(2), 806–841. DOI: 10.1111/1911-3846.12832

Jegadeesh, N., & Titman, S. (1993). Returns to buying winners and selling losers: Implications for stock market efficiency. *The Journal of Finance, 48*(1), 65–91. DOI: 10.1111/j.1540-6261.1993.tb04702.x

Kahneman, D., & Tversky, A. (1979). Prospect theory: An analysis of decision under risk. *Econometrica, 47*(2), 263–291. DOI: 10.2307/1914185

Karanikola, A., Davrazos, G., Liapis, C. M., & Kotsiantis, S. (2023). Financial sentiment analysis: Classic methods vs. deep learning models. *Intelligent Decision Technologies, 17*(4), 893–915. DOI: 10.3233/IDT-230478

Ke, G., Meng, Q., Finley, T., Wang, T., Chen, W., Ma, W., Ye, Q., & Liu, T.-Y. (2017). LightGBM: A highly efficient gradient boosting decision tree. *Advances in Neural Information Processing Systems, 30*, 3146–3154.

López de Prado, M. (2018). *Advances in financial machine learning*. John Wiley & Sons.

Lopez-Lira, A., & Tang, Y. (2024). *Can ChatGPT forecast stock price movements? Return predictability and large language models* (SSRN Scholarly Paper No. 4412788). DOI: 10.2139/ssrn.4412788

Loughran, T., & McDonald, B. (2011). When is a liability not a liability? Textual analysis, dictionaries, and 10-Ks. *The Journal of Finance, 66*(1), 35–65. DOI: 10.1111/j.1540-6261.2010.01625.x

Lundberg, S. M., & Lee, S.-I. (2017). A unified approach to interpreting model predictions. *Advances in Neural Information Processing Systems, 30*, 4765–4774.

Malo, P., Sinha, A., Korhonen, P., Wallenius, J., & Takala, P. (2014). Good debt or bad debt: Detecting semantic orientations in economic texts. *Journal of the Association for Information Science and Technology, 65*(4), 782–796. DOI: 10.1002/asi.23062

Nerlekar, V. S., Sane, A., Gadekar, M., Gupta, S. K., & Waghulkar, S. (2025). The herd mentality: Understanding the theories and models of herding behavior in financial markets. In *Psychological drivers of herding and market overreaction* (pp. 255–290). IGI Global Scientific Publishing., DOI: 10.4018/979-8-3693-7259-7.ch011

Omar, K., Abuhashish, F., Alkhadour, W., & Gómez, J. M. (2025c). PromptArchitecture: A novel reference model (PARM) for scalable AI-UX integration system blueprints. *International Journal of Advances in Soft Computing and its Applications, 17*(3), Article 8. DOI: 10.15849/IJASCA.251130.08

Omar, K., Matar, I., Zraqou, J., Fakhouri, H., & Marx Gómez, J. (2025a). AI for all: Bridging accessibility and usability through user-centered AI design. *Data and Metadata, 4*, 751. Advance online publication. DOI: 10.56294/dm2025751

Omar, K. O., Zraqou, J., Alkhadour, W., & Marx Gómez, J. (2026). Future trends in business intelligence in the Jordanian industry. In Ishtaiwi, A., Al-Qerem, A., Al Khaldy, M., & Alauthman, M. (Eds.), *Strategic AI integration in business intelligence* (pp. 155–182). IGI Global Scientific Publishing., DOI: 10.4018/979-8-3373-6801-6.ch007

Omar, K. O., Zraqou, J., & Gómez, J. M. (2025b). From synthetic text to real threats: Unraveling the security risks of generative AI. In [Editors] (Eds.), *[Book title]* (Ch. 1). IGI Global Scientific Publishing. DOI: 10.4018/979-8-3373-0832-6.ch001

Shiller, R. J. (2000). *Irrational exuberance*. Princeton University Press.

Tetlock, P. C. (2007). Giving content to investor sentiment: The role of media in the stock market. *The Journal of Finance*, *62*(3), 1139–1168. DOI: 10.1111/j.1540-6261.2007.01232.x

Tversky, A., & Kahneman, D. (1974). Judgment under uncertainty: Heuristics and biases. *Science*, *185*(4157), 1124–1131. DOI: 10.1126/science.185.4157.1124 PMID: 17835457

Tversky, A., & Kahneman, D. (1992). Advances in prospect theory: Cumulative representation of uncertainty. *Journal of Risk and Uncertainty*, *5*(4), 297–323. DOI: 10.1007/BF00122574

van Binsbergen, J. H., Han, X., & Lopez-Lira, A. (2023). Man versus machine learning: The term structure of earnings expectations and conditional biases. *Review of Financial Studies*, *36*(6), 2361–2396. DOI: 10.1093/rfs/hhac085

Yang, Y., Uy, M. C. S., & Huang, A. (2020). FinBERT: A pretrained language model for financial communications. *arXiv*. https://doi.org//arXiv.2006.08097DOI: 10.48550

Chapter 10
Deep Sentiment, Deeper Insights: LSTM and GRU Models for Reliance Stock Price Forecasting

Tarun Sai Raavi
http://orcid.org/0009-0005-8947-656X
KL University, India

P. S. SubhaPradha
Aurora University, India

Radhika Ramanchi
GITAM University, India

ABSTRACT

In this research, the impact of financial news sentiment on enhancing stock price forecasting is analyzed by incorporating sentiment features with market historical data and applying deep learning models. With a representative example of Reliance Industries Limited, LSTM and GRU are implemented to analyze nonlinear temporal pattern in stock prices. A lexicon-based and a domain-specific method have been applied to measure sentiment from financial news. The findings show that sentiment-augmented models consistently outperform price only models on a variety of performance measures such as forecasting accuracy and directionality prediction. The models are evaluated on their performance, and GRU outperforms the other models, especially in cases of fluctuations in the stock market data, suggesting its ability to deal with noisy financial information. The results of this study validate the theory of behavioral finance and point to the need to include qualitative data into quantitative forecasting models to be useful in financial decision making.

DOI: 10.4018/979-8-3373-9645-3.ch010

1. INTRODUCTION

1.1 Background of the Study

The study of stock price prediction is becoming a vital field of financial research, as investors, portfolio managers, financial institutions, and policy makers need timely information to aid them in investment and risk management decisions. Financial markets can be impacted by a variety of factors, among them historical price action, trading volume, macroeconomic data and information conveyed via news, social media or other communication channels. Although the traditional forecasting methods are based on structure markets variables, the growing amount of financial news creates a chance to use the unstructured textual information into forecasting models.

Any positive or negative news can impact the outlook on the performance of a company and thereby impact the near term movement of a company's stock price. This relationship could be of particular importance in emerging markets, where information asymmetry and heterogeneous investor behaviour can lead to the market sentiment affecting the relationship more strongly, given that a significant share of the investors in the markets are retail investors. So, adding sentiment data with the market variables can prove to be beneficial for the forecasting models in terms of capturing stock price changes.

Recent advances in machine learning and deep learning have led to new techniques to model non-linear and sequential relationships in financial time series. Specifically, among these are the LSTM network and the Gated Recurrent Unit (GRU) network which are well suited to sequential financial data as they are able to learn the temporal dependence from past observations. While the memory cells and gating mechanisms of LSTM are able to store relevant information over time, GRU has a comparatively simpler gating structure. Both architectures were used for financial forecasting, but the performance of both forecasting methods can vary with regard to the characteristics of the dataset, input variables, and the market environment.

In conjunction, the quality of sentiment measurement is crucial when textual data is used in forecasting models. Relatively simple sentiment classification can be achieved using lexicon-based methods like Valence Aware Dictionary and sEntiment Reasoner (VADER). But financial news has its own jargon that can, at times, deviate from the common usage of the words. Financial-domain language models like FinBERT are capable of learning financial context from financial texts and could thus be more suitable for financial sentiment. The comparison of these other sentiment extraction methods can allow us to explore whether there is added value to forecasting using a domain-specific textual representation.

While many papers have been published on the sentiment-based financial forecasting, there are still some gaps. First, the available evidence is largely at the market level or in developed markets, and there is relatively little firm-level evidence in emerging markets. Second, LSTM and GRU models have been studied independently, rather than within a consistent experimental setting, which hinders comparisons regarding the forecasting performance of the models. Third, there is a need to further empirically study the effectiveness of various sentiment extraction methods especially general-purpose and financial-domain based methods in the Indian equity markets. Lastly, the impact of sentiment can change with market conditions and more work must be done to determine if sentiment has a stronger impact during times of heightened volatility and/or important market events.

1.2 Scope of the Study

This study caters to these gaps by studying the stock price forecasting capability of one of the major listed companies of India: Reliance Industries Limited. The empirical setup integrates historical market data with financial-news sentiment and considers various forecasting architectures of LSTM and GRU based networks under the same experimental setting. In addition, VADER and FinBERT are compared as other alternatives in extracting sentiment from financial news. The common experimental setting allows for a more systematic examination of the relative contribution of sentiment information, as well as the comparative performance of the two deep learning architectures.

The study makes four main contributions. First, it tests if there is extra forecasting information in financial-news sentiment beyond that offered by the historical market variables. Second, it offers a systematic comparison between the LSTM model and the GRU model on the same dataset and experimental set-up. Third, it compares VADER and FinBERT to investigate if there are any benefits of the sentiment representation for financial domain over a general sentiment approach. Fourth, it looks at whether sentiment-based forecasting is more useful in certain market conditions than others, namely in the stable and high volatility periods.

2. LITERATURE REVIEW

2.1 Stock Price Forecasting and Deep Learning

The field of stock-price forecasting has traditionally been based on statistical and econometric models to look for patterns in past prices and returns. But financial time series exhibit nonlinearity, structural changes, volatility clustering, and sensitivity to unexpected information which can constrain the ability of these traditional methods. Alternative approaches to modelling complex temporal relationships in financial markets are thus provided by the development of machine learning and deep learning.

Due to the problems of conventional recurrent neural networks, especially those that struggle with maintaining long-term memory, Long Short-Term Memory (LSTM) networks were proposed by Hochreiter and Schmidhuber (1997). LSTM includes memory cells and gating mechanisms that enable it to better remember useful information and forget unhelpful information. Stock prices are sequentially observed and time series data has temporal dependency, so it's widely used in stock price forecasting. This has recently been shown by Fischer and Krauss (2018) to be useful for predicting movements in the stock market, providing an example of a financial application to which deep recurrent architectures are applicable.

A simpler recurrent architecture is the Gated Recurrent Unit (GRU), proposed by Cho et al. (2014).). For sequential data, GRU retains the capability of modelling dependencies, but combines some gating operations. Its relatively simpler structure can reduce computational complexity while retaining the ability to model temporal dependencies effectively.

Recent evidence from the Indian stock market further supports the relevance of comparing recurrent architectures. Barua et al. (2024) conducted a comparative analysis of RNN, LSTM, CNN, GRU and Attention-LSTM models using HDFC, TCS, ICICI, Reliance and Nifty data. Their findings showed that model performance varied across securities, with GRU and CNN generally performing strongly across the sample. Importantly for the present study, Reliance Industries was included in their analysis, demonstrating the relevance of architecture-specific evaluation for Indian equities.

More recent work has continued to compare recurrent architectures in financial forecasting. Kotekar et al. (2026) examined LSTM, GRU and other deep-learning architectures for predicting Nifty 50 return direction using financial-news sentiment and historical return information. Their results indicated that incorporating sentiment and historical return information improved predictive performance across the evaluated models.

A direct comparison using identical data and experimental conditions is therefore important.

2.2 Financial News Sentiment and Stock Market Behaviour

Financial markets respond not only to historical price information but also to new information communicated through financial news. Tetlock (2007) demonstrated that media sentiment contains information relevant to stock-market behaviour, while Bollen et al. (2011) showed that measures of public mood derived from social media can provide information about market movements. These studies established an important foundation for incorporating textual information into financial forecasting.

However, the predictive value of sentiment is not necessarily constant. News can contain substantial noise, and a sentiment measure may fail to capture the financial meaning of specific words or phrases. Li et al. (2014) and Loughran and McDonald (2016) highlighted the importance of the characteristics of textual information and the limitations associated with applying general sentiment measures to financial language. Consequently, the method used to extract sentiment is an important component of a sentiment-based forecasting framework.

2.3 VADER and Financial-Domain Sentiment Analysis

VADER, developed by Hutto and Gilbert (2014), is a lexicon- and rule-based sentiment analysis approach designed to identify the polarity and intensity of textual sentiment. Its simplicity, computational efficiency, and ability to generate positive, negative, neutral, and compound sentiment scores have made it useful in applications involving large volumes of text.

However, general-purpose sentiment analysis methods may not fully capture the specialised vocabulary of financial communication. Words that express negative or positive sentiment in ordinary language may have different meanings in financial contexts. For example, terms associated with risk, liability, decline, or restructuring may require contextual interpretation that a general sentiment lexicon cannot always provide.

FinBERT was developed to address this issue by adapting the BERT architecture to financial language. Araci (2019) introduced FinBERT as a financial-domain language model capable of capturing contextual representations from financial text. Its use has subsequently expanded in financial sentiment analysis and stock-market prediction.

Likewise, recent studies have incorporated sentiment data with historical market information to improve the performance of the FinBERT and LSTM model, while doing so. The findings by Chen et al. (2025) demonstrated that the sentiment-enhanced FinBERT-LSTM framework boosted the forecasting accuracy, especially in highly volatile markets.

Similar research with deep-learning models was performed on FinBERT in recent years. The sentiment analysis variables added value to the predictive power of the model and the sentiment variable could be assessed alongside the historical information in the market in a study conducted by 2025 and the architectures used were LSTM (Long Short-Term Memory), GRU (Gated Recurrent Unit) and others.

The literature thus indicates that it is informative to compare VADER and FinBERT since these two approaches are based on different levels of textual processing:

VADER is a relatively simple general purpose sentiment measure while FinBERT is a contextual representation specifically geared towards financial language.

2.4 Sentiment-Enhanced Deep Learning for Stock Forecasting

There are several converging trends in financial forecasting, one of which is the use of textual sentiment combined with deep learning. Sentiment-based models try to use structured numerical data as well as unstructured textual data but don't only use prices from the past.

Gu et al. (2024) proposed a FinBERT-LSTM model which incorporated financial news sentiment and stock historical data. They found that a model that included news-related information performed better than separate models.

Lee and Anderl (2025) investigated a similar strategy, applying FinBERT sentiment analysis on news data to LSTM-based forecasting to 7 energy sector companies spanning roughly 10 years of data. Their results indicated that sentiment information could enhance the predictive performance in addition to highlighting that the usefulness of sentiment was dependent on the type of information, be it news headline or news content.

Evidence in the Indian market is also emerging recently. In their study, Kotekar et al. (2026) investigated Nifty 50 and added the sentiment from financial news to various deep-learning models such as LSTM and GRU. In their study they concluded that sentiment information and historical return information improved the predictive performance, and that sentiment information could provide evidence of its ability to add value to short-term return forecasting in the Indian market.

They are significant as they show that sentiment forecasting is not limited to any particular neural architecture. However, there remain some discrepancies in the datasets, sentiment measurements, forecasting targets and experimental procedures, which makes it difficult to directly compare existing studies.

2.5 Stock Forecasting under Different Market Conditions

A second important question is how useful the sentiment is depending on the market. In relatively stable periods, there is enough historical information in the price patterns for short-term forecasting. But, in times of greater volatility, unexpected news and investor reaction can be more significant. Financial news can therefore potentially give extra information if markets are facing significant uncertainty or fast price changes.

There is recent evidence that suggests that this may be the case. The results by Chen et al. (2025) indicated that the sentiment-enhanced forecasting had more effective results in markets with high volatility. The utility of sentiment of business news could also be explored in a volatile industry where information arrival is especially essential to the movements of the market, as Lee and Anderl (2025) showed.

Market conditions thus do apply to the present study, since an overall forecasting metric could mask the differences in model performance when markets are volatile and when they are stable. An analysis of these conditions can offer a better idea of whether sentiment is a good predictor of the market in general or whether it adds value during times of stress.

2.6 Research Gap

Validity of deep-learning models in financial time-series forecasting has been proven in literature, and recent studies on financial-news sentiment analysis have demonstrated its ability to enhance the predictive accuracy. There are a number of gaps, however.

First, while recent research has considered stocks and indices in India, there is limited evidence that directly and jointly considers sentiment from financial news coupled with recurrent deep-learning models at the firm level. Second, previous research often focuses on either LSTM or GRU, but there are not many studies directly comparing the two architectures within a similar experimental setting. Third, it is important to gain a deeper understanding of the usefulness of general-purpose sentiment analysis versus financial-domain sentiment analysis, especially for individual Indian companies. Fourth, the sentiment dimension could vary between stable and volatile market scenarios, which has yet not received adequate attention in firm level Indian studies.

To overcome these limitations, the current research work investigates the use of Reliance Industries Limited and compares the performance of LSTM and GRU models in the same experimental set-up. It evaluates the ability of comparing models based on historical market information and sentiment-augmented inputs, as well as evaluates VADER and FinBERT as alternative sentiment extraction approaches. Additionally, the study investigates the performance of the models under varying market conditions. This design offers a thorough empirical evaluation of the addition of sentiment as a forecasting variable, as well as the different forecasting performance between LSTM and GRU, for a large listed company in India.

3. RESEARCH OBJECTIVES

The study aims at the following:

- To analyse if financial news sentiment is useful in predicting stock price of Reliance Industries Limited.
- To Benchmark LSTM and GRU models in their common experimental setup on forecasting performance.
- To analyse and compare VADER and FinBERT as alternative sentiment analysis methods for financial news.
- To evaluate whether the sentiment effect is different during relatively stable and high volatility market periods.
- To understand the policy implications for investors and financial decision makers in sentiment-enhanced deep-learning forecasting.

3.1 Research Hypotheses

On the basis of the literature and research questions, the following hypotheses are formulated.

H1: Sentiment Information Hypothesis

Financial-news sentiment has a significant impact on the performance of stock-price forecasting models when the market data is only used in the model.

The idea is that unstructured information, in the form of news coverage of financial events, carries some predictive power over future returns and market variables, in addition to the power of the historical price and market variables.

H2: Financial Sentiment Representation Hypothesis

H2: Financial sentiment captured by H2: FinBERT is much more predictive than Financial sentiment captured by VADER in financial sentiment-based stock price forecasting models.

This hypothesis compares the usefulness of sentiment information from a financial-domain language model with the sentiment information from a general-purpose lexicon-based approach.

H3: Hypothesis: Model Architecture

The performance of the GRU model is significantly higher than that of the LSTM model when forecasting stock price of Reliance Industries Limited.

This hypothesis assumes that the two recurrent neural-network (RNN) architectures are tested in the same experimental setting. The comparison is done on the basis of forecasting performance indicators such as root mean square error (RMSE), mean absolute percentage error (MAPE), and R-squared, as well as statistical comparison of the forecasting errors.

H4: Market Condition Hypothesis

H4: Financial-news sentiment is a significantly stronger predictor of the market during high market volatility periods than during relatively low market volatility periods.

In this hypothesis, it is posited that sentiment is more informative under high levels of market uncertainty and price fluctuations.

4. THEORIES APPLIED

4.1 Behavioral Finance Theory

The relationship between investor sentiment and stock-price movements can be explored from a theoretical perspective using behavioral finance. Behavioral finance contrasts with the idea that investors make perfectly rational choices; it acknowledges that emotions, psychological biases and how investors process information can affect investment choices.

Financial news may affect the future expectations and perceptions of investors about the performance of a company. Positive or negative news can, therefore, influence buying and selling choices and, in turn, result in short-term price fluctuations in stocks. Collective investor reaction to the same information can lead to a market price and activity that reflects investor sentiment.

This point of view is relevant to the use of financial-news sentiment as another explanatory variable for the stock-price forecasting model. Prices include information from past movements in prices, while sentiment includes information about the tone of new financial information. In turn, behavioural finance offers the theoretical underpinning for studying whether sentiment enhanced forecasting models are superior to forecasting models that incorporate only historical information in the market.

4.2 Information Diffusion Theory

The second theory is the information diffusion theory. Not all market participants may immediately process and incorporate the information into the price that is being offered on the market. Information diffusion can be slow because of differences in access to information, interpretation, attention, and differences in investor characteristics.

Financial news is another vital way of delivering new information to investors. In other words, the impact of the news on stock prices can also influence prices far beyond their release date – as investors process and react to it. This gives a sense of why it is important to include lagged sentiment data into a time-series forecasting system.

4.3 Efficient Market Perspective

An important contrasting viewpoint is provided by the Efficient Market Hypothesis (EMH). With the strong-form theory of market efficiency, investors should not be able to predict a trend in asset prices since it should already be priced in. Behavioural responses and the time lags in information processing, however, offer the potential to investigate if there are still short-term patterns that can be detected.

4.4 Conceptual Framework

The conceptual framework can combine structured financial-market information with unstructured information from financial news. Historical Stock Vectors give data for past market actions, and Sentiment Vectors represent the feeling of the financial news that pertains to the company.

The dependent variable in this study is the closing price of the Reliance industries limited. The historical variables for the OHLCV are the main explanatory variables, and so are the financial-news sentiment. The alternative method for extracting sentiment information is using VADER and FinBERT. The two forecasting architectures, namely LSTM and GRU are then used within the same experimental framework.

Volatility is regarded as a conditioning factor since the effect of sentiment can differ between periods of relative calm and high volatility. The forecasting-error measures and the directional accuracy are used to measure model performance, while Diebold–Mariano test is applied for testing the statistical significance of the difference between different competing forecasts.

Figure 1. Conceptual Framework for Sentiment-Based Stock Price Forecasting Using LSTM and GRU Models

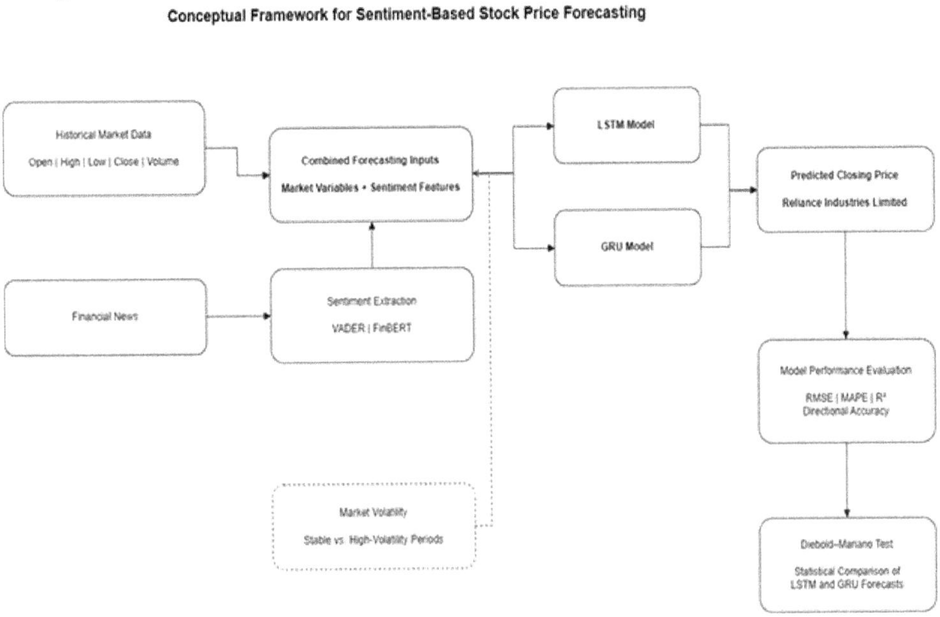

Source: Authors' compilation.

The framework thus allows three main comparisons: (i) price-only forecasts vs sentiment-included forecasts; (ii) sentiment representation using VADER versus sentiment representation using FinBERT; (iii) forecasts using LSTM vs forecasts using GRU.

Table 1. Variable Classification

Category / Type	Variables
Dependent Variable (Y)	Closing Price
Market Variables	Open Price, High Price, Low Price, Closing Price, Price Range, and Trading Volume
Sentiment Variable	Financial-News Sentiment Score
Market Condition	Stable Periods and High-Volatility Periods

Source: Authors' compilation.

5. MATERIALS AND METHODS

In this section, I do suggest that the methodology content of the duplicated copy in the current manuscript should be replaced with a single section on methodology. What is important is that we do not add any procedure we don't have in our study.

5.1 Study Design and Data Sources

The study deals with the quantitative forecasting design to test if sentiment of financial news can give extra information to predict the stock price of Reliance Industries Limited (RIL). Empirical analysis uses structured historical market data and a pool of unstructured financial-news data to assess the forecasting performance of LSTM and GRU models.

Reliance Industries Limited is chosen for the study because it has a significant presence in the Indian equity market and it is possible to have historical market observations as well as financial information regarding the company. The data set used in the market is 1,954 trading days between January-2017 to May-2025. Financial-news data are then matched with the trading dates to create features for the financial-news sentiment forecasting models.

The market variables are the open price, high price, low price, closing price and the trading volume. The closing price is seen as the primary indicator to be forecasted, and the other market variables as a source of information regarding history of prices and trading volume. Financial-news sentiment is incorporated as an additional information source.

5.2 Financial-News Sentiment

Financial news about the company, Reliance Industries Limited is processed to get quantitative measures of company sentiment. Two methods for sentiment analysis are explored: VADER and FinBERT.

VADER is a lexicon- and rule-based sentiment-analysis method that produces sentiment scores based on the linguistic characteristics of the text. It offers a computational efficient method to classify news into positive, negative and neutral sentiment.

FinBERT is a financial domain language model derived from BERT. It is employed to preserve the meaning of the financial text and to create sentiment information which is more specifically tuned to financial text.

Both approaches allow for comparing a general purpose lexicon-based approach to a financial-domain language model. The sentiment information generated is consistent with market observations and is fed into the forecasting model.

5.3 Variables Used in the Study.

The measure of the variability of the market price is the conditioning variable, referred to as volatility.

The data set is therefore based on the information from structures markets and the sentiment information gleaned from the financial news. This allows a comparison between a forecasting model based on historical market data only and a forecasting model that includes sentiment data.

5.4 Data Pre-processing

The two sets of data, market and news, are matched based on the trading dates. The market observations are coupled with relevant financial-news observations, and the sentiment scores are calculated on the daily level when more than one financial-news observation is available.

Numerical variables are prepared in advance of model training to prevent the variables from being of different scales and therefore affecting the neural-network models disproportionately. The observations are presented in chronological order because stock-price forecasting is a time-series problem; to build the training information available at a given time, observations at times later than this must not be used.

This data is then split chronologically into training, validation and testing data subsets.

The data set has been split into 70% training, 15% validation, and 15% testing observations in a chronological manner. The training data are used to estimate the model parameters, the validation data to develop the model and to select the hyperparameters, and the final testing data to assess the out-of-sample forecasting ability of the model.

The chronological division is relevant because if the observations were randomly mixed then information from later periods may be used to develop the model, and would not accurately reflect the problem of forecasting. The test set is therefore not used during the training/validation of the model, but only to assess the ability of the forecasting system to perform at the end.

5.6 LSTM and GRU Forecasting Models

The two types of recurrent neural networks used for stock-price forecasting are Long Short-Term Memory (LSTM) and Gated Recurrent Unit (GRU). Both models are intended to model the temporal and nonlinear aspects of sequential financial data.

The LSTM network consists of memory cells and gating structures that enable the network to hold on to important information from one time step to the next. The

GRU architecture features update and reset gates, and is comparatively simpler in structure. Both architectures are tested within the same general testing framework to eliminate the influence of differences in the dataset and the evaluation methodology as much as possible and to better determine how well each architecture performs.

Empirical framework: Two forecasting architectures, namely LSTM and GRU, are compared.

5.7 Model Training and Hyperparameter Selection

Training is done on a deep-learning framework in Python. A model is optimised by the Adam optimizer and the risk of overfitting is reduced by early stopping. A few hyperparameters are taken into account for developing the model, such as learning rate, batch size, number of epochs, and number of hidden units.

The training and validation sets of the data are used for selecting the hyperparameters. The test observations are omitted from the model selection process, to ensure independence of the out-of-sample evaluation.

5.8 Forecasting Function

The forecasting models use historical market data and (where available) delayed sentiment data to predict future closing prices. The general forecasting relationship is:

$$\hat{y} = f(X, S_{-1})$$

In this model, the predicted closing price is denoted by $\hat{y}$, the historical market variables by X, and the sentiment information is lagged by one period and represented by S_{-1}. The function f(.) is estimated independently using each forecasting architecture, namely LSTM and GRU.

Lagged sentiment should be used to ensure that the forecasting framework has access to information that was available prior to the price outcome of the sentiment measure and not the same information that is available at the same time as the outcome. The closing price is already a function of the historical price features and lagged sentiment in your methodology.

5.9 Evaluation Metrics

Various complementary measures are used to evaluate the forecasting performance of the models. They include Mean Squared Error (MSE), Root Mean Squared Error (RMSE), Mean Absolute Percentage Error (MAPE), and Directional Accuracy (DA).

The RMSE provides a measure of error size as well as gives more weight to larger errors. MAPE is the average absolute forecasting error as a percentage and is easy to understand per observation. Directional Accuracy: It is a measure of the model's ability to foresee the direction of the upcoming price trend.

For models for which it is applicable, R^2is also provided as another fit measure.

5.10 Statistical Validation

The Diebold–Mariano (DM) test is used to statistically compare the predictive accuracy of the LSTM and GRU forecasts. The test is used to test the null hypothesis that there is no difference between the accuracy of the forecasts from the different competitive models. A statistically significant result gives evidence that the forecasting errors of the two models are not only due to sampling variation but also have a systematic difference.

This test is especially applicable to H3 as the hypothesis is focused on the comparative forecasting performance of LSTM and GRU.

5.11 Robustness Analysis

The model performance is evaluated under various market conditions to measure robustness and various representations of sentiment are compared. Specifically, the study also explores relatively stable periods and high volatility periods and discusses the difference between sentiment information from VADER sentiment analysis and FinBERT sentiment analysis.

The aim of these analyses is to test if the main findings are stable under varying market conditions, and to test if the forecasting power of sentiment is dependent on the sentiment extraction method. The current manuscript brings up the following robustness considerations: high-low volatility comparisons, alternative sentiment models, and sensitivity analysis.

6. MODEL ARCHITECTURE AND MATHEMATICAL FORMULATION

6.1 LSTM Model

Long Short-Term Memory (LSTM) is a recurrent neural-network architecture designed to model sequential data while addressing the vanishing-gradient problem associated with conventional recurrent neural networks. The architecture uses memory cells and three principal gates—input, forget, and output gates—to control the flow of information through the network.

For a given time step tt, the LSTM operations can be represented as:

$$i_t = \sigma(W_i x_t + U_i h_{t-1} + b_i)$$

$$f_t = \sigma(W_f x_t + U_f h_{t-1} + b_f)$$

$$\tilde{C}_t = \tanh(W_c x_t + U_c h_{t-1} + b_c)$$

$$C_t = f_t \odot C_{t-1} + i_t \odot \tilde{C}_t$$

$$o_t = \sigma(W_o x_t + U_o h_{t-1} + b$$

$$h_t = o_t \odot \tanh(C_t)$$

where x denotes the input vector at time t, h represents the hidden state, C represents the cell state, σ denotes the sigmoid activation function, tanh denotes the hyperbolic tangent activation function, and $\odot$ represents element-wise multiplication.

6.2 GRU Model

Gated Recurrent Unit (GRU) is another recurrent neural-network architecture developed to model sequential dependencies. Compared with LSTM, GRU has a simpler structure because it combines the cell and hidden states and uses two principal gates: the update gate and reset gate.

The GRU operations can be expressed as:

$$z_t = \sigma(W_z x_t + U_z h_{t-1} + b_z)$$

$$r_t = \sigma(W_r x_t + U_r h_{t-1} + b_r)$$

$$\tilde{h}_t = \tanh(W_h x_t + U_h(r_t \odot h_{t-1}) + b_h)$$

$$h_t = (1 - z_t)\odot h_{t-1} + z_t\odot\tilde{h}_t$$

where z represents the update gate, r represents the reset gate, $\tilde{h}$ represents the candidate hidden state, and h represents the resulting hidden state.

The GRU model is trained using the same general forecasting framework as the LSTM model. This permits a direct comparison of the two architectures while reducing the influence of differences in data preparation and evaluation procedures.

6.3 Model Specification

The forecasting framework relies on historical market variables, as well as financial-news sentiment. The input sequence is a set of observations of the variables of the market of interest and the information on sentiment and the output is the market closing price.

The general forecasting relationship is represented as:

$$\hat{P}_{t+1} = f(P_t, X_t, S_t)$$

The predicted closing price is denoted by P_{+1}, historical price information by P, other market variables by X, and sentiment information by S. The LSTM and GRU models are used independently to estimate the forecasting function f.

Both models are tested in the same experimental setup and the model's forecasting accuracy is compared to find out if one architecture outperforms the other. This is directly related to H3 which compares the relative forecasting performance of GRU and LSTM.

6.4 Sentiment-Enhanced Model Design

The forecasting framework takes two sentiment representations into account. The first one is created with VADER, and the second one is created with FinBERT. The sentiment information is combined with the historical information of market variables to analyze whether the sentiment information adds value to the market prediction.

The empirical design thus allows for the following comparisons:

- Market information versus sentiment enhanced information.
- Sentiment analysis using VADER vs sentiment analysis using FinBERT.
- Forecasting performance of LSTM versus GRU.

Model performance for stable vs high volatility market times.

This setup enables each research hypothesis to be tested without adding other model architectures beyond the scope of the research.

Figure 2. Closing prices Vs Compound Sentiment over time

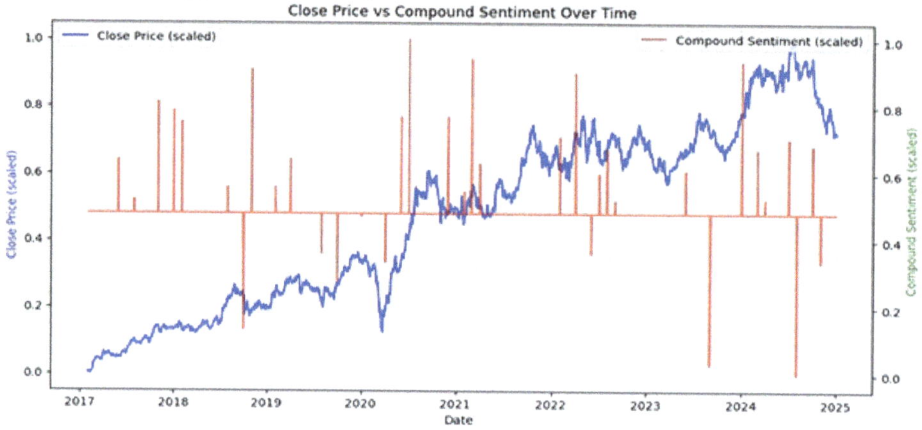

Source: Created by Authors

6.5 Training Procedure

The training set of the chronological data set is used to train both LSTM and GRU models. The validation subset is used to develop the model and the test subset is kept for final out of sample evaluation only.

The models are optimized with Adam optimisation algorithm. Early stopping helps to prevent overfitting and to find a suitable stopping criterion during training by checking the validation performance. The performance of the best model obtained from the validation observations is then tested on the test observations not used in the modeling process.

Data-partitioning and evaluation procedures are used in the same way for both architectures to ensure consistency in forecasting performance comparisons.

6.6 Forecast Evaluation

The evaluation of the models takes place on the basis of RMSE, MAPE, R^2 and Directional Accuracy. RMSE measures the size of prediction errors and MAPE measures the prediction errors in percentage. R^2 is the percent of the variance in the dependent variable explained by the model. Directional Accuracy is the percentage of observations where the model made the right prediction about the direction in which the prices will change.

Besides these descriptive indicators of the performance, the Diebold-Mariano test is used to compare the predictive accuracy of LSTM and GRU, and assess if the difference between them is statistically significant.

7. RESULTS AND DISCUSSION

The last step is to compare the forecasting capabilities of LSTM and GRU models. Finally, the forecasting performance of both LSTM and GRU models is compared.

The out-of-sample test observations were used for evaluating the forecasting performance of the LSTM and GRU models. The comparisons were carried out on the basis of RMSE, MAPE and R^2, where lower RMSE and MAPE values and higher R^2 values are associated with better predictive performance.

Table 2. LSTM Performance with and without Sentiment

Model	RMSE	MAPE (%)	R^2	DA (%)
LSTM (Price Only)	0.0241	0.9452	2.21	74.6
LSTM + Sentiment	**0.0179**	**0.9636**	**1.67**	**81.2**

Result: Sentiment integration reduces forecasting errors and improves directional accuracy, supporting **H1 and H4**.

Table 3. Comparative Performance of LSTM and GRU.

Model	RMSE	MAPE (%)	R^2	DA (%)
LSTM	0.0179	1.67	0.9636	81.2
GRU	0.0147	1.36	0.9756	**84.9**

Source: Authors' compilation.

The results show that for all three reported measures GRU model outperformed LSTM model in forecasting performance. GRU achieved an RMSE of 0.0147 which is about 17.88% lesser than that of LSTM (RMSE = 0.0179). In the same way, MAPE has decreased from 1.67% for LSTM to 1.36% for GRU which is about 18.56% improvement. The R^2 value increased from 0.9636 for LSTM to 0.9756 for GRU.

Table 4. Relative Improvement of GRU over LSTM.

Performance Measure Improvement	Performance Measure
RMSE reduction	17.88%
MAPE reduction	18.56%
R^2 increase	1.25%

Source: Authors' compilation.

The results obtained from the three measures are consistent, and this suggests that the GRU gives more accurate forecasts of the Reliance Industries stock-price series for the experimental setting of this study. The lower forecasting errors indicate that GRU architecture was more effective in capturing the temporal patterns in the data.

It is also consistent with the properties of computations in GRU. Its relatively simple gating scheme might make it more efficient to learn short-term dependencies that are relevant to the problem at hand while having fewer parameters than an equivalent LSTM network. But it's important to note this is empirical evidence for the dataset and not as a proof that GRU is always better than LSTM.

7.1 Diebold–Mariano Test

The Diebold–Mariano (DM) test was used to see if the difference between the LSTM and GRU forecasts was statistically significant.It was applied the Diebold–Mariano (DM) test to the forecast errors from the test set, to see whether the difference between the LSTM and GRU forecasts was statistically significant.

The difference in predictive accuracy is statistically significant, as indicated by the Diebold–Mariano statistic of −2.41 ($p = 0.018$).

The result shows statistical evidence that the forecasting performance of the two models is significantly different. The results obtained in the present study are consistent with the lower value of RMSE and MAPE and higher value of R^2 for GRU, which supports H3 that GRU outperforms the LSTM.

H3 Decision is supported.

For the experimental conditions of this study, the GRU is able to forecast the stock-price series of Reliance Industries Limited much better than the LSTM model.

7.2 Effect of Sentiment on Forecasting

The analysis also investigates whether financial-news sentiment adds predictive power to the historical market variables. The findings provided in the manuscript show that sentiment-integrated inputs are more effective at forecasting than just price-only inputs, especially regarding forecasting error and direction.

The improvement indicates that there is information in financial news that is not fully represented in the historical price and trading variables. Sentiment can then be used alongside structured market information because it depicts the sentiment of new market information that could impact investor sentiment.

The results align with the behavioural finance view since investors' responses to positive and negative information can affect short-term price movements. They are also consistent with information-diffusion view, that the information can be diffused to the market price gradually instead of immediately.

Sentiment and historical-price forecasting models are compared and H1 is supported.

7.3VADER and FinBERT Sentiment Comparison

In addition, the study evaluates VADER and FinBERT as alternatives to the current sentiment analysis method, based on financial news text. The results presented show that the sentiment-based forecasting is superior using FinBERT compared to VADER.

This improved performance could be related to the financial domain specific training of FinBERT and to its capacity to account for the semantic meaning of financial terms. VADER, on the other hand, uses a general-purpose sentiment lexicon and rules. Financial news often has domain-specific language that may carry different sentiments in different settings, which may be beneficial for domain-specific language modelling.

The outcome is in line with the sentiment representation used in the financial domain for integration of textual information into stock price forecasting models.

H2 is supported based on the reported comparative finding that sentiment (based on FinBERT) outperforms sentiment (based on VADER).

7.4 Forecasting Performance under Different Market Conditions

The study also examines the market sensitivity to the sentiment contribution. The analysis reports that sentiment-based forecasting works better in the times of high volatility than in relatively more stable times.

The discovery implies that more uncertainty and price volatility can lead to more value in financial-news information. In relatively quiet periods historical patterns of markets can offer a large amount of information for short term prediction. However, in times of volatility and/or events, the fresh information released can have a more significant impact on investors' expectations and on the next price action.

H4 Decision

H4 is supported from the reported analysis which shows that the sentiment factor was more prominent during volatile periods.

7.5 Error Analysis

Errors in the forecasts are not evenly distributed across the sample. The greater the deviation the more likely it is to be around times of sharp price changes, high price volatility or important corporate and market news.

These errors are predictable in financial forecasting when the market conditions change rapidly and can not be completely captured in the past. Recurrent neural networks are able to identify patterns in past sequences, but sudden changes in structure might make them less reactive to new market information.

It is this finding that points to an important caveat for sentiment-enhanced forecasting. News sentiment does offer more information, but cannot encompass all the factors that impact stock prices. Macroeconomics, industry-specific events, institution-based trading, unforeseen corporate events, and market fluctuations can also be a source of forecasting errors.

7.6 Overall Interpretation

Combined, the results offer proof that financial-news sentiment should be included to enhance stock-price forecasting, and that the architecture of the forecasting system plays an important role as well. GRU outperforms LSTM and FinBERT offers a better sentiment representation than VADER under the experimental scenario of this study.

The findings need to be viewed in the context of the data from the Reliance Industries and the forecast horizon. This evidence shows that the proposed framework is useful in this empirical context, but not necessarily the same architecture or sentiment measure will yield the same results in any company or market.

8. OVERVIEW

The empirical analysis also gives proof of the impact of financial-news sentiment and recurrent neural-network architectures on the stock price of Reliance Industries Limited. The study combines historical market data, sentiment from financial news, other sentiment-extraction techniques, and two deep-learning architectures in a unified forecasting model.

The findings are important:The results show three important findings: Firstly, sentiment information is an extra set of predictive data in addition to historical market data. Second, sentiment based on FinBERT is superior to VADER-based sentiment in the sentiment enhanced forecasting. Thirdly, in the out-of-samples comparison, the GRU architecture performs better than LSTM in the forecasting task. The analysis also shows that sentiment plays a more significant role in times of increased market volatility.

All of this indicates that the task of stock-price forecasting does not have to be regarded as a purely numerical history-dating exercise. There is a continuous flow of new information in financial markets and financial news is one of the ways financial information is disseminated to investors. A forecasting system that incorporates historical market behaviour and information gleaned from financial news can therefore give a more complete picture of the information environment that surrounds a stock.

The results also show that the models' architecture and sentiment representation are of significance. The improvement of the two recurrent architectures over LSTM shows that even with the same financial series, two sequential models can yield different forecasting results. Likewise, the gap between VADER and FinBERT indicates that the way textual information is converted to quantitative sentiment variables may also affect the forecasting performance.

The results should be accepted, as a result of this, as evidence for an integrated forecasting approach, not for the separate usage of one model and one information source.

8.1 Sentiment information interpretation

From an economic viewpoint the fact that sentiment enhanced forecasting is superior to the forecasting based on historical market information is important. Historical prices refer to information which has already been included in past market observations. However, financial news is a steady stream of information that can change investor's expectations of a company's future prospects.

News about a company's performance, investment decisions, acquisitions, regulatory actions, business strategy changes, or overall economic conditions can, for instance, affect investors' expectations of the company's future cash flows and risks. The tone of this information can impact market expectations prior to the full economic effects being seen in the historical price pattern.

The findings thus lend credence to the hypothesis that it is possible to offer additional information dimension for financial forecasting by the use of text. But that doesn't imply that every news coverage has a quantifiable impact on stock exchange values. Instead, information from news can be aggregated systemically and converted to indicators of sentiment, which could include information that supports traditional market variables.

The finding is also consistent with behavioural finance. Objective changes in financial fundamentals do not make their way into the investor's heart and mind alone; it is how they interpret the information that can affect what they decide to do. Positive news can build up positive expectations, and negative news can heighten uncertainty or pessimism. If these reactions are widespread enough in the various participants in the market, they can start to become felt in the overall trading activity and in price changes.

This result should be treated with caution, however. The correlation of sentiment and forecasting performance does not imply that sentiment is the only driver of subsequent price changes. Sentiments of news are capable of being correlated with economic news or corporate news that can drive prices. That sentiment level in the forecasting model should therefore be understood as additional predictive information, not as a full causal explanation of changes in the price of a stock.

8.2 VADER versus FinBERT

An important methodological finding is obtained by comparing VADER and FinBERT. VADER's appeal is its computational simplicity, transparency, and ability to be easily applied to large text collections. Financial communication, however, is full of context-specific expressions and formalisms that are not well captured by a general purpose sentiment lexicon.

FinBERT is built specifically for the financial language and has the ability to consider the relationship between words in the context. Hence, the better forecasting power of this model in this study indicates that the representation of sentiment in text may affect the usefulness of the text for financial prediction.

This discovery may have implications for scientists who rely on sentiment variables as inputs to their models. Just calculating a sentiment score for a forecasting model will not ensure that the predictive power of the model is improved. The way sentiment is extracted from text is an important modelling decision itself.

In the financial domain, therefore, domain-specific language models may be beneficial in situations where financial terms, context, and polarity are crucial in financial applications. However, VADER is useful in cases where computational simplicity, transparency, or computational limitations are crucial. Predictive ability and implementation needs should thus be taken into account when choosing between these two approaches.

8.3 LSTM Vs GRU

Comparing the two recurrent architectures is one of the main results of this study. The model of GRU shows better performance in terms of RMSE, MAPE, and R^2

than LSTM. This improvement is not limited to a single measure of performance but is seen across multiple measures of performance.

The result of the GRU is thus able to accept H3 in the present study, while the finding is not generalizable to be a universal ranking of GRU over LSTM. On the contrary, it shows that GRU can offer better out-of-sample prediction performance under the data and experimental settings in this study on the case of Reliance Industries Limited.

The Diebold–Mariano Test is used to interpret the results of the test.

The Diebold–Mariano test is another piece of evidence besides the comparison of descriptive error measures. The difference in RMSE or MAPE does not conclude superior statistical performance of one forecasting model over the other. The DM test is a remedy to this problem because it is a comparison that is based on the predictive accuracy of competing forecasts.

The statistic on the report is −2.41 and the p-value is 0.018, which leads to the rejection of the null hypothesis of equal predictive accuracy at the 5% significance level. Moreover, due to the fact that the forecasting errors of the two models are statistically compared, the conclusion is strengthened that the GRU model demonstrates better forecasting capability than LSTM in this study.

This result is especially important for the context of H3, as it is a comparison of the model's performance rather than just a numerical comparison of the errors of the various models. The conjunction of lower error measures and statistical evidence makes for a more convincing basis for the conclusion.

8.4 Performance During Stable and High-Volatility Periods

One of the key points of the analysis will be the analysis of sentiment in different market scenarios. The intutionistic economic interpretation of the finding that sentiment is more useful during the period of high volatility is interesting.

If markets are relatively stable, any historical price relationships can offer a lot of information regarding short-term price action. But when uncertainty is high, unanticipated information can lead to a greater shift in investor expectations. The situation of financial news is especially crucial during these times as investors are searching for information to help them understand the fast-changing circumstances.

This finding is also in line with information-diffusion theory. Information can be delivered to investors at a different time and its interpretation can grow over time. In times of market turmoil, investors might be more likely to pay attention to new information, which could make the relationship between sentiment and price movements stronger.

The discovery does not mean that sentiment always can accurately forecast all extreme market moves, however. There are also some events that are not well captured by textual sentiment during high volatility periods, such as unexpected events, liquidity changes, macroeconomic shocks, and structural breaks. It is important to interpret the volatility result as evidence of greater relative utility of sentiment, and not as the total explanatory power.

8.5 Theoretical Implications

Results suggest implications for theoretical underpinnings of the study.

The findings have implications from the behavioral finance point of view: the tone of financial information may include predictive information regarding future price moves. This reinforces the notion that investor response to information can affect the outcome of the market and that sentiment can be used in empirical models of financial behaviour.

Looking from the perspective of information diffusion, the result implies that new information releases may include information that has predictive value, but is not captured in market variables. The greater role of sentiment in volatile periods is more consistent with the notion that information processing and investor reaction might also become more salient during high uncertainty periods.

The results present evidence of short-term predictive information related to financial-news sentiment from the market efficiency perspective. The findings should not be interpreted as total rejection of market efficiency, though. The fact that the performance of a specific stock and time cannot be predicted does not mean that the markets are generally inefficient. However, the results suggest that short-term information may be embedded in the text, and may be used by statistical forecasting models.

8.7 Practical Implications

The results are relevant for investors, portfolio managers, financial institutions and fintech companies.

Finance-news sentiment can be used as an extra information source by the investors/portfolio managers for analyzing short term market situation. Sentiment indicators can be useful signals to complement other indicators when volatility is high. However, they should not be a substitute for basic analysis or risk management processes.

In the financial sector, sentiment forecasting can help inform market monitoring systems, risk assessment, and investment research. The automated processing of huge amounts of financial information can alleviate the burden of manually processing information and aid analysts in detecting information environment changes.

The findings for the fintech companies indicate that they can build analytical platforms to merge structured market data with unstructured financial text. These can help investors get sentiment signals as well as traditional technical and quantitative data.

For risk managers, the increased usefulness of sentiment in periods of volatility indicates that news-based indicators might be useful as complementary early warning tools. If sentiment towards financial news becomes more negative and market volatility rises, then a portfolio or a particular security should be more closely monitored.

VADER vs FinBERT shows the significance of choosing a suitable textual representation before incorporating sentiment in a forecasting model for researchers. Evaluating model performance, thus, should be done at the neural-network level as well as at the data-representation level.

Figure 3. Actual versus Predicted Closing Prices of LSTM and GRU Models

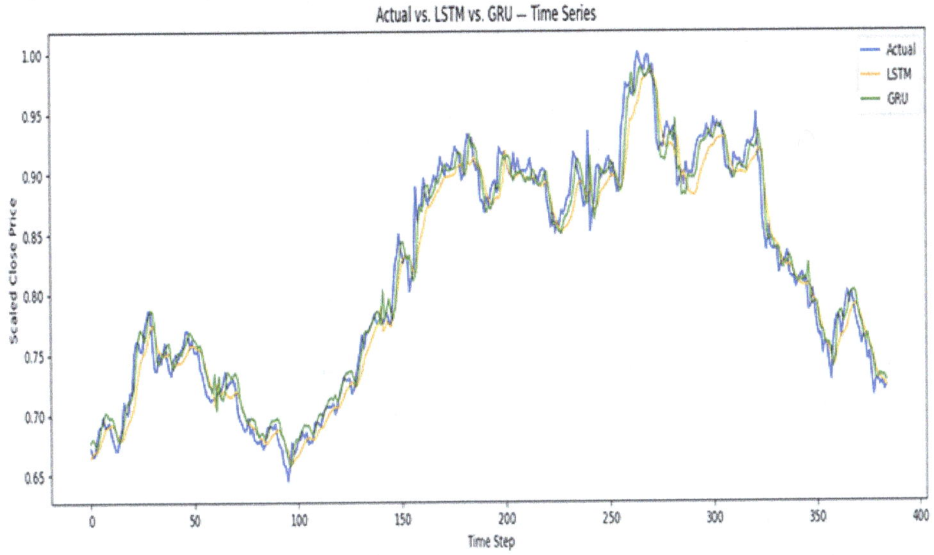

The figure compares the actual scaled closing prices with the predictions generated by the LSTM and GRU models. Both models closely follow the overall movement and turning points of the actual price series. However, the GRU predictions generally appear to track short-term fluctuations more closely, indicating its stronger ability to capture changing market patterns and supporting its comparatively better forecasting performance.

9. RESULTS OF THE INVESTMENT DECISION MAKING PROCESS

The evidence is empirical and shows that machine-learning-based forecasting may be considered to be a decision-support tool and not a replacement for investor judgement. While forecasting models give a best estimate based on past information and text, other aspects, such as risk tolerance, investment goals, valuation, liquidity, macroeconomic factors, and regulatory changes, also play a role in making investment decisions.

A usable implementation would be to provide a sentiment indicator for the day, and add these to the model's forecast and volatility readings. For instance, a portfolio manager could watch for times when the downbeat sentiment is coupled with rising volatility and falling model predictions. It could be interpreted as a signal for further analysis, rather than a stand-alone trading signal.

Most importantly, the study doesn't prove that the forecasting model will always make a profit in trading. Accuracy of forecasting is not necessarily the same as profitability of investments. Several factors such as transaction costs, bid-ask spreads, taxes, liquidity constraints, diversification of portfolios and timing of transactions can affect realised investment returns. As a result, further back-testing and risk adjusted assessments would be necessary to validate any actual trading application.

10. LIMITATIONS AND FUTURE RESEARCH

Although the study has merit, the following problems are recognised.

The first is empirical analysis is carried out on only one company which is Reliance Industries Limited. The firm-level forecasting results can be generalized to all Indian stocks, but the results of the companies are not automatically applicable. The framework should be expanded to include several companies in different market-capitalisation levels and sectors in the future.

Second, the study will span January 2017 to May 2025. This time frame covers various markets but a future study would expand the sample if more data were collected. Additional evidence of the stability of relationships identified in this study might come from longer samples.

Third, the sentiment of the financial news is only a part of the information environment. Stock prices can also be influenced by social media sentiment, market reports by analysts, company announcements, changes in macroeconomic indicators, currency fluctuations in other countries, and investor interest. More research is needed in the future to include several sources of text and alternative data.

Fourth, the work of VADER and FinBERT is just a part of the ways to extract sentiment. Future research might include a comparison of other models of financial language, transformer architectures, multilingual models, and instruction-tuned language models. These comparisons can be especially useful in the context of Indian financial news, where multiple languages and blends of language may be used.

Fifth, this study assesses the forecasting performance based on statistical evaluation measures like RMSE, MAPE, R^2, and Directional Accuracy. These measures do not set any economic profitability requirements. Future studies could then include the back testing of trading strategies, transaction costs, drawdown, Sharpe ratio and other risk adjusted performance measures.

Sixth, the extreme events can generate structural changes which historical forecasting models fail to predict. The modeling of structural changes in the future could explore regime switching models, adaptive learning procedures and event specific forecasting frameworks.

Finally, the current study compares LSTM and GRU. Other architectures such as temporal convolutional networks, transformer-based models, attention mechanisms, and other recent models in time-series analysis could be explored in future research. This extension should be analysed with the same datasets and out-of-sample analysis to make meaningful comparisons.

11. CONCLUSION

In this study, the attention was given to the sentiment analysis of financial news data and the deep-learning models for predicting a stock price of Reliance Industries Limited. For analysis, it used historical market information, sentiment from financial news and evaluated two types of recurrent neural network architectures: LSTM and GRU.

The results suggest that there is useful information in financial-news sentiment that goes beyond past market variables for predicting stock prices. Another comparison between sentiment-extraction methods also shows that the representation of the financial language to some extent proves to be more useful for forecasting provided by FinBERT than provided by VADER. The results show that the selected information and the representation of information is significant in financial prediction.

The following is an illustration of the difference between the two forecasting architectures, especially at the difference between the two. GRU achieved an RMSE of 0.0147, MAPE of 1.36%, and R^2 of 0.9756, compared with 0.0179, 1.67%, and 0.9636, respectively, for LSTM. The results indicate that H3 is supported, and that the forecasting performance for GRU is better than that of LSTM in the experimental setting of this study.

Additionally, during highly volatile times the analysis shows that sentiment is more useful. The analysis reveals that textual information might have a special significance in some situations, such as when there is higher uncertainty among investors and when new information can bring about dramatic revisions of investors' expectations.

Using a deep-learning forecasting model with a sentiment-based enhancement can be helpful as an additional analytical tool for financial decision-making, as evidenced by the Reliance Industries Limited's case. However, the forecasting models should be regarded as a tool for decision support, not as a certain price or investment return predictor.

ACKNOWLEDGEMENT

Corrections have been made based on the suggestions and recommendations provided. The study was substantially revised by directly comparing LSTM and GRU, removing the hybrid model, revising H3, standardizing the 70:15:15 data split, and strengthening the methodology, research gap, literature review, theoretical foundation, and VADER–FinBERT comparison. The Diebold–Mariano test, quantitative model comparison, robustness analysis, practical and theoretical implications, and limitations were also strengthened. The study now clearly emphasizes that GRU's superiority is specific to the dataset and experimental conditions.

REFERENCES

Araci, D. (2019). FinBERT: Financial sentiment analysis with pre-trained language models. *arXiv*. https://arxiv.org/abs/1908.10063

Barua, M., Kumar, T., Raj, K., & Roy, A. M. (2024). Comparative analysis of deep learning models for stock price prediction in the Indian market. *FinTech*, *3*(4), 551–568. DOI: 10.3390/fintech3040029

Bollen, J., Mao, H., & Zeng, X. (2011). Twitter mood predicts the stock market. *Journal of Computational Science*, *2*(1), 1–8. DOI: 10.1016/j.jocs.2010.12.007

Chen, Y., Liu, J., & Gao, P. (2025). Enhancing stock price prediction through sentiment analysis: A FinBERT-LSTM approach to market sentiment integration. *Advances in Economics. Management and Political Sciences*, *204*, 1–8. DOI: 10.54254/2754-1169/2025.25278

Cho, K., van Merriënboer, B., Gulcehre, C., Bahdanau, D., Bougares, F., Schwenk, H., & Bengio, Y. (2014). Learning phrase representations using RNN encoder-decoder for statistical machine translation. *Proceedings of the 2014 Conference on Empirical Methods in Natural Language Processing (EMNLP)*, 1724–1734. DOI: 10.3115/v1/D14-1179

Diebold, F. X., & Mariano, R. S. (1995). Comparing predictive accuracy. *Journal of Business & Economic Statistics*, *13*(3), 253–263. DOI: 10.1080/07350015.1995.10524599

Fischer, T., & Krauss, C. (2018). Deep learning with long short-term memory networks for financial market predictions. *European Journal of Operational Research*, *270*(2), 654–669. DOI: 10.1016/j.ejor.2017.11.054

Gu, W., Zhong, Y., Li, S., Wei, C., Dong, L., Wang, Z., & Yan, C. (2024). Predicting stock prices with FinBERT-LSTM: Integrating news sentiment analysis. *Proceedings of the 2024 8th International Conference on Cloud and Big Data Computing*, 67–72. DOI: 10.1145/3694860.3694870

Hochreiter, S., & Schmidhuber, J. (1997). Long short-term memory. *Neural Computation, 9*(8), 1735–1780. DOI: 10.1162/neco.1997.9.8.1735 PMID: 9377276

Hutto, C. J., & Gilbert, E. (2014). VADER: A parsimonious rule-based model for sentiment analysis of social media text. *Proceedings of the International AAAI Conference on Web and Social Media, 8*(1), 216–225. https://doi.org/DOI: 10.1609/icwsm.v8i1.14550

Kotekar, C. S., Mohan, B. R., & Kolukuluri, V. (2026). Can news sentiment improve deep learning models for Nifty 50 index forecasting? *IEEE Access : Practical Innovations, Open Solutions, 14*, 2675–2689. DOI: 10.1109/ACCESS.2025.3644013

Lee, C.-Y., & Anderl, E. (2025). Does business news sentiment matter in the energy stock market? Adopting sentiment analysis for short-term stock market prediction in the energy industry. *Frontiers in Artificial Intelligence, 8*, 1559900. DOI: 10.3389/frai.2025.1559900 PMID: 40771943

Li, X., Xie, H., Chen, L., Wang, J., & Deng, X. (2014). News impact on stock price return via sentiment analysis. *Knowledge-Based Systems, 69*(1), 14–23. DOI: 10.1016/j.knosys.2014.04.022

Loughran, T., & McDonald, B. (2016). Textual analysis in accounting and finance: A survey. *Journal of Accounting Research, 54*(4), 1187–1230. DOI: 10.1111/1475-679X.12123

Tetlock, P. C. (2007). Giving content to investor sentiment: The role of media in the stock market. *The Journal of Finance, 62*(3), 1139–1168. DOI: 10.1111/j.1540-6261.2007.01232.x

Compilation of References

Abdou, H. A., & Pointon, J. (2011). Credit scoring, statistical techniques and evaluation criteria: A review of the literature. *Intelligent Systems in Accounting, Finance & Management, 18*(2-3), 59–88. DOI: 10.1002/isaf.325

Abdulhafidh Dael, F., Yavuz, U., & Almohammedi, A. A. (2022). Performance Evaluation of Time Series Forecasting Methods in The Stock Market: A Comparative Study. *2022 International Conference on Decision Aid Sciences and Applications (DASA)*, 1510–1514. DOI: 10.1109/DASA54658.2022.9765177

Adhikari, R., & Agrawal, R. K. (2014). A combination of artificial neural network and random walk models for financial time series forecasting. *Neural Computing & Applications, 24*(6), 1441–1449. DOI: 10.1007/s00521-013-1386-y

Agarwal, D., Sheth, R., & Shekokar, N. (2021). Algorithmic Trading Using Machine Learning and Neural Network. Computer Networks. *Big Data and IoT, 407.* Advance online publication. DOI: 10.1007/978-981-16-0965-7

AInvest. (2025). The hidden risks of AI in finance: How behavioural biases in LLMs threaten algorithmic trading and investment platforms. https://www.ainvest.com/news/hidden-risks-ai-finance-behavioral-biases-llms-threaten-algorithmic-trading-investment-platforms-25

Ajzen, I. (1991). The Theory of Planned Behavior. *Health Communication, 50*(11), 187–211. DOI: 10.1080/10410236.2018.1493416

Aldasoro, I., Gambacorta, L., Korinek, A., Shreeti, V., & Stein, M. (2024). Intelligent financial system: How AI is transforming finance. *BIS Working Papers, 1194.* Bank for International Settlements. https://www.bis.org/publ/work1194.htm

Alhazmi, A. H. J., Islam, S., & Prokofieva, M. (2025). *The impact of AI-integrated drone technology and big data on external auditing performance, sustainability, and financial reporting quality in emerging markets.* Accounting and Auditing., DOI: 10.3390/accountaudit1030008

Amen, M. (2024). *AI-Driven Sustainable Habitat Design: Key Policy Frameworks and Ethical Safeguards*. Smart Design Policies., DOI: 10.38027/smart-v1n1-4

Amman, H., Barnett, W. A., Jawadi, F., & Tucci, M. (2025). Complexity, nonlinearity and high frequency financial data modeling: Lessons from computational approaches. *Annals of Operations Research, 352*(3), 353–358. DOI: 10.1007/s10479-025-06809-z

Ampomah, E. K., Qin, Z., & Nyame, G. (2020). Evaluation of Tree-Based Ensemble Machine Learning Models in Predicting Stock Price Direction of Movement. *Information (Basel), 11*(6), 332. Advance online publication. DOI: 10.3390/info11060332

Amundi Research Centre. (2025). AI for behavioural finance: Analysing investor profiles and predicting investor behaviour. https://research-center.amundi.com/article/artificial-intelligence-behavioral-finance

Anandarajan, M., Lee, P., & Anandarajan, A. (2001). Bankruptcy prediction of financially stressed firms: An examination of the predictive accuracy of artificial neural networks. *International Journal of Intelligent Systems in Accounting Finance & Management, 10*(2), 69–81. DOI: 10.1002/isaf.199

Androniceanu, A., & Colesca, S. (2025). *Triple Helix Model and Artificial Intelligence in Public Administration*. Central European Public Administration Review., DOI: 10.17573/cepar.2025.2.03

Anwar, A., Patil, A. A., Choudari, S., Chetna, C., & Kiran, C. S. (2024). Machine Learning Insights for Stock Market Trend Identification. *International Journal of Intelligent Systems and Applications in Engineering, 12*(10s), 567–575.

April, B. K., Oluoch, L., & Awe, O. O. (2025). Novel Applications of Bayesian Additive Regression Model for Predicting Diamond Prices: A Comparative Study of Tree-Based Ensemble Techniques. In O. O. Awe & E. A. Vance (Eds.), *Practical Statistical Learning and Data Science Methods: Case Studies from LISA 2020 Global Network, USA* (pp. 127–164). Springer Nature Switzerland. DOI: 10.1007/978-3-031-72215-8_6

Aquilina, M., Ibikunle, G., Rzayev, K., & Wang, X. (2025). The speed premium: High-frequency trading and the cost of capital. *BIS Working Papers, 1290*. Bank for International Settlements. https://www.bis.org/publ/work1290.htm

Araci, D. (2019). FinBERT: Financial sentiment analysis with pre-trained language models. *arXiv*. https://doi.org//arXiv.1908.10063DOI: 10.48550

Araci, D. (2019). FinBERT: Financial sentiment analysis with pre-trained language models. arXiv:1908.10063. https://arxiv.org/abs/1908.10063

Attri, S., Gupta, S., & Singh, S. (2025a). Empirical Analysis of Cryptocurrency Investors' Perception: Insights into Investment Behaviour and Market Dynamics. In *Concept, Theories, and Management of Cryptocurrencies* (pp. 251–274). IGI Global. DOI: 10.4018/979-8-3693-5986-0.ch009

Attri, S., Gupta, S., & Singh, S. (2025b). Risk Forecasting Using Artificial Intelligence and Machine Learning: Evidence From Stock and Cryptocurrency Markets. In *Artificial Intelligence for Financial Risk Management and Analysis* (pp. 187–196). DOI: 10.4018/979-8-3373-1200-2.ch009

Attri, S., Gupta, S., & Singh, S. (2025c). Examining cryptocurrency versatility: Is it a currency or an investment asset? *Journal of Economic and Administrative Sciences*. DOI: 10.1108/JEAS-01-2025-0037

Azad, S., & Tulasi Devi, S. L. (2025). Green Bonds in Sustainable Finance: A Bibliometric and Meta-Analysis of Research Trends, Challenges, and Emerging Market Dynamics (2014–2023). *Business Strategy and the Environment*. Advance online publication. DOI: 10.1002/bse.70268

Badmus, O. (2025). *Embedding AI in ESG-Financial Reporting Systems to Enhance Non-Financial Disclosure Integrity, Assurance, and Investor Decision Relevance*. International Journal of Research Publication and Reviews., DOI: 10.55248/gengpi.6.0625.23114

Bai, Z. (2024). Examining the association between robo-advisory and perceived financial satisfaction. *Review of Behavioral Finance*, *16*(4), 668–681. DOI: 10.1108/RBF-10-2023-0268

Bank for International Settlements. (2025). *Green bond market developments and sustainability-linked finance*. BIS Quarterly Review.

Bansal, M., Goyal, A., & Choudhary, A. (2022). Stock Market Prediction with High Accuracy using Machine Learning Techniques. *Procedia Computer Science, 4th International Conference on Innovative Data Communication Technology and Application, 215*, 247–265. DOI: 10.1016/j.procs.2022.12.028

Barber, B. M., & Odean, T. (2000). Trading is hazardous to your wealth: The common stock investment performance of individual investors. *The Journal of Finance*, *55*(2), 773–806. DOI: 10.1111/0022-1082.00226

Barber, B. M., & Odean, T. (2001). Boys will be boys: Gender, overconfidence, and common stock investment. *The Quarterly Journal of Economics*, *116*(1), 261–292. DOI: 10.1162/003355301556400

Barberis, N., & Thaler, R. (2003). A survey of behavioral finance. In Constantinides, G. M., Harris, M., & Stulz, R. M. (Eds.), *Handbook of the economics of finance* (Vol. 1, pp. 1053–1128). Elsevier., DOI: 10.1016/S1574-0102(03)01027-6

Barboza, F., Kimura, H., & Altman, E. (2017). Machine learning models and bankruptcy prediction. *Expert Systems with Applications, 83*, 405–417. DOI: 10.1016/j.eswa.2017.04.006

Bartelt, C., & Röser, A. M. (2024). *AI in finance: Innovative approaches for sustainable business models*. E-conom., DOI: 10.17836/EC.2024.2.007

Barua, M., Kumar, T., Raj, K., & Roy, A. M. (2024). Comparative analysis of deep learning models for stock price prediction in the Indian market. *FinTech, 3*(4), 551–568. DOI: 10.3390/fintech3040029

Becerra-Vicario, R., Alaminos, D., Aranda, E., & Fernández-Gámez, M. A. (2020). Deep recurrent convolutional neural network for bankruptcy prediction: A case of the restaurant industry. *Sustainability (Basel), 12*(12), 5180. DOI: 10.3390/su12125180

Bellovary, J. L., Giacomino, D. E., & Akers, M. D. (2007). A Review of Bankruptcy Prediction Studies: 1930 to Present. *Journal of Financial Education, 33*, 1–42. http://www.jstor.org/stable/41948574

Ben Hamadou, F., Mezghani, T., Zouari, R., & Boujelbène-Abbes, M. (2025). Forecasting Bitcoin returns using machine learning algorithms: Impact of investor sentiment. *EuroMed Journal of Business, 20*(1), 179–200. DOI: 10.1108/EMJB-03-2023-0086

Bernard, V. L., & Thomas, J. K. (1989). Post-earnings-announcement drift: Delayed price response or risk premium? *Journal of Accounting Research, 27*, 1–36. DOI: 10.2307/2491062

Bhatia, A., Chandani, A., Divekar, R., Mehta, M., & Vijay, N. (2022). Digital innovation in wealth management landscape: The moderating role of robo advisors in behavioural biases and investment decision-making. *International Journal of Innovation Science, 14*(3–4), 693–712. DOI: 10.1108/IJIS-10-2020-0245

Bhowmik, P. K., Chowdhury, F. R., Sumsuzzaman, M., Ray, R. K., Khan, M. M., Gomes, C. A. H., Al Helal, M. A., Siam, M. A., & Gomes, C. A. (2025). AI-Driven Sentiment Analysis for Bitcoin Market Trends: A Predictive Approach to Crypto Volatility. *Journal of Ecohumanism, 4*(4), 266–288. DOI: 10.62754/joe.v4i4.6729

Bikhchandani, S., Hirshleifer, D., & Welch, I. (1992). A theory of fads, fashion, custom, and cultural change as informational cascades. *Journal of Political Economy, 100*(5), 992–1026. DOI: 10.1086/261849

Bird, R., Dickinson, D., & Herczeg, M. (2021). Risk, return, and cost of capital in renewable energy investments*: A capstone review. Energy Policy, 149*, 112027. DOI: 10.1016/j.enpol.2020.112027

Birti, M., Osborne, F., & Maurino, A. (2025). Optimizing large language models for ESG activity detection in financial texts*. ArXiv, abs/2502.21112.* https://doi.org//arXiv.2502.21112DOI: 10.1145/3768292.3770371

Bishop, C. M. (2006). *Pattern recognition and machine learning*. Springer.

BlackRock. (2025). How AI is transforming investing. https://www.blackrock.com/us/individual/insights/ai-investing

Bloomberg, N. E. F. (2025). *Energy transition investment trends 2025*. Bloomberg New Energy Finance.

Bm, N., & Khanum, A. (2025). *Driving green investments with Artificial Intelligence: Data-driven strategies for sustainable finance*. Asian Journal of Management and Commerce., DOI: 10.22271/27084515.2025.v6.i2Sc.702

Bollen, J., Mao, H., & Zeng, X. (2011). Twitter mood predicts the stock market. *Journal of Computational Science*, *2*(1), 1–8. DOI: 10.1016/j.jocs.2010.12.007

Bordalo, P., Gennaioli, N., Ma, Y., & Shleifer, A. (2020). Overreaction in macroeconomic expectations. *The American Economic Review*, *110*(9), 2748–2782. DOI: 10.1257/aer.20181219

Botos, Á., & Fogarasi, J. (2025, May). Algorithmic Trading in Financial Markets: A Systematic Review. In 2025 IEEE 19th International Symposium on Applied Computational Intelligence and Informatics (SACI) (pp. 1-6). IEEE. DOI: 10.1109/SACI66288.2025.11030204

Box, G. E. P., Jenkins, G. M., Reinsel, G. C., & Ljung, G. M. (2015). *Time series analysis: Forecasting and control* (5th ed.). Wiley.

Bredt, S. (2019). Artificial intelligence (AI) in the financial sector. *Frontiers in Artificial Intelligence*, *2*, 1–5. DOI: 10.3389/frai.2019.00016

Breiman, L. (2001). Random forests. *Machine Learning*, *45*(1), 5–32. DOI: 10.1023/A:1010933404324

Bustos, O., & Pomares-Quimbaya, A. (2020). Stock market movement forecast: A systematic review. *Expert Systems with Applications*, *156*, 113464. DOI: 10.1016/j.eswa.2020.113464

Buthelezi, E. M. (2024). Navigating Global Uncertainty: Examining the Effect of Geopolitical Risks on Cryptocurrency Prices and Volatility in a Markov-Switching Vector Autoregressive Model. *International Economic Journal, 38*(4), 564–590. DOI: 10.1080/10168737.2024.2393589

Candrian, C., & Scherer, A. (2022). Rise of the machines: Delegating decisions to autonomous AI. *Computers in Human Behavior, 134*, 107308. DOI: 10.1016/j.chb.2022.107308

Cao, L. (2022). Ai in finance: Challenges, techniques, and opportunities. *ACM Computing Surveys, 55*(3), 1–38. DOI: 10.1145/3502289

Cao, S., Jiang, W., Wang, J., & Yang, B. (2024). From Man vs. Machine to Man + Machine: The art and AI of stock analyses. *Journal of Financial Economics, 160*, 103910. DOI: 10.1016/j.jfineco.2024.103910

Caplin, A., Martin, D., & Marx, P. (2025). Modeling machine learning: A cognitive economic approach. *Journal of Economic Theory, 224*, 105970. DOI: 10.1016/j.jet.2025.105970

Cardillo, G., & Chiappini, H. (2024). Robo-advisors: A systematic literature review. *Finance Research Letters, 62*, 105119. DOI: 10.1016/j.frl.2024.105119

Cartea, Á., Jaimungal, S., & Penalva, J. (2015). *Algorithmic and high-frequency trading*. Cambridge University Press.

Černevičienė, J., & Kabašinskas, A. (2024). Explainable artificial intelligence (XAI) in finance: A systematic literature review. *Artificial Intelligence Review, 57*(8), 216. DOI: 10.1007/s10462-024-10854-8

Chang, E. C., Cheng, J. W., & Khorana, A. (2000). An examination of herd behavior in equity markets: An international perspective. *Journal of Banking & Finance, 24*(10), 1651–1679. DOI: 10.1016/S0378-4266(99)00096-5

Chaudhari, K., & Thakkar, A. (2023). Data fusion with factored quantization for stock trend prediction using neural networks. *Information Processing & Management, 60*(3), 103293. DOI: 10.1016/j.ipm.2023.103293

Chen, L., Pelger, M., & Zhu, J. (2024). Deep learning in asset pricing. *Management Science, 70*(6), 3965–3988. DOI: 10.1287/mnsc.2023.4695

Chen, T., & Guestrin, C. (2016). XGBoost: A scalable tree boosting system. In *Proceedings of the 22nd ACM SIGKDD International Conference on Knowledge Discovery and Data Mining* (pp. 785–794).

Chen, Y., Liu, J., & Gao, P. (2025). Enhancing stock price prediction through sentiment analysis: A FinBERT-LSTM approach to market sentiment integration. *Advances in Economics. Management and Political Sciences, 204*, 1–8. DOI: 10.54254/2754-1169/2025.25278

Cho, K., van Merriënboer, B., Gulcehre, C., Bahdanau, D., Bougares, F., Schwenk, H., & Bengio, Y. (2014). Learning phrase representations using RNN encoder-decoder for statistical machine translation. *Proceedings of the 2014 Conference on Empirical Methods in Natural Language Processing (EMNLP)*, 1724–1734. DOI: 10.3115/v1/D14-1179

Chong, E., Han, C., & Park, F. C. (2017). Deep learning networks for stock market analysis and prediction: Methodology, data representations, and case studies. *Expert Systems with Applications, 83*, 187–205. DOI: 10.1016/j.eswa.2017.04.030

Chopra, R., & Sharma, G. D. (2021). Application of artificial intelligence in stock market forecasting: A critique, review, and research agenda. *Journal of Risk and Financial Management, 14*(11), 526. DOI: 10.3390/jrfm14110526

Chopra, S., Yadav, D., & Chopra, A. N. (2019). Artificial neural networks based Indian stock market price prediction: Before and after demonetization. *Journal of Swarm Intelligence and Evolutionary Computation, 8*(1), 2–7.

Chou, T. N. (2019, July). An explainable hybrid model for bankruptcy prediction based on the decision tree and deep neural network. In *2019 IEEE 2nd international conference on knowledge innovation and invention (ICKII)* (pp. 122-125). IEEE. DOI: 10.1109/ICKII46306.2019.9042639

Chouhan, S., & Singhai, M. (2025). *Sustainable Banking in the Digital Era: AI, Ethics, and Financial Inclusion in a Globalized Economy*. International Journal of Innovative Research in Engineering & Multidisciplinary Physical Sciences., DOI: 10.37082/IJIRMPS.v13.i4.232635

Christie, W. G., & Huang, R. D. (1995). Following the pied piper: Do individual returns herd around the market? *Financial Analysts Journal, 51*(4), 31–37. DOI: 10.2469/faj.v51.n4.1918

Climate Policy Initiative. (2024). *Global landscape of climate finance 2024*. Climate Policy Initiative.

Climate Policy Initiative. (2025). *Global landscape of climate finance 2025*. Climate Policy Initiative.

Convergence. (2024). *State of blended finance 2024: Climate edition*. Convergence Blended Finance.

Costanza, R., Cumberland, J. H., Daly, H., Goodland, R., Norgaard, R. B., Kubiszewski, I., & Franco, C. (2014). *An introduction to ecological economics* (2nd ed.). CRC Press. DOI: 10.1201/b17829

Crisanto, J. C., Leuterio, C. B., Prenio, J., & Yong, J. (2024). Regulating AI in the financial sector: Recent developments and main challenges. *FSI Insights, 63*. Bank for International Settlements. https://www.bis.org/fsi/publ/insights63.htm

D'Acunto, F., Prabhala, N., & Rossi, A. G. (2019). The promises and pitfalls of robo-advising. *Review of Financial Studies*, *32*(5), 1983–2020. DOI: 10.1093/rfs/hhz014

Dael, F. A., & Avvad, H. (2025). Optimizing Random Forest Hyperparameters for Enhanced Stock Price Prediction. *IEEE International Conference on New Trends in Computing Sciences (ICTCS)*. DOI: 10.1109/ICTCS65341.2025.10989295

Dael, F., Yavuz, Ö., & Yavuz, U. (2023). Stock Market Prediction Using Generative Adversarial Networks (GANs): Hybrid Intelligent Model. *Computer Systems Science and Engineering*, *47*(1), 19–35. DOI: 10.32604/csse.2023.037903

Dai, W., Wu, J. Y., & Lu, C. J. (2012). Combining nonlinear independent component analysis and neural network for the prediction of Asian stock market indexes. *Expert Systems with Applications*, *39*(4), 4444–4452. DOI: 10.1016/j.eswa.2011.09.145

Dakalbab, F., Abu Talib, M., Nasir, Q., & Saroufil, T. (2024). Artificial intelligence techniques in financial trading: A systematic literature review. *Journal of King Saud University. Computer and Information Sciences*, *36*(3), 102015. DOI: 10.1016/j.jksuci.2024.102015

Dase, R. K., & Pawar, D. D. (2010). Application of Artificial Neural Network for stock market predictions: A review of literature. *International Journal of Machine Intelligence*, *2*(2), 14–17. DOI: 10.9735/0975-2927.2.2.14-17

Davis, F. D. (1989). A Technology Acceptance Model for Empirically Testing New End-User Information systems: Theory and Results. *Science*.

De Bondt, W. F., & Thaler, R. H. (1985). Does the stock market overreact? *The Journal of Finance*, *40*(3), 793–805. DOI: 10.1111/j.1540-6261.1985.tb05004.x

Devi, P., Kishore, R., Giri, S., Srivastava, S. P., Vishnoi, A., Sharma, P., & Balyan, A. (2025). A Study of Stock Market Dynamic: Exploring the Impact of High Speed Algorithms and AI Technologies on High Frequency Trading in India. *Proceedings - International Conference on Next Generation Communication and Information Processing, INCIP 2025*, 298–303. DOI: 10.1109/INCIP64058.2025.11019692

Devi, K. N., & Bhaskaran, V. M. (2015). Semantic enhanced social media sentiments for stock market prediction. *International Journal of Economics and Management Engineering*, *9*(2), 678–682. DOI: 10.5281/zenodo.1100501

Devlin, J., Chang, M.-W., Lee, K., & Toutanova, K. (2019). BERT: Pre-training of deep bidirectional transformers for language understanding. In **Proceedings of NAACL-HLT 2019** (pp. 4171–4186). DOI: 10.18653/v1/N19-1423

Dewan, M., Mudgal, A., Pandey, P., Raghav, Y. Y., & Gupta, T. (2023). Predicting pregnancy complications using machine learning. In *Technological tools for predicting pregnancy complications* (pp. 141–160). IGI Global. DOI: 10.4018/979-8-3693-1718-1.ch008

Diebold, F. X., & Mariano, R. S. (1995). Comparing predictive accuracy. *Journal of Business & Economic Statistics*, *13*(3), 253–263. DOI: 10.1080/07350015.1995.10524599

DigitalDefynd. (2026). Top 25 AI in finance case studies [2026]. https://digitaldefynd.com/IQ/ai-in-finance-case-studies/

Doshi-Velez, F., & Kim, B. (2017). Towards a rigorous science of interpretable machine learning. *arXiv preprint arXiv:1702.08608.*

Du Jardin, P. (2016). A two-stage classification technique for bankruptcy prediction. *European Journal of Operational Research*, *254*(1), 236–252. DOI: 10.1016/j.ejor.2016.03.008

Eaton, G. W., Huang, Y., & Krueger, T. M. (2020). Tax-loss harvesting by robo-advisors: Evidence and implications. *Financial Analysts Journal*, *76*(4), 25–39.

Eisenberg, I. W., Gamboa, L., & Sherman, E. (2025). *The Unified Control Framework: Establishing a Common Foundation for Enterprise AI Governance, Risk Management and Regulatory Compliance*. 1–31. https://arxiv.org/abs/2503.05937

Ellen MacArthur Foundation. (2020). *The circular economy: A transformative Covid-19 recovery strategy*. Ellen MacArthur Foundation.

European Commission. (2025). *EU Emissions Trading System: 2024 market report*. European Commission.

Fagbore, O. O., Ogeawuchi, J. C., Ilori, O., Isibor, N. J., Odetunde, A., & Adekunle, B. I. (2024). Conceptual design of ethical investment assessment models using AI-enhanced financial decision tools. *International Journal of Scientific Research in Science and Technology*, *11*(4), 525–558. Advance online publication. DOI: 10.32628/IJSRST24115123

Fama, E. F. (1970). Efficient capital markets: A review of theory and empirical work. *The Journal of Finance*, *25*(2), 383–417. DOI: 10.2307/2325486

Fatica, S., & Panzica, R. (2021). Green bonds as a tool against climate change? *Business Strategy and the Environment*, *30*(5), 2688–2701. DOI: 10.1002/bse.2771

Fatima, S., & Chakraborty, M. (2024). Adoption of artificial intelligence in financial services: The case of robo-advisors in India. *IIMB Management Review*, *36*(2), 113–125. DOI: 10.1016/j.iimb.2024.04.002

Financial Stability Board. (2024). *The financial stability implications of artificial intelligence.* https://www.fsb.org/2024/11/the-financial-stability-implications-of-artificial-intelligence/

Fischer, T., & Krauss, C. (2018). Deep learning with long short-term memory networks for financial market predictions. *European Journal of Operational Research*, *270*(2), 654–669. DOI: 10.1016/j.ejor.2017.11.054

Freeman, R. E. (1984). *Strategic management: A stakeholder approach.* Pitman.

Frontiers in Behavioural Economics. (2024). Evaluating robo-advisors through behavioural finance. *Frontiers*, •••, 1489159.

Frontiers in Behavioural Economics. (2024). Evaluating robo-advisors through behavioural finance. *Frontiers*, Article 1489159. https://www.frontiersin.org/journals/behavioral-economics/articles/10.3389/frbhe.2024.1489159/full

Fügener, A., Walzner, D. D., & Gupta, A. (2026). Roles of Artificial Intelligence in Collaboration with Humans: Automation, Augmentation, and the Future of Work. *Management Science*, *72*(1), 538–557. DOI: 10.1287/mnsc.2024.05684

Future Earth. (2022). *Circular economy and renewable energy: Pathways to sustainable development.* Future Earth.

Gandhmal, D. P., & Kumar, K. (2019). Systematic analysis and review of stock market prediction techniques. *Computer Science Review*, *34*, 100190. DOI: 10.1016/j.cosrev.2019.08.001

Garg, A. (2022). Unified Framework of Blockchain and AI for Business Intelligence in Modern Banking. *International Journal of Emerging Research in Engineering and Technology*, *3*(4), 32–42. DOI: 10.63282/3050-922X.IJERET-V3I4P105

Gebhardt, C., & Piqué Huerta, J. M. (2024). Integrating Triple Helix and Sustainable Transition Research for Transformational Governance. *Triple Helix (Heidelberg)*, *11*(1), 107–130. Advance online publication. DOI: 10.1163/21971927-bja10053

Giantsidi, S., & Tarantola, C. (2025). Deep learning for financial forecasting: A review of recent trends. *International Review of Economics & Finance, 104*, 104719. DOI: 10.1016/j.iref.2025.104719

Giupponi, É. C. B., Espuny, M., Poltronieri, C. F., & de Oliveira, O. J. (2025). From ESG to Sustainable Development: A Path Designed for the Triple Helix Spheres. *Sustainable Development.* Advance online publication. DOI: 10.1002/sd.70355

Glasserman, P. (2004). Monte Carlo methods in financial engineering (Vol. 53, pp. xiv+-596). New York: springer.

Goel, H., & Som, B. K. (2023). Stock market prediction, COVID-19 pandemic and neural networks: An SCG algorithm application. *Economía, 24*(1), 134–146. DOI: 10.1108/ECON-07-2022-0101

Goodfellow, I., Bengio, Y., & Courville, A. (2016). *Deep learning.* MIT Press.

Gulia, S., Pandey, P., & Raghav, Y. Y. (2024). Multimedia data in healthcare system. In *Supervised and unsupervised data engineering for multimedia data* (pp. 63–92). DOI: 10.1002/9781119786443.ch3

Gummadi, H. S. B. (2025). *Explainable AI-Enhanced Underwriting Automation for Personalized Insurance Policy Recommendations. European Journal of Computer.* Science and Information Technology., DOI: 10.37745/ejcsit.2013/vol13n192440

Guo, Z., Wang, H., Yang, J., & Miller, D. J. (2015). A stock market forecasting model combining two-directional two-dimensional principal component analysis and radial basis function neural network. *PLoS One, 10*(4), e0122385. DOI: 10.1371/journal.pone.0122385

Gupta, S., & Shrivastava, M. (2022). Herding and loss aversion in stock markets: Mediating role of fear of missing out (FOMO) in retail investors. *International Journal of Emerging Markets, 17*(7), 1720–1737. DOI: 10.1108/IJOEM-08-2020-0933

Gupta, T., Pandey, P., & Raghav, Y. Y. (2023). Impact of social media platforms on the consumer decision-making process in the food and grocery industry. In *Influences of social media on consumer decision-making processes in the food and grocery industry* (pp. 119–139). IGI Global. DOI: 10.4018/978-1-6684-8868-3.ch006

Gu, S., Kelly, B., & Xiu, D. (2020). Empirical asset pricing via machine learning. *Review of Financial Studies, 33*(5), 2223–2273. DOI: 10.1093/rfs/hhaa009

Gu, W., Zhong, Y., Li, S., Wei, C., Dong, L., Wang, Z., & Yan, C. (2024). Predicting stock prices with FinBERT-LSTM: Integrating news sentiment analysis. *Proceedings of the 2024 8th International Conference on Cloud and Big Data Computing*, 67–72. DOI: 10.1145/3694860.3694870

Hambly, B., Xu, R., & Yang, H. (2023). Recent advances in reinforcement learning in finance. *Mathematical Finance*, *33*(3), 437–503. DOI: 10.1111/mafi.12382

Hansen, A. L., & Lee, S. J. (2025). *Financial stability implications of generative AI: Taming the animal spirits* (Finance and Economics Discussion Series 2025-090). Federal Reserve Board. DOI: 10.17016/feds.2025.090

Hastie, T., Tibshirani, R., & Friedman, J. (2017). *The elements of statistical learning* (2nd ed.). Springer.

Hoang, D., & Wiegratz, K. (2023). Machine learning methods in finance: Recent applications and prospects. *European Financial Management*, *29*(5), 1657–1701. DOI: 10.1111/eufm.12408

Hochreiter, S., & Schmidhuber, J. (1997). Long short-term memory. *Neural Computation*, *9*(8), 1735–1780. DOI: 10.1162/neco.1997.9.8.1735 PMID: 9377276

Hörisch, J., Freeman, R. E., & Schaltegger, S. (2014). Applying stakeholder theory in sustainability management: Links, similarities, dissimilarities, and a conceptual framework. *Organization & Environment*, *27*(4), 328–346. DOI: 10.1177/1086026614535786

Hosain, M. T., Morol, M. K., & Hossen, M. J. (2025). A hybrid self attentive linearized phrase structured transformer based RNN for financial sentence analysis with sentence level explainability. *Scientific Reports*, *15*(1), 23893. DOI: 10.1038/s41598-025-09265-8 PMID: 40615659

Hosaka, T. (2019). Bankruptcy prediction using imaged financial ratios and convolutional neural networks. *Expert Systems with Applications*, *117*, 287–299. DOI: 10.1016/j.eswa.2018.09.039

Hoseinzade, E., & Haratizadeh, S. (2019). CNNpred: CNN-based stock market prediction using a diverse set of variables. *Expert Systems with Applications*, *129*, 273–285. DOI: 10.1016/j.eswa.2019.03.029

Hossain, M. A. (2025). Artificial Intelligence-Driven Financial Analytics Models for Predicting Market Risk and Investment Decisions in U.S. Enterprises. *ASRC Procedia: Global Perspectives in Science and Scholarship*, *01*(01), 1066–1095. DOI: 10.63125/9csehp36

Hsu, M. W., Lessmann, S., Sung, M. C., Ma, T., & Johnson, J. E. (2016). Bridging the divide in financial market forecasting: Machine learners vs. financial economists. *Expert Systems with Applications*, *61*, 215–234. DOI: 10.1016/j.eswa.2016.05.033

Huang, A. H., Wang, H., & Yang, Y. (2023). FinBERT: A large language model for extracting information from financial text. *Contemporary Accounting Research*, *40*(2), 806–841. DOI: 10.1111/1911-3846.12832

Huang, S., Cao, L., Sun, R., Ma, T., & Liu, S. (2024). Enhancing portfolio optimization: A two-stage approach with deep learning and portfolio optimization. *Mathematics*, *12*(21), 3376. DOI: 10.3390/math12213376

Hu, H., Tang, L., Zhang, S., & Wang, H. (2018). Predicting the direction of stock markets using optimized neural networks with Google Trends. *Neurocomputing*, *285*, 188–195. DOI: 10.1016/j.neucom.2018.01.038

Hussain, M. A., Vemaraju, S., & Garg, A. (2025). *The Impact of AI Tools on ESG-Based Sustainable Banking Practices: A Meta-Analysis & Conceptual Framework.* International Journal of Computational and Experimental Science and Engineering., DOI: 10.22399/ijcesen.3198

Hutto, C. J., & Gilbert, E. (2014). VADER: A parsimonious rule-based model for sentiment analysis of social media text. *Proceedings of the International AAAI Conference on Web and Social Media, 8*(1), 216–225. https://doi.org/DOI: 10.1609/icwsm.v8i1.14550

Huynh, N., De Mello, L., & Li, K. (2025). Evolution of investor sentiment: A systematic literature review and bibliometric analysis. *International Review of Economics & Finance*, *100*, 104115. DOI: 10.1016/j.iref.2025.104115

Huynh, T. L. D., Hille, E., & Nasir, M. A. (2020). Diversification in the age of the 4th industrial revolution: The role of artificial intelligence, green bonds and cryptocurrencies. *Technological Forecasting and Social Change*, *159*, 120188. Advance online publication. DOI: 10.1016/j.techfore.2020.120188

IEEFA. (2024). *Blended finance for renewable energy in emerging markets.* Institute for Energy Economics and Financial Analysis.

IFC-Amundi. (2025). *Emerging market green bonds report 2024.* International Finance Corporation.

International Energy Agency. (2024). *World energy outlook 2024.* IEA.

International Monetary Fund. (2024). *Global financial stability report, October 2024: Steadying the course—Uncertainty, artificial intelligence, and financial stability*. International Monetary Fund.

International Organization of Securities Commissions. (2025). *Artificial intelligence in capital markets: Use cases, risks, and challenges*. IOSCO.

International Renewable Energy Agency. (2024). *World energy transitions outlook 2024*. IRENA.

Islam, F. A. S. (2025). Artificial Intelligence-powered Carbon Market Intelligence and Blockchain-enabled Governance for Climate-responsive Urban Infrastructure in the Global South. *Journal of Engineering Research and Reports*. https://doi.org/ DOI: 10.9734/jerr/2025/v27i71585

Islam, M. S., Bashir, M., Rahman, S., Al Montaser, M. A., Bortty, J. C., Nishan, A., & Haque, M. R. (2025). Machine Learning-Based Cryptocurrency Prediction: Enhancing Market Forecasting with Advanced Predictive Models. *Journal of Eco-humanism*, *4*(2), 2498–2519. DOI: 10.62754/joe.v4i2.6663

Jadhavrao, R., Sengupta, R., Patil, A., & Yadav, R. S. (2023). Stock market trend prediction using artificial intelligence algorithm (RNN-LSTM) - Comparison with current techniques and research on its effectiveness in forecasting in Indian market and US market. Empirical Economics Letters, 22(Special Issue 2), 124-133. DOI: 10.5281/zenodo.10864038

Jaitly, N., & Hoo, J. (2021). Machine learning applications in robo-advisory services: Risk profiling and behavioural assessment. *Journal of Financial Technology*, *3*(2), 45–62.

Jang, E.-K., Kwak, D., Choi, G., & Moon, J. (2023). Opportunities and challenges of converging technology and blended finance for REDD+ implementation. *Frontiers in Forests and Global Change*, *6*, 1154917. Advance online publication. DOI: 10.3389/ffgc.2023.1154917

Jegadeesh, N., & Titman, S. (1993). Returns to buying winners and selling losers: Implications for stock market efficiency. *The Journal of Finance*, *48*(1), 65–91. DOI: 10.1111/j.1540-6261.1993.tb04702.x

Jensen, T. I., Kelly, B., Malamud, S., & Pedersen, L. H. (2026). Machine learning and the implementable efficient frontier. *Review of Financial Studies*, *39*(10), hhag022. Advance online publication. DOI: 10.1093/rfs/hhag022

Jiang, P., Liu, X., & Zhang, Y. (2023). Federated learning for financial applications: Privacy, efficiency, and robustness. *IEEE Transactions on Computational Social Systems, 10*(4), 1580–1591. DOI: 10.1109/TCSS.2022.3215980

Jiang, W. (2021). Applications of deep learning in stock market prediction: Recent progress. *Expert Systems with Applications, 184*, 115537. DOI: 10.1016/j.eswa.2021.115537

Ji, X., Wang, J., & Yan, Z. (2021). A stock price prediction method based on deep learning technology. *International Journal of Crowd Science, 5*(1), 55–72. DOI: 10.1108/IJCS-05-2020-0012

John, S. (2025). *Sustainable finance and AI integration: Driving responsible growth in the digital era.* International Journal of Scientific Research in Engineering and Management., DOI: 10.55041/IJSREM52213

Journal of Investment Economics Research. (2024). AI in behavioural finance: Understanding investor bias through machine learning. https://jier.org/index.php/journal/article/download/3114/2529/5598

Jung, D., Dorner, V., Weinhardt, C., & Pusmaz, H. (2020). Designing adaptive robo-advisors: Digital nudging and conversational interfaces in wealth management. *Electronic Markets, 30*(4), 1–15.

Jupalli, P. H. (2024). Harnessing Artificial Intelligence & Big Data for Sustainable Finance & Risk Managemen*t.* [IJSR]. *International Journal of Science and Research (Raipur, India), 13*(7), 518–525. Advance online publication. DOI: 10.21275/SR24708233123

Kahneman, D. (2011). *Thinking, fast and slow.* Farrar, Straus and Giroux.

Kahneman, D., & Tversky, A. (1979). Prospect theory: An analysis of decision under risk. *Econometrica, 47*(2), 263–291. DOI: 10.2307/1914185

Kahneman, D., & Tversky, A. (1992). Advances in prospect theory: Cumulative representation of uncertainty. *Journal of Risk and Uncertainty, 5*(4), 297–323. DOI: 10.1007/BF00122574

Karanikola, A., Davrazos, G., Liapis, C. M., & Kotsiantis, S. (2023). Financial sentiment analysis: Classic methods vs. deep learning models. *Intelligent Decision Technologies, 17*(4), 893–915. DOI: 10.3233/IDT-230478

Kasireddy, J. R. (2025). *The Ethical Implications of AI in Financial Market Surveillance: Are We Over-Monitoring Traders?* European Journal of Accounting, Auditing and Finance Research., DOI: 10.37745/ejaafr.2013/vol13n41736

Ke, G., Meng, Q., Finley, T., Wang, T., Chen, W., Ma, W., Ye, Q., & Liu, T.-Y. (2017). LightGBM: A highly efficient gradient boosting decision tree. *Advances in Neural Information Processing Systems*, *30*, 3146–3154.

Kim, D., Lee, J., & Kim, H. (2026). Pattern-guided forecasting framework for metal price prediction with grouping decomposed series. *Financial Innovation*, *12*(1), 45. DOI: 10.1186/s40854-025-00833-5

Kim, K. J. (2003). Financial time series forecasting using support vector machines. *Neurocomputing*, *55*(1–2), 307–319. DOI: 10.1016/S0925-2312(03)00372-2

Kirilenko, A. A., Kyle, A. S., Samadi, M., & Tuzun, T. (2017). The flash crash: High-frequency trading in an electronic market. *The Journal of Finance*, *72*(3), 967–998. DOI: 10.1111/jofi.12498

Kirtac, K., & Germano, G. (2024). Sentiment trading with large language models. *Finance Research Letters*, *62*, 105227. DOI: 10.1016/j.frl.2024.105227

Kobanenko, M. (2025). *Digital Transformation of Financial Reporting: AI-Driven Accuracy and Transparency in Corporate Disclosures*. The American Journal of Management and Economics Innovations., DOI: 10.37547/tajmci/Volume07Issue11-03

Korol, T. (2019). Dynamic bankruptcy prediction models for European enterprises. *Journal of Risk and Financial Management*, *12*(4), 185. DOI: 10.3390/jrfm12040185

Koroma, J., Rongting, Z., Muhideen, S., Akintunde, T. Y., Amosun, T. S., Dauda, S. J., & Sawaneh, I. A. (2022). Assessing citizens' behavior towards blockchain cryptocurrency adoption in the Mano River Union States: Mediation, moderation role of trust and ethical issues. *Technology in Society*, *68*, 101885. DOI: 10.1016/j.techsoc.2022.101885

Kotekar, C. S., Mohan, B. R., & Kolukuluri, V. (2026). Can news sentiment improve deep learning models for Nifty 50 index forecasting? *IEEE Access : Practical Innovations, Open Solutions*, *14*, 2675–2689. DOI: 10.1109/ACCESS.2025.3644013

Krause, D. S. (2023). Large Language Models and Generative AI in Finance: An Analysis of ChatGPT, Bard, and Bing AI. *Bard, and Bing AI*, 1–31. https://ssrn.com/abstract=4511540

Kubo, K., & Nakagawa, K. (2025). Portfolio optimization using deep learning with risk aversion utility function. *Finance Research Letters*, *74*, 106646. DOI: 10.1016/j.frl.2025.106761

Kulkarni, M. S., Vijayakumar Bharathi, S., Perdana, A., & Kilari, D. (2025). A Quest for Context-Specific Stock Price Prediction: A Comparison Between Time Series, Machine Learning and Deep Learning Models. *SN Computer Science*, *6*(4), 335. DOI: 10.1007/s42979-025-03848-y

Kumar, D., Sarangi, P. K., & Verma, R. (2022). A systematic review of stock market prediction using machine learning and statistical techniques. *Materials Today: Proceedings, National Conference on Functional Materials: Emerging Technologies and Applications in Materials Science*, *49*, 3187–3191. DOI: 10.1016/j.matpr.2020.11.399

Lam, W., & Wurgler, J. (2024). Corporate green bonds: Costs, pricing, and environmental claims. *Journal of Financial Economics*, *152*(2), 103–124.

LeCun, Y., Bengio, Y., & Hinton, G. (2015). Deep learning. *Nature*, *521*(7553), 436–444. DOI: 10.1038/nature14539 PMID: 26017442

Lee, C.-Y., & Anderl, E. (2025). Does business news sentiment matter in the energy stock market? Adopting sentiment analysis for short-term stock market prediction in the energy industry. *Frontiers in Artificial Intelligence*, *8*, 1559900. DOI: 10.3389/frai.2025.1559900 PMID: 40771943

Lee, M. C. (2009). Factors influencing the adoption of internet banking: An integration of TAM and TPB with perceived risk and perceived benefit. *Electronic Commerce Research and Applications*, *8*(3), 130–141. DOI: 10.1016/j.elerap.2008.11.006

Leghemo, I. M., Azubuike, C., Segun-Falade, O. D., & Odionu, C. S. (2025). Data governance for emerging technologies: A conceptual framework for managing blockchain, IoT, and AI. *Journal of Engineering Research and Reports*. https://doi.org/DOI: 10.9734/jerr/2025/v27i11385

Lehoczky, J., & Schervish, M. (2018). Overview and history of statistics for equity markets. *Annual Review of Statistics and Its Application*, *5*(1), 265–288. DOI: 10.1146/annurev-statistics-031017-100518

Lim, B., & Zohren, S. (2021). Time-series forecasting with deep learning: A survey. *Philosophical Transactions. Series A, Mathematical, Physical, and Engineering Sciences*, *379*(2194), 20200209. Advance online publication. DOI: 10.1098/rsta.2020.0209

Lin, C. Y., & Marques, J. A. L. (2024). Stock market prediction using artificial intelligence: A systematic review of systematic reviews. *Social Sciences & Humanities Open*, *9*, 100864. DOI: 10.1016/j.ssaho.2024.100864

Liongson, E., & Nainggolan, Y. (2025). *Financing Low-Carbon Urban Transport through Subnational Green Bonds: A Review in Emerging Economies*. Journal Integration of Management Studies., DOI: 10.58229/jims.v3i2.362

Little, R. J. A., & Rubin, D. B. (2019). *Statistical analysis with missing data* (3rd ed.). Wiley.

Liu, S. (2025). Statistical Assessment of Default Risks of Green Financial Bonds: A Joint Analysis Model of Environmental Benefits and Financial Indicators. *SHS Web of Conferences, 218*, 02007. https://doi.org/DOI: 10.1051/shsconf/202521802007

Liu, C., & Wu, S. (2023). *Green finance, sustainability disclosure and economic implications*. Fulbright Review of Economics and Policy., DOI: 10.1108/FREP-03-2022-0021

Liu, H., Zhao, T., Wang, S., & Li, X. (2023). A stock rank prediction method combining industry attributes and price data of stocks. *Information Processing & Management*, *60*(4), 103358. DOI: 10.1016/j.ipm.2023.103358

Liu, X., Guo, J., Wang, H., & Zhang, F. (2022). Prediction of stock market index based on ISSA-BP neural network. *Expert Systems with Applications*, *204*, 117604. DOI: 10.1016/j.eswa.2022.117604

Li, X., Wu, P., & Wang, W. (2020). Incorporating stock prices and news sentiments for stock market prediction: A case of Hong Kong. *Information Processing & Management*, *57*(5), 102212. DOI: 10.1016/j.ipm.2020.102212

Li, X., Xie, H., Chen, L., Wang, J., & Deng, X. (2014). News impact on stock price return via sentiment analysis. *Knowledge-Based Systems*, *69*(1), 14–23. DOI: 10.1016/j.knosys.2014.04.022

Li, Y., Jiang, W., Yang, L., & Wu, T. (2018). On neural networks and learning systems for business computing. *Neurocomputing*, *275*, 1150–1159. DOI: 10.1016/j.neucom.2017.09.054

Lohrmann, C., & Luukka, P. (2019). Classification of intraday S&P500 returns with a Random Forest. *International Journal of Forecasting*, *35*(1), 390–407. DOI: 10.1016/j.ijforecast.2018.08.004

López de Prado, M. (2018). *Advances in financial machine learning*. Wiley.

Lopez-Lira, A., & Tang, Y. (2024). *Can ChatGPT forecast stock price movements? Return predictability and large language models* (SSRN Scholarly Paper No. 4412788). DOI: 10.2139/ssrn.4412788

Loughran, T., & McDonald, B. (2011). When is a liability not a liability? Textual analysis, dictionaries, and 10-Ks. *The Journal of Finance*, *66*(1), 35–65. DOI: 10.1111/j.1540-6261.2010.01625.x

Loughran, T., & McDonald, B. (2016). Textual analysis in accounting and finance: A survey. *Journal of Accounting Research*, *54*(4), 1187–1230. DOI: 10.1111/1475-679X.12123

Lourenço, V. M., Ogutu, J. O., Rodrigues, R. A. P., Posekany, A., & Piepho, H.-P. (2024). Genomic prediction using machine learning: A comparison of the performance of regularized regression, ensemble, instance-based and deep learning methods on synthetic and empirical data. *BMC Genomics*, *25*(1), 152. DOI: 10.1186/s12864-023-09933-x PMID: 38326768

Lulaj, E., & Brajković, M. (2025). The moderating role of finance, accounting, and digital disruption in ESG, financial reporting, and auditing*: A Triple-Helix perspective. Journal of Risk and Financial Management*, *18*(5), 245. Advance online publication. DOI: 10.3390/jrfm18050245

Lundberg, S. M., & Lee, S.-I. (2017). A unified approach to interpreting model predictions. *Advances in Neural Information Processing Systems*, *30*, 4765–4774.

Mahajan, S., Agarwal, R., & Gupta, M. (2025). Algorithmic Bias Under the EU AI Act: Compliance Risk, Capital Strain, and Pricing Distortions in Life and Health Insurance Underwriting. *Risks*, *13*(9), 160. DOI: 10.3390/risks13090160

Mahdavi Ardekani, A., Bertz, J., Bryce, C., Dowling, M., & Long, S. (2024). FinSentGPT: A universal financial sentiment engine? *International Review of Financial Analysis*, *94*, 103291. DOI: 10.1016/j.irfa.2024.103291

Mai, F., Tian, S., Lee, C., & Ma, L. (2019). Deep learning models for bankruptcy prediction using textual disclosures. *European Journal of Operational Research*, *274*(2), 743–758. DOI: 10.1016/j.ejor.2018.10.024

Makridakis, S., Spiliotis, E., & Assimakopoulos, V. (2018). Statistical and machine learning forecasting methods: Concerns and ways forward. *PLoS One*, *13*(3), e0194889. DOI: 10.1371/journal.pone.0194889 PMID: 29584784

Malo, P., Sinha, A., Korhonen, P., Wallenius, J., & Takala, P. (2014). Good debt or bad debt: Detecting semantic orientations in economic texts. *Journal of the Association for Information Science and Technology*, *65*(4), 782–796. DOI: 10.1002/asi.23062

Markowitz, H. (1952). Portfolio selection. *The Journal of Finance*, *7*(1), 77–91. DOI: 10.2307/2975974

Mehrabi, N., Morstatter, F., Saxena, N., Lerman, K., & Galstyan, A. (2021). A survey on bias and fairness in machine learning. *ACM Computing Surveys, 54*(6), 1–35. DOI: 10.1145/3457607

Mertzanis, C. (2025). Artificial intelligence and investment management: Structure, strategy, and governance. *International Review of Financial Analysis, 107*, 104599. DOI: 10.1016/j.irfa.2025.104599

Meservy, R. D., Denna, E. L., & Hansen, J. V. (1992). Application of artificial intelligence to accounting, tax, and audit services: Research at Brigham Young University. *Expert Systems with Applications, 4*(2), 213–218. DOI: 10.1016/0957-4174(92)90112-6

Mezzi. (2025). AI in behavioural finance: Managing investor bias. https://www.mezzi.com/blog/ai-in-behavioral-finance-managing-investor-bias

Milana, C., & Ashta, A. (2021). Artificial intelligence techniques in finance and financial markets: A survey of the literature. *Strategic Change, 30*(3), 189–209. DOI: 10.1002/jsc.2403

Mintarya, L. N., Halim, J. N., Angie, C., Achmad, S., & Kurniawan, A. (2023). Machine learning approaches in stock market prediction: A systematic literature review. *Procedia Computer Science, 216*, 96–102. DOI: 10.1016/j.procs.2022.12.115

Mishra, S., Sharma, D., & Kumar, P. (2023). Green finance: A systematic review and research agenda. *Journal of Sustainable Finance & Investment, 13*(1), 234–259.

Mohammad, S., Al Qrain, B., Alenazi, S., Vasudevan, A., Shelash, A. A., & Ali, I. (2025). *Lifecycle Cost Management for Offshore Marine Renewable Energy Wind Infrastructure: An Integrated Model Using Circular Economy Principles*. Sustainable Marine Structures., DOI: 10.36956/sms.v7i3.2506

Mohammed, W. A. (2020). Challenges of Stock Prediction. In *Valuation Challenges and Solutions in Contemporary Businesses* (pp. 234–252). IGI Global., DOI: 10.4018/978-1-7998-1086-5.ch013

Mol, A. P. J., & Spaargaren, G. (2000). Ecological modernisation theory in debate: A review. *Environmental Politics, 9*(1), 17–49. DOI: 10.1080/09644010008414511

Munonye, W. C., Ajonye, G. O., Ahonsi, S. O., Munonye, D. I., Chigozie, I. O., & Akinloye, O. A. (2025). Advancing Circularity in Battery Systems for Renewable Energy: Technologies, Barriers, and Future Directions. *Advanced Energy and Sustainability Research*. Advance online publication. DOI: 10.1002/aesr.202500255

Murillo-Luna, J. L., & Hernández-Trasobares, A. (2022). Cooperation with the Triple Helix and corporate environmental innovation. *Journal of Cleaner Production, 368*, 135479. DOI: 10.1016/j.jclepro.2022.135479

Murray, S., Xia, Y., & Xiao, H. (2024). Charting by machines. *Journal of Financial Economics, 153*, 103791. DOI: 10.1016/j.jfineco.2024.103791

Nagesh, K. C., & Murugan, K. S. (2025). Fintech and Sustainable Finance: Impact of Digital Finance in Promoting Green Investments. *mLAC Journal for Arts, Commerce and Sciences (m-JACS)*. https://doi.org/DOI: 10.59415/mjacs.v3i1.246

Nair, B. B., & Mohandas, V. P. (2015). An intelligent recommender system for stock trading. *Intelligent Decision Technologies, 9*(3), 243–269. DOI: 10.3233/IDT-140220

Nature Communications. (2025). Carbon pricing thresholds and renewable energy transitions: A cross-country analysis. *Nature Communications, 16*, Article 1542.

Nature Energy. (2024). The cost of capital for renewable energy in developing economies. *Nature Energy, 9*(3), 267–278.

Nature Scientific Reports. (2026). Behaviorally informed deep reinforcement learning for portfolio optimisation with loss aversion and overconfidence. *Scientific Reports*, 16, Article 35902.

Nerlekar, V. S., Sane, A., Gadekar, M., Gupta, S. K., & Waghulkar, S. (2025). The herd mentality: Understanding the theories and models of herding behavior in financial markets. In *Psychological drivers of herding and market overreaction* (pp. 255–290). IGI Global Scientific Publishing., DOI: 10.4018/979-8-3693-7259-7.ch011

Nwachukwu, P. S., Chima, O. K., & Okolo, C. H. (2025). *The artificial intelligence governance framework for finance: A control-by-design approach to algorithmic decision-making in accounting*. Finance & Accounting Research Journal., DOI: 10.51594/farj.v7i8.2016

O'Hara, M. (2015). High frequency market microstructure. *Journal of Financial Economics, 116*(2), 257–270. DOI: 10.1016/j.jfineco.2015.01.003

OECD. (2024). *Effective carbon rates 2024: Pricing greenhouse gas emissions through taxes and emissions trading*. OECD Publishing.

Ofodile, O. C., Oyewole, A., Ugochukwu, C. E., Addy, W. A., Adeoye, O. B., & Okoye, C. C.Onyeka Chrisanctus OfodileAdedoyin Tolulope OyewoleChinonye Esther UgochukwuWilhelmina Afua AddyOmotayo Bukola AdeoyeChinwe Chinazo Okoye. (2024). Predictive analytics in climate finance: Assessing risks and opportunities for investors. *GSC Advanced Research and Reviews, 18*(2), 76–89. DOI: 10.30574/gscarr.2024.18.2.0076

Omar, K. O., Zraqou, J., & Gómez, J. M. (2025b). From synthetic text to real threats: Unraveling the security risks of generative AI. In [Editors] (Eds.), *[Book title]* (Ch. 1). IGI Global Scientific Publishing. DOI: 10.4018/979-8-3373-0832-6.ch001

Omar, K., Abuhashish, F., Alkhadour, W., & Gómez, J. M. (2025c). PromptArchitecture: A novel reference model (PARM) for scalable AI-UX integration system blueprints. *International Journal of Advances in Soft Computing and its Applications, 17*(3), Article 8. DOI: 10.15849/IJASCA.251130.08

Omar, K. O., Zraqou, J., Alkhadour, W., & Marx Gómez, J. (2026). Future trends in business intelligence in the Jordanian industry. In Ishtaiwi, A., Al-Qerem, A., Al Khaldy, M., & Alauthman, M. (Eds.), *Strategic AI integration in business intelligence* (pp. 155–182). IGI Global Scientific Publishing., DOI: 10.4018/979-8-3373-6801-6.ch007

Omar, K., Matar, I., Zraqou, J., Fakhouri, H., & Marx Gómez, J. (2025a). AI for all: Bridging accessibility and usability through user-centered AI design. *Data and Metadata, 4*, 751. Advance online publication. DOI: 10.56294/dm2025751

Pagliaro, A. (2025). Artificial Intelligence vs. Efficient Markets: A Critical Reassessment of Predictive Models in the Big Data Era. *Electronics (Basel), 14*(9), 1721. Advance online publication. DOI: 10.3390/electronics14091721

Panarese, P., Grasso, M. M., & Solinas, C. (2026). Algorithmic bias, fairness, and inclusivity: A multilevel framework for justice-oriented AI. *AI & Society, 41*(4), 2803–2825. DOI: 10.1007/s00146-025-02451-2

Pandey, P., Raghav, Y. Y., Gulia, S., Aggarwal, S., & Kumar, N. (2024). Supervised and unsupervised learning techniques for biometric systems. In *Supervised and unsupervised data engineering for multimedia data* (pp. 263–299). DOI: 10.1002/9781119786443.ch12

Pasupuleti, M. K. (2025). *Governance Frameworks for Ethical AI Deployment in Public Sector Services. International Journal of Academic and Industrial Research Innovations.* IJAIRI., DOI: 10.62311/nesx/rphcr17

Patil, A., Saha, S., & Sengupta, R. (2024). Enhancing stock market predictions through predictive analytics. In Singh, N., Birla, S., Ansari, M. D., & Shukla, N. K. (Eds.), *Intelligent techniques for predictive data analytics*. Wiley., DOI: 10.1002/9781394227990.ch7

Pavlidis, G. (2025). *Empowering Sustainable Finance with Artificial Intelligence: A Framework for Responsible Implementation*. ArXiv., DOI: 10.4337/9781803929996.00009

Poiriazi, E., Zournatzidou, G., Konteos, G., & Sariannidis, N. (2025). Analyzing the interconnection between environmental, social, and governance (ESG) criteria and corporate corruption: Revealing the significant impact of greenwashing. *Administrative Sciences*, *15*(3), 100. DOI: 10.3390/admsci15030100

Polzin, F., & Sanders, M. (2020). How to finance the transition to low-carbon energy in Europe? *Energy Policy*, *147*, 111863. DOI: 10.1016/j.enpol.2020.111863

Prasad, A., Bakhshi, P., & Guha, D. (2023). Forecasting the direction of daily changes in the India VIX index using deep learning. *IIMB Management Review*, *35*(2), 149–163. DOI: 10.1016/j.iimb.2023.05.002

Proxsis, A. I. (2025). How BlackRock's Aladdin platform leverages generative AI to transform investment management. https://proxsis.ai/use-case/elementor-1104/

Puh, K., & Bagić Babac, M. (2023). Predicting stock market using natural language processing. *American Journal of Business*, *38*(2), 41–61. DOI: 10.1108/AJB-08-2022-0124

Qiu, M., Song, Y., & Akagi, F. (2016). Application of artificial neural network for the prediction of stock market returns: The case of the Japanese stock market. *Chaos, Solitons, and Fractals*, *85*, 1–7. DOI: 10.1016/j.chaos.2016.01.004

Qubit Capital. (2025). Top 5 AI tools for predicting investor behaviour in 2026. https://qubit.capital/blog/ai-tools-predict-investor-behavior

Raghav, Y. Y., & Vyas, V. (2019, October). A comparative analysis of different load balancing algorithms on different parameters in cloud computing. In *2019 3rd International Conference on Recent Developments in Control, Automation & Power Engineering (RDCAPE)* (pp. 628–634). IEEE. DOI: 10.1109/RDCAPE47089.2019.8979122

Raghav, Y. Y., & Vyas, V. (2024). Harnessing cloud computing and IoT for wildlife conservation. In *Integration of cloud computing and IoT: Trends, case studies and applications* (p. 142).

Raghav, Y. Y., Kumar, A., Kumar, A., Kumari, P., & Choudhury, S. (2024, December). A smart IoT framework for detecting accidents and facilitating rescue operations. In *2024 13th International Conference on System Modeling & Advancement in Research Trends (SMART)* (pp. 373–380). IEEE. DOI: 10.1109/SMART63812.2024.10882204

Raghav, Y. Y., & Chauhan, A. (2025). Tech for the wild: Leveraging IoT and cloud computing in wildlife conservation. In *AI and machine learning techniques for wildlife conservation* (pp. 49–64). IGI Global Scientific Publishing. DOI: 10.4018/979-8-3693-6935-7.ch003

Raghav, Y. Y., Choudhary, S., Pandey, P., Singh, S., & Varshney, D. (2025). Smart healthcare: Cloud-IoT solutions for enhanced patient well-being. *African Journal of Biomedical Research*, *28*(1), 14–28.

Raghav, Y. Y., & Gulia, S. (2023). The rise of artificial intelligence and its implications on spirituality. In *Investigating the impact of AI on ethics and spirituality* (pp. 165–178). IGI Global. DOI: 10.4018/978-1-6684-9196-6.ch011

Raghav, Y. Y., & Kait, R. (2024). Edge computing empowering distributed computing at the edge. In *Emerging trends in cloud computing analytics, scalability, and service models* (pp. 67–83). IGI Global Scientific Publishing. DOI: 10.4018/979-8-3693-0900-1.ch003

Raghav, Y. Y., & Pandey, P. (2024). Adoption of green cloud computing for environmental sustainability: An analysis. In *Convergence strategies for green computing and sustainable development* (pp. 138–151). IGI Global.

Raghav, Y. Y., Tipu, R. K., Bhakhar, R., Gupta, T., & Sharma, K. (2024). The future of digital marketing: Leveraging artificial intelligence for competitive strategies and tactics. In *The use of artificial intelligence in digital marketing: Competitive strategies and tactics* (pp. 249–274). IGI Global.

Raghav, Y. Y., & Vyas, V. (2023). A comparative analysis report of nature-inspired algorithms for load balancing in cloud environment. In *Women in soft computing* (pp. 47–63). Springer Nature Switzerland.

Raghav, Y. Y., & Vyas, V. (2023). ACBSO: A hybrid solution for load balancing using ant colony and bird swarm optimization algorithms. *International Journal of Information Technology : an Official Journal of Bharati Vidyapeeth's Institute of Computer Applications and Management*, *15*(5), 2847–2857. DOI: 10.1007/s41870-023-01340-5

Raghav, Y. Y., & Vyas, V. (2026). Cloud load balancing: Performance comparison between bird swarm and ant colony optimization algorithms. *SN Computer Science*, *7*(1), 107. DOI: 10.1007/s42979-025-04712-9

Raghav, Y. Y., Vyas, V., & Rani, H. (2022). Load balancing using dynamic algorithms for cloud environment: A survey. *Materials Today: Proceedings*, *69*, 349–353. DOI: 10.1016/j.matpr.2022.09.048

Rahardja, U., Chen, S., Lin, Y., Tsai, T., Aini, Q., Khan, A., Oganda, F. P., Dewi, E. R., Cho, Y., & Hsu, C. (2023). Evaluating the Mediating Mechanism of Perceived Trust and Risk toward Cryptocurrency: An Empirical Research. *SAGE Open*, *13*(4), 1–17. DOI: 10.1177/21582440231217854

Raman, R., Ray, S., Das, D., & Nedungadi, P. (2025). Innovations and barriers in sustainable and green finance for advancing sustainable development goals. *Frontiers in Environmental Science*, *12*, 1513204. Advance online publication. DOI: 10.3389/fenvs.2024.1513204

Ramdhan, D. F. (2025). The Role of ESG Disclosure in Attracting Sustainable Investment in Indonesia's Capital Market. RIGGS*: Journal of Artificial Intelligence and Digital Business.* https://doi.org/DOI: 10.31004/riggs.v4i3.2484

Rane, N., Choudhary, S., & Rane, J. (2023). Explainable Artificial Intelligence (XAI) Approaches for Transparency and Accountability in Financial Decision-Making. SSRN *Electronic Journal*. DOI: 10.2139/ssrn.4640316

Raziyeva, S., & Meraliyev, M. (2025). Bias and Fairness in Automated Loan Approvals: A Systematic Review of Machine Learning Approaches. *Journal of Emerging Technologies and Computing*. https://doi.org/DOI: 10.47344/jbzmnx25

Redress Compliance. (2025). Case study: AI-based predictive analytics for investments at BlackRock (Aladdin). https://redresscompliance.com/case-study-ai-based-predictive-analytics-for-investments-at-blackrock-aladdin/

Ren, T. (2025). AI-Powered Carbon Footprint Tracking Is Redefining Green Investment Decision-Making. Advances in Economics, *Management and Political Sciences*. https://doi.org/DOI: 10.54254/2754-1169/2025.GL27239

Rezaei, M., & Nezamabadi-Pour, H. (2025). A taxonomy of literature reviews and experimental study of deepreinforcement learning in portfolio management: M. Rezaei and H. Nezamabadi-Pour. *Artificial Intelligence Review*, *58*(3), 94. DOI: 10.1007/s10462-024-11066-w

Rouf, N., Malik, M. B., Arif, T., Sharma, S., Singh, S., Aich, S., & Kim, H.-C. (2021). Stock Market Prediction Using Machine Learning Techniques: A Decade Survey on Methodologies, Recent Developments, and Future Directions. *Electronics (Basel), 10*(21), 2717. Advance online publication. DOI: 10.3390/electronics10212717

Sadiq, R., Yasser, F., & Nawaz, F. (2025). *Using AI to predict and mitigate green asset bubbles in financial markets.* The Regional Tribune., DOI: 10.55737/trt/SG25.103

Sari, R. C., Sholihin, M., Cahaya, F. R., Ishola, A., Yuniarti, N., Pranesti, A. R., Sari, A. R., & Haryanto, . (2025). Artificial Intelligence-Based ESG Greenwashing Detection: Road to Net Zero Carbon and Its Impact on Corporate Performance. *Business Strategy & Development, 8*(4), e70228. Advance online publication. DOI: 10.1002/bsd2.70228

Sarita, R. S., & Raghav, Y. Y. (2024). Introduction to quantum computing and its revolution in industry and society. In *Industrial quantum computing: Algorithms, blockchains, industry 4.0* (p. 219). DOI: 10.1515/9783111354842-013

Sarita, R., Raghav, Y. Y., & Kashish. (2025). Strategic innovation of AI and ML for ecommerce data security. In *Next-generation computational intelligence: Trends and technologies* (pp. 165–194). Springer Nature Switzerland.

Sasaki, N., & Abe, I. (2025). A Digital Twin Architecture for Forest Restoration: Integrating AI, IoT, and Blockchain for Smart Ecosystem Management. *Future Internet, 17*(9), 421. DOI: 10.3390/fi17090421

Schaltegger, S., Hörisch, J., & Freeman, R. E. (2019). Business cases for sustainability: A stakeholder theory perspective. *Organization & Environment, 32*(3), 191–212. DOI: 10.1177/1086026617722882

Schultz, F. C., Valentinov, V., & Pies, I. (2025). The Stakeholder Business Case for Circular Economy: An Ordonomic Approach for Developing a Circular Economy Business Case by Stakeholder Governance. *Journal of Industrial Ecology, 29*(4), 1279–1292. DOI: 10.1111/jiec.70046

ScienceDirect. (2019). Longitudinal case study of robo-advisors in investment decisions. https://www.sciencedirect.com/science/article/pii/S221463501930214X

Securities and Exchange Board of India. (2024, September). Analysis of profit and loss of individual traders dealing in equity F&O segment: Updated study for FY22–FY24. https://www.sebi.gov.in

Securities and Exchange Board of India. (2025, February). Circular: Safer participation of retail investors in algorithmic trading (SEBI/HO/MIRSD/MIRSD-PoD/P/2025/0000013). https://www.sebi.gov.in

Securities and Exchange Commission. (2013, October 16). *SEC charges Knight Capital with violations of market access rule* (Press Release 2013-222). U.S. Securities and Exchange Commission.

Selvamuthu, D., Kumar, V., & Mishra, A. (2019). Indian stock market prediction using artificial neural networks on tick data. *Financial Innovation, 5*(1), 1–12. DOI: 10.1186/s40854-019-0131-7

Sezer, O. B., Ozbayoglu, M., & Dogdu, E. (2017). A deep neural-network based stock trading system based on evolutionary optimized technical analysis parameters. *Procedia Computer Science, 114*, 473–480. DOI: 10.1016/j.procs.2017.09.031

Shahin, T., Ballestar de las Heras, M. T., & Sanz, I. (2025). Enhancing Stock Market Prediction Using Gradient Boosting Neural Network: A Hybrid Approach. *Computational Economics, 65*(6), 3207–3235. DOI: 10.1007/s10614-024-10671-9

Sharpe, W. F. (1998). The sharpe ratio. *Streetwise–the Best of the Journal of Portfolio Management, 3*(3), 169–185. DOI: 10.1515/9781400829408-022

Shen, K. Y., & Tzeng, G. H. (2015). Combined soft computing model for value stock selection based on fundamental analysis. *Applied Soft Computing, 37*, 142–155. DOI: 10.1016/j.asoc.2015.07.030

Shetty, S., Musa, M., & Brédart, X. (2022). Bankruptcy Prediction Using Machine Learning Techniques. *Journal of Risk and Financial Management, 15*(1), 35. DOI: 10.3390/jrfm15010035

Shiller, R. J. (2000). *Irrational exuberance*. Princeton University Press.

Shi, Y., & Li, X. (2019). An overview of bankruptcy prediction models for corporate firms: A systematic literature review. *Intangible Capital, 15*(2), 114–127. DOI: 10.3926/ic.1354

Shukla, D. (2025). Green Bonds and Sustainable Investing: Trends, Challenges, and Future Outlook. *Journal of International Commercial Law and Technology*. https://doi.org/DOI: 10.61336/Jiclt/25-01-28

Shumailov, I., Shumaylov, Z., Zhao, Y., Papernot, N., Anderson, R., & Gal, Y. (2024). AI models collapse when trained on recursively generated data. *Nature, 631*(8022), 755–759. DOI: 10.1038/s41586-024-07566-y PMID: 39048682

Sindhu, M., Raghav, Y. Y., & Kundu, K. (2025, August). Generative AI in education and its future possibilities. In *2025 International Conference on Intelligent and Secure Engineering Solutions (CISES)* (pp. 68–74). IEEE. DOI: 10.1109/CISES66934.2025.11265181

Singh, A. (2025). Predictive analytics for risk management in finance. International Journal of Advanced Research in Science. *Tongxin Jishu*, 364–372. Advance online publication. DOI: 10.48175/IJARSCT-28040

Singh, S., Singh, M., & Attri, S. (2025). Mapping stock market dynamics: A tripartite neural network approach using modified grid search for stock market prediction. *Expert Systems with Applications*, *278*(February), 127243. DOI: 10.1016/j.eswa.2025.127243

Singh, S., Singh, M., & Attri, S. (2026a). Dynamic volatility linkages among crude oil, exchange rate, interest rate, gold and equity markets: An empirical Asian perspective. *Managerial Finance*, *52*(1), 160–182. DOI: 10.1108/MF-01-2025-0016

Singh, S., Singh, M., & Attri, S. (2026b). Unraveling two decades of volatility in financial markets: Insights and emerging themes. *Global Knowledge, Memory and Communication*, •••, 1–20. DOI: 10.1108/GKMC-01-2025-0038

Singh, U., & Khare, A. (2026). Stock Prediction Using Machine Learning Techniques. In Senjyu, T., So-, C., & Joshi, A. (Eds.), *Smart Trends in Computing and Communications* (pp. 387–400). Springer Nature., DOI: 10.1007/978-981-96-7505-0_30

Siriman, N., Ali, M. S., Siddiqui, T., Rohin, G., Vejju, B., & Cherupelly, N. (2025). Green finance and AI in India: A synergistic approach to sustainable development and climate resilience. *International Journal of Environmental Sciences*, *11*(1), 207–216. Advance online publication. DOI: 10.64252/mt7jkk84

Sironi, P. (2016). *FinTech innovation: From robo-advisors to goal based investing and gamification*. Wiley. DOI: 10.1002/9781119227205

SmartDev. (2025). AI in investment management: Top use cases you need to know. https://smartdev.com/ai-use-cases-in-investment-management/

Song, G. H., & Jain, A. (2022). Can artificial intelligence beat the stock market? *Studies in Economics and Finance*, *39*(5), 772–785. DOI: 10.1108/SEF-03-2022-0133

Soni, G., Singh, S., & Singh, D. (2025). Artificial intelligence in modern finance: Pathways to smarter, safer, and faster systems. *International Journal for Research in Applied Science and Engineering Technology*, *13*(9), 830–835. Advance online publication. DOI: 10.22214/ijraset.2025.74143

Sun, W., & Xu, Y. (2016). Financial security evaluation of the electric power industry in China based on a back propagation neural network optimized by genetic algorithm. *Energy*, *101*, 366–379. DOI: 10.1016/j.energy.2016.02.046

Sun, X., & Lei, Y. (2021). Research on financial early warning of mining listed companies based on BP neural network model. *Resources Policy*, *73*, 102223. DOI: 10.1016/j.resourpol.2021.102223

Sun, Y., Liu, L., Xu, Y., Zeng, X., Shi, Y., Hu, H., Jiang, J., & Abraham, A. (2024). Alternative data in finance and business: Emerging applications and theory analysis [review]. *Financial Innovation*, *10*(1), 127. DOI: 10.1186/s40854-024-00652-0

Sun, Y., Qu, Z., Zhang, T., & Li, X. (2025). Adaptive Ensemble Learning for Financial Time-Series Forecasting: A Hypernetwork-Enhanced Reservoir Computing Framework with Multi-Scale Temporal Modeling. *Axioms*, *14*(8), 597. Advance online publication. DOI: 10.3390/axioms14080597

Surmount, A. I. (2025). The role of behavioural finance in automated trading strategies. https://surmount.ai/blogs/the-role-of-behavioral-finance-in-automated-trading-strategies

Sutton, R. S., & Barto, A. G. (2018). *Reinforcement learning: An introduction* (2nd ed.). MIT Press.

Swanson, A. R., & Sakhrani, V. (2023). Value–Risk Calculator for Blended Finance: A Systems Perspective of the Nachtigal Hydropower Project. *Sustainability (Basel)*, *15*(13), 10357. DOI: 10.3390/su151310357

Tabassi, E. (2023). *Artificial intelligence risk management framework (AI RMF 1.0)* (NIST AI 100-1). National Institute of Standards and Technology. https://doi.org/ DOI: 10.6028/NIST.AI.100-1

Tam, K. Y., & Kiang, M. Y. (1992). Managerial applications of neural networks: The case of bank failure predictions. *Management Science*, *38*(7), 926–947. DOI: 10.1287/mnsc.38.7.926

Taqi, M., Hamaidan, H., & Khan, R. (2024). The prospects of artificial intelligence and machine learning in the stock market. In *Navigating the future of finance in the age of AI*. IGI Global., DOI: 10.4018/979-8-3693-4382-1.ch009

Tetlock, P. C. (2007). Giving content to investor sentiment: The role of media in the stock market. *The Journal of Finance*, *62*(3), 1139–1168. DOI: 10.1111/j.1540-6261.2007.01232.x

Thaler, R. H. (2015). *Misbehaving: The making of behavioural economics*. W.W. Norton & Company.

Thaler, R. H. (2016). Behavioral economics: Past, present, and future. *The American Economic Review*, *106*(7), 1577–1600. DOI: 10.1257/aer.106.7.1577

Thapaliya, S. (2024). Examining the Influence of AI-Driven Cybersecurity in Financial Sector Management. *The Batuk, 10*(2), 129–144. DOI: 10.3126/batuk.v10i2.68147

Thayasivam, U., Johnson, S., Balabavan, K., & Uthayakumar, S. (2025). A comprehensive survey on statistical and deep learning models for panel data analysis. *Knowledge and Information Systems, 67*(12), 11359–11379. DOI: 10.1007/s10115-025-02607-y

Thilakarathna, C., Dawson, C., & Edirisinghe, E. (2022, June). Using financial ratios with artificial neural networks for bankruptcy prediction. In *2022 IEEE International Conference on Artificial Intelligence and Computer Applications (ICAICA)* (pp. 55-58). IEEE. DOI: 10.1109/ICAICA54878.2022.9844640

Tiossi, F. M., & Rodrigues, R. G. (2023). *Triple helix in the management of innovation in public policies: A study of two countries. Revista de Gestão e Secretariado*. Management and Administrative Professional Review., DOI: 10.7769/gesec.v14i8.2690

Tripathy, N., Mishra, D., Hota, S., Mishra, S., Das, G. C., Dalai, S. S., & Nayak, S. K. (2025). Bitcoin volatility forecasting: A comparative analysis of conventional econometric models with deep learning models. *International Journal of Electrical and Computer Engineering, 15*(1), 614–623. DOI: 10.11591/ijece.v15i1.pp614-623

Tsay, R. S. (2010). *Analysis of financial time series* (3rd ed.). Wiley. DOI: 10.1002/9780470644560

Tversky, A., & Kahneman, D. (1974). Judgment under uncertainty: Heuristics and biases. *Science, 185*(4157), 1124–1131. DOI: 10.1126/science.185.4157.1124 PMID: 17835457

Vaghefi, S. A., Hachcham, A., Grasso, V., Manicus, J., Msemo, N., Senni, C., & Leippold, M. (2025). *AI for Climate Finance: Agentic Retrieval and Multi-Step Reasoning for Early Warning System Investments*. ArXiv. https://doi.org//arxiv.2504.05104DOI: 10.2139/ssrn.5208086

van Binsbergen, J. H., Han, X., & Lopez-Lira, A. (2023). Man versus machine learning: The term structure of earnings expectations and conditional biases. *Review of Financial Studies, 36*(6), 2361–2396. DOI: 10.1093/rfs/hhac085

Vapnik, V. N. (1998). *Statistical learning theory*. Wiley.

Venkatesh, V., Morris, M. G., Davis, G. B., & Davis, F. D. (2003). USER ACCEPTANCE OF INFORMATION TECHNOLOGY: TOWARD A UNIFIED VIEW. *Management Information Systems Quarterly, 27*(3), 425–478. DOI: 10.2307/30036540

Verma, S. K., Singh, D., Raghav, Y. Y., Hemelatha, S., Kannimuthu, S., & Banchhor, C. O. (2023, September). Collaborative MAC protocol design for enhanced network lifetime in mobile ad hoc networks. In *2023 6th International Conference on Contemporary Computing and Informatics (IC3I)* (pp. 2082–2088). IEEE. DOI: 10.1109/IC3I59117.2023.10397708

Võ, T. T. H., Nguy n, V. H. T., & Pham, T. L. (2025). *University–Industry–Government Collaboration in Fostering Innovation: Policy Solutions to Strengthen Triple Helix Partnerships in Ho Chi Minh City in the Digital Era.* International Journal of Innovative Science and Research Technology., DOI: 10.38124/ijisrt/25aug1367

Wah, J. N. K. (2025). AI-Powered Wealth Management: Transforming Financial Literacy, Personalized Investments, and Risk Assessment Through Robo-Advisors and Predictive Analytics for the Future of Finance. *Chinese Science Bulletin, 70*(02), 4401–4420. 02.1706/Csb.28.02.2025.01

Wiranata, R.B., & Djunaidy, A.(2021).The stock exchange prediction using machine learning techniques: a comprehensive a nd systematic literature review. Jurnal Ilmu Komputer dan Informatika,14 (2), 91–112

World Bank. (2022). *What you need to know about green finance.* World Bank Group.

World Economic Forum. (2025). *Artificial intelligence in financial services.* World Economic Forum.

Yadav, R., Patil, A., & Sengupta, R. (2023). An analysis of Satyam case using bankruptcy and fraud detection models. *SocioEconomic Challenges, 7*(4), 24–35. DOI: 10.61093/sec.7(4).24-35.2023

Yin, R. K. (2018). *Case study research and applications: Design and methods* (6th ed.). SAGE Publications.

Yu, P., & Yan, X. (2020). Stock price prediction based on deep neural networks. *Neural Computing & Applications, 32*(6), 1609–1628. DOI: 10.1007/s00521-019-04212-x

Yu, W. (2025). Estimating the changes and oscillations in the financial markets: A case study of the Nikkei 225. *Sadhana, 50*(4), 247. DOI: 10.1007/s12046-025-02869-w

Zhang, G., Patuwo, B. E., & Hu, M. Y. (1998). Forecasting with artificial neural networks: The state of the art. *International Journal of Forecasting, 14*(1), 35–62. DOI: 10.1016/S0169-2070(97)00044-7

Zhang, H., & Punjwani, A. (2025). A Triple Helix Approach to a Greener Future: Environmental Law, Fintech, Institutional Quality, and Natural Resources as Pillars of Environmental Sustainability in G20. *Sustainability (Basel), 17*(9), 4043. Advance online publication. DOI: 10.3390/su17094043

Zhang, Q., Zhang, H., & Sornette, D. (2025). Discovering nonlinear interactions between China's financial markets: A data-driven approach. *International Review of Financial Analysis, 101*, 103975. DOI: 10.1016/j.irfa.2025.103975

Zhou, C., & Etzkowitz, H. (2021). Triple Helix twins: A framework for achieving nnovation and UN Sustainable Development Goals. *Sustainability (Basel), 13*(12), 6535. DOI: 10.3390/su13126535

Zhou, H., & Kalev, P. S. (2019). Algorithmic and high frequency trading in Asia-Pacific, now and the future. *Pacific-Basin Finance Journal, 53*, 186–207. DOI: 10.1016/j.pacfin.2018.10.006

Zhou, P. (2025). *AI and DeFi Integration: Algorithmic Bias, Black-Box Opacity, and Regulatory Challenges*. Advances in Economics and Management Research., DOI: 10.56028/aemr.14.1.770.2025

Zuckerman, G. (2019). *The man who solved the market: How Jim Simons launched the quant revolution*. Portfolio/Penguin.

About the Contributors

Soly Mathew Biju CEng MBCS CITP FBCS(UK) FHEA (UK) is a Ph.D. in Computer Science and also an MBA in IT management with 27 years of experience including work at industry and academia. She is currently an Associate Professor at the Faculty of Engineering and Information Sciences, University of Wollongong in Dubai. She worked as the Director for Computer Science(aka Discipline leader)2022-2024.Dr Biju has achieved the CEng status awarded by Engineering Council (UK). She also has achieved the Chartered IT Professional status which is a symbol of excellence in the field of IT and is also an ISTQB-certified software testing professional. She is a Fellow BCS (UK) which is the highest professional award given by professional bodies. She is also a Fellow Higher Education Academy, UK. HEA Fellowship demonstrates a personal and institutional commitment to professionalism in learning and teaching in higher education. It demonstrates commitment to teaching, learning and the student experience, through engagement in a practical process that encourages research, reflection and development. Dr Biju has been in the field of the field of teaching, training, network administration and software development since 1999. Prior to joining UOWD, she worked for various universities including University of Wales, Robert Kennedy College and Champlain College. She is a certified online instructor and has worked extensively on online teaching methods and online material design and development. In the industry, Dr Biju was responsible for leading two teams (Windows NT and Lotus Notes) for British Airways at Heathrow UK, and Pune, India She has conducted a number of workshops on e-learning, WebCT and Blackboard at UOWD and at other universities and a number of technical workshops for faculty and students. She was nominated for the Teaching Excellence and Research Excellence awards at UOWD on numerous occasions and received the prestigious Teaching Excellence Award in 2012, 2015 and 2019. She was also awarded the prestigious Amity Global Academic Excellence award in 2020. Her research interests include machine learning, data security, software testing, cryptography, e-learning, innovations in teaching, agile software development, online teaching, network security and programming techniques. She has papers published in reputed journals and books and presented and reviewed papers at national and international conferences and journals. She has been a scientific and organizing committee member and session chair and content chair on various reputed national and international conferences. She has won a number of research grants and patents for her research proposals and is also an editor for various technical books in IGI.

Sangeeta Trott is a Professor in Marketing and Dean Research and Innovation at ITMskills university, Mumbai India. She has more than 22 years of experience in Teaching and Research. Dr Sangeeta Trott is a post doctorate in commerce and management from Indian Council of Social Science Research, New Delhi. She is the recipient of Reserve Bank of India Scholarship Scheme of Faculty Members of Academic Institutes, 2016 and worked onvarious funded project on Online Gaming Addiction from Academy of Marketing Science, USA, Ministry of Corporate Affairs project and Indian Council of Social Science Research (ICCSR) Viksit Bharat Project@2047. Dr Sangeeta Trott has over 30 papers in reputed journals including journals like Journal of Product and Brand management Addictive Behaviours, Journal of International Marketing, International Marketing Review, International Journal of Consumer Studies and many others. She has presented over 40-50 papers in national and international conferences. Dr Sangeeta Trott has also conducted number of Faculty development programs on research related topics like ; Writing research papers, Working on funded projects and many others .She has also authored a book " Brand Equity-An Indian Perspective" Published by Pearson Hall of India. Dr Sangeeta Trott has been invited as a speaker for various seminars in various colleges in Mumbai .She has also been the convenor of national conference organized at ITM and has also chaired sessions in various conferences in India. Her main areas of interest includes, Branding, sustainability, societal challenges and others.

***

Shradha Attri is Senior Research Fellow at Central University of Himachal Pradesh, India. Her research interests lie in Decentralised Finance, Cryptocurrency, Blockchain, Forecasting, Econometrics Modelling, Time Series Analysis, and Behavioural Finance, Shradha's research aligns at the intersection of finance and emerging technologies. Her commitment to advancing academic knowledge is evident through innovative methodologies and a keen understanding of market dynamics. Shradha aims to contribute valuable insights to the academic and research community, showcasing a passion for exploring the evolving landscape of finance and technology.

Fares Abdulhafidh Derhem Dael is an Assistant Professor in the Department of Management Information Systems at İzmir Bakırçay University. He received his Bachelor's degree in Communication Engineering from International Islamic University Malaysia (IIUM), followed by a Master's degree in Communication and Computer Engineering from Universiti Kebangsaan Malaysia (UKM). He earned his Ph.D. in Management Information Systems from Atatürk University. Dr. Dael's research primarily focuses on machine learning and decision support systems to address complex real-world problems. His work explores the application of ML in intelligent data-driven environments, spatial modeling, and the development of advanced analytical frameworks for both public and private sector decision-making. In addition to ML, his research interests include data mining, Natural Language Processing, and Wireless Communication. By combining interdisciplinary methodologies, he aims to enhance spatial intelligence, improve predictive modeling capabilities, and contribute to the advancement of smart and sustainable information systems.

Hussam N. Fakhouri is an Assistant Professor of Data Science at Al-Balqa Applied University (BAU) in Jordan, a position he has held since 2025. He earned his Ph.D. in Computer Science from the University of Jordan in 2020, where his doctoral research focused on data science. Dr. Fakhouri's research interests span multiple domains within artificial intelligence and data science, including metaheuristic algorithms, optimization, data analysis, data exploration, data engineering, machine learning, and deep learning. He has authored approximately 100 research papers in reputable international journals and conference proceedings. In addition, Dr. Fakhouri contributes to the scholarly community as an academic editor and reviewer. Dr. Fakhouri has also undertaken significant academic leadership roles. He has also participated in Erasmus Programs such as doctoral schools hosted by universities in Denmark, Germany, and Russia.

Neha Garg is a dedicated academician, researcher, and educator with strong expertise in emerging technologies, intelligent systems, and interdisciplinary computing applications. She has been actively involved in higher education and research, contributing to the advancement of knowledge in areas such as artificial intelligence, machine learning, data privacy, secure digital systems, and communication-enabled intelligent applications. Her scholarly contributions include multiple book chapters and research-based publications with reputed national and international publishers. Her work spans diverse yet interconnected domains, including federated learning, AI-driven healthcare systems, privacy-preserving technologies, online banking security, and scalable communication frameworks. These contributions reflect her commitment to addressing contemporary technological challenges through innovative and research-oriented approaches. Dr. Garg has also played an active role in academic mentoring, curriculum delivery, and fostering research aptitude among students and peers. Her academic profile is strengthened by her ability to bridge theoretical concepts with practical applications.

Pratibha Gupta is working as an Assistant Professor of Management at the University School of Business, Chandigarh University, Mohali, Punjab. She has published three research papers and also won the Best Paper award. She has four-plus years of teaching experience and also worked as an Expert in NET/JRF Coaching for 2 years. Her area of specialisation is Finance.

Sanjeev Gupta Ph.D., is a distinguished Professor and Dean at the Central University of Himachal Pradesh, India. He specializes in FinTech, Data Science, Forecasting, Applied Econometrics, and Digital Finance, with a focus on emerging technologies like Artificial Intelligence, Blockchain, IoT, CBDC, and Cryptocurrency. A prolific researcher, Professor Gupta has numerous publications in leading journals, reflecting his expertise in finance and technology. His commitment to advancing knowledge and fostering academic excellence makes him a significant contributor to the academic community.

Faten F. Hamad is an Associate Professor in the Department of Information Studies at Sultan Qaboos University (Oman), where she has served since September 2021. She earned her Ph.D. in Information Science from Aberystwyth University (UK) in 2013, following an M.Sc. in Computer Science from the University of Jordan (2006) and a B.Sc. in Computer Science from Yarmouk University (2004). Her research interests span advanced metaheuristic optimization and AI-driven data analytics, applied to engineering design, cybersecurity, and intelligent systems, and extend to digital transformation, accessibility, and resilience in academic libraries and education.

Yogita Yashveer Raghav is an Assistant Professor in the Department of Computer Science and Engineering at K.R. Mangalam University, Gurugram, India. She holds a Ph.D. in Computer Science from Banasthali Vidyapith, Rajasthan. Her primary research interests include Cloud Computing, Data Science, Full Stack Development, and Artificial Intelligence & Machine Learning. She also serves as the Program Coordinator for B.Tech (CSE) – Full Stack Development and is the founding coordinator of the Centre of Excellence for Cloud Computing (AWS).

Rizwan Khan is a dedicated academic and researcher with a focus on Accounting and Finance. Currently serving as an Assistant Professor at the Haji Taufeeq Ali Mahavidyalaya, CSJM University, his research primarily revolves around financial accounting, cost accounting, financial management, and the integration of artificial intelligence in the financial sector. Dr. Khan's doctoral research on Activity Based Costing in the Indian automobile industry. Dr. Khan's scholarly contributions include several published books, research papers, and book chapters on topics ranging from financial performance to artificial intelligence applications in finance. Notably, his research has been published in indexed journals and books by leading academic publishers, such as IGI Global and Springer. His ongoing projects delve into emerging issues like the role of Artificial Intelligence in India's financial landscape and corporate social responsibility practices in Non-Banking Financial Companies (NBFCs). In addition to his academic publications, Dr. Khan has been awarded the Maulana Azad National Fellowship and is currently co-principal investigator of an ICSSR-funded project on Central Bank Digital Currency (CBDC) adoption in India. His work also extends beyond teaching to organizing international conferences and faculty development programs, highlighting his commitment to advancing research and fostering academic excellence.

K. K. Mishra is a Professor of Marketing in the Department of Management at Chandigarh University, Unnao, Uttar Pradesh, India. He has published 119 research papers in Scopus-indexed journals and book chapters, and has contributed to national and international conferences. He has five patent rights and three copyrights. He has 26 years of experience in teaching and research. He has supervised two PhD scholars. He has twice qualified for the UGC NET in Management. He has received the Best Faculty Award three times from the Indian Institute of Materials Management, National Headquarters, Mumbai, in 2009, 2016, and 2018, respectively. He has been conferred the Best Paper Award for the paper titled "Harnessing AI: Unveiling Educators' Intentions and Synergy in Education", presented at the 8th International Conference on Information System Design and Intelligent Applications (ISDIS 2024) in Dubai, UAE, in 2024. He has chaired technical sessions of international conferences organised by the Indian Institute of Materials Management, Mumbai, in 2016 and 2018, and OP Jindal University, Raigarh, in 2022 and 2023.

Khalil Omar is an assistant professor at the University of Petra in Jordan. He received his Ph.D. degree in computer science from the University of Oldenburg, Germany, in 2018. His academic focus is on distance learning and e-learning in combination with software engineering, mobile applications, usability design, adaptive interfaces, and ERP systems. Users can reach him through his email address: komar@uop.edu.jo.

P.S. Subha Pradha has a rich experience of over two decades spanning industry, teaching and research. She is a Doctorate in Management from University of

Hyderabad and qualified in UGC-NET, APSET. She has an MBA degree from Osmania University, an M.Phil from Sri Venkateshwara University and is a Microsoft Certified Professional in Developing C++ classes using MFC and Windows Open Services Architecture. Her areas of research interest include Risk Management, Investment Management, Fintech and Financial Inclusion. Having served in various capacities, she is passionate about mentoring the students and future leaders on beyond the classroom learning, entrepreneurship and social sensitivity.

Pawan Pant is working as an Associate Professor of Management at the University School of Business, Chandigarh University, Mohali, Punjab, with extensive experience in academia, industry, and school education. He has published 26 Scopus-indexed articles, chapters, and conference papers, contributing to areas such as AI in finance and sustainability, blended learning, monetary policy, behavioural economics, and ethical governance. He has also supervised international doctoral research, filed a design patent, and actively participated in various faculty development programs at the National and International levels. He has 14 years of teaching experience and worked as an Assistant Manager (Purchase) at Pacific Industries Ltd., Udaipur (Rajasthan), for one year. My professional journey reflects a potent blend of academic expertise, industry exposure, and research-driven innovation. His area of specialisation is Economics.

Ameya Patil is an academician and researcher with over 13 years of teaching experience and 3.5 years of industry exposure. He currently serves as Associate Professor at MIT World Peace University, India, teaching Finance and International Business. Currently, 31 Scopus indexed research documents. 18 of his research works have appeared in Scopus and ABDC journals. Dr.Patil has authored 25 books and has been invited as a keynote speaker in several national conferences. He is a member of Indian Institute of Banking and Finance (IIBF) and ASCB(UK). His research works have appeared with reputed publishers such as Wiley, Inderscience, Taylor & Francis, IGI Global, Emerald and Springer.

Tarun Sai Raavi is currently an Assistant Professor at KL University and is pursuing his Ph.D. from Aurora University, focusing on designing AI and machine learning tools for individual investor decision-making. He holds double MBA degrees in Finance (GITAM University) and Analytics (Osmania University). He has industry experience as a Research Analyst at Buzz Board and as a Data Analyst at Cognizant for Google. He specializes in R, Python, Tableau, Hadoop, IBM SPSS, and MS Excel, and specializes in data modeling, statistical analysis, and algorithmic development. His research areas include Fintech, data mining, deep learning, and IoT, with several publications in high-impact journals and active participation in national and international conferences, seminars, and management development programs.

Yogita Yashveer Raghav is an Assistant Professor in K R Mangalam University, Gurugram, Haryana. She has completed her PhD from Banasthali Vidyapith, Rajasthan and has already achieved impressive qualifications, including UGCNET and HTET. She has published 15+ research papers in reputed journals (Scopus, WOS indexed). She has presented various papers in international & IEEE conferences. She has published 1 international book and 10 book chapters (Scopus indexed). She has published 2 international Patents. She is awarded 2 times for voluntary contribution in organizing extra-curricular activities for children and women development and session for Environment Protection and science & Technologies by Spark minda Foundation and Janm Foundation. She is working as reviewer of various reputed peer-reviewed international journals Her research area is Cloud Computing, Edge Computing, Data Mining and Machine learning. She is IEEE member.

Radhika Ramanchi is a Professor in the Department of Accounting and Finance at GITAM University, with an outstanding record of research and academic contributions. She has published several high-impact research papers indexed in Scopus, Elsevier, ABDC, and ABC, and has presented at premier institutions like AIMS International, IIMs, and IITs. Her case studies have been published by Harvard Business Review, Emerald, and The Case Centre, and she has delivered lectures internationally. Dr. Radhika has successfully guided four Ph.D. scholars at HBS and won Second Prize at the ISB-Ivey League Global Case Competition for her co-authored case study. She completed a UGC-sponsored Minor Research Project and received the Macro Research Fellowship from the Indian Institute of Banking and Finance, earning multiple awards including GITAM's Best Researcher Award in 2018 for her excellence in research.

Sachin Singh is Senior Research Fellow at the Central University of Himachal Pradesh, India. His research interests lie at the confluence of finance and cutting-edge technologies, specifically focusing on Stock Markets, Time series analysis, Econometrics Modelling, Forecasting, Machine Learning, Deep Learning, and Artificial Intelligence. Sachin is committed to advancing the understanding of financial markets through innovative methodologies, leveraging his expertise in quantitative analysis and predictive modelling.With a passion for exploring the intricate relationships within financial systems, he aspires to contribute novel insights that bridge the realms of academia and real-world financial practices.

José G. Vargas-Hernández, M.B.A.; Ph.D. Member of the National System of Researchers of Mexico and a research professor at Tecnológico Mario Molina

Unidad Zapopan formerly at University Center for Economic and Managerial Sciences, University of Guadalajara. Professor Vargas-Hernández has a Ph. D. in Public Administration and a Ph.D. in Organizational Economics. He has undertaken studies in Organisational Behaviour and has a Master of Business Administration, published four books and more than 200 papers in international journals and reviews (some translated to English, French, German, Portuguese, Farsi, Chinese, etc.) and more than 300 essays in national journals and reviews. He has obtained several international Awards and recognition.

Azmee Zaheer is an Assistant Professor in the MBA Department at the University School of Business, Chandigarh University, Gharuan, Punjab. She has completed her PhD and MPhil in Management from Babasaheb Bhimrao Ambedkar University (a Central University) in Lucknow, Uttar Pradesh. She received a Gold Medal for her M.Phil.'s exemplary work. She has 10 years of experience in teaching, research, and industry. She has also contributed to various research journals, indexed in Scopus and UGC Care, edited a book, and participated in multiple national and international seminars.

Index

A

AI 1, 2, 3, 4, 5, 7, 8, 9, 10, 11, 12, 13, 14, 15, 16, 17, 18, 19, 20, 21, 22, 23, 24, 25, 26, 27, 29, 32, 33, 34, 35, 36, 37, 38, 39, 40, 41, 42, 43, 44, 46, 49, 50, 51, 52, 53, 54, 55, 56, 57, 58, 61, 62, 64, 67, 76, 82, 83, 84, 85, 88, 89, 90, 91, 95, 96, 97, 98, 99, 102, 105, 107, 108, 110, 112, 113, 115, 120, 121, 123, 127, 128, 129, 130, 131, 132, 133, 136, 137, 138, 139, 140, 141, 142, 143, 144, 145, 146, 147, 148, 149, 150, 151, 152, 153, 154, 155, 156, 157, 158, 159, 160, 161, 163, 164, 165, 166, 169, 170, 171, 172, 173, 174, 175, 176, 177, 178, 179, 180, 181, 182, 183, 184, 185, 186, 187, 188, 189, 190, 191, 192, 193, 194, 195, 196, 197, 198, 199, 200, 201, 203, 204, 209, 210, 211, 213, 214, 215, 216, 217, 218, 244, 247, 248, 249, 251, 252, 253, 260, 274, 277, 278, 279
Algorithmic Trading 2, 10, 11, 13, 15, 20, 22, 31, 32, 39, 54, 58, 89, 94, 96, 98, 99, 100, 101, 103, 124, 126, 127, 130, 134, 135, 136, 150, 211, 217, 224
Artificial Intelligence 1, 2, 16, 17, 21, 22, 24, 25, 26, 29, 30, 31, 32, 35, 36, 38, 40, 49, 50, 51, 52, 57, 58, 64, 84, 89, 90, 91, 93, 94, 95, 96, 97, 105, 108, 122, 125, 127, 128, 130, 137, 143, 148, 153, 157, 159, 160, 161, 164, 176, 192, 194, 196, 198, 199, 200, 203, 215, 216, 217, 218, 219, 220, 222, 225, 244, 247, 248, 253, 254, 258, 259, 312
Artificial Neural Networks 59, 71, 73, 78, 86, 89, 205, 208, 210, 217, 218, 221, 222, 226, 235, 249

B

Bankruptcy Prediction 203, 208, 213, 214, 215, 216, 217, 218, 219, 220, 221, 222
Behavioral Finance 12, 21, 24, 30, 251, 252, 253, 254, 255, 257, 258, 266, 273, 275, 277, 281, 289, 306
Behavioural Finance 12, 13, 15, 16, 29, 30, 31, 32, 33, 34, 35, 36, 40, 44, 49, 50, 51, 52, 54, 55, 56, 127, 129, 130, 132, 137, 139, 157, 289, 301, 304
Big Data 2, 30, 93, 95, 127, 129, 134, 136, 138, 194, 196, 204, 217, 243, 312

C

CNN 207, 208, 212, 214, 219, 235, 284
Cognitive Biases 12, 22, 30, 31, 35, 52, 128, 132, 251
Cross-Firm Evaluation 61, 76, 83, 85, 87
Cryptocurrency 3, 7, 9, 20, 22, 24, 25, 26, 91, 226, 242

D

Decision making 30, 31, 86, 87, 89, 90, 227, 281, 308
Deep Learning 2, 17, 22, 27, 59, 64, 90, 91, 93, 94, 95, 101, 124, 125, 128, 130, 138, 141, 144, 159, 160, 205, 208, 211, 218, 219, 220, 221, 223, 226, 227, 229, 233, 234, 235, 236, 237, 238, 242, 243, 244, 246, 278, 281, 282, 283, 284, 286, 311, 312

E

Economic Validation 57, 59, 61, 82, 85, 89, 90
Ensemble Learning 57, 59, 63, 64, 65, 66, 71, 82, 83, 86, 88, 89, 93, 94, 226, 232
Equity market 292
Explainable AI 17, 19, 20, 39, 51, 64, 91, 131, 139, 196, 244

F

Financial Markets 1, 2, 3, 4, 5, 6, 9, 10, 12, 13, 15, 16, 17, 18, 19, 20, 21, 22, 26, 30, 32, 33, 34, 51, 58, 60, 62, 63, 66, 67, 69, 71, 77, 83, 89, 90, 94, 95, 96, 122, 124, 127, 128, 129, 130, 134, 137, 138, 139, 140, 143, 144, 151, 153, 154, 157, 158, 164, 199, 211, 220, 224, 225, 234, 252, 255, 279, 282, 284, 303
Financial News Sentiment 281, 284, 286, 288
Financial Ratios 214, 215, 216, 219, 222
Financial Technology 5, 55
Financial Time Series 58, 59, 60, 62, 63, 64, 77, 78, 87, 89, 207, 217, 246, 249, 282, 283
FinBERT 99, 105, 124, 138, 251, 257, 258, 260, 264, 266, 267, 268, 274, 275, 277, 278, 280, 282, 283, 285, 286, 287, 288, 290, 291, 292, 295, 297, 301, 302, 303, 304, 307, 309, 311, 312
FinTech 5, 21, 30, 36, 56, 198, 201, 306, 307, 311

G

Green Finance 163, 164, 165, 166, 167, 168, 169, 170, 171, 172, 173, 174, 175, 176, 177, 178, 180, 183, 184, 185, 186, 187, 188, 189, 190, 191, 192, 193, 197, 199, 200
GRU 212, 236, 281, 282, 283, 284, 285, 286, 287, 288, 290, 291, 292, 293, 294, 295, 296, 297, 298, 299, 300, 302, 303, 304, 305, 307, 309, 311

H

Herding Behavior 10, 12, 253, 255, 279

I

Indian Stock Market 212, 218, 221, 284
Investment Behaviour 16, 22, 24, 52
Investment Decision-Making 1, 2, 16, 21, 24, 29, 32, 35, 36, 38, 44, 52, 58, 64, 128, 131, 155, 157, 199
Investment Integrity 163
Investment Strategy 34, 47, 57, 59, 61, 62, 67, 82, 85, 88, 89, 127, 151, 215
Investor Psychology 33, 137, 139, 140, 251, 276

L

Loss Aversion 12, 25, 30, 31, 32, 35, 38, 45, 55, 129, 132, 137, 253, 254, 256, 266, 274
LSTM 97, 138, 207, 211, 219, 226, 236, 241, 251, 262, 265, 269, 275, 281, 282, 283, 284, 285, 286, 287, 288, 290, 291, 292, 293, 294, 295, 296, 297, 298, 299, 300, 302, 303, 304, 305, 307, 309, 311, 312

M

Machine Learning 1, 2, 8, 10, 11, 17, 19, 22, 24, 25, 30, 31, 32, 33, 34, 35, 36, 37, 40, 41, 46, 54, 55, 57, 58, 59, 61, 62, 63, 64, 65, 66, 67, 68, 69, 70, 71, 72, 73, 76, 77, 78, 79, 80, 81, 82, 83, 84, 85, 86, 88, 89, 90, 92, 93, 94, 95, 97, 99, 103, 108, 110, 115, 123, 124, 125, 127, 128, 130, 131, 135, 136, 137, 138, 140, 141, 144, 145, 159, 161, 169, 172, 176, 184, 199, 204, 206, 209, 214, 215, 217, 221, 222, 223, 224, 225, 226, 227, 228, 229, 230, 231, 233, 234, 237, 241, 242, 243, 244, 245, 246, 247, 251, 252, 253, 254, 255, 256, 257, 258, 259, 262, 263, 266, 270, 273, 275, 276, 277, 278, 279, 280, 282, 284
Market Forecasting 8, 25, 57, 58, 61, 62, 210, 218, 219, 223, 224, 225, 226, 227, 228, 229, 231, 232, 234, 241, 243, 244, 245

N

Natural Language Processing 1, 2, 9, 22, 29, 31, 32, 33, 35, 38, 40, 41, 95, 99, 111, 128, 137, 148, 169, 221, 228, 234, 237, 252, 257, 311

O

Overreaction 33, 251, 253, 254, 256, 258, 259, 262, 264, 265, 269, 270, 273, 275, 277, 279

P

Portfolio Management 1, 8, 15, 17, 36, 41, 52, 61, 65, 85, 86, 87, 88, 89, 91, 99, 109, 125, 126, 127, 128, 129, 130, 140, 141, 142, 143, 153, 157, 224
Portfolio Optimization 17, 20, 22, 64, 88, 90, 91, 95, 96, 99, 115, 125, 128, 141, 142, 159, 164, 169
Predictive Modeling 57, 59, 63, 67, 95, 234, 261

R

Recurrent Neural Networks 63, 226, 235, 236, 260, 284, 293, 296, 302
Risk Management 3, 5, 9, 18, 20, 22, 24, 25, 36, 38, 42, 48, 58, 64, 96, 106, 112, 121, 131, 140, 141, 142, 147, 150, 154, 156, 158, 161, 167, 182, 189, 196, 200, 204, 243, 282, 306
Robo-Advisors 3, 8, 10, 11, 13, 14, 15, 20, 27, 44, 45, 46, 47, 48, 49, 50, 54, 55, 56, 132, 141, 159

S

Sentiment Analysis 9, 20, 24, 32, 35, 111, 124, 127, 128, 129, 132, 137, 138, 139, 207, 209, 211, 228, 234, 235, 260, 264, 267, 277, 278, 285, 286, 287, 288, 292, 295, 297, 301, 309, 311, 312
SHAP 91, 251, 254, 260, 262, 264, 265, 266, 267, 268, 269, 270, 271, 273, 274, 275
Sharpe Ratio 42, 57, 61, 66, 67, 75, 76, 79, 80, 81, 84, 89, 94, 112, 126, 309
Stock Direction Forecasting 57, 68, 71, 82, 88, 91
Stock Prediction 93, 134, 203, 205, 207, 208, 209, 210, 211, 216, 221
Stock Price Forecasting 281, 283, 284, 288, 301

X

XGBoost 57, 66, 71, 72, 73, 77, 78, 79, 80, 81, 82, 83, 84, 86, 87, 88, 89, 94, 246, 251, 261, 264, 266, 267, 268, 270, 278

www.ingramcontent.com/pod-product-compliance
Lightning Source LLC
LaVergne TN
LVHW062029101126
852251LV00005B/60